Reconciliation and Reification

Reconciliation and Reification

*Freedom's Semblance and Actuality from Hegel
to Contemporary Critical Theory*

TODD HEDRICK

OXFORD
UNIVERSITY PRESS

OXFORD
UNIVERSITY PRESS

Oxford University Press is a department of the University of Oxford. It furthers
the University's objective of excellence in research, scholarship, and education
by publishing worldwide. Oxford is a registered trade mark of Oxford University
Press in the UK and certain other countries.

Published in the United States of America by Oxford University Press
198 Madison Avenue, New York, NY 10016, United States of America.

Library of Congress Cataloging-in-Publication Data
Names: Hedrick, Todd, 1978–author.
Title: Reconciliation and reification : freedom's semblance and actuality from
Hegel to contemporary critical theory / Todd Hedrick.
Description: New York, NY, United States of America : Oxford University Press, [2019] |
Includes bibliographical references and index.
Identifiers: LCCN 2018013717 (print) | LCCN 2018036741 (ebook) |
ISBN 9780190634032 (updf) | ISBN 9780190634049 (epub) |
ISBN 9780190634025 (cloth : alk. paper)
Subjects: LCSH: Critical theory. | Reconciliation. | Reification. | Social change. | Liberty.
Classification: LCC HM480 (ebook) | LCC HM480.H44 2018 (print) |
DDC 303.4—dc23
LC record available at https://lccn.loc.gov/2018013717

1 3 5 7 9 8 6 4 2

Printed by Sheridan Books, Inc., United States of America

To my grandmother, Ellen Sax

CONTENTS

ACKNOWLEDGMENTS

To start these acknowledgments, I would like to go back some ways to my time as an undergraduate at Swarthmore College, and thank Richard Eldridge, who first sparked my interest in Hegel and encouraged me to think of him as both a pivotal figure in philosophy and a cannily prescient one in modern social theory. In graduate school at Northwestern, I had the fortune to study with Terry Pinkard and Thomas McCarthy: two virtuoso scholars who, respectively, gave me whatever bedrock understanding of Hegel and Habermas that I have. They conveyed both the incredible depth and complexity of those theories without losing sight of the basic, intuitable outlook that informs them. Cristina Lafont also added a lot to my development during this time, especially in giving me a sense of critical theory as an ongoing research concern. Over the last nine years as a faculty member in the Michigan State University philosophy department, I have had the backing of two tremendous chairs, Dick Peterson and Matthew McKeon, who were as supportive as can be of my work. Among the many students and colleagues with whom I have had the fortune to have relationships at Michigan State, I would like to single out my friend Christian Lotz: the opportunity to team teach a year-long seminar on the foundations of critical theory broadened my perspective on Lukács, Adorno, and Marx, among others, stimulated my interest in psychoanalysis, and consistently challenged the perspective that I take (hopefully in a refined form, thanks to him) in this book. I also learned a lot from Fred Rauscher's knowledge of Hegel and Rawls. Thanks go to my students from Advanced Topics in the Philosophy of Law for helping me stumble through some of my early ideas about *The Philosophy of Right*, and to great graduate students like Xinmiao Li, Mladjo Ivanovic, Dustin Byrd, and Aidan Sprague-Rice for their conversation and input.

I presented pieces of the book's arguments at several iterations of the Critical Theory Roundtable, and the critical theory gatherings in Prague and Rome. I profited a great deal from those meetings, which tended to inspire the bursts of compositional activity that got this thing done. In particular, I would like to mention James Gledhill, Verena Erlenbusch, Marjan Ivković, Timo Jütten, David Ingram, Amy Allen, Christopher Zurn, and Jeff Flynn. Other friends and colleagues who offered feedback and support and generally gave me things to think about include Lily Woodruff, Matthew Handelman, Danny Mendez, Corinne Painter, Yelena Kalinsky, Chad Belfor, and Kyle Whyte. I am grateful to my family—Ty and Ann, and my parents, Nancy and Mike—for the love and care we offer each other through life's ups and downs.

Lucy Randall has been a wonderful, encouraging editor, who patiently guided me through this long process. Thanks also to Hannah Doyle for her help putting together the final version of this manuscript. Two anonymous reviewers from Oxford helped give the book much sharper definition with their incisive criticism. Special thanks to Frederick Neuhouser for his invaluable feedback on the entire manuscript.

Some of the ideas presented in this book I first worked out in article form, small bits of which are scattered throughout in a revised and expanded form. Portions of Chapters 1, 2, and 5 draw from "Democratic Constitutionalism as Mediation: The Decline and Recovery of an Idea in Critical Social Theory," *Constellations* 19, no. 3 (2012): 383–400; and "Reifying and Reconciling Class Conflict: From Hegel's Estates to Habermas' Interchange Roles," *European Journal of Social Theory* 16, no. 4 (2013): 522–540. Parts of Chapters 2 and 4 draw from "Reification In and Through Law: Elements of a Theory in Marx, Lukács, and Honneth," *European Journal of Political Theory* 13, no. 2 (2014): 178–198. I am grateful to the publishers for permission to reproduce this material.

ABBREVIATIONS FOR FREQUENTLY CITED WORKS

Jean-Jacques Rousseau

DI   *Discourse on the Origin of Inequality*
SC   *On the Social Contract*

G. W. F. Hegel

A   *Lectures on Fine Art*
PhG   *The Phenomenology of Spirit*
PR   *Outlines to the Philosophy of Right*

Karl Marx

C   *Capital*, vol. 1
CPR   "Critique of Hegel's *Philosophy of Right*"
GI   *The German Ideology* (with Friedrich Engels)
MCP   "The Manifesto of the Communist Party" (with Engels)
OJQ   "On the Jewish Question"
PN   "From the Paris Notebooks"

Georg Lukács

CC   "Class Consciousness" (in *History and Class Consciousness*)
RCP   "Reification and the Consciousness of the Proletariat" (in *History and Class Consciousness*)

Theodor W. Adorno

DE   *Dialectic of Enlightenment* (with Max Horkheimer)
MM   *Minima Moralia*

Max Horkheimer

AS   "The Authoritarian State"

TCT   "Traditional and Critical Theory"

John Rawls

CP   *Collected Papers*
JF   *Justice as Fairness: A Restatement*
LHMP   *Lectures on the History of Moral Philosophy*
LHPP   *Lectures on the History of Political Philosophy*
PL   *Political Liberalism*
TJ   *A Theory of Justice*

Axel Honneth

COP   *The Critique of Power*
D   *Disrespect*
FR   *Freedom's Right*
IW   *The I in the We*
NEL   "The Normativity of Ethical Life"
OPL   "Of the Poverty of Our Liberty"
PIF   *Pathologies of Individual Freedom*
POR   *Pathologies of Reason*
R   "Reification and Recognition" (in *Reification*)
RJ   "Rejoinder" (in *Reification*)
RR   *Recognition or Redistribution?* (with Nancy Fraser)
SR   *The Struggle for Recognition*

Jürgen Habermas

BFN   *Between Facts and Norms*
BNR   *Between Naturalism and Religion*
CD   "Constitutional Democracy"
CES   *Communication and the Evolution of Society*
CHD   "The Concept of Human Dignity and the Realistic Utopia of
           Human Rights"
IO   *Inclusion of the Other*
KHI   *Knowledge and Human Interest*
LC   *Legitimation Crisis*
MCCA   *Moral Consciousness and Communicative Action*
PDM   *The Philosophical Discourse of Modernity*
PT   *Postmetaphysical Thinking*
TCA1   *Theory of Communicative Action*, vol. 1
TCA2   *Theory of Communicative Action*, vol. 2
T&J   *Truth and Justification*
TRS   *Towards a Rational Society*

Reconciliation and Reification

Introduction

Authors observing how pervasive the rhetoric of freedom is in modern political discourse—across both left- and right-wing movements, the political philosophy of the Enlightenment and its dissenting offshoots—often add a warning that this ubiquity threatens to cross into vacuousness.[1] Indeed, when finding myself having to talk about my professional competence in Western political thought to a member of the general public (or when teaching intermediate level classes on the topic), I am sometimes vaguely embarrassed by the sense that for as much as the core topics canvassed therein—e.g., civic virtue, the just society, principles of liberalism and democracy, etc.—matter as public concerns, and that choices among libertarianism, liberal capitalism, social democracy, communism, etc., have big impacts on peoples' material conditions, there can be something overly abstract or pious in talking about such matters in terms of freedom. Part of the reason for this is my hunch that most people in my (admittedly non-representative) milieu take themselves (accurately or not) to be free, to a tolerable degree and in an unexciting way. Namely, we casually think of ourselves as possessing the kind of liberty that mainstream, canonical thinkers like Locke, Rousseau, or Rawls seem to talk about, i.e., something brought about in a certain kind of political system, as legally secured freedom of choice and/or the positive capacity to engage in public life. We have, after all, not had to wrest freedom from the clutches of tyrants, nor are we, in most (not all) cases, manning barricades; most of us (again, not all) have not put explicitly political activity central at the very center of our life project, and so conceptions of freedom that see it as a more or less universal aspiration that is realized through the core functions of the political system can seem arid and dispassionate.[2]

---

[1] Most famously, see Isaiah Berlin, *Four Essays on Liberty* (New York: Oxford University Press, 1990); see also Charles Taylor, *Philosophical Papers*, vol. 2: *Philosophy and the Human Sciences* (Cambridge, MA: Harvard University Press, 1985), 230–247. Axel Honneth offers a less jaundiced interpretation of this phenomenon; see "Rejoinder," *Critical Horizons* 16, no. 2 (2015): 206–213.

[2] The same sort of point could be made about the metaphysics of free will: while the question of whether my will is "really" free is not necessarily irrelevant to whether I think of myself as free

At the same time, things like legal rights, equitable public policies, and a legitimate democratic process clearly have *something* to do with lived freedom: I would, after all, miss them if they were terribly degraded, and I would like to think that whatever personal self-determination I carve out for myself is cheapened to the extent that the social system purchases it through the toil and bloody exclusion of others (even though a little reflection on history makes clear that this is, at some level, surely the case). Moreover, while my sense of leading a worthwhile, meaningful life may not have a first order relationship to the political system's commanding heights, it also seems that, since I have chosen neither to live "off the grid" nor in iconoclastic opposition to society, it must have a good deal to do with the way I interact with social institutions underlying these commanding heights: how I incorporate them into everyday life, appropriate their values and norms, impacts whether I feel that I am acting as truly myself when conforming to their demands.

Since the enterprise of critical theory, in Max Horkheimer's canonical formulation, stakes its claim to superiority over other forms of normative reflection on being grounded in a real emancipatory interest that people have vis-à-vis society, it seems important to think about the ways in which we can understand freedom as meaningfully realizable in people's lives, as they are and as they could be.[3] To this extent, I am very much in sympathy with Axel Honneth's method, in *Freedom's Right*, of tethering a theory of justice to an analysis of the ways that freedom is actualized in social practices. Despite the fact that (for specific reasons enumerated in Chapter 4) Honneth ends up not being the hero of this book, its overall approach to critical theory is probably most similar to his. In that spirit, the kind of freedom-actualizing social practices that *have* been important to me in my adult life seem better captured in academic literature on, say, the sociology of professions than in most moral and political philosophy. For instance, Steven Brint has argued that professions in recent decades have come to be characterized less by a specialized pedigree that allows one to serve in perennial areas of human concern (i.e., the classic "trusteeship" definition), than by a status that facilitates "self-directing dignity."[4] Self-directing dignity is not a libertarian fantasy of mastery over one's world and destiny; it is not opposed to institutions and accepts that one is deeply shaped by those that make professional life possible; it also accepts dependence upon peers' recognition, and a broader public that implicitly accepts the institutions that confer value on professional activity. Autonomous professional persons, on this view, allow

---

in a more social or practical sense, it stands at an uncertain distance from such matters. See Taylor, *Philosophical Papers*, vol. 2, 211–229.

[3] A similar thought, drawing on different philosophical sources (existentialism), animates Mariam Thalos, *A Social Theory of Freedom* (New York: Routledge, 2016).

[4] See Steven Brint, *In an Age of Experts: The Changing Role of Professionals in Politics and Public Life*, 2nd ed. (Princeton, NJ: Princeton University Press, 1996).

education, discipline, enculturation, etc., to mold their impulses and native abilities into norms and values that give purpose and direction. This molding hopefully is not just repressive conditioning but puts them in a position to have an appropriative and critical relationship to these norms and values. If all goes decently well along the way, they acquire the capital (cultural and financial) to be a well-rounded person who participates in central areas of social life beyond the purview of a credentialed competence (e.g., have a family, appreciate the arts, form political opinions, etc.). Such participation may not be all that successful or sophisticated, but professionals can nevertheless acquire in this way a view of the whole: what society is, what it offers, how it works, and how one's activity contributes to it. Ideally, it produces a state of self-satisfaction or self-possession that is relatively (though of course not wholly) free from stormy anxieties about whether it all means anything—such an ideal resonates with colloquial expressions like "being comfortable in one's own skin."

I make no pretense that this—what I will be calling either "lived freedom," or (in a more theorized form, and following Honneth) "social freedom"[5]—is the only kind of freedom worth its name: more romantic, non-conformist cultural currents continue to roil modern society, and transcendent conceptions of freedom as an escape from the bondage of self can have both cultural appeal and intellectual currency. Nor do I wish to defend the claim that it is, morally speaking, the best kind of life aspiration, since ones defined by religious callings or, say, secular passions for social justice may not be aptly characterize-able in terms of freedom, at all. More pointedly, the fact that I sought to introduce the idea of social freedom by gesturing toward the lifestyle aspirations of modern professionals is, of course, a dead giveaway: in our society, this kind of freedom exists as privilege, restricted by class and race, forcing conformity to masculine careerist norms among those positioned to take part in them in the first place. The dual trends of outrage over historically unprecedented levels of income inequality, on the one hand, and demands for greater inclusivity along lines of race, gender, sexual orientation, culture, and nationality, on the other, are currently straining nearly all Western social systems in a way that may ultimately reveal the professionalized version of this ideal to be necessarily a matter of bourgeois privilege, if it cannot be made compatible with these political demands.[6] And maybe that is all that it is, or can be—at the conclusion of this book, I acknowledge

---

[5] In general, I use "lived freedom" to denote peoples' more or less pre-theoretical sense of themselves as self-determining and at home in their everyday existence, and "social freedom" to refer to the theorization of how the former is actualized.

[6] See Albert Dzur, *Democratic Professionalism: Citizen Participation and the Reconstruction of Professional Ethics, Identity, and Practice* (University Park: The Pennsylvania State University Press, 2008).

that this is a possibility. I also acknowledge that its discredit and disintegration could auger a future in which persons do not aspire to be free in any recognizably Enlightenment sense, or where (and this may be roughly the same thing) freedom does not attach to social positions and ego strivings in the same way. But that said, the fact that the vision of freedom involved in "self-directing dignity" can read as pedestrian seems to me less an indictment and speaks more to its potential as a universal aspiration, as the sort of freedom that a society like ours promises to (and to some extent prescribes for) its members. To that extent, it strikes me as a useful way to intuitively elucidate the emancipatory interest that critical theory seeks to ground itself in, if one is concerned to avoid spinning that interest into an abstractly utopian notion that transcends the horizon of the social world we live in, thereby unmooring it from the motivations of actual people to be free in their lives, as they actually are. To be universalizable, however, it would plainly have to expand well beyond the confines of professional life, to be institutionalized more broadly and inclusively in ways that I cannot guarantee are possible.[7]

As I read him, when Hegel takes up the model of freedom as self-legislation familiar to him from Rousseau, Kant, and Fichte, while criticizing the way they concentrate it in practices of civic virtue or moral rectitude that stand apart from everyday social life, he is essentially concerned with understanding freedom in terms of the social, lived self-determination that I have just tried to sketch. The fact that Hegel makes vocational associations (i.e., the Estates and corporations) a crucial ingredient in the way that "ethical life" "actualizes" freedom is only an initial indication of this.[8] His notion of freedom as "being at home with one's self in another" is an action-orienting ideal that requires individuals to make some degree of peace with what society makes and demands of them. This is accompanied by Hegel's insistence that conceptions of freedom that attempt to realize it outside of social life are impoverished (e.g., Stoicism and romantic irony), contradictory (the Kantian "moral worldview"), or incoherent (the flight from self found in mysticism). Despite the fact that Hegel's picture of what freedom actually looks like in the modern world is prosaic—it basically involves people doing their jobs, fulfilling their familial roles, trusting their laws—his formulations of it, like his philosophy as a whole, are dense and sometimes exotic-sounding. Aside from Hegel's infamous writing style perhaps lending itself to this, I would contend that a great deal actually is needed in order to explain why this kind of ease and comfort in self deserves to be called freedom,

---

[7] For some interesting reflections along these lines, see Margaret Walker, *Moral Contexts* (Lantham, MD: Rowman and Littlefield, 2003), 189–203.

[8] Also emphasizing this sort of thing, see Emile Durkheim, *Professional Ethics and Civic Morals* (Glencoe, IL: The Free Press, 1958).

rather than repressive, or ideological, conditioning that makes people content within unduly limited prospects. As Hegel sees it—and in this regard, he follows Rousseau, whose conception of civil liberty involves a similar mixture of objective social conditions and their self-conscious affirmation by individuals—he needs to explain why the institutions giving shape to individuals' prospects are, in fact, "rational" (in the specific sense of promoting freedom) and knowable as such. In recent years, scholarship, particularly focusing on *The Philosophy of Right*, has explored the "objective" side of this equation, with less attention to the latter, "subjective" dimension. I suspect that part of this is due to the latter's close association with Hegel's concept of "reconciliation." Hegelian reconciliation is usually thought to make it incumbent upon people in the modern world to swallow the claim that their institutions represent the culmination of history (i.e., the infamous "end of history" thesis), and hence not something contemporary philosophers are eager to defend.[9]

One of the main contentions of this book, which I try to demonstrate in Chapter 1 and put into practice in the rest, is that what Hegel actually means by reconciliation—in particular, how it is accomplished by and for ordinary modern people—has not been well understood, and so its relevance for the subsequent currents of left Hegelian critical theory (which has been leery of the triumphalism associated with Hegel's philosophy of history) has been obscured. On my reading, Hegel's idea of reconciliation arises from a modern condition where a) the justification of basic social arrangements depends increasingly on rational discourse rather than inherited and prescribed worldviews, even while b) the impersonal division of labor and functional differentiation of social spheres associated with the "rationalization of society" has a tendency to alienate individuals from their social roles, by making them seem contingent, meaningless, and sometimes oppressive, which overall diminishes their capacity to rationally identify with them. Reconciliation (as I will ordinarily be using the term, which I take to be basically continuous with Hegel's sense of it) involves a process wherein the social roles we adopt (with varying degrees of voluntariness), and the socialization processes that go into the constitution of the self, can be accurately perceived as impartially justifiable, of a piece with an overall rational, justifiable way of ordering social life. To be reconciled, in this sense, is emancipatory to the extent that we may justifiably (though of course, not literally) regard our social identity as rationally self-authored. Although Hegel's conception of reconciliation involves more of a fraught, ongoing, and politicized process than usually thought, it still probably too closely resembles the idea that freedom is a matter of coming to *see* the social world in a certain

---

[9] See Robert Pippin, *Interanimations: Receiving Modern German Philosophy* (Chicago: University of Chicago Press, 2015), 91–93.

way to entirely skirt Marx's objection, from the 1840s, that it is passive, contemplative, and therefore, a hollow semblance of freedom. Not only is Hegel's imagination lacking concerning the institutions he takes as "necessary" for freedom, but he lacks the social psychology to distinguish between scenarios wherein the individual's incorporation into social systems is reflective and emancipatory, as opposed to repressive and disciplinary. Nevertheless, it will be my contention that a cogent enough conception of reconciliation can be reconstructed out of Hegel that centers around transparent and responsive politics (as opposed to philosophy), and that critical theory's intermittent dialogue with psychoanalysis provides resources for conceptualizing the conditions under which the reflective, liberatory scenario predominates over the repressive one.

It would behoove critical theory to develop a more affirmative relationship to Hegel's concept of reconciliation, since it has struggled mightily, ever since confidence waned in the class theory and philosophy of history that buoyed the normative projections of Marx and Lukács, to ground its critical perspective immanently in society without being resigned to the group oppression and psychic repression that undergirds its historical genesis and current maintenance. But much of contemporary critical theory can be configured around a normative lodestone of reconciliation without too much textual violence, and this has the benefit both of clarifying the relationship between a) the emancipation of the individual's psyche and b) the rational organization of society at the level of law and politics. Both (a) and (b) should be of roughly co-equal concern to anyone that holds true to Horkheimer's formulation of critical theory as a form of reflection on society with a built-in interest in emancipating people from the forms of socially-induced blindness, oppression, and repression that prevent them from realizing their potentials, and I take a large part of the reconciliation paradigm's appeal to be its capacity to discuss both in the same breath.

Here, the second main category of this book—reification—becomes pertinent: for reasons spelled out in Chapters 1 and 2, I reject conceptions of freedom-through-reconciliation that think of it as an explicitly utopian ideal, and so I do not want to conclude that reconciliation is realizable only in an optimally just society. This obliges me to explain why, if reconciliation is to some extent achievable in the existing social world, it is not more progressively and universally achieved. While I by no means believe that reification is the only thing that prevents people in modern societies from being free—this would be an absurd contention, given the array of group-based exclusions from full "participational parity"[10] that are hardly "hidden" in a way that would require

---

[10] See Nancy Fraser, *Scales of Justice: Reimagining Political Space in a Globalizing World* (New York: Columbia University Press, 2010).

a concept of reification to account for—defending the notion that reconciliation represents a universal aspiration for modern societies, against which their legitimacy should be assessed, requires grounds for finding that its present actualization as professionalized class privilege is unnecessarily stunted, as opposed to being a semblance providing ideological cover for an essentially domineering form of life. To fill this need, I reconstruct a working concept of reification more psychologically grounded than Lukács', while less totalizing than Adorno's. I believe that reification, especially once linked to a psychoanalytically informed conception of ego formation, can help explain apparent motivational deficits among persons to access or press for non-repressive ways of incorporating themselves into social systems: reification suggests that such persons do not grasp themselves or their society as things amenable to reconciliation (due, e.g., to the opacity of social systems, the perceived immutability of society and/or the psyche, etc.). But while I follow Adorno in employing a psychology of ego formation to explain why modern individuals are *subject* to reifying pathologies, the conception of reification that I endorse is closer to Habermas' by being rooted in formalized institutional patterns not sustained through democratic will formation. This is meant to dovetail with the more explicitly political cast that I give to the concept of reconciliation in my interpretation of Hegel, while explaining that although reification is more pervasive than, say, Honneth would have it, it is not so inevitable (*á la* Lukács and Adorno) as to require revolutionary social transformation in order to make reconciliation a meaningful possibility on a broad enough basis so as to be considered a universal.

In short, I do not hold that the paradigm of reconciliation and reification should wholly supplant more straightforwardly moral criticism of societal practices (e.g., post-Rawlsian justificatory liberalism, the capabilities approach or G. A. Cohen's value-based egalitarianism, or Rainer Forst's moral-theoretic version of critical theory), or modes of theory aiming to disrupt or negate existing norms and institutions (e.g., Judith Butler or Jacques Ranciére). Norms and institutions do need to be morally criticized, so that they might be dismantled or reformed, and patterns of injustice do need to be disrupted, when they are stubbornly entrenched; and this book is not rife with formulations or strategies for doing either. I do, however, try to demonstrate that reconciliation and reification is the most compelling paradigm available for assessing the legitimacy of modern social orders in a way that connects to persons' experiences of integration in and exclusion from them, and in that sense, is urgently useful, perhaps necessary, for connecting theory to practice, at least when considering regimes, social orders, ways of life, as wholes, and thereby avoiding piecemeal analyses and abstract negations.

My argument proceeds in the manner of a historical reconstruction: very roughly, Chapter 1 develops what I take to be the most applicable and defensible conception of freedom through reconciliation in Hegel (via Rousseau), which aims to explain what his conception of freedom is, why reconciliation is necessary for being "at home" with one's self in the modern world, and the manner in which it can be achieved on a broad basis, mainly through the mediating institutions at the frontier between civil society and the state. Chapter 2 follows the trajectory of left Hegelian social theory from Marx to Lukács to Horkheimer and Adorno in order to marshal what those authors take to be increasingly definitive objections to reconciliation's prospects for actualization in modern society. Through this reconstruction, I formulate a series of hurdles that a theory needs to surmount in order to rehabilitate the idea of freedom as reconciliation today:

Hurdle 1: it should conceive of the political process through which reconciliation is accomplished in a more participatory and inclusive manner than Hegel does.

Hurdle 2: it should conceptualize this process in such a way as to ward off the problem of reification as it affects individuals' relationship to social institutions (the law, in particular).

Hurdle 3: it should supply an account of subject formation that supports the notion that emancipation can be realized in and through society.

Chapters 3–5 examine a series of more contemporaneous theorists—Rawls, Honneth, and Habermas—gauging the extent to which they can be read as putting into practice a paradigm of reconciliation and reification with different theoretical resources, and under changed historical circumstances. I argue that Rawls represents an object lesson on attempts to spell out a conception of social freedom that bypasses the left Hegelian critique of reconciliation—namely, he ends up with a one-sided, overly affirmative conception of law. He thus runs afoul of the charge leveled at *The Philosophy of Right* by the first left Hegelians, namely, that Hegel projects a false unity onto the state that papers over the strife of civil society. Honneth, on the other hand, explicitly critiques conceptions of freedom that conceive of law as the privileged site for its actualization, instead focusing on the general conditions for successful socialization. He performs a fascinating renewal of critical theory's dialogue with psychoanalysis, and a compelling reinterpretation of Hegel's method of "normative reconstruction." But Honneth is actually not a theorist of reconciliation: he does not think reflection on society is an integral component of freedom's actualization. This, I argue, makes his theory hostage to implausible contentions about the transparency of social reproduction. On my reckoning, Habermas' theory represents the most cogent combination of reconciliation and reification, when one reads the proceduralist paradigm of law from *Between Facts and Norms* as addressing reification effects of lifeworld colonization described in *Theory of Communicative Action*. And yet, his way of combining these elements depends on a very malleable conception of the psyche, and results in a picture of reconciliation that has an arid, almost ironical quality, which as I have tried to indicate in this introduction, it is advisable for a critical theory that claims to anchor its perspective a real emancipatory interest to avoid. The book closes by considering whether this reveals an inherent limitation of the reconciliation paradigm—on the contrary, I pose the suggestion that psychoanalytic concepts that Honneth draws from Winnicott can outline a relationship between self and society that grounds the self's autonomy amidst the highly provisional assurance of correctness of roles and norms that Habermas' framework provides, while the latter's form of reflection on society could compensate for Honneth's inability to distinguish emancipated from adaptive ego formations.

1

Reconciling Individuality and Sociality in Hegel's *Philosophy of Right*

Hegel's *Philosophy of Right* is, notoriously, an ideologically ambiguous text. While there are several reasons for this, most vexations over Hegel's stance on individualism versus collectivism, or whether he is ultimately a booster for liberal progress or reaction, stem from his complicated relationship to the positions he groups under the heading of "the Enlightenment." This term can mean a great many things, but as far as Hegel's political thought is concerned, its main reference points are the French Revolution and its aftermath, what he takes to be its intellectual forerunner in Rousseau's political philosophy, and Kant's doctrine of moral autonomy, along with his call to cast aside the "self-imposed immaturity" of custom in order to think for oneself. These admittedly selective references reflect the way that Enlightenment political thought frequently makes recourse to a conception of the relationship between state and citizenship, on the one hand, and civil society and private personhood, on the other, where the latter pairing is characterized by particular desires and interests, and values of personal liberty or independence; the former by universality, impartiality, and values of autonomy and public freedom. Rightness and legitimacy, on this model, are based on the latter pairing, on concepts like basic rights, the common good, and reasons that all can share—i.e., on subsuming particularity under the universal.

From Hegel's perspective, this model suffers from an underdeveloped—and hence, "indeterminate"—conception of freedom due to the cleavage it posits between particularity and universality. The Enlightenment represents European modernity's most highly developed attempt to assure persons that their way of doing things is justifiable. However, the conception of freedom that follows from it is, Hegel argues, devoid of content: attempts to settle on action norms by abstracting away from existing institutions and practices come up empty—they direct individuals *not* to follow tradition, convention, etc. without providing real direction ("determination"). But since, practically speaking, agents in the world must act in accordance with some norm or other, efforts to put Enlightenment into practice oscillate ambiguously between the thought that individuals should pursue their self-interest within the constraints of the rule of law, or that they should submit themselves to whatever stands for "the universal" at a given moment.

Hegel aims to rectify this deficit without abandoning the real advance he thinks the Enlightenment represents.[1] In particular, he urges that an adequate conception of freedom cannot tolerate a gulf between particular persons and what sociality (i.e., the universal) demands of them. Rather, freedom should be understood as something realized *in* social life, as opposed to the private life of the mind, or by transcending one's social identity. To many subsequent readers, however, Hegel's commitment to this point is belied by his relatively modest political vision, which makes peace with the emerging capitalist market and retains a number of traditional elements, from patriarchy to the "Estates" to monarchy.[2] For as much as Hegel insists that modern ethical life liberates by "mediating" between persons' particularity and society's universality through these institutions, it can be hard to see why incorporation into it amounts to more than submission to another set of historically given institutions.

Is there anything to this charge, and if so, is there nevertheless a plausible and appealing conceptualization of freedom available in Hegel's work? I answer both of these questions in the affirmative. Hegel powerfully articulates a conception of freedom as something that develops ontogenetically through the socialization of the individual, phylogenetically in the history of objective Spirit, and finally in the twining of the two. But it is very easy to criticize his institutional imagination, since in several regards it fails to keep pace with progressive political developments of his time; the ease with which such criticisms can be made suggests that Hegel's conception of freedom is too malleable—i.e., too accommodating to extant hierarchies—to be emancipatory. This is a legitimate worry. However, unless we take philosophy to be in a position to concretely specify the institutional shape of a free society—as Marx and Lukács to some extent do, but the various iterations of the Frankfurt School do not—then we need some way of picturing what an emancipatory form of socialization would be, absent a blueprint for a society in which it is maximally realized. This, I argue, Hegel does, or at least makes great strides in doing.

Hegel's core notion of freedom is captured in the phrase "being at home with oneself in another." Although his formulations can sound exotic, this idea is actually quite intuitive and resonant: put colloquially, Hegel thinks that to be free is to have a kind of personal wholeness, i.e., a consonance between what

---

[1] See Stephen Houlgate, "Hegel's Critique of the Triumph of *Verstand* in Modernity," *Hegel Bulletin* 18, no. 1 (1997): 54–70.

[2] See David McGregor, *Hegel, Marx, and the English State* (Boulder, CO: Westview, 1992).

one understands one's self to be in terms of deeply held needs and values, and what one's social existence allows and requires.[3] The fact that Hegel regards this wholeness as a cognitive and practical achievement means that he is not thinking of modern subjects as mere cultural dopes, conditioned to affirm the hierarchies that put them in their place. For as much as he thinks modern people are free and should find themselves at home in their social relations, this "finding" needs to be both self-conscious and justified (i.e., persons should realize that they are at home by recognizing objective features of their social world that make it worthy of being a home). And this is by no means automatic: societies with modern institutions can fail to actualize the rational potential of those institutions; and individuals can fail to recognize the rationality that is possible, notably when it is not displayed with sufficient publicity. Hegel is, in many ways, the first philosopher of modernity, insofar as he initiates the tradition—running through Marx, Weber, Durkheim, Parsons, and Habermas—that thinks of modern societies' social integration as distinctive in that it depends less on a collective bonding experience than the interplay of increasingly distinct and specialized forms of discourse and institutions. Therefore, Hegel's core definition of freedom as being at home with oneself among the social world's role obligations has to be joined to his concept of reconciliation, because he believes that modern society, despite its underlying rationality, contains an ineliminable moment of alienation, such that, for all practical purposes, being at home in the social world requires one to learn to see it in such a way where one is no longer alienated. Freedom requires both that society be a certain kind of social union, *and* that ethical life socialize persons in such a way that these objectively rational features are discernable.[4] My specific aim in this chapter is to spell out a particular way of understanding how Hegel brings his idea of reconciliation into view in *The Philosophy of Right*.[5] We have to understand not only what reconciliation is and how it relates to "being with oneself in another," but how it is accomplished ("actualized") through the activity of the state. I present the complex of institutions that mediate between

---

[3] See Robert Williams, "Freedom as Correlation: Recognition and Self-Actualization in Hegel's *Philosophy of Spirit*," in *Essays on Hegel's* Philosophy of Subjective Spirit, ed. David Stern (Albany: SUNY Press, 2013), 155–180.

[4] The issue of what "objective" features of institutions make them rational, i.e., freedom actualizing, is the focus of Frederick Neuhouser, *The Foundations of Hegel's Social Theory: Actualizing Freedom* (New York: Cambridge University Press, 2000). My focus on reconciliation, by contrast, highlights the question of how this objective rationality is brought to consciousness. I see this more as a difference of emphasis than anything else, and my understanding of Hegel owes a great deal to this work.

[5] For a systematic discussion of the concept of reconciliation, see Michael Hardimon, *Hegel's Social Philosophy: The Project of Reconciliation* (New York: Cambridge University Press, 1994), 84–123.

civil society and the state—the *Polizei* and the rule of law, the Estates and their role in the legislature, and the constitution of the state—as pivotal in this regard. Grasping those institutions, their activity, our participation in them, and what they— working altogether—aim to do, is basically what it is to be reconciled, or so I will argue. Beyond this, I aim to explain why Hegel thinks this comprehension and activity makes us free, and what he thinks philosophy has to do with this enterprise.

Although the kind of personal wholeness, and harmony between individual and society, associated with the concept of reconciliation has had an almost bewitching appeal in the critical theory tradition, Hegel's own way of spelling it out in *The Philosophy of Right*—which has been variously understood as conservative, passive, and contemplative—has not enjoyed similar acclaim. The key to understanding this notion more appreciatively is to grasp the extent to which much of the work of reconciliation is accomplished through reflection on the institutions of ethical life ("objective Spirit")—the way an ongoing legal and political process publicly relates the individual to a reasonably ordered social whole—more than a specifically philosophical cognition ("Absolute Spirit") about the nature of freedom, and indeed, of reality itself.[6] To draw this out, I begin with some extended reflections on Jean-Jacques Rousseau. Although Rousseau may not be foremost among Hegel's self-conscious influences, my contention is that his path-breaking ideas about the social nature of the self, and freedom through submission to the general will, strikingly prefigure Hegel's notion of freedom—more so than Kant's—and that a lot can be learned by seeing how Hegel seeks to rectify the problems he keenly perceives in Rousseau.

1. Rousseau's Dialectic of Enlightenment

Rousseau is the first thinker to theorize what Horkheimer and Adorno later dub the dialectic of enlightenment: according to him, rationality has both a social origin and an emancipatory potential, yet its social origins tend to bind human beings together in slavish, opaque, and hostile interdependence that stymies their ability to be guided by their own, true self. Furthermore, rational (i.e., technical) progress in human affairs tends to tighten the entwinement of reason to bondage, rather than unraveling it as enlightenment forecasts hoped.[7] Nevertheless, a

---

[6] On the way that other, not specifically philosophical branches of Absolute Spirit—art, in particular—can contribute to national identity, see Lydia Moland, *Hegel on Political Identity: Patriotism, Nationality, Cosmopolitanism* (Evanston, IL: Northwestern University Press, 2011), 126–148.

[7] See Rudiger Bubner, *The Innovations of Idealism* (New York: Cambridge University Press, 2003), 145–161.

transparently mutual form of society that combines rationality with freedom—one organized around the general will—is possible. As Rousseau sees it, Hobbes and Locke could never understand how society could be anything other than a shackling compromise (albeit a rationally desirable one) because they treat the allegedly natural human beings that initiate the social compact as fully formed individuals with a conception of their personal interest. As such, they cannot see how this type of human being represents a fall, and so neither can they see the possibility of redemption through its overcoming.

Rousseau's *Second Discourse* decisively alters the anthropologically fictitious representations of the state of nature that informed earlier social contract theories and argues that humans become individuated, rational, and reflective beings by learning to see themselves through the eyes of others, whose interests they must take account of and whose cooperation they require (DI, 144ff). To really imagine "Man's natural state" (134) is to imagine a smart animal existing prior to any but the most rudimentary forms of sociality (e.g. mating, child bearing and rearing), who, because of relative isolation, has no conception of who "he" (as a self-directing, individuated ego) is, precisely because he has no impetus to conceptualize how he stands vis-à-vis others. He acts only on impulses arising from basic instincts (142), i.e., sating needs, sometimes moved by an unreflective sense of compassion at signs of suffering among others of his species.[8] This state of rugged independence is not only innocent but happy, albeit in an unreflective way that is unimaginable for careworn products of civilization like ourselves:

> I know that we are repeatedly told that nothing would have been more miserable as man in this state . . . I should very much like to have it explained to me what kind of misery there can be for a free being, whose heart is at peace, and body in health. (149–50)

So, if we imagine a state in which human beings are unsocialized and have little to do with one another, we are imagining beings that are serene and contented: having no cause to acquire a social identity, they are untroubled by thoughts about how their condition could be other than it is.

Rousseau consistently describes such people as "independent," or having "natural freedom," but not "free" in the full sense that he eventually associates with the possession of "civil liberty." They are free in that their actions spring from no other source than themselves, yet Rousseau shares with classical thinkers like Plato and Aristotle the sense that an elevated form of human life should involve not just pleasurable contentment but self-mastery, which the philosophical

---

[8] See Joshua Cohen, "The Natural Goodness of Humanity," in *Reclaiming the History of Ethics: Essays for John Rawls*, eds. Andrews Reath, Barbara Herman, and Christine Korsgaard (New York: Cambridge University Press, 1997), 102–139.

tradition has typically viewed in terms of reason's dominion over unruly desire. Although Rousseau is not very specific about the rationale (in the way that, say, Kant or Mill are), he considers moral liberty, achieved within a just democratic state, to make for a life more worthwhile and dignified than the bucolic independence of the state of nature. Only by virtue of being thrown together with others in a way that reveals the survival advantages of cooperative behavior does the natural human being have to reckon with who "he" is.[9] The emergence of a self is, Rousseau sees, absolutely necessary for psychic space to open up for a rational self to restrain reaction, inclination, impulse, etc., and therefore for any sort of morally dignified existence to be possible.

The rational capacity to survey the world from an impersonal perspective and steer the will in accordance with insight is not one that Rousseau thinks we can ascribe to natural human beings: if rationality involves taking an impersonal, objectivating view of things, this third person perspective presupposes a cognitive capacity to crisply distinguish between self and world that human beings do not naturally acquire. The capacity to act in accordance with some conception of what one "should" do requires an ability to relate reasons to a self (in order to have an idea of *what* I should do, I require some sense of *who* I am), and therefore requires stable interaction contexts (i.e., relationships that involve role expectations) that spur the self's development.[10] According to Rousseau's most innovative argument here, this capacity in turn has its source in the development of a second-person perspective—Honneth later encapsulates precisely this thought with his thesis that "recognition must precede cognition" (R, 46). It should be emphasized that this concern for others is not rooted in the natural disposition for pity. The latter, being unreflective, does not necessarily involve any recognition of the other's identity; by the same token, the recognition of others at the seat of cognition does not necessarily involve any sympathy for them, but is rather driven by a need to understand how I am perceived by others. The ability to situate one's self in relation to others opens a new avenue for taking satisfaction in self: the natural, unproblematic, unreflective thriving that Rousseau calls "love of self" (*amour de soi*) becomes pleasure that is contingent upon

---

[9] Rousseau goes on at some length about the events that might have led a hitherto asocial being to begin establishing repeatable forms of social cooperation. While his musings about the originally isolated condition of human beings are not grounded in any historical record, nothing much hangs on the accuracy of his reconstruction (even according to Rousseau himself; see DI, 159). All things considered, though, Rousseau's general sense that rational thought must have a social origin has, we can now see, considerable empirical support. See Michael Tomasello, *The Cultural Origins of Human Cognition* (Cambridge, MA: Harvard University Press, 2001).

[10] Christine Korsgaard argues for a similar connection between "practical identity" and reasons for action; see *The Sources of Normativity*, ed. Onora O'Neill (New York: Cambridge University Press, 1996), 115ff.

how I *compare* to others (*amour-propre*) (DI, 218). Thus, the emergence of the rational self is far from an innocuous bit of natural history, as it implies that a basic form of narcissism lies at the root of any articulated identity: reasons for action must be reasons for *me* to act, and once the self is invoked, *amour-propre* becomes involved, with all the grandiosity, envy, and fear that can accompany it.

Rousseau diverges from the entire philosophical tradition preceding him in seeing how the emergence of rationality alters our affective makeup in a way that makes it impossible to directly connect rationality with virtuous self-determination: the self's inward, reflective turn stirs up prideful self-regard—from here on, more-or-less innocent natural instincts compete with impulses stemming from one's attachment to a social identity. Once it becomes possible to distinguish between *my* interests and others', it occurs to me that the others' misfortune does not *have to* meaningfully impact my self, and so one becomes capable of indifference that the innate disposition of pity would have made hitherto impossible.

> It is reason that engenders *amour-propre*, and reflection that reinforces it; reason that turns man back on himself; reason that separates him from everything that troubles and afflicts him: It is Philosophy that isolates him; by means of Philosophy he secretly says, at the sight of a suffering man, perish if you will, I am safe. (153)

Amour-propre, despite being the source of collective irrationality, is a child of reason. It is essentially comparative and therefore involves the ability to switch perspectives on one's self, to envision states other than what is directly present; it churns up feelings of shame and pride based on comparisons of status, worth, etc., and therefore ensures that individuals have an (often overweening) concern with how they are perceived. Socially induced suffering stems from a condition where they are deeply dependent upon one another, but within opaque conditions, where they struggle to advance their perception of personal interest against others. But while such conditions have so far prevailed in all developed societies, Rousseau does not think that genuine freedom and happiness is therefore something that lies beyond sociality. Rather, ethical and fulfilling human lives require a rapprochement between individual self-interest and the demands of social order.

2. Completing Sociality: Freedom and the General Will

Despite these unappealing consequences of rational selfhood, Rousseau does not hold that socially developed dispositions are inherently avaricious, as this passage from *The Social Contract* illustrates:

This transition from the state of nature to the civil state produces a most remarkable change in man by substituting justice for instinct in his conduct, and endowing his actions with the morality they previously lacked. Only then, when the voice of duty succeeds physical impulsion and right succeeds appetite, does man, who until then had only looked to himself, see himself forced to act on other principles, and to consult his reason before listening to his inclination. (SC, 53)

Rousseau is downplaying the ambivalent nature of sociality here, but clearly, he thinks that the self is capable of internalizing moral/objective/other-regarding reasons for action. However, it is equally clear that the refinement of one's social identity—something driven by the technical advance of civilization connected to a more elaborate, specialized division of labor—tends to render increasingly stark the boundaries between one's own interests and others' in a way that hardly encourages unqualified moral commitments.

Rousseau appears to have posed a dilemma for himself: freedom, in a sense that rises above animal independence, requires the existence of a rational self. This is, in turn, dependent upon socially developed relations of mutual dependence. These may not appear to necessitate selfishness or antagonism, since there is manifestly an array of intimate and civic relations that involve a high degree of solidarity. But most hitherto existing forms of solidarity are secured through forms of recognition where one's worth depends on comparative assessments to other groups and individuals. In other words, one's sense of well-being is hostage to existing hierarchies and the opinions of others. So, what often passes for self-possession is really a toxic mix of self-aggrandizement and sycophancy.[11]

Although I cannot give a complete overview of Rousseau's famous general will, with all of its attendant controversies, we are in a position to appreciate the purpose with which he introduces it: persons that transform themselves into citizens by positing a shared will that advances the mutual well-being of all, and in turn are governed by it, unravel the knot of civilization and oppression. In such a polity, citizens affirm dependence on others as *consonant* with their identity and interests, as opposed to being a fetter upon them. For as much as Rousseau acknowledges that socialized human beings have their own particular purposes, his proposal for rapprochement between individuality and sociality notoriously

---

[11] It would be misleading to claim that Rousseau sees this as wholly a social and political problem. The system of education described in *Emile* has the aim of uncoupling the pupil's sense of self-worth from the opinions of others, so that he might take satisfaction simply in the experience of self. But Rousseau certainly sees this effort as swimming against strong currents, so long as society persists as a system of domesticated antagonism. See Neuhouser, *Rousseau's Theodicy of Self-Love: Evil, Rationality, and the Drive for Recognition* (New York: Oxford University Press, 2008), 155–183.

seems weighted in favor of social order. He poses the problem of how to achieve it as follows:

> To find a form of association that will defend and protect the person and goods of each associate with the full common force, and by means of which each, uniting with all, nevertheless obey only himself and remains as free as before. (49–50)

Paradoxical as this formulation may be, Rousseau imagines that the general will solves the problem of combining sociality and freedom straightforwardly: if we join with others in affirming a system of laws for the sake of our common good, and genuinely identify ourselves with that system, then in a very real sense the laws governing us are self-imposed, an extension of our own will more than impositions upon it—when we obey the law, we will be obeying our own self.

This conceptual elegance belies considerable difficulties putting these ideas into practice. Rousseau has an acute sense of how human socialization makes it difficult to identify with the common good in the thoroughgoing way the general will demands. But it is possible: in addition to being private persons, we are also capable of thinking of ourselves as sharing interests with circles of compatriots. In a society where this form of identification is credible and encouraged, it can coalesce around an ethic of citizenship. As his references to Spartan civic life attest, Rousseau thinks that tight-knit societies have the merit of sternly discouraging any form of loyalty other than to the common weal. And while he is not put off by Spartan militarism, the key advantage they have is not so much that as their simplicity in rank, as the following, different example shows:

> When, among the happiest people in the world, troops of peasants are seen attending to affairs of State underneath an oak tree and always acting wisely, can one help despising the refinements of other nations which make themselves illustrious and miserable with so much art and mystification? (121)

Although Rousseau does not have a theory of modernization, per se, plainly he finds that geographically far-flung societies with complicated political systems, lots of specialized commercial activity, etc. create an environment where personal interest is pressing and visceral, while duty to the state is distant and inessential. If this tendency is more or less inescapable in our time, then reorientation toward the general will requires something like a turning of the soul among not just isolated individuals, but a populace.

Rousseau never explains whether such a thing is likely, or how it might come about. What he does offer is a recommendation: once we recognize that a society constituted as a system of legally structured, self-interested competition tends toward general immiseration, it is advisable for individuals to embrace their identity as citizens who think in terms of what is equally in the interests of all. He wants readers to appreciate that a life devoted to private pursuits over civic duty is Sisyphean and unfree: it binds the self to a pattern of social relations that is at once symbiotic and antagonistic, where my sense of well-being depends on both the diminishment of and recognition conferred by others.

3. Rousseau's Uneasy Modernity

A common objection to Rousseau's general will is that it is overly nebulous, making it difficult to explain how individuals can *correctly* identify its content. Before getting into the substance of this charge, note that it is usually thought to raise a problem about how to rationally adjudicate competing claims about what the general will stands for.[12] This is certainly an issue; however, I want to highlight a related problem that Hegel will be keen to correct for: Rousseau thinks that in order to be free, it is important that citizens *know* that their laws express the general will, yet under most conditions, it is not very clear how this is possible. The general will impartially wills what is equally in the interests of all citizens, making it a forerunner to Kant's identification of moral rightness with universalizable reasons for action.[13] But unlike Kant's categorical imperative, Rawls' original position, or Habermas' principle of universalization, Rousseau does not formalize the general will as a decision procedure. Perhaps he simply does not attend to this issue, but there are some reasons for thinking that he does not believe that it is possible.

Rousseau's reticence on this point is evident in his being torn about the prospects for institutionalizing the general will. Anticipating Hegel, one of the aspects of Greek civic life that Rousseau admires is the immediate, intuitive way Greeks understood what their general will was, what it required of them, and the ease with which they made this will their own. But this immediacy seems lost to us: modern nation-states that are much more far-flung and functionally differentiated, not to mention culturally plural, than the *polis* require considerably more elaborate machinery of state. It then becomes an open question whether the ongoing operation of that machinery reflects the general will; providing an affirmative answer to this in turn requires what I will be calling, following Rawls, institutional reference points that satisfy *publicity conditions*. At least under modern conditions, in order to identify the general will, citizens

[12] See Patrick Riley, "Rousseau's General Will," in *The Cambridge Companion to Rousseau*, ed. Patrick Riley (New York: Cambridge University Press), 124–153.

[13] See J. B. Schneewind, *The Invention of Autonomy: A History of Modern Moral Philosophy* (New York: Cambridge University Press, 1998), 487–492.

require some concrete (i.e., exemplified in positive law) preunderstanding of what it is, along with some reasonable expectation that it is being carried out in the ongoing administration of public affairs. Such a preunderstanding can be schematic, but should be concrete enough to specify that *these* laws, customs, practices, etc. may provisionally be regarded as representative of the general will. This point needs to be underscored: for Rousseau, freedom is an essentially collective aspiration, and since we are neither ancient Spartans nor peasants settling our affairs under an oak tree, we need assurance that our fellow citizens are likewise oriented toward the general will, and that this orientation is reflected in the laws that impact our life prospects. Without these assurances, any personal orientation toward the general will is in vain.

But where would this knowing come from, for modern people lacking the intuitive self-assurance of the Greeks and the intimate proximity of the peasants? This is a difficult issue for Rousseau, as he is clear that the general will *does not* provide answers to local, specific questions of public policy, but rather only pertains to something like society's fundamental laws, e.g., what Rawls dubs "the basic structure of society." Rousseau writes, "[the general will] loses its natural rectitude when it tends toward some individual and determinate object" (62). In a society where day-to-day public affairs are to a large extent understood as a matter of applying settled custom, this is not usually problematic. For this reason, Rousseau urges that laws be kept as simple as possible (121). But this is vanishingly possible in a state of any scale.

For as much as it is the theoretical tradition stemming from Locke that tends to be dubious of expansive state power, in *The Social Contract* Rousseau expresses a quite jaundiced view of government. It should be noted that, for Rousseau, government is not identical to the sovereign power constituted by the general will. Rather, it serves as an "intermediate body" between the people considered as a sovereign whole (83), whose power is vested in the legislative function of the state, and the people considered as individual subjects. That is, "government" refers to permanently institutionalized state administration (by "Magistrates"); it is not the direct object of citizens' allegiance and duty (62). Government by magistrate obviously contrasts to the authority of the general will. Being subject to the latter is emancipatory due to its impersonal character: "each, by giving himself to all, gives himself to no one" (50). Government's legitimacy depends on it being duly deputized to execute the laws, and is revocable. Furthermore, Rousseau thinks that magistrates are not necessarily reliable bearers of the general will, as they tend to develop a group interest in preserving the machinery of state, particularly their corner of it. Acknowledging that particular decisions and government by magistrate are, at best, less than directly expressive of the general will amounts to a troubling concession, though, since citizens in modern states are subject to a vast accumulation of laws made by specific officials for particular policy reasons at discrete moments in the past, and professionally administered subsequently. If I am only free under the law when the law reflects the general will, the prospects for freedom are diminished if I cannot assess whether the bulk of the laws I am subject to reflect the general will or not.

It would be hasty to say that this problem is intractable: we *can* seek to ascertain whether the general will is embodied in the basic structure of our society and institutionalized in the political process. As indicated, I consider this to be a crucially Rawlsian idea, but it is presaged in Rousseau. Consider the following passage: "In effect, so soon as a matter of fact or particular right is in question on a point which has not been regulated by a previous convention, the affair becomes contentious" (63). A lot obviously hinges here on what it means for a decision to be "regulated." I would suggest that a particular decision *can* be consonant with the general will if it takes place within a framework that has been established through the general will. It seems reasonable to attribute to Rousseau something like the following position: a) the general will pertains most directly to questions about institutions and policies that impact the life prospects of all (or at any rate, the preponderance of) citizens, affecting them in a similar manner; b) more specific, localized policies, or temporary measures, cannot be deduced from the general will; c) nevertheless particular political acts can be *contrary* to the general will, and citizens are entitled to have them made within a procedural infrastructure that guarantees minimum thresholds of equal treatment, and within which they can be confident that their interests and preferences are taken account of, undertaken by officials who at least act in the spirit, so to speak, of the general will.

For example, the question of whether a local highway project should be funded is not a matter of universal concern: some citizens will benefit from it, a few may be harmed; all citizens will contribute taxes to an infrastructure upgrade that affects most in only a circuitous way. Nevertheless, most all have a roughly similar interest in living in a society with a functional transportation system, and so particular decisions are imbued with the spirit of the general will, as it were, by virtue of being made within a decision-making framework that provides for such things. However, even here, some citizens, for whatever reason (disability, disinterest in travel, geographical isolation), may have a much slighter, less direct interest in such matters, and there will be an array of different views on things like: how high of a spending priority should transportation be? how it should be divided between rural and urban areas, balanced against things like wilderness conservation, etc.? And so, the general will is most fully on display in the foundations of a political system that establishes a process whereby the basic needs of the citizenry (transportation, healthcare, education, etc.) are provided for in a way that consistently treats all citizens as having an equal voice and stake. Moreover—and here, the publicity conditions come into play—the connections between these levels (the highway funding decision, the system of transportation planning and funding, the constitutional structure of the state) need to be visible, manifest in a way that goes beyond mere procedural validity.

So, particular decisions should flow from the general will, but the question of how to specify this flowing-from relation are mysterious, and one that Rousseau never solves. In fact, he addresses it only in a negative way: what social theorists generically call "complexity" diminishes the general will's presence in the capillary action of the state—in his view, the sense in which the general will animates the day-to-day legislative and administrative activities of the state diminishes proportional to the size of the permanent administrative apparatus of the state ... which is nevertheless absolutely necessary in a complex, functionally differentiated society, where a large, strong state is needed in order to bring the populace to an awareness that they are bound together as citizens under a general will in the first place.

It should be clear by now that Rousseau's general will, like so much of his philosophy, has an ambiguous relationship to reason. The general will's existence plainly depends on the reflective distancing from instinct, internalization of norms, and self-possession that only the rational self makes possible. Yet, he cannot say how—apart from being opposed to the particular—rational thought specifies its content. Rousseau seems aware of this problem, but his main way of dealing with it is to posit various instruments for rallying the citizenry around symbols of civic virtue, so that disagreements about the general will do not break out in the first place. Moreover, while Rousseau thinks that the terms of the social contract reserve final legislative authority for the assembled people, as the most authentic expression of the general will, he acknowledges that for all practical purposes, legislative power needs to have some determinate institutional form. But he notably does not think that the form it takes has any particular epistemic function. That is, we might think that democratic lawmaking is in part a process where a polity's reflection on itself is institutionalized in a way that seeks to ensure that outcomes are arrived at through an exchange of reasons—and that the way this process is structured can affect the quality of that exchange. But this is simply not Rousseau's view: rather, he holds that upright citizens should be able to intuit the general will:

> If, when an adequately informed people deliberates, the Citizens had no communication among themselves, the general will would always result from a large number of small differences, and the deliberations would always be good. (60)

These comments are today usually regarded as an unfortunate obstacle toward Rousseau's inclusion in the canon of deliberative democrats, but probably not essential to his position. And while in the above passage, context suggests that Rousseau's main worry concerns factional maneuvering within the legislative body itself, the view expressed reflects a core doctrine: while Rousseau does not argue that communication about the general will is inherently corrupting, he also does not have confidence that institutional procedures can do much to rationally restore a fractured consensus, or forge a new one. Hence, the key lies in preventing such disagreements from breaking out in the first place. So, Rousseau sees that a constitution can become an enduring representation of the way a polity has committed to instantiating the general will; however, he sees fit to augment this with the suggestion—in the otherwise puzzling sections "On the Legislator" and reflections on civil religion (68–72; 142–151)—that citizens should regard their laws as having an inspired, divine foundation.[14] Yet even before we account for ethical and cultural plurality, or forms of ideological disagreement that Rousseau was not yet acquainted with, the division of specialized labor by itself seems to indicate that ascertaining the general will is not a reliably straightforward matter, requiring some legislative and administrative sensitivity to the needs and circumstances of different groups. A specific institutional setup can never satisfy the general will—once some constituency credibly claims that it does not, there is nothing within the space of reasons to gainsay it.

4. Hegel's Translation of the Rousseauian Problematic

Rousseau's casting of the problem of social freedom has proven immensely influential; Kant and Hegel both offer sympathetic, but quite different, receptions of it. Kant follows Rousseau in identifying autonomy with self-legislation in accordance with norms endorsable from an impartial point of view.[15] Kant, however, does not regard freedom as an *achievement*, so much as something that we *are*.[16] We can, of course, fail to live up to the dignity of our rational nature, but for Kant, we are equipped to actualize reason in practice, not through socially cultivated sensibility, so much as reason's own process of testing the universalizability of maxims. By depoliticizing it, Kant sidesteps the problems Rousseau has in explaining how the general will could be embodied in law: laws should respect the freedom that we have, rather than be responsible for bringing it about. Hegel

[14] See Christopher Kelly, "'To Persuade without Convincing': The Language of Rousseau's Legislator," *American Journal of Political Science* 31, no. 2 (1987): 321–335.

[15] See Immanuel Kant, *Groundwork of the Metaphysics of Morals*, in *Practical Philosophy*, ed. and trans. Mary Gregor (New York: Cambridge University Press, 1996), 89–90 (4:440–441).

[16] See ibid., 95–96 (4:448).

consistently rails against Kant's notion that the rational subject is, by virtue of its nature, capable of freely determining itself, and insists that reason cannot be actualized in the individual subject, monologically self-legislating in accordance with universal maxims. Rather, it can only be actualized collectively, through the human community's (i.e., Spirit's) reflection on its own, existing practices.

Hegel's objections to Kantian ethics have been thoroughly explored,[17] but we should note that, in making this critique, Hegel returns to precisely those elements of Rousseauian freedom that Kant discarded. Like Rousseau, he thinks of freedom as being possible for human beings only once they reflect on the re-lationship of self to other and world. Therefore, it has a socio-historical origin, and should not be hypostatized as our essential nature.[18] Furthermore, Rousseau and Hegel both conceive of freedom as a self-consciously achieved harmony be-tween the self's inner needs and purposes, and the identity and roles made avail-able to (or foisted on) it by society. Indeed, Hegel sometimes characterizes this set of ideas in a way that closely echoes Rousseau:

> Freedom in action issues . . . from the fact that the rationality of the will wins actualization. This rationality the will actualizes in the state. In a state which is really articulated rationally all the laws and organ-izations are nothing but a realization of freedom in its essential char-acteristics. When this is the case, the individual's reason finds in these institutions only the actuality of his essence, and if he obeys these laws, he coincides, not with something alien to himself, but simply with what is his own. (A, 98)

The un-Rousseauian element here is Hegel's emphasis on rationality. Hegel's comprehensive account of social freedom contains conceptual innovations captured in the following phrases: "being at home with oneself in another," and "reconciliation." The first formulation is, when considered by itself, familiar from *Discourse on the Origin of Inequality*'s account of the rational self's emergence from nature. It refers to the idea that we are constituted as persons through giving and receiving recognition of our ability to appropriately think, speak, and act. It extends to the idea that we can find liberation in realizing that the social world's requirements are commensurate with our inner needs and convictions; this is analogous to Rousseau's idea that giving ourselves to the general will and

---

[17] For a summation of the current state of the debate, see Robert Stern, *Kantian Ethics: Value, Agency, and Obligation* (New York: Oxford University Press, 2015), 139–156.

[18] To be fair, Kant does have a considerable amount to say (e.g., in his anthropological writings) about how cultural development and natural history shape our propensity for rationality. See Patrick Louden, *Kant's Impure Ethics: From Rational Beings to Human Beings* (New York: Oxford University Press, 2000).

receiving its laws in return makes us free, by virtue of being "at home" in the world wrought by the general will. The concept of reconciliation, on the other hand, does not have a counterpart in Rousseau. The word itself suggests that, in order to be free in the social world, we need to *realize* something about it, i.e., that we come to see something that *appeared* alienating as in fact being expressive of our highest interests.

Notably, Hegel thinks that the practical need for reconciliation arises in the modern world. There are two takeaways from this: a) realizing the truth about the modern world (i.e., why its core institutions and practices are the way they are) should reconcile us to it; but b) there may be something about ordinary consciousness that does not intuitively ("immediately") grasp this truth—we need to be *re*-conciled to it. While, as I stressed, an element of self-consciousness is present in Rousseauian civil liberty (i.e., laws' satisfaction of the general will should be public knowledge), this sense of being liberated by using reason to *reveal* something about the world is not. It also suggests a passive, contemplative view of freedom: liberation is not a matter of changing the world, but of knowing how it is. However, even if we follow Hegel in thinking that being fully at home in the social world requires reconciliation, and therefore something more cognitively demanding than Rousseau, the gulf between them is not as yawning as it appears, or so I shall argue: reconciliation is to a large extent accomplished through the visible and ongoing political organization of society. To that extent, reconciliation does not strictly imply a contemplative conception of freedom.

Although some interpreters have heard echoes of Rousseau in Hegel,[19] the degree to which we can understand Hegel as overcoming shortcomings in Rousseau's idea of the general will has been underappreciated for, I think, two reasons:

a)   Hegel does not appear to be much influenced by Rousseau, nor does he seem to have understood him very well. Hegel is either unaware of, or does not acknowledge, the way Rousseau's account of the self's genesis in *Discourse on the Origin of Inequality* anticipates his own. And while Rousseau is careful to distinguish the general will from an aggregation of personal preferences, which he calls "the will of all," Hegel repeatedly identifies the former with the latter.[20] This unjustly assimilates Rousseau to the voluntarist, rational choice versions of the social contract more characteristic of his predecessors.

---

[19]   Again, Neuhouser's work has been very instructive for me in this regard. See *The Foundations of Hegel's Social Theory*, chap. 2.

[20]   For example, see Hegel, *Lectures on the History of Philosophy*, vol. 3, *Medieval and Modern Philosophy*, trans. E. S. Haldane and Frances Simson (Lincoln: University of Nebraska Press,

b) *Philosophy*, not politics, is the medium through which reconciliation takes place, on most understandings of Hegel. After all, the passage where he most famously introduces the concept runs as follows:

> To recognize reason as the rose in the cross of the present and thereby to enjoy the present, this is the rational insight which *reconciles* us to actuality—the reconciliation which philosophy affords to those in whom there has once arisen an inner voice bidding them to comprehend. (PR, 15; see also PhG, §7/4–5, and A, 54–55)

Regarding (a), I claim no direct path of profound influence between Rousseau and Hegel, but I do contend that despite misunderstanding the general will, Hegel has a lively sense of its shortcomings. Regarding (b), as the above passage makes clear, Hegel does explicitly say that reconciliation is the work of philosophy (even though he does not say that it is *exclusively* the work of philosophy). In order to truly be at home in social life, I have to comprehend why society—and what it has made of me—has the shape it does, and finally, why that shape is rational. Through Hegel's philosophy, one acquires the most complete, erudite comprehension of this. Thus, in keeping with what appears to be Hegel's official position, cultural institutions that furnish people with a sense of what life is all about ("Absolute Spirit" in the form of art, religion, and philosophy) seem to bear the decisive burdens of bringing reconciliation about. In the following sections, I counterbalance these considerations by arguing that reflective participation in the modern state offers an appreciation of the rationality of ethical life as a whole, to a degree that allows Hegel to judge that people in the modern world *are* (by and large) free, even though most of them have at most a diluted version of the cognition of what truly is (i.e., "the Absolute") that his philosophy provides. Modern citizens have a capacity to understand how their society works—rationally, for the common good—through inclusion in the activity of the state, and thus participation in objective Spirit does much of the heavily lifting of reconciliation. In other words, I will argue that, although Hegel's philosophy often uses reconciliation to refer to a cognitive *state* where I grasp the rationality of what is, it is at the same time a state of the will wherein I affirm the rationality of what is, and moreover, has a more practically relevant sense of being consciously included in a *process* whereby the state strives to make the social world a home for me and those groups of others to whom I am related.[21]

1995), 400–402. On Hegel's misreading, see Robert Williams, *Hegel's Ethics of Recognition* (Berkeley: University of California Press, 1997), 276–281.

[21] On reconciliation as a state and a process, see Hardimon, *Hegel's Social Philosophy*, 95ff.

In order to see why the apparently contemplative notion of reconciliation is in fact structurally similar to the emancipation on offer in Rousseau's general will—while at the same time Hegel finds these Rousseauian ideas deficient in terms of rationality—a few words are in order about what it would mean for thought to achieve the kind of cognitive repose that Hegel's conception of freedom involves. A succinct way of moderating Hegel's apparent intellectualism is to observe that, for him, philosophy is an erudite expression of concepts that orient the cognitive lives of real historical communities—philosophy grasps its time in thought (PR, 16). Accordingly, we can understand "Spirit" to refer to the set of norms and practices for justifying claims about how things are and what should be done—i.e., persons' theoretical and practical self-understanding— that have authoritative sway in a given community.[22] Part of what Hegel claims here—and what the sections on "Consciousness" in the *Phenomenology* purportedly establish—is that making a justifiable claim (to knowledge, proper conduct, etc.) necessarily involves some logically prior notion of what it is to make a justifiable claim. Such conceptions are not naturally occurring in the human mind, and most are practically unsustainable in the long run. Hegel famously calls Spirit's phenomenology "the path of *doubt*" (PhG, §78/49)[23] because he thinks its development can be reconstructed as a very long series of responses to problems (e.g., social disintegration, cognitive aporias, etc.) it encounters while attempting to enact its self-understanding. This means that Spirit has, in effect, the aim of conceiving of itself (i.e., its conception of what is, how it is knowable, and the place of human beings in it—Hegel calls this set of categorical types "the Concept") free from the contradictions, conflicts, and skeptical problems that caused prior shapes of Spirit to go under ("the Concept" actualized in this way is "the Idea").

Of course, there are important differences between Hegel's approach and Rousseau's. For one, Hegel moves beyond *The Social Contract*'s conception of the state and its positive laws as *the* locus of norms that need to be affirmatively incorporated into the subjects' self-understanding, taking the full gamut of formal/political and informal/cultural sources of normativity into account. Second, and more importantly for present purposes, Hegel clearly thinks that reconciliation requires self-consciousness about why *these* norms and practices have authority for us—he begins *The Philosophy of Right* urging that a philosophical treatment of "right" should be devoted to discerning the traces of reason

---

[22] See Terry Pinkard, "What Is a 'Shape of Spirit'?" in *Hegel's* Phenomenology of Spirit: *A Critical Guide*, eds. Dean Moyar and Michael Quante (New York: Cambridge University Press, 2010), 112–129.

[23] I am modifying the Miller translation of the *Phenomenology* with the aid of Pinkard's version, available here: http://terrypinkard.weebly.com/phenomenology-of-Spirit-page.html.

in the actually existing accumulation of norms posited to govern human conduct. Rousseau does not seem to think that the general will can be understood
as the result of "right's" progressive development in history, nor is he able to
justify the conviction that one set of laws reflects the general will and others do
not. Again, this makes the general will's relation to reason ambiguous, making
allegiance to a specific social order grounded more in affect more than rationally motivated consensus. Absent an account of why *these* norms deserve the
authority they have, submission to the general will—even though its formal impartiality depersonalizes its authority—can *only* be submission.

5. Science: Grasping What Is as a Result and as a Whole

Although Hegel shares with Rousseau the sense that freedom should be
characterized as a kind of wholeness or self-possession, he thinks these notions
should be conceived of as a justified cognitive achievement. In order to clarify the
form that such an achievement would need to take, why Hegel regards the lack
of a cognitive dimension in Rousseau as a deficit, and how he seeks to remedy
it, I turn to the idea of "Science" (*Wissenschaft*) outlined in the *Phenomenology*'s
preface—what it is, and its relationship to both philosophy and lived individual
freedom. While this focus on a text written fairly early in Hegel's career may
seem artificial, the preface contains a programmatic statement of his system's
goals that holds mostly steady through subsequent writings. Getting a handle on
these goals elucidates what it means in *The Philosophy of Right* for freedom to be
actualized through reconciliation with ethical life.

Before getting into this exposition, I want to address the issue of where this
situates me in the interpretive controversies between metaphysical and non-
metaphysical readings of Hegel.[24] My main concern here is with the notion of
freedom running through *The Philosophy of Right*. I do not doubt that Hegel himself thinks that the structure of ethical life described therein, which culminates
in the concrete universal of the state, and the philosophy of objective Spirit's
progression through increasingly determinate conceptions of right (abstract
right, morality, ethical life), reflects the logic of the Idea. In my opinion, he probably also thinks that these aspects of *The Philosophy of Right* are underwritten
or grounded by the logic of the Idea. But I do not see why that work becomes
indefensible or incomprehensible without this grounding relationship—in this
specific sense, I have a "non-metaphysical" reading of *The Philosophy of Right*.

---

[24] See Frederick Beiser, *Hegel* (New York: Routledge, 2005) for a forceful defense of the metaphysical reading.

That said, my position is that Hegel's theoretical philosophy is very relevant for understanding *The Philosophy of Right*'s aims—to that extent, I am opposed to readings of it as a freestanding political philosophy.[25] This opposition, however, is tempered by my sense that a reading of the *Phenomenology* as defending a basically pragmatist conception of agency and a coherentist conception of truth is sufficient for these purposes, and I take questions of whether or not there is more involved in Hegel's overall project—e.g., an ontologically expressed identity of subject and object, Spirit and nature—to be mostly apart from my concerns.[26]

Hegel incorporates self-consciousness about what it is that makes truth contents accessible to cognition into the heart of his conception of knowledge. This move connects the following well-known but often puzzling theses:

a) Genuine knowing is not a matter of grasping isolated propositions, but can only be expressed by displaying their systematic interconnectedness: "The true shape in which truth exists can only be the scientific system of such truth" (§5/3).

b) Knowledge must be expressed as the result of the development of this system:

> The true is the whole. However, the whole is only the essence completing itself through its development. This much must be said of the absolute: it is essentially a *result*, and only at the *end* is it what it is in truth. Its nature consists precisely in this: to be actual, to be subject, that is, to be the becoming-of-itself. (§20/11; see also §3/2)

To illuminate Hegel's point, consider the following (admittedly reductive) example: let us say that we became convinced (as Hegel is definitely *not*) that natural science represents *the* privileged method available to us for making justifiable claims (because, say, it establishes correspondence to reality). Suppose further that physicists successfully elaborate a grand final theory, expressed in a series of discrete propositions that capture the fundamental elements and forces of the universe, and how they interact. Would these propositions, for Hegel, be the truth about what is, i.e., the Absolute? The answer is clearly "no"; he considers such a conception of the Absolute severely "one-sided." To round it out, we would need an account of how and why these propositions came to have

---

[25] See Allen Wood, *Hegel's Ethical Thought* (New York: Cambridge University Press, 1990), for what is perhaps the founding version of this reading.

[26] See Robert Brandom, *Tales of the Mighty Dead: Historical Essays in the Metaphysics of Intentionality* (Cambridge, MA: Harvard University Press, 2002), 210–234.

authority for us. Now, Hegel is not the first philosopher to suggest that, in order for something to count as knowledge, true belief needs to be supplemented by a justification for that belief. But he is unique in terms of what is involved in successful justification by introducing a level of reflexivity about justificatory practices themselves: while acknowledging that our claim-making ability is parasitic on what Spirit makes available, those claim-making practices themselves can be rationally redeemed if they can be understood as having come about for good reasons. In this example, it is not so much that we would need a detailed history of the natural sciences, but they do need to be grasped as more than a brute "way things are done." We would need to understand them as practices institutionalized for sound, tested reasons, which represent an advance over relevant historical alternatives; plus, a sense of how they relate to (and became differentiated from) other claim-making discourses (e.g., faith and common sense, ethics and art). The *Phenomenology*'s figurative sketches of the articulation and breakdown of shapes of Spirit purportedly confirm that they are determinate results of a social learning process.

Hegel thus radicalizes the self-conscious element of knowledge that Descartes began stressing, but which finds fuller expression in Kant's apperceptive unity of consciousness and deduction of the categories.[27] For Hegel, confirmation of claim-making practices' soundness should be a historical actuality, realized by actual knowers, as opposed to the formal possibility Descartes' *Meditations* and Kant's first *Critique* make it. This radical self-consciousness, when added to Hegel's insistence that Absolute knowing can only properly be conceived systematically and as a result, comes together in the idea of Science. Science is the shape that philosophy must take in order to adequately express what is. Although Hegel's rhetoric in the preface and conclusion of the *Phenomenology* appear to be continuous with the tradition of substance metaphysics, the preceding considerations indicate that this cannot be quite right. For one thing, an essential feature, Hegel thinks, of *what is* is that it is not just *knowable*, but that at a certain historical juncture it *becomes known*. This is why Hegel's idealism does not amount to the claim that mind is the basic substance of reality, but to the thesis that it is incoherent to cede metaphysical priority to subject or object: "Philosophy is idealism because it does not acknowledge either one of the opposites as existing for itself in its abstraction from the other."[28] Thus, when Hegel makes the claim that "everything hangs on apprehending and expressing

---

[27] See Dietmar Heidemann, "Substance, Subject, System: The Justification of Science in Hegel's *Phenomenology of Spirit*," in *Hegel's* Phenomenology of Spirit: *A Critical Guide*, 1–20.

[28] Hegel, *Faith and Knowledge*, trans. Walter Cerf and H. S. Harris (Albany: SUNY Press, 1977), 68. See Sally Sedgwick, *Hegel's Critique of Kant: From Dichotomy to Identity* (New York: Oxford University Press, 2012), 128–162.

the true not as *substance*, but rather even more as *subject*" (PhG, §17/10), he is saying that truth involves a grasp not so much of the basic stuff of reality, but of how we developed cognitive practices whereby things become knowable. What makes *what is* rational is that it is ascertained through reason, which grasps it through reflection (not intuition, or Kant's "the understanding"):

> Hence, reason is misunderstood if reflection is excluded from truth and is not taken to be a positive moment of the Absolute. Reflection is what makes truth into the result, but it is likewise what sublates the opposition between the result and its coming to be . . . This is for the first time its actuality. (§21/11–12)

Thus, to know the truth of what is essentially involves self-consciously being at home amongst the web of cognitive practices that make this knowing possible, which comes about through reflection on Spirit. Later, in the *Encyclopedia*, Hegel treats metaphysics not as a type of discourse that comprehends reality through its own means (e.g., rational intuitions), but as the enterprise that seeks to see how things hang together at the most general level by concerning itself with the "universal determinations of thought" that comprise "the diamond net into which everything is brought and thereby first made intelligible."[29]

It is notable that the cognitive practices that comprise Spirit are plural, spanning the types of claiming-making that are possible in human communities, and rather than reducing them to or grounding them in a metaphysical master discourse, Spirit reaches its apogee as Science by reflecting on how these practices have become fully sufficient for the purposes of inquiry and action coordination. Hegel is beginning to grapple with an aspect of modernity that later social theorists (Talcott Parsons, Niklas Luhmann) dub "functional differentiation": briefly, the development of specialized forms of inquiry and action coordination that involve qualitatively distinct value orientations and modes of justification. Contrary to societies of antiquity, centered around cults given visible shape in art, and medieval ones centered around religious life, Spirit in the modern world has fractured into a constellation of specialized discourses— forms of inquiry, prescriptions for social conduct—none of which ground the others, per se. Even philosophy—the mode of Absolute Spirit that has superseded art and religion as the one most appropriate to modern times—does not ground them, so much as reveal them to be the result of reason's free development. Hegel thinks that contemporaries who read differentiation as fracture (e.g., the romantics) fail to appreciate that "the actuality of this simple whole consists in those embodiments which, having become moments of the whole,

---

[29] Hegel, *Encyclopedia of the Philosophical Sciences*, part 2, *The Philosophy of Nature*, trans. A. V. Miller (New York: Oxford University Press, 1970), §246R/11.

once again develop themselves anew and give themselves embodiment" (§12/ 7). There are a host of questions about this stance, e.g., does Hegel have anything approaching an adequate idea of the natural sciences? Can the emphatic claims to ultimate meaning made by art and religion—and occasionally, philosophy— really be relegated to niches, possessing only qualified truth? Can secular forms of morality and law be motivationally efficacious without backing from such emphatic forms of meaning? But the basic point that Hegel strives to make plausible is: Spirit becomes fully "for itself" by affirming through reflection that the modern constellation of specialized discourses, when appropriately ordered, is fully adequate for the mutually justifiable ordering of human affairs across its perennial concerns. As he writes in the *Encyclopedia*, "[the Idea's] content is none other than the concept in its determinations."[30]

Now, Hegel is aware that there is something bloodless about this conclusion: to laypersons, the assurance that Hegelian philosophy offers—basically, that at some highly abstruse level beyond what art and religion can illuminate, human life makes sense—is likely not something that imparts meaning/ purpose ("spiritual life") to individual lives in the way art and religion did for bygone ages. Hegel does not shrug off this issue: freedom requires the reflective internalization of Science's perspective in contingent individual lives that do not equally participate in, much less master, the full gamut of specialized discourses. This is enabled by an affective identification with the Idea, but this is something that Science, by itself, does not motivate (as, e.g., art did in Greek ethical life). In order to be rooted in a community's spiritual life, the Idea must have some concrete, ascertainable shape: "Only what is completely determined is at once exoteric, comprehensible, and capable of being learned and possessed by everybody." But again, Science itself does not seem to have this, so earlier in this passage, he writes, "Without this development, science has no general intelligibility, and it seems to be the esoteric possession of only a few individuals" (§13/7). Yet, all *should* be able to intelligibly grasp the whole, that they might be at home in their contingent and partial place within it—and so, Science (its gist, at any rate) should be accessible to ordinary consciousness: "To achieve rational knowledge through our own intellect is the rightful demand of a consciousness which is approaching the status of Science." The issue is similar to that of publicity conditions in Rousseau: if freedom involves not just inhabiting certain objectively correct conditions, but knowing this and affectively identifying with them, then there needs to be something public and tangible to identify *with*.

---

[30] Hegel, *Encyclopedia of the Philosophical Sciences in Basic Outline*, part 1, *Science of Logic*, ed. and trans. Klaus Brinkmann and Daniel Dahlstrom (New York: Cambridge University Press, 2010), §213/282.

In fact, far from neglecting the problem of affectively anchoring Spirit such that individuals may regard its customs, practices, norms, etc. as their own, a concern with the possibility of ways of life degenerating into "dead" systems of authority is a guiding thread in Hegel's thought, extending back to his earliest writings, where he considers both Christianity and Kant's secular morality to be threatened with this sort of decline.[31] One of his most striking accounts of this sort of regression is the one that takes place between Greek ethical life and a Roman world that is dominated by "excessive legality" and "formalism."[32] To put it colloquially, Hegel thinks that Romans acquired their main sense of who they were and how their society hung together not from art, nor religion, nor science, but from the law—and the law had become disconnected from those more cognitively satisfying and emotionally nourishing forms of Absolute Spirit:

> The Spirit of the Roman world is domination by abstraction (i.e. by dead law), the demolition of beauty and joyous customs, the suppression of the family *qua immediate* natural ethical life, in general the sacrifice of individuality which surrenders itself to the state and finds its cold-blooded dignity and intellectual satisfaction in obedience to abstract law. (A, 541)

In the Greece of Hegel's imagination, instead of experiencing the particular forms of behavior prescribed by settled mores and obligations owed to the state as something externally imposed, Greeks unproblematically identify themselves with these roles. After Greece's beautiful but unreflective form of life fractures under the weight of internal conflicts, however, it is succeeded by a Roman one that is not so beautiful and fails to inspire a similar kind of spontaneous identification with its prescribed roles. Rome compensates for this lack of identification with a highly developed legal system: "ethical consciousness is *immediately* directed toward the law" (PhG, §475/289). By this, I take Hegel to mean that the ties that bind Roman society consist largely in a body of law identifying persons essentially as property holders with enumerable rights and responsibilities. This body of law is experienced by its subjects, not as consonant with rules persons would choose to impose on themselves (as in modern social contract theory), nor as the institutional embodiment of a people's normative self-conception

---

[31] See Hegel, *Early Theological Writings*, trans. T. M. Knox (Philadelphia: University of Pennsylvania Press, 1975), 67–181.

[32] Compared to the attention given to Hegel's (and many of his romantic contemporaries') idealized view of Greek life, little has been written concerning his ideas about Roman society. See, however, Terry Pinkard, *Hegel's* Phenomenology: *The Sociality of Reason* (New York: Cambridge University Press, 1994), 146–150, 250.

(as in Greek ethical life), but as "the simple necessity of an empty fate" (§476/290)—that is, an impersonal, authoritative determination of social reality.

Since this "dead," "abstract" system of law is understood as the backbone of order that makes possible social interaction in Roman society, it should be no surprise that Hegel deems it to be an asocial, atomized polity: "as a legal person, each exists for himself, and he excludes continuity with others through the absolute, unaccommodating nature of his point-like existence" (§481/293). In *The Philosophy of Right*, he attributes some of the cruelty of Roman society, in particular the status of dependents in family law, to the preponderance of law.

> One of the blackest marks against Roman legislation is the law whereby children were treated as slaves. This offense against the ethical order in its innermost and most tender life is one of the most important clues for understanding the place of the Romans in the history of the world and their tendency toward legal formalism (PR, §175/174).

When societies transition from a form of social integration that takes place through mutually recognized participation in a shared way of life, to one where it depends on a network of legal statuses and permissible actions that persons accede to as given, the need to recognize persons as active agents in the repro-duction of their social life recedes and they tend to become reduced to their immediate appearance within this formal system. To wit, family dependents in Rome are, for legal purposes, entirely subject to the decision-making authority of heads of households. Of course, we would now want to maintain that these dependents are also vulnerable persons with their own needs and interests. But in a society where relations are overwhelmingly conceived as legally structured, how persons appear in the legal system effectively defines what they are—in this case, children, treated as akin to property by Roman law, come to be regarded as basically that: property of the father, to be disposed of at his arbitrary discre-tion. In other words, the spiritual deficits of Roman political life—it inspires not affective identification, but sullen submission—damages the overall quality of communal life, and is in turn detrimental to freedom: if freedom is being with oneself in another, and ethical life is the primary medium through which individuals are related to one another, then ethical substance (e.g., Roman law) that integrates society without being anchored in the affective identification of its members leaves them to a large extent spiritually empty, unable to be at home in the world. So, to the extent that Hegel at least countenances the worry that the ethical substance of the modern world might be crumbling into diffuse systems of authority, unanimated by Spirit, he must have some reason to think this will not be its fate. But the triumphalist rhetoric at the conclusion of the *Phenomenology* belies the fact that he does not seem to offer much to assuage this worry there; however, in *The Philosophy of Right*, with the conception of ethical life, he does.

6. Hegel's Critique of Rousseau in Summation

Before examining how we might see ethical life as publicizing functional differentiation and reconciling individuals to it, we can finish with Rousseau by seeing how, from Hegel's perspective, he founders badly on the issue of matching the citizens' affective identification to the general will with laws and institutions that would give it public visibility and substance. Rousseau reconciles citizens to their *sociality* (i.e., their mutual dependence) without reconciling them to *society* (i.e., the division of labor, and the instruments of government that shape it). Such reconciliation is unreal to the extent that it tends to produce alienation from "right" as it exists. When Hegel ascribes to what we might call Rousseauianism responsibility for the French Revolution's self-immolating trends, he is pointing out that citizens must identify *something* as the general will in order that they might know themselves as free, but because a) the general will is not "a result" of predecessor shapes of Spirit so much as a break with them, and b) it cannot specify concrete institutions, it is hazy what this "something" is. This is not to say that individuals cannot be convinced that this or that (leader, political party, constitutional interpretation, etc.) stands for the general will; yet there are no publicly authoritative standards or procedures for assessing claims about whether any such identification warrants everyone's assent. As Hegel writes, "it cannot amount to a positive work, that is, it can neither amount to universal works of language, nor to those of actuality, nor to the laws and universal institutions of *conscious* freedom, nor to the deeds and works of *willing* them" (PhG, §588/358; see also PR, §258R/230). We should recall here Rousseau's skepticism toward the idea that any institution, permanently established and professionally administered, could reliably convey the general will. This reflects the larger fact that Rousseau is uncomfortable with functional differentiation: he thinks the differentiation of society into spheres that require individuals to occupy particular roles fosters comparison, which breeds faction. The general will is geared to move our sense of self *beyond* this differentiation, rather than reconcile us to it . . . while leaving the differentiation of social spheres intact. Rather than representing an ongoing procedure of consensus formation for ordering differentiated social spheres, the general will can only be conceptualized as permanent suspicion toward the structures and powers that institutionalize them: "there remains for it only the *negative* act. It is merely the *fury* of disappearing" (PhG, §589/359).

At a conceptual level, this misunderstands how freedom could be manifest in the will. For the will to be free, a moment of abstraction is plainly

involved: simply being determined by something exogenous to the will is antithetical to freedom. So, if we think that actions normally issue from impulses
shaped by existent habits and norms, then the free will must exercise a capacity
to abstract away from these possible determinations; it must realize that none
of them are necessary, that I *could* do *any* of these things—at this point, the will
is free "in itself" (PR, §10A/35). In some circles, e.g., for varieties of mysticism
(or, for Hegel, "fanaticism"), this moment of "indeterminacy" is considered
freedom, full stop, where freedom is a flight from the conventionality and fixity
of the self (§5R/29). But, such a will is unfree insofar as it cannot experience
itself in any particular action: "it would become truly free only as truly determinate content. At that point it is free for itself, has freedom as its object, and
is freedom" (§10A/35). Hegel associates the indeterminate moment of the will
with arbitrariness (*Wilkür*) or paralysis, the "bad infinity" of endless possibility,
and alienation from the social sources of action norms. To be *actually* (in Hegel's
technical sense) free, the will must will *something*, and that something has to
be reflectively continuous with the agent's sense of self. So, the actualized free
will is the unity of these moments of determinacy and indeterminacy—unity
in the sense of a harmonious interrelation rather than fusion. However, the will
is by no means naturally in such a state of harmony. Not coincidentally, Hegel's
conception of the free will's actuality parallels the way persons who understand
themselves as dependent upon Spirit, but comprehend Spirit as Science, obtain
the stance of Absolute knowing: while they cannot understand themselves as
wholly originary sources of action, they *can* be reflectively aware of their socialization into a rational form of life, and thus be assured in their appropriation of
its action norms.[33]

In contrast to Rousseau who, at least in moments, favors highly local, homogenous, plebiscite democracy (e.g., SC, 90–92), Hegel appreciates how the actualization of a freedom that synthesizes the particular and universal moments
of the will must contend with the complexity of modern societies through a
differentiated set of institutions and practices that mediate between individuals
occupying different social positions. Hegel's innovative approach to this dilemma is to differentiate the concept of autonomy into a set of institutionally
anchored forms of recognition that confer on persons the statuses of a) unique,
dependent beings (the family); b) independent, rational, and responsible agents
(the market and rule of law); c) members of communities of solidarity and

---

[33] Although we can understand the sense in which Stern characterizes Hegelian normativity as
"intuitionistic," insofar as it concedes that different values and action norms are appropriate for different institutional spheres, I think that the fact that, for Hegel, modern ethical life has this kind of
normative authority for us because we can see that it, overall, actualizes freedom, belies this point.
See Stern, *Kantian Ethics*, 145–149.

shared interests (corporations and estates); and d) citizens involved in the articulation of universal principles (the state).

7. Ethical Life: Reconciling Individuality and Sociality

We should now be in a position to see why Hegel introduces ethical life as "*the Idea of freedom . . . the concept of freedom developed into the existing world and the nature of self-consciousness*" (PR, 154/142). The institutional infrastructure of modern life socializes persons with the ability to freely appropriate ethical life's action norms into their sense of self, as opposed to being subject to them by either explicit coercion or unconscious conditioning. Moreover, this incorporation is based on a recognition of ethical life as mutual and rational, even while it permits everyone to be their own self—this recognition is made possible by the public and transparent nature of the state's activity. In contradistinction to Rousseau, who urges individuals to anchor their sense of what is truly important to them beyond the particularity and partiality of everyday life, ethical life folds individual subjectivity into a social whole that can visibly be grasped to rationally work for the well-being of all and to be the result of progressive social learning (i.e., over Greek ethical life, feudalism, Enlightenment atomism).[34]

In order to see how this enfolding takes place, we need to consider how Hegel understands the relationship between civil society and the state. Civil society is the sphere of modern life that valorizes individual self-expression and self-interest. Its main institutions—the impartial rule of law and the market economy—establish the individual's formal independence from more collective institutions like family

---

[34] Readers may notice that my account has not emphasized Hegel's philosophy of history. This lack of emphasis is intentional, for although the extent to which Hegel is committed to some kind of historical determinism, or an "end" to history (whatever that might mean), plus how he thinks "great" individuals and events contribute to change, are open to interpretation, Such matters are not essential to my purposes. There is no doubt that Hegel's lectures on world history and Absolute Spirit are Eurocentric, implying that non-Western peoples either do not have history, or at any rate not in the dynamically progressive way that the West does. Given that Hegel's conception of normativity is dependent on recognizing the institutions of modern ethical life as rational progress, and that this outlook seems quite tied up with comparative assessments of the value and worth of non-Western peoples as lesser, Amy Allen has trenchantly argued that the whole "left Hegelian grounding strategy" is stuck in a vain struggle to extricate itself from Eurocentrism. See Allen, *The End of Progress? Decolonizing the Normative Foundations of Critical Theory* (New York: Columbia University Press, 2016). Although it is hard to believe that, genetically, Hegel's own thoughts about the rationality of Occidental development did not involve comparative judgments about peoples he considered lesser, what is essential here is the ability that Hegel thinks is afforded to people in *his* society to recognize *their* institutions as rational developments vis-à-vis *their* past, e.g., feudalism and antiquity. For a reading of Hegel's philosophy of history along these lines, see Joseph McCarney, *Hegel on History* (New York: Routledge, 2000).

and state, allowing them to pursue their preferences without obligation to the common good. Participants in civil society conceive of one another as independent, autonomous individuals pursuing their own interests. It is, ultimately, an alienated world: there is a deep chasm between the institutions of civil society, in which the needs of individuals are linked together through "a system of all-round interdepend- ence" (§183/181) that gives relations between them "mediation through the form of *universality*" (§182/181), on the one hand, and the way that individuals compre- hend this interdependence *qua* members of civil society, on the other. Hegel's use of the term "form" here signals that he regards this mode of universality as incom- plete. If, in general, we can think of the actualization of freedom as "the unity and interpenetration of universality and individuality" (§258R/229), in civil society, universality and individuality exist side-by-side, but in an unreconciled manner. Individuality exists as a bundle of "needs" and "natural necessity" (§182/180– 181). The laws of political economy through which preference-satisfiers are univer- sally related to one another are uncomprehended by the individuals involved. Or, rather, to the extent that they are comprehended (e.g., by political economists), they are understood as quasi-natural laws that operate behind the backs of individuals. Certainly, the ability to participate in civil society does not require persons to un- derstand the mechanisms through which they are universally related to others: "the interest of the Idea" is one "which these are as such unconscious" (§187/184).

Civil society's unruly tendencies are symptomatic of the one-sided, incom- plete kind of freedom instantiated therein: individuals may do as they please, but only within a scope defined by the laws of political economy and the rule of law. As such, they experience these boundaries as externally imposed constraints on their liberty of choice: "In civil society, universality is necessity only" (§229A/ 215).[35] In civil society, forces outside of their control and comprehension buffet individuals about. Hegel is often given a lot of credit for predicting the crisis- ridden character of the market economy—in particular, how the unfettered operation of supply and demand mechanisms could result in crises of overpro- duction, resulting in chronic unemployment and poverty among workers, who

---

[35] This also helps explain Hegel's interpretation of Kant's principle of right: "Any action is right if it can coexist with everyone's freedom in accordance with a universal law, or if on its maxim the freedom of choice of each can coexist with everyone's freedom in accordance with a universal law ..." *The Metaphysics of Morals*, in *Practical Philosophy*, 387 (6:230). In Kant's social contract, the principle of right is universally willed by all rational beings, but at least on Hegel's reading, it amounts to a vol- untary limitation on the free will of the subject. So long as we understand political right as primarily concerned with constraining arbitrary will, the rule of law appears as "only a negative determination," in which "the rational can come onto the scene only as a restriction on the type of freedom which this principle involves, and so also not as something immanently rational but only as an external, formal universal" (PR, §29A/46–47). This echoes the younger Hegel's concern that Kant's moral system is purely positive, amounting to rigid subjection before the moral law. See Hegel, *Early Theological Writings*, 204–224.

form an exploitable underclass forced to live by their daily labor ("the rabble"). So, in addition to being chaotic and self-undermining, civil society is only an apparent domain of freedom, but is equally one of compulsion, where other persons are experienced as obstacles and antagonists.

Despite all this, Hegel treats civil society with ambivalence, not condemnation: it institutionalizes "the principle of subjectivity," which grants individual personality "the right to develop launch forth in all directions" (§184/ 181). Civil society allows particularity space to develop of its own accord. Concomitantly, individuals in a modern society, Hegel seems to realize, identify themselves to a much greater extent with this particularity: it is central to who they are rather than just an inessential accident of their existence. He concedes that the principle of subjectivity institutionalizes a sort of pettiness (of the sort Rousseau deplored) that prevents the modern state from being the beautiful unity that he associates with ancient Greek city-states. The virtue of the modern world lies in its institutionalization of reflection, not in the nobility of its heroes—the differentiated nature of the forms of reflection variously institutionalized in the modern "way of life" makes it ill-suited to artistic depiction: unlike "the beautiful days of Greek art . . . the conditions of our present time are not favorable to art" (A, 11).[36] But he criticizes Greek life for giving insufficient weight to particularity, since the well-being of the individual is all but completely subsumed under the interests of the whole, and he views the freedom on offer in modern societies as ultimately richer and more fully developed than what was possible in previous eras (PR, §260A/235). So, Hegel is convinced that the principle of subjectivity represents a real and important dimension of freedom, and a significant achievement of the modern world. While he casts the state as that form of modern community that reconnects myopically self-interested members of civil society to one another through their universal identity as citizens, it does so not by overwhelming the particular identities and interests of individuals.

> The principle of modern states has prodigious strength and depth because it allows the principle of subjectivity to progress to its culmination in the self-sufficient extreme of personal particularity, and yet at the same time brings it back to the substantial unity and so maintains this unity in the principle of subjectivity itself. (§260/235)

So, Hegel tasks the modern state with preserving individuality while overcoming its dysfunction as a self-sufficient conception of freedom.

---

[36] For the claim that perhaps not art, but aesthetic imagination, nevertheless plays a significant role in Hegel's conception of modern social relations, see Jason Miller, "The Role of Aesthetics in Hegelian Theories of Recognition," *Constellations* 23, no. 1 (2016): 96–109.

The key here, for Hegel, is to conceptualize how individuals can, when pursuing their self-interest, have a background awareness that this action orientation is licensed by the whole, i.e., that the state arranges this area of social life with the expectation that people will be self-interested within it. In order that the state respect self-legislating rationality, modern persons should be able to understand the state as something consciously willed by the citizens in tandem, not as a traditional, "merely positive" institution that they find themselves subject to. But, unlike Rousseau, these shared reasons should *license* personal particularity (by institutionalizing it in civil society) rather than seeking to erase or overcome it. So, Hegel here involves himself in a characteristic balancing act: the particularity of civil society threatens to dissolve society into atomistic chaos, while a state based on solely universal principles proves to be empty and self-destructive. Consequently, a rationally ordered modern state acknowledges the principle of subjectivity, while being true to the equally modern insight that the state should be based on reasons that all share.

It is notable that, in contradistinction to the shapes of Spirit the *Phenomenology* progresses through, the dysfunction that civil society creates is *containable*—it does not negate the whole order. The existence of the "*Polizei*"—a kind of proto-welfare state—is indicative of the kind of institutionalized reflexivity that Hegel expects from a modern state: *qua* members of civil society, individuals normally do not care to inform themselves how their self-interest refracts through market mechanisms to contribute to collective outcomes; but *qua* citizens, they expect that the view of the whole that the state enjoys allows it to manage potential disruptions. So, for example, "differing interests of producers and consumers may come into collision with each other" in ways that have the potential for both class conflict and serious privations (§236/217). But a state able to anticipate this collision can provision for its consequences without unduly undermining the market's dynamism. I should emphasize here that Hegel thinks it is important that citizens be aware of how the *Polizei* ensure that particularity by and large contributes to universal interests. This awareness contributes to the background understanding that persons occupying their roles as member of civil society have of the state as the active agent of the common good.

Stepping back momentarily, we can see that Hegel should not be numbered among social theorists who think of markets as natural. The variety of shapes of Spirit canvassed in the *Phenomenology* indicates that they comprise systems of action wherein participants recognize one another as acting for legitimate reasons, that there are a wide range of types of actions that can be considered reasonable and appropriate by a given collectivity, and that persons are generally motivated to act in such a way as to satisfy social expectations. In fact, Hegel's account of dispositional and motivational psychology, such as it is, is considerably more plastic than Rousseau's, who had already advanced a fair distance away from a static account of human nature, toward more of a cultural conditioning model.[37] Hegel seems to think that individual human beings are primarily driven by a need to have an integrated identity, and be confirmed and recognized in their way of doing things, rather than by bare self-interest.[38] So, self-regarding market actors must (overall, in general) believe that their way of doing things will be recognized as legitimate. Now, Hegel is enough of a Smithean to think that, in a qualified way, markets *do* promote the common good (by expanding trade and industry), but this fact would not explain why individuals are assured of their legitimacy, since this is specialized knowledge that participants do not ordinarily possess. Insofar as Hegel thinks that people *do* think of self-interested market behavior as socially legitimate in our time, background awareness of its legitimacy has to be actively promoted and maintained by the state.

It should be said that, from our contemporary perspective, the *Polizei*'s tools for dealing with macroeconomic problems (supply and demand imbalances, unemployment) are not terribly sophisticated. Mainly, they consist in price controls and last-resort safety nets, plus the possibility of public works programs. Ever since Marx, Hegel has been widely criticized for not recognizing how much of a contagion "the rabble" could be for the system's legitimacy, and the inadequacy of his measures for dealing with it.[39] But whatever the retrospective adequacy of Hegel's policies here, the crucial thing to notice is how he thinks market problems *can be* contained, and what this says about freedom through reconciliation. In keeping with Hegel's effort to conceive of modern Spirit as a unity of specialized discourses—the comprehension of which constitutes Absolute knowing—we can attain consciousness of the particularity in civil society as *a moment* of modern life. It is an ingredient in a well-led life that *can*, in a rationally organized society, be harmonized with other equally essential dimensions of life (e.g., intimacy, public deliberation). But this harmony is not the natural state of things and requires active mediation. This invocation of mediation—an important concept for the explication of Hegel's logic, which indicates that the nature or identity of a thing is bound up with its relationship to something else—is quite important.[40] Philosophy may provide (or at least crucially informs) this

[37] See Katie Padgett Walsh, "Reasons Internalism, Hegelian Resources," *Journal of Value Inquiry* 44, no. 2 (2010): 225–240, and Pinkard, *Hegel's Naturalism: Mind, Nature, and the Final Ends of Life* (New York: Oxford University Press, 2012), 53–64.

[38] Although I hazard this as a general take on Hegel's point, there are a welter of issues about why he thinks this is and what it could mean that I do not have the space to explore. See Robert Pippin, *Hegel on Self-Consciousness: Desire and Death in* The Phenomenology of Spirit (Princeton: Princeton University Press, 2011).

[39] See Frank Ruda, *Hegel's Rabble: An Investigation into* The Philosophy of Right (New York: Continuum, 2011).

[40] See Hegel, *Encyclopedia of the Philosophical Sciences*, part 1, *Science of Logic*, ed. and trans. Klaus Brinkmann and Daniel Dahlstrom (New York: Cambridge University Press, 2010), §62–65/

consciousness, as it prepares us to think of the Idea as something actualized *through the work of reason*. Readers of the *Logic* can anticipate that the wholeness of a particular person is not self-contained, but is rather attained by relating itself to the universal (the state). But *The Philosophy of Right* describes an ongoing process of mediation that takes place through citizens' cognizance of (and to a limited extent, participation in) a political process wherein particularity is circumscribed, but given its due; and wherein the state works out, on an ongoing basis, how different group interests can be made to cooperatively (though competitively) complement each other, while the groups recognize each other as essential components of a self-reproducing whole. Comprehending how ethical life works as a whole allows individuals to see the various aspects of their particularity through the lens of the universal.

In addition to the *Polizei*, there are a series of institutions at the border of civil society and the state that perform this mediation. They do so in a way that, despite being intricate, aims at transparency, i.e., being understandable without mystification or specialized knowledge. This point warrants underscoring: while philosophy comprehends the activity of the universal in terms of the Idea's logic, ordinary social consciousness grasps the Idea's actualization in a way that, while perhaps lacking the rigor of philosophy, nevertheless does not require the abstracting simplifications of the lesser forms of Absolute Spirit (art and religion). In short, Hegel thinks that laypersons can basically understand how their society works—and that, *qua* individuals, their freedom depends on this comprehension.

8. Politics as the Mediation of Universal and Particular: The Constitution and the Rule of Law

When considered in isolation, the previous points about civil society and the *Polizei* may seem unconvincing: why should the fact that the *Polizei* are needed in order to contain economic crisis and widespread pauperism indicate the ultimately harmonious nature of ethical life, as opposed to its precariousness, i.e., that it is held together only through continuous, coercive state intervention? More broadly, we might take the upshot of Hegel's reflections on the prominence of civil society to be that modern life is very fractured: individuals are compelled to assume multiple roles, adapt to and transition between a variety of institutional contexts with very different, incompatible systems of action. Like his romantic contemporaries, Hegel is prepared to regard this fragmentation as detrimental to one's ability to forge an

---

110–116. See also, Brian O'Connor, "The Concept of Mediation in Hegel and Adorno," *Bulletin of the Hegel Society of Great Britain*, 39/40, no. 1–2 (1999): 84–96.

integrated identity, and therefore as a loss of freedom. But we are in a position to see that his philosophy is geared to recoup a sense of wholeness amidst Spirit's differentiation; more specifically, he thinks there must be a nodal center for the mediational activity that relates specialized social spheres to the whole; moreover, in the interests of publicity, this nexus must be concretely representable. Hegel thinks that Rousseau (and by extension, the Enlightenment) failed utterly in handling this latter requirement. But, while Hegel raises this issue in the *Phenomenology*, it is hard to see how he solves it there. Earlier in the chapter, I indicated that we ought to look at ethical life in *The Philosophy of Right* to find Hegel's most complete answer to this challenge. In particular, two elements of modern ethical life are particularly relevant in disclosing it as both concrete and a universal system of mediation: the constitution and the Estates.

The fracturing of modern ethical life into functionally differentiated spheres can, by Hegel's reckoning, be reconciled by the constitution of a well-ordered modern state. The constitution represents a vantage point from which the differentiation of these social spheres—and the various roles and identities entailed by them—can be understood as being jointly willed by the members of society. To be sure, Hegel's idea of constitutionalism is not ours, being less legalistic and formal. It refers to both the more narrow "political" constitution (PR, §267/ 240) (the basic legal norms governing the production of legitimate law and binding political decisions) and, more broadly, the constitution as the backbone of institutions through which a society can understand itself as a social whole—something like Rawls' "basic structure of society."[41] This distinction can be fuzzy, since there is plainly a reciprocal relationship between the two senses: the welfare of individuals secured by the institutions of family, civil society, and the Estates (i.e., the broad constitution) form the "firm foundation of the state," while individuals' "self-awareness" of the narrower political constitution as that which preserves these institutions and their well-functioning interrelation grounds their "political disposition" of habitual "trust" toward the state, i.e., patriotism (§268/240).

It is in this context that we can understand Hegel when he writes: "The constitution is essentially a system of mediation" (§302A/290). Conceived on such terms, a constitution is a complex of institutions and norms through which citizens can understand themselves as individual persons, separate from others, with their own dignity, interests, and identities, but who know that these

---

[41] See PR, §264–5/239–240. A careful commentary on this point can be found in Ludwig Siep, "Constitution, Fundamental Rights, and Social Welfare in Hegel's *Philosophy of Right*," in *Hegel on Ethics and Politics*, eds. Otfried Höffe and Robert Pippin (New York: Cambridge University Press, 2004), 268–290. See also Andrew Buchwalter, "Law, Culture, and Constitutionalism: Remarks on Hegel and Habermas," in *Beyond Liberalism and Communitarianism: Studies in Hegel's* Philosophy of Right, ed. Robert Williams (Albany: SUNY Press, 2001), 207–228.

interests and identities are generated through intersubjective processes of recognition, and that, therefore, their well-being (not just their security, but their very sense of self) is tied to the fates of others in a common enterprise. Certainly, a given constitutional order may fail to do all of this. For one thing, the political culture must be such that the citizens actually comprehend themselves as being connected to one another in the manner just referred to. In this regard, Hegel notes the dangers of despotism and excessive legalism, whereby the constitutional order can degenerate into an instrument for group domination (§297/283–284).[42] The upshot of these reflections is that, for a constitution to be successful in its mediational function, it must a) be recognizably concrete in the sense that citizens need to be able to perceive themselves as bound together within *this particular* institutional order, and b) provide a normative framework whereby all members understand their relationships to others (economic, social, and political) as justified by the lights of their shared reasons. In order to satisfy (a), the norms of the constitution must be public and knowable, that is, they must be already established and "positive." But in order to satisfy (b), the constitution must not be merely positive: for citizens to make it their own and have the norms governing their relationship to each other be the work of their own reason-giving activities, the content of the constitution should continually be shaped and renewed. Again, Hegel may be justly criticized for the very limited amount of participation "in the universal business of the state" that he envisions being feasible for the average citizen to take part in. However, the foregoing should make clear his opposition to static, overly foundational models of constitutionalism: constitutional norms can only be made meaningful through some kind of rational activity—they undergo "progressive development" through ongoing legislation (§298A/284–285).[43] In order to actualize the democratic potential in this conception, we would, to be sure, have to supplement or replace Hegel's account of how the content of this ongoing legislation takes place—his examples are subtle but impactful changes in the administration of property and justice by royal elites—with one that views it as the result of broad-based rational discourses on issues of public concern.

This broad notion of constitutionalism, together with opposition to Roman-style legalism, is very much of a piece with what Hegel says earlier in *The Philosophy of Right* about the rule of law and the administration of justice. There,

---

[42] Also interesting in this regard are the young Hegel's reflections on the dissolution of what he viewed as Germany's calcified constitution: see Hegel, "The German Constitution," in *Political Writings*, eds. Laurence Dickey and H. B. Nisbet, trans. H. B. Nisbet (New York: Cambridge University Press, 1999), 6–101.

[43] See also ibid., 23–24, where he seems more favorably disposed toward broader based participation.

while he allows that state administration requires professionalization, he is hostile to the notion that the law can only be known by expert jurists:

> The legal profession, possessed of a specialized knowledge of the law, often claims this knowledge as its monopoly and refuses to allow any layman to discuss the subject . . . Right is concerned with freedom, the worthiest and holiest thing in humanity, the thing a human being must know if it is to have obligatory force for him. (§215/204)

Hegel's rationale for this view should be clear: the actualization of the Idea in ethical life requires self-transparency; the actualization of freedom for individuals requires them to understand how their (contingent and partial) lives relate to the social whole. In general, this means that the basic terms according to which society functions should be accessible to ordinary consciousness, and specifically, if law is the medium that connects specialized social spheres together and works to ensure their complementarity, that medium cannot itself be a specialized sphere of discourse (at least not one with high entry barriers). In this context, Hegel is a moderate legal codifier: in keeping with his screed in *The Philosophy of Right*'s preface against forms of political rationalism that attempt to break with extant forms of right, he is certainly against root-and-branch transformations of the law according to a model code. But reforms that make the laws "well-arranged and clear cut" are laudable: they offer ordinary citizens a concrete (if schematic) sense of what their laws *are* (i.e., what they stand for, where generic burdens of proof lie, differences among areas of law, etc.).[44] This sense that the law both has a specific shape and character (concrete), while being the medium that knits society together (universal), trickles upward into his understanding of constitutionalism.

In sum, we might say that Hegel conceives of the constitutional order as a unity of difference, whereby individuals are recognized in their particularity, but are related to one another through rational and transparent norms that they can understand as an extension of their own will, as something universal. I have been highlighting the importance of the concept of mediation in Hegel's account and the state's specific task in mediating between universality and particularity: the constitutional order should be instantiated through a particular system of positive law that involves the citizens in the development of an order that has universal validity, containing the chaos of civil society by preserving the particularity instantiated therein, while embedding individuality within a larger order that legitimates the pursuit of self-interest as a part—but only a part—of modern life.

---

[44] On Hegel's position in contemporary natural law/positivism debates, see Thom Brooks, "Natural Law Internalism," in *Hegel's* Philosophy of Right, ed. Thom Brooks (Malden, MA: Blackwell, 2012), 167–179.

9. Mediation and the Division of Labor: The Estates

As we have just seen, the state's constitution lays out the terms according to which citizens can meaningfully understand themselves as members of *this* society, and understand what causes society's differentiated spheres to hang together as a whole. The role of the constitution in facilitating freedom is more cognitive than the equivalent role that the general will plays in Rousseau, insofar as the constitution has a concrete explanatory role in our understanding of how society works, which is not true of the general will. That said, if we were to isolate the constitution and consider it to be *the* central mediator between private individuals and the universal state, this would not be terribly different from Rousseau's proposal. It would be hard to see how Hegel would evade the charge that he levels against Rousseau and Kant, namely, that they posit an abstract, unmediated juxtaposition of individual and society. It seems important to Hegel for individuals to have some tangible grasp of *how* the system works on an ongoing basis to represent *their* interests, while configuring their type of particularity with that of others in the division of labor—by itself, the constitution represents more of a bare declaration that the state *does* represent universal interests, work for mutual benefit, etc. The *Polizei* does some of this work, but it functions more in the mode of paternalistic crisis management. Hegel's main way of dealing with this issue is to insist that individuals should be members of one of the Estates, which represent the mains types of social labor in a modern society (agriculture, business/trade, and civil service), and that the Estates should play a direct role in the legislature. The fact that the Estates strike most readers as quasi-medieval makes this one of the less-celebrated aspects of Hegel's political philosophy, and masks the distinctiveness and importance of his ideas here. In granting the Estates a compulsory and legislative role, Hegel is breaking from Enlightenment political thought's (and contemporary liberalism's) frequent recourse to a model of the relationship between state and citizenship, on the one hand, and civil society and private personhood, on the other, where the latter pairing is characterized by particular desires and interests, the former by universality and impartiality. This association of legitimate politics with universality has never much appealed to more empirically oriented thinkers, who note that it bears little resemblance to the way that actual citizens in modern democracies behave;[45] and liberalism's critics often argue that its discourse of universalism

---

[45] See Raymond Geuss, *Philosophy and Real Politics* (Princeton, NJ: Princeton University Press, 2008). For a bracing survey of empirical data, see Christopher Achen and Larry Bartels, *Democracy for Realists: Why Elections Do Not Produce Responsive Government* (Princeton, NJ: Princeton University Press, 2016).

can serve as cover for the assertion of privileged interests.[46] Hegel is one of the few thinkers with a generally affirmative relationship to liberalism who breaks from this vision of a universalistic discourse of citizenship defining the legitimate terms of politics. So, while some of the common criticisms of the Estates are well justified, his ideas about why institutions like these are important are well worth paying attention to.

Given that the modern world seems to indelibly feature decentered markets, expert bureaucracies, and religious and cultural pluralism, Rousseau's hope for the re-emergence of something like ancient Sparta in the middle of 18th-century Europe has struck many as a vain protest. Hegel accords with this objection; by the time of composing *The Philosophy of Right*, he had abandoned any similar yearning for Greek ethical life, which he views as rationally deficient due to its unreflective identification of the individual with the whole (§260A/235). While the most commented-upon aspect of Hegel's break with the Rousseauian model concerns his view of civil society, two related points have equal significance: first, Hegel does not believe that freedom requires the kind of concentrated public-spiritedness that Rousseau does. This is partly a consequence of the fact that Hegel hardly expects modern people to be consumed by the affairs of state, since their nations are sufficiently complex to require bureaucracies whose competency outstrips what could be expected from members of the general public. As a result, the subjective stance of patriotism, which Hegel *does* think is called for, is more passive: an attitude of trust toward the state, associated with a habitual desire to respect the law, but not ordinarily requiring selfless dedication.[47]

Second, the modern division of labor is, on Hegel's account, such that the existence of distinct groups performing significantly different forms of labor is inevitable. This prevents him from believing that a general will concerning what is equally in the interests of all can spontaneously emerge from civil society (§308R/294). So, while Hegel thinks, along with Rousseau and Kant, that freedom requires us to conceive of ourselves as willing the laws that bind us, and thus some sense that we are part of and active in the state, this sense cannot be very direct. Thus, intermediary institutions, situated between private individuals and the universal state, are needed to furnish a more tangible sense of belonging. The Estates do this by operating as "a mediating organ" between particular individuals and the state (§302/289–290). In brief, Hegel's idea is that membership in an estate allows individuals to discern how their activity contributes to

---

[46] See Catherine MacKinnon, *Toward a Feminist Theory of the State* (Cambridge, MA: Harvard University Press, 1989).

[47] See Moland, "History and Patriotism in Hegel's *Rechtsphilosophie*," *History of Political Thought* 28, no. 3 (2007): 496–519.

one of the main spheres of labor central to the reproduction of the social totality of which they are a part, and subsequently grasp how their interests and way of life are represented in the lawmaking process, which synthesizes them with other occupational spheres.[48] As we will see, the political function of the Estates accomplishes this synthesis, while the visibility of this process brings its accomplishment to consciousness, as Hegel stresses here:

> The Estates have the function of bringing the universal interest into existence not only *in itself,* but also *for itself,* i.e., bringing into existence the moment of subjective *formal freedom,* public consciousness as the empirical universality of the thoughts and opinions of the many. (§301/287)

Our first inclination may be to think of the Estates as class-based organizations, but this is misleading in that they are vertically stratified institutions. For example, the members of the agricultural estate are not only farmers, but everyone involved in agriculture, including the landed gentry. Different members of an estate share something substantial: not so much a similar material condition, as a shared way of life.

To appreciate the distinctiveness and relevance of Hegel's view, two points are crucial: first, the Estates are more like classes in the modern sense than, say, the social classes of feudal society (whose existence is to a greater extent based on "positive" traditions and authority), by virtue of the fact that *we,* Hegel thinks, have come to regard the existence of these groups as *the result* of economic processes that lead types of labor to "converge, owing to the universality inherent in their content, and become distinguished into *general groups*" (§201/193). The solidarity of estate membership is not so much ascribed by tradition as based on the recognition of shared material interests *and* ways of life that result from the contingencies of market development.[49] As such, the Estates blend elements of both Marxian classes and Weberian status groups, although Hegel does seem to hold that cultural factors associated with the latter will continue to be more important for defining group identity. Moreover, this is perhaps the main place where Hegel indicates that "ordinary consciousness" can grasp the institutions of modern ethical life as a "result," i.e., a progressive development out of feudal, traditional social formations.

---

[48] For an explanation of how the Estates develop the talents of particular individuals and educate them in virtue, see Christopher Yeomans, *The Expansion of Autonomy: Hegel's Pluralistic Philosophy of Action* (New York: Oxford University Press, 2015).

[49] On the idea that the modern conception of solidarity is rooted in the recognition of shared contingency, see Hauke Brunkhorst, *Solidarity: From Civic Friendship to Global Legal Community* (Cambridge, MA: MIT Press, 2005).

Second, Hegel introduces the Estates as part of civil society, that is, prior to the state—individuals are members of them as private persons, not citizens. Noting this offers some nuance to Hegel's portrait of civil society: usually understood as the sphere of modern life where self-interest is given its moment of free reign, it is also the sphere of work and association. Hence, actors in it are driven by motives more varied than bald self-interest: in addition to preference fulfillment, they seek *"recognition"* of their labor's value. Hegel repeatedly speaks of the "honor" of belonging to an estate (§207/196; §253/225–226), and for a person lacking one (the major category being unskilled wage laborers), "his isolation reduces his business to mere self-seeking" (§253R/226). Thus, the Estates are crucial for persons' ability to view themselves as "at home" (literally, to have a "place" [*Stand*]) in modern society. Modern societies are highly differentiated and complex and, if left on their own, individuals have difficulty comprehending how their particular efforts connect to the reproduction of the social whole, unable to see themselves as other than an isolated cog, buffeted by alien forces.

This is especially a problem for the commercial estate: whereas Hegel attributes to the agricultural estate a kind of earthy wisdom and attachment to tradition, and civil servants are occupied with the universal as a matter of professional interest, businesspersons' incentives and daily habits incline them toward an intense focus on their personal interests (§250/224). Lacking the traditional community of agriculture, and the *esprit de corps* of the civil service, they do not naturally gravitate toward communities of solidarity—their livelihood is also more insecure. Hence, in addition to formal membership in the commercial estate, they should also belong to associations more particular to their trades—this is "the corporation."[50] This demonstrates that Hegel specifically intends the Estates and corporations to counteract the alienation inherent in civil society and prepare them, as were, to connect to the universal; it stands to reason that those whose lives are mostly occupied with civil society would have a proportionally greater need to have their perspective enlarged.

To contemporary critics, part of what makes Hegel's Estates objectionable is the directly political function he grants them, which seems intended to filter out popular participation, making state administration the business of a technocratic elite, and lawmaking that of a clubby association of noblemen and captains of industry. The legislative function is dominated by representatives elected by gatherings of the Estates (§309–311/295–297). While elections within the Estates are supposed to expose members to debates about current affairs, giving

---

[50] For more detail about the corporation—how its organization differs from the Estates, the relationship between corporations and the commercial estate, etc.—see Bernard Cullen, "The Mediating Role of Estates and Corporations in Hegel's Theory of Political Representation," in *Hegel Today*, ed. Bernard Cullen (Brookfield: Gower, 1988), 22–41.

them a political education, Hegel also spends a good portion of these passages disparaging "unmediated" notions of popular sovereignty, making it clear that he envisages a process of elite selection, rather competitive elections based on broad suffrage.[51] For Marx, Hegel's thoughts here sink below the level of the French Revolution, which while twisted by bourgeois egoism, at least sought to abolish feudal privilege, which Hegel is simply too conservative to dispose of.[52] Concluding our interpretation here, however, prevents us from raising questions about why Hegel feels the need to amend the vision he is familiar with from thinkers more sympathetic to the French Revolutionary model of a universal, rational state that citizens participate in as equals, regardless of differences in class, status, etc.

An already-noted weakness of Rousseau's program that Hegel reacts to is the former's wish for the essential business of the state to be conducted by the citizens themselves, while doubting ordinary persons' ability to do so with upright resolve; hence Rousseau wishes that it be as uncomplicated as possible, based on simple laws and settled mores. Hegel has little truck with such thinking, accepting the existence an administrative apparatus staffed by professionals who carry out the everyday business of the state as their livelihood and specialized competence, rather than as a matter of occasional, patriotic public service (§235/ 216–217). It would be a stretch to conclude that Hegel has more confidence than Kant or Rousseau in the capacity of modern persons to deliberate and act on the basis of the common good. But he wrestles innovatively with a problem that Kant does not much address, and that Rousseau poses as a dilemma: how is a coherent conception of social freedom in the modern world possible, if on the one hand we must pay fealty to the normative principle that citizens ought to somehow author the laws that bind them, yet their ability to comprehend their individual activity as contributing to reproduction of the whole is stunted by social complexity and limited opportunities to participate meaningfully in the state? Hegel's Estates serve to mediate universal and particular by a) giving recognition that individuals' general type of labor is crucial for the reproduction of society; b) ensuring that they do not deteriorate materially below the level of social participation; and c) allowing them to perceive that their estate's particular values and interests are represented in a legislative process that (hopefully) balances and synthesizes them with others.

From a certain perspective, it is fair to view the Estates as a check on participation by ordinary citizens. The other side of Hegel's view, however, is a conception

---

[51] For a more comprehensive account of the Estates' role in the legislature, see ibid., and Hardimon, *Hegel's Social Philosophy*, 192–202.

[52] This objection is explored in Houlgate, "Hegel's Critique of the Triumph of *Verstand* in Modernity."

of politics much more tolerant of clashes of interests than one might expect, especially compared to Rousseau's.[53] Although "deputies are selected to deliberate and decide on universal matters" (§309/295), they are not expected to become "abstract individuals," but rather should "retain within their very determination the distinctions between Estates" (§304/292). Indeed, the large part of why Hegel thinks representatives of the Estates, not professional bureaucrats, should be responsible for making public policy—even though the latter "have a deeper and more comprehensive insight into the nature of the state's organization" (§301/288)—is that they are better acquainted with, and more sympathetic to, their estates' concerns (§311/296–297). They represent a check on indifferent technocracy. Perhaps even more importantly, ordinary individuals are aware that they represent this; the direct presence of the Estates in the lawmaking heart of the state should dispel the possible suspicion that they are ruled by distant elites or faceless bureaucrats, increasing citizens' capacity for justifiable, if habitual, trust and identification with the state: "The real significance of the Estates lies in the fact that it is through them that the state enters subjective consciousness of the people and the people begins to participate in the state" (§301A/289). The representation of these in the legislative process "implies the possibility, though no more, of harmonization, and the equally likely possibility of hostile opposition" (§304/292).

All this duly noted, Hegel is certainly not envisioning the legislative process becoming a field of interest group struggle, where legislation is the product of battles and deals between the Estates. It is true that there is no magic bullet in Hegel's arsenal to foreclose this possibility. To a more a jaundiced eye, his Estates-centric view of politics was prescient, but not in the way he imagined: while the Estates themselves did not have a future in the modern nation-state, the picture he arguably ends up with—interest groups and elites clashing, coexisting, and disposing of a high volume of state business in a shadowy netherworld between civil society and the formal political process—presages trends toward corporatism and interest group pluralism, as well as more overtly cynical conceptualizations of politics as insider manipulation. Yet Hegel demands that the state be transparent and rationally oriented toward the public good. He probably hopes that a shared sense of patriotism—thin though we have seen that his conception of that is—will prevent politics from degenerating into rent-seeking

---

[53] See Norbert Waszek, "Hegelianism and the Theory of Political Opposition," in *Politics, Religion, and Art: Hegelian Debates*, ed. Douglas Moggach (Evanston, IL: Northwestern University Press, 2011), 147–163. As Waszek observes, although Hegel is not explicit in the published text of *The Philosophy of Right*, it does not rule out the legitimacy of a loyal opposition, and the Heidelberg text from 1817–18 forthrightly endorses one. Hegel, *Lectures on Natural Right and Political Science* (Berkeley: University of California Press, 1995), §156, 290–292.

squabbles. The representatives elected from the Estates ought to be high-minded enough not to assert their parochial interests past the point where they become an overt drag on public welfare (§309/295). And intriguingly, for as much as his discussion of public opinion echoes classical objections to populism as shrill and volatile, he allows that it is a "repository" of "the eternal, substantial principles of justice, the true content and result of legislation, the whole constitution, and the universal condition in general" (§317/299). So, "the formal subjective freedom of individuals" demands that it be allowed to form, and it should be listened to (§316/299). But, for as much as wisdom sediments in public opinion, in the short term it is decentered (and therefore cannot be reasoned *with*) and unpredictable, with no publicly available criteria for determining whether it is operating as a force of blind reaction or commonsensical wisdom. So, while Hegel does not think that legislation and administration should be overly concerned to swiftly respond to public opinion, the fact that it is too pervasive and powerful in modern society for state officials to safely ignore means that it compels them to attend to concerns more ecumenical than those of their narrow constituencies.

10. Conclusion

Is there a sense in which the accusation that Hegel's view is excessively sunny is true? From the preceding, it can be hard to give credence to the rosy gloss of rational mediation he applies to the modern social order, even given his own description of it. Hegel maintains that the rational potentials of modernity *are* being actualized in the state, which not only contains but harmonizes the dissonances of modern societies. In my opinion, he can mostly be forgiven for not considering the ideological conflicts, and civil rights and decolonial struggles that came after his time (whether he can be forgiven for his treatment of the substantive issues of race and gender that gave rise to them in the first place is another matter). But as it is, he sees that modern societies are faced with problems of mass participation, secularism and religious pluralism, alienation, class conflict, and poverty. Against this array of explosive challenges stand a coalition of bureaucrats, businessmen and old world aristocrats, and a figurehead monarch. Of course, when considering things as Hegel does, the issue is not whether we find this leadership cohort inspiring. His philosophy is awash with initially grandiose-sounding claims about Spirit culminating in Science and achieving Absolute knowing, and the Idea actualizing freedom in the social world. Yet, this is always paired with an unapologetically prosaic vision of what this world looks like: specialized and unheroic individual vocations within a fractured and diffuse social whole, overseen by anonymous bureaucracies and legal procedures. It is only when reflecting on the way the state mediates these parts, weaving them into a transparently self-reproducing whole, that modern society starts to seem a sublime work of reason. As a way of life, Hegel never pretends that it is as rousing as the vision of Greek heroes manning the ramparts and joyously celebrating the gods. He hopes we can see that the accumulation of institutional rationality in ethical life warrants confidence that a decent and fair institutional infrastructure is in place whose ongoing functionality makes for a society that citizens may justly regard as *good*, in a way that does not depend on inspired leadership—one in which all at least nominally recognize each other as in it together, while each is allowed to be his or her own person, and furthermore, that this is the case without the irrationality, exclusion, and oppression that attends traditional forms of ethical life centered around admittedly more galvanizing public symbols.

It is worth repeating that to be reconciled to the social world is not to deem it without moral failing. For Hegel, unhappy marriages, poverty and burdensome labor, and wars are all features, not bugs, of modern ethical life, all of which are ruinous for large numbers of people.[54] Reconciliation takes place through the insight that the institutional skeleton of the modern world is arranged to deliver the forms of care, belonging, and self-realization normally constitutive of a satisfyingly whole human life. Individuals are subject to caprice and contingency, and no human life obtains all of these goods without struggle and failure, in addition to all of the other things (sickness, tragedy, etc.) that can go wrong—to claim that reconciliation is a possibility woven into the fabric of modern life does not attach to any firm assurance that these aspects of personhood *will* obtain in a given life. But it does hold that individuals should *not* be able to cogently attribute obstacles encountered and misfortunes suffered to the system itself, i.e., they should not find that the system purchases the well-being and privilege of others at their expense. However, Hegelian ethical life is obviously far from fully egalitarian in terms of the privileges and material outcomes it allows. The legitimacy of the system hinges on our assessment of how it—in particular, the political system—works with the differences that nature and history furnish as initial givens, to make them function for the good of all, or, where that is not possible, ensure that they are not unduly burdensome. In this sense, I see Hegel as an important exponent of what Christopher Zurn calls a "developmentalist" conception of legitimacy, which will be crucial in my assessment of Habermas in Chapter 5, and my argument for how reconciliation functions as an orienting goal of critical theory.[55] I would urge that our assessment of Hegel's political thought should not hinge on his own assessment of early 19th-century Prussia,

---

[54] See Hardimon, *Hegel's Social Philosophy*, 228–250.

[55] See Christopher Zurn, "The Logic of Legitimacy: Bootstrapping Paradoxes of Constitutional Democracy," *Legal Theory* 16, no. 3 (2010): 191–227.

which is at any rate ambiguous. It is safe to assume that he is more sanguine than we are likely to be about hierarchies and the deprivations afflicting his society, and ours. But Hegel's own application of the framework he develops is of less interest than the framework itself, which adds up to a conception of the legitimacy of the modern social order in terms of how the state configures and preserves its core social spheres. Acquiring a sense that one's social order is legitimate is emancipatory. A rational, justified social order is liberating, but not in a radical sense of releasing people from coercion and toil, or making them into equals bound by love and solidarity. It liberates by allowing individuals to undertake the process of a) internalizing the roles and action norms of ethical life, b) incorporating them into their sense of self based on insight, not just conditioning, c) coming to see what society has made of them, and d) deeming it reflective of a reasonable, mutually justifiable way to organize society. This is what reconciliation for individuals amounts to; it can be spelled out into a framework for assessing societies based on the degree to which they furnish or stymie this process.

That the structure of reconciliation mirrors that of Spirit achieving the standpoint of Science is not coincidental. To the extent that philosophy has an indefeasible function in completing reconciliation, it is in recognizing this parallel and thereby understanding that coming to be at home in the social world *is what freedom is*, as far as individuals are concerned. But this structural parallel should not obscure an important modal difference: in the *Phenomenology*, Spirit achieves repose in the standpoint of Science—it becomes complete and self-sufficient. On the other hand, as I have sought to understand it, the sense of reconciliation as a process is more relevant than the sense of it as a state of achieved wholeness: it is a matter of the political system reckoning with different group needs, historical contingency and change, and a constellation of social problems that, while tractable, cannot be resolved with any finality. More precisely, reconciliation is the recognition of this process and one's place within it, together with the recognition that this process *is freedom* as it is actualized in history. But the process itself, while taking place within a framework of ethical life that has a firm shape, does not culminate or achieve repose, as the movement of Spirit allegedly does. The rhetoric of finality characteristic of the *Phenomenology* should not be conflated with the in-process—and oft times vexing and incomplete—way freedom is actualized in *The Philosophy of Right*.

Going forward, I will be regarding these features of freedom through reconciliation—how it is accomplished through an ongoing political process wherein one's interests and values are recognized, balanced and synthesized with others', and made to contribute to the universal—to be major (and mostly overlooked) points in favor of Hegel's conception. In the present context, however, things are more ambiguous. As mentioned a moment ago, it seems quite possible to look at the society Hegel describes in *The Philosophy of Right* and see not a system of legal mediations that reconcile individuality and sociality, but a society fractured among hierarchically ordered social spheres, subject to technocratic control, stabilized by elite collusion, and burnished by nationalism for a veneer of legitimacy. Since Hegel readily acknowledges that even a rational society will be beset by not only personal tragedy and international conflict, but persistent problems of equitable inclusion and macrosocial steering, it seems inappropriate to think that difference between a social order that facilitates reconciliation with reasonable parity across social groups, and an illegitimate one that does not, can be assessed by applying a criteria of substantive justice—i.e., what Zurn calls a "threshold" conception of legitimacy. It depends, rather, on an inevitably holistic assessment of the efficacy, responsiveness, and equity of the state's mediational activity. The issue here is not so much with this holism itself, or whether Hegel gives us reason to think that publicity and public spiritedness will triumph over alienation and elite collusion, but rather that it is not at all clear how we would discern which scenario predominates. Hegel may think that philosophy enters here to assure us that the former predominates, reasoning that our ability to conceive of the state as the mediational node between particularity and universality would not be possible unless the actual world reflected that characterization. But unless we take Hegel's *Doppelsatz* (*"What is rational is actual and what is actual is* rational" [14]) to be the uncritical worship of the present that his harshest critics have taken it to be, this will not do. It is more charitable to read Hegel as saying that existing ethical life represents a framework through which the state *can* undertake this mediation—but whether it does or not depends on just the holistic package of considerations just adverted to. And reconciliation requires more than just a formal possibility of our mediational incorporation into the whole, but the knowledge that it is actually happening.

When dealing with the set of problems he inherits from Rousseau, Hegel takes two steps forward and one back. Despite the sophisticated way that he parses the forms of recognition and mediational institutions he takes to be involved in reconciling individual and society, he threatens to fall back into the nebulous ambiguity about the general will that he justly faults Rousseau for. Rousseau feels that the citizen portion of our identity should be actively expressed in patriotic service and ceremonial enactments of togetherness. Hegel, on the other hand, tends more to the view that the state's public facade should display the rationality of ethical life. Although Hegel's picture of what the actualization of freedom looks like is concrete in a way that Rousseau's is not, individuals mostly just receive this display and are supposed to trust that it is indicative of an underlying mediational rationality. Although mediating institutions like the constitution, the rule of law, and the *Polizei* allow cognizance of how society works, activities of citizenship, and our cognizance of how specific interests and values are represented and configured with those of other, are cloistered in the Estates. As we have seen, Hegel thinks that *something* like the Estates is needed in order to give citizens a concrete sense of where/how they are embedded in the social whole, but they also threaten to program their members' perspective to be rather parochial. It is all well and good that Hegel sees patriotism, and to some extent public opinion (which does not germinate in the Estates), counterbalancing this parochialism, but his setup raises the suspicion that the interests/values represented in the legislative process are restricted to those that allow the Estates to reproduce themselves as centers of institutional power. This is akin to a common worry about political parties in parliamentary democracies: are they vehicles for the articulation of interests and values, or rent-seeking power structures that filter the political agenda to make it compatible with their own self-preservation?[56] The Estates' generally prescriptive nature suggests the latter: despite membership being formally voluntary, overwhelmingly people are born into them; they acclimate members to hierarchies associated with ways of life that may or may not be compatible with, e.g., their class interest. One does not have to regard the Estates as overtly corrupt in order find that they insulate lawmaking from the kind of discursive besiegement that would lend patriotic trust in the state some rationality.

Finally, there is some worry about possible vicious circularity in Hegel's method that first appeared while introducing his notion of Science, insofar as it seemed to involve assessing norms and practices from the perspective of the system that generated them in the first place. My present concern is not with whether an idealist epistemology like Hegel's is question-begging, but to observe that there is (unsurprisingly) a parallel issue in his political thought, which is disquieting whatever one's opinion of coherentist theories of truth. As indicated earlier, Hegel does not really have a social psychology that is distinct from his account of Spirit, which tends to make his views about motivation and affect very plastic: by and large, people internalize the norms and practices constitutive of their shape of Spirit, take satisfaction in being recognized for their role performances, and affectively respond to gestures of mutuality. While Hegel does not regard human beings as cultural dopes, he does not sufficiently reckon with the question of whether they can be programmed to act monstrously or contrary to their interests, because he thinks that shapes of Spirit are, at least in a qualified way, rational. Individuals embedded in a shape of Spirit are in a position to undertake critique when cracks open in that shape's capacity to reproduce itself—that is, neither Hegel's philosophy of history nor his phenomenological account of determinate negation suggest that progressive change takes

---

[56] See Lawrence Jacobs and Robert Shapiro, *Politicians Don't Pander: Political Manipulation and the Loss of Democratic Responsiveness* (Chicago: University of Chicago Press, 2000).

place through group demands to utilize a form of life's untapped potentials for freedom and equity (what Honneth calls a "normative surplus"). But in these concluding remarks, I have been raising the possibility that, even if the structure of modern ethical life (i.e., its differentiation into distinct social spheres involving different types of recognition and action orientation) has the outward appearance of rationality, this does not certify that the mediational activity needed in order to actualize this rationality, thereby making freedom a lived reality, is taking place. But Hegel's philosophy of subjective Spirit describes persons primed to find themselves at home in the institutions that socialize them, to a degree that the stable persistence of that institutional configuration would, from their perspective, certify its rationality. In other words, Hegel's insistence that the distinction between reconciliation and resignation is conceptual, not merely a matter of whether subjects *perceive* a loss of rationality in their institutional roles, is, if the preceding suspicions are not unfounded, not of much relevance to ordinary consciousness. This might support an interpretation of Hegel that has him investing philosophy with a weighty, indefeasible role in actualizing freedom. But it would otherwise undercut what I have been arguing makes the conception of freedom as reconciliation appealing and relevant.

2

Totality Fractured,
Reconciliation Deferred

From Marx to Lukács, to Horkheimer
and Adorno

This chapter traces the influence trajectory of Hegel's idea of freedom as reconciliation between individuality and sociality in the critical theory tradition, as it develops in the hundred-plus years after Hegel. Its main interpretive question is why Marx, Lukács, Horkheimer, and Adorno have an increasingly dim view of the legal-political manner in which Hegel fills this conception out, while nevertheless retaining allegiance to its broad strokes. I attempt to read these authors as progressively spelling out a more coherent rationale for this position, with Lukács filling in gaps in Marx's critique of Hegelian reconciliation, and Horkheimer and Adorno doing something similar for Lukács. This of course involves some selective interpretation and criticism, but with the purpose of setting up the next part of the book, wherein I examine the more recent work of Rawls, Honneth, and Habermas. The evaluative framework I bring to bear on these attempts I develop in the present chapter: do Rawls, Honneth, and/ or Habermas have resources within their theories for cogently replying to the criticisms of Hegelian reconciliation that develop from Marx through Lukács, to Horkheimer and Adorno?

1. *The Philosophy of Right* in Left Hegelian
Social Thought

Our customary narratives about the essential core of Hegel's thought, and its legacy, have quite naturally been refracted through the oft-acrimonious debates about it in the aftermath of his death in 1831, which after all did so much to set the agenda for the next century of continental thought.[1] These lenses tend to consign *The Philosophy of Right* to a less well-regarded corner of Hegel's corpus, at least as far as the critical theory tradition until Honneth is concerned. The lenses I am referring here to are a) the split between the official guardians of that legacy, the right Hegelians, and the young Hegelians, students keen to move Hegel's thought toward radical social criticism; and b) the fact that the most ultimately consequential thinkers from this period (roughly, the 1840s)—Kierkegaard, the young Marx, to a lesser extent, Feuerbach—regard Hegel as at once a figure of unparalleled achievement, but one who nevertheless represents something almost monstrous.[2] The right Hegelians promulgate a religiously freighted view of Hegel, highlighting his triumphalist view of history, foregrounding the theodicy seemingly implied by his *Doppelsatz*. The young Hegelians (and, I would contend, the critical theory tradition generally—again, up to Honneth) largely accept this as an accurate rendering of Hegel's substantive views about objective Spirit. They draw more nourishment from the system's account of subjective Spirit, in particular, its methodological aspects, e.g., dialectic, the historical embeddedness of subjectivity, and the negativity of experience (PN, 87). On the one hand, the young Hegelians share the intuition that these methodological considerations, when appropriately harnessed and contextualized, point to an emancipatory view of human agency, but on the other hand, that Hegel's method of grasping things as actual and rational implies, for him, that emancipation, since it had not been actualized in the form of emancipatory politics, should be thought to be crowned where it *is* most developed, i.e., in thought, and more specifically, the apprehension of the Idea in philosophy. For Marx, as well as Kierkegaard and Feuerbach, there is something subsumptive and anti-individualistic about Hegel's thought (119–123),[3] tendencies they associate with the very notion of philosophy, and which make Hegel (and philosophy, generally) unable to grasp what is most true and authentic about human existence. To this extent, their view of Hegel as *the* philosopher (and it is striking to observe how much Marx and Kierkegaard credit Hegel with successfully grasping the nature of rational thought) is a decidedly ambiguous appellation.

---

[1] This framing excludes the "revolt against idealism" and the effect this had on the reception of Hegel's political philosophy in the English-speaking world. See Eric Lee Goodfield, *Hegel and the Metaphysical Frontiers of Political Theory* (New York: Routledge, 2014), 11–46.

[2] As does Schopenhauer who, casting himself as Kant's true heir, views his more-lauded colleague as a peddler of "charlantry." See Stephen Houlgate, *Hegel, Nietzsche, and the Critique of Metaphysics* (New York: Cambridge University Press, 1986).

[3] See also Søren Kierkegaard, *Concluding Unscientific Postscript*, in *The Essential Kierkegaard* (Princeton, NJ: Princeton University Press, 2000), 200–220.

My present aim is not so much to rehash this history,[4] as to point out how it has colored *The Philosophy of Right*'s reception in the critical theory tradition. As the main, mature statement of objective Spirit, *The Philosophy of Right* came to stand for the bad Hegel in left Hegelian thought, e.g., Hegel at his most reactionary, peddling the perverse conclusion that the institutional infrastructure of post-Napoleonic Prussia is necessary for freedom, and that the people living there, between the crumbling edifices of feudalism and the atomistic chaos of the emerging capitalist market, could actualize freedom simply by becoming conscious of this. In this light, spelling out freedom as a self-conscious reconciliation between individuality and sociality appears an exercise in rank status-quo apologetics, so long as it takes place under the conditions Hegel was surveying. Marcuse encapsulates this sentiment when he writes (in a book whose overall goal is to extricate Hegel from associations with a Germanic *Sonderweg*!):

> Hegel shifts the task of materializing the order of reason from civil society to the state. The latter, however, does not displace civil society, but simply keeps it moving . . . The authoritarian trend that appears in Hegel's political philosophy is made necessary by the antagonistic structure of civil society.[5]

On this view, civil society is exploitative, crisis-ridden, and alienating, and these shortcomings, rather than being surmounted at the universal level of the state, are instead falsely legitimated by a politics that anesthetizes the real divisions in civil society. Marx initiates this line of criticism by diagnosing in Hegel a tendency to project a false unity onto the state, which he links to Hegel's idealism. Hegel may claim that the alienation of civil society is overcome in the state, but this is an illusion characteristic of the German ideology.

The Philosophy of Right's influence on left Hegelian thought, however, is not necessarily as truncated as the preceding would lead one to assume. In order to see this, it is worth parsing different layers of Hegel's thesis on the actualization of freedom in modern ethical life in ways he is not always careful to.

a) At the surface layer is Hegel's view concerning ethical life's institutional structure in its specificity, e.g., the patriarchal family, the marketized system of needs, estates and corporations, his account of the legislative process

---

[4] See Karl Löwith, *From Hegel to Nietzsche: The Revolution in 19th Century Thought* (New York: Columbia University Press, 1991); and Pinkard, *German Philosophy, 1760–1860: The Legacy of Idealism* (New York: Cambridge University Press, 2002).

[5] Herbert Marcuse, *Reason and Revolution: Hegel and the Rise of Social Theory* (New York: Humanity Books, 1999), 202. See also Theodor Adorno, *Hegel: Three Studies* (Cambridge, MA: MIT Press, 1993), 26–32.

and monarchy, interstate relations, etc. As I argued in the previous chapter, Hegel is onto something extremely important here with his insistence on the need for mediating institutions between the bare particularity of civil society and the universalism of the state; furthermore, his conception of constitutionalism is (perhaps surprisingly) prescient and compelling. Yet even if we appreciate this, no contemporary reader's reaction to this level of Hegel's thesis is liable to be all that positive, and he does make some strong-sounding claims about the necessity of something closely approximating this institutional structure.

b) A level deeper lies Hegel's view that freedom should not be understood as some kind of heroic or romantic individualism, but that, as a universal aspiration, it must involve some kind of reconciliation to the division of labor as it necessarily exists in a modern society, and the partiality of individual lives that results from it. Rejecting Hegel's affirmation of the rationality of the specific institutions of ethical life does not force us to reject his view that, as individuals, we know ourselves as something universal by grasping ourselves as incorporated in a division of labor that is being politically and legally configured in an overall rational manner, through a process that we are somehow present in—as indicated in Chapter 1, I find much that is appealing and defensible about this idea.

c) At the deepest level, there is Hegel's overall conception of freedom as the Idea (i.e., as the highest aspiration for a rational society), actualized by an interpenetration of particularity and universality—I have been preferring the formulation "reconciliation between individuality and sociality" for this, but of course other formulations for roughly the same notion are possible, for example, an emancipatory interest in a freely integrated identity.

Now, despite the fact that Kierkegaard notably rejects (c),[6] nearly the entire stream of critical theory to the present does not. However, since nearly everyone roundly rejects (a), I believe that the extent to which Hegel views this reconciliation more generally as mediated through an ongoing public, political, and legal process (b), which I drew out in the last chapter, has been obscured. This is partly because, as left Hegelianism flowed into Marxism, and then Western Marxism and critical theory, the (mostly justified) rejection of (a) bled into the (more contestable) rejection of (b). Indeed, for Marx and Lukács, (a) and (b) are of a piece: together, they represent the idea that emancipation is something achieved *in mente*, by grasping a process that unfolds external to our own

---

[6] See Merold Westphal, "Kierkegaard and Hegel," in *The Cambridge Companion to Kierkegaard*, eds. Alasdair Hannay and Gordon Daniel Marino (New York: Cambridge University Press, 1998), 101–125.

agency, and given its most erudite expression in philosophy rather than in lived, practical activity.[7] Although I do not have the space here to evaluate their metacritique of philosophy, I take this conflation of (a) and (b) to be grounds for criticizing Marx's and Lukács' rejection of legally-politically mediated reconciliation, since to be conclusive it would require an account of subject formation that elucidates how the relationship between individuality and sociality in a capitalist society is necessarily a one-sided matter of forceful conditioning of the former by the latter—although Lukács' conception of reification advances farther than Marx, neither substantiates this. Horkheimer and Adorno, on the other hand, do provide cogent grounds for rejecting (b), and since I am interested here to see what can be recovered from Hegel's politically mediated notion of reconciliation, their reasons for doing so need to be taken seriously. I take these figures up in turn.

2. Marx

This section surveys the young Marx's reasons for holding that the kind of personal wholeness that Hegel's conception of freedom aspires to is incompatible with the kinds of legally sanctioned personal particularity that an antagonistic society, like the one Marx takes Hegel to be describing, countenances. It goes on to examine how Marx later begins developing a notion of how legal categorization and commodity exchange naturalize a gulf between self and society, which prevents their reconciliation. I argue, however, that he fails to flesh out what the unmediated/unreconciled incorporation of the individual into the social whole amounts to, how and why it happens, etc., which will motivate our turn to Lukács, then Horkheimer and Adorno.

a. Individuality, Emancipation, and the Division of Labor

Perhaps fatefully, Marx and Lukács—easily the most influential left Hegelians of the century after Hegel's death—adopt something close to an all-or-nothing view on the conditions for reconciliation between individuality and sociality. They judge it to require social transformations more radical than anything Hegel entertains, and argue that visions of emancipation within a still-antagonistic social whole should be regarded as stunted, ideological semblances of "real, human emancipation." For them, the fact that civil society is characterized not just by

---

[7] See Marx, "Theses on Feuerbach," in *Early Political Writings*, ed. and trans. Joseph O'Malley (New York: Cambridge University Press, 1994), 116–118.

personal avarice and competition (as Hegel readily acknowledges), but class antagonism between workers and owners, implies that the discourse of universal
citizenship present in the state is hollow. While Hegel argues that estates and
corporations serve as mediating organs that help individuals locate their place
and interests within the social whole, Marx believes that the combination of class
and status identification found in them, which serve to muffle bare-knuckled
class struggle, will ultimately prove untenable under capitalism: the unbridled
egoism of capitalism eats away at the traditional hierarchies of feudalism, as
"the infinite fragmentation of interest and rank"[8] characteristic of what Weber
calls status orders gives way to a radically simplified, dualistic class structure in
which the proletariat comes to the rightful realization that the material interests
they share as a result of being contingently subject to asocial market forces are
incompatible with the present structure of society. Genuine reconciliation can
only occur once class has been abolished, the division of labor overcome.[9] The
issue of what it would mean to overcome the division of labor, however, and
why such a thing is absolutely required for real, human emancipation is murky.
While Marx's comments about "hunting in the morning and fishing in the after-
noon... and after supper to criticize" (GI, 132) have been much derided, neither
he nor Lukács can seriously be thought to imagine that an emancipated, rationally organized, modern society should be one with no particular role functions
or specialized labor whatsoever. So, we need to gather some sense of what they
think makes the forms of personal particularity found in Hegel's civil society incompatible with emancipated individuality.

Throughout Marx's early writings, one finds a close association between
freedom, emancipation, and individuality, joined with a forthright affirmation
of individuality as both genetically a social phenomenon and one that reaches its
apogee in an emancipated community (PN, 96). Although the contours of this
idea constellation are similar to Hegel's, Marx gives considerably less quarter to
the inevitable contingency or partiality of modern life, i.e., that one must occupy
these roles, *this* place, *this* function in a division of labor. His reasons for doing
so go beyond the thought (which, of course, he also has) that the conditions
of civil society are considerably nastier in an industrializing society than Hegel
concedes. The deeper problem, as Marx sees it, is that a division of labor that
individuals are thrust into by contingency or compulsion horns them into pre-
existing, pre-defined social categories that calibrate the social intercourse they

---

[8] Marx, *Capital: A Critique of Political Economy*, vol. 3 (New York: International Publishers,
1967), 886.

[9] For what Marx has in mind as far as overcoming the division of labor is concerned, see Sean
Sayers, *Marx and Alienation: Essays on Hegelian Themes* (New York: Palgrave Macmillan, 2011),
133–157.

can subsequently have. Thus, Marx calls a feudal society, where individual places in the division of labor are determined by the fate of being born into legally/traditionally defined roles, "the animal history of mankind, its zoology" (CPR, 19)[10]: individuals are their classification.

Estimations of the degree to which this has changed under capitalism can easily be overstated: although the forces determining who occupies what social roles have shifted from having a social to an asocial character, the degree of self-determination that many individuals have to freely select their roles has not dramatically shifted, nor (perhaps more significantly) has individuals' freedom vis-à-vis the roles that they do inhabit, i.e., their ability to appropriate and define them for themselves. The fact that, in modern civil society, the legally defined roles that people occupy are the result of some combination of pluck and circumstance does not change the essential point that their social existence is calibrated (and subsequently restricted) by the sum of their acquired or ascribed roles; in particular (or rather, at the most general), they become members of a class: "the communal relationship into which individuals of a class entered, and which was conditioned by their common interests in the face of a third party, was always a community to which these individuals belonged only as average individuals" (GI, 89). By contrast, in the emancipated community of revolutionary proletarians, "The conditions under which individuals interact with one another . . . are conditions that belong to their individuality and not external to them" (91). Or, as he puts it in the Paris manuscripts,

> each individual man, however particular he be—and it is precisely his particularity that makes him an individual and an *actual individual* species being—is just as much the *totality*: both the *ideal* totality, i.e., the subjective existence of society present to itself in thought and feeling; and in the actual world, in his actual contemplation and actual enjoyment of social existence, a totality of manifestations of life. (PN, 81)

For Hegel, the process of reconciliation not just involves, but is constituted by subjects internalizing the conditions that make them individuals while becoming aware of those conditions as rational. But in the above quotation, one finds Marx archly claiming that it is he and not Hegel who is treating freedom and individuality in their actuality: to be a free, emancipated, individual is to *feel* in the course of one's lived existence that one's activity is an expression of an inner need or desire; that the social whole respects and incorporates this interiority in the course of action coordination; and that any duties to the community are freely arranged, given altruistically, and with due deference to one's

---

[10] See also David Leopold, *The Young Karl Marx: German Philosophy, Modern Politics, and Human Flourishing* (New York: Cambridge University Press, 2007).

own way of contributing.[11] As Marx urges, it is a terrible mistake to believe one's freedom to be located in something external to one's own agency and feeling ("an intermediary").

But if this is a mistake, intellectuals and laypersons alike make it over and over again. Does Marx have an explanation for this pattern? Not an especially deep one: although it remains untheorized in his work, it seems that Marx countenances a persistent human drive that Honneth eventually spells out: the need for a freely integrated identity. The fact that this drive can, under hitherto existing conditions, only be achieved in abstract thought means that it satiates itself by projecting the semblance of harmoniously integrated species-being onto the social whole (i.e., the state), and then treating identification with and conformity to this projection as if it were the actualization of one's own freedom. From Marx's perspective, Hegel's claim that individuals affirm and internalize the social conditions that allow them to be individuals describes a process that *does* occur, but which is only partially rational: society is able to reproduce itself, but individuals within it do not *freely* affirm, nor really understand, their contributions to this reproduction. Therefore, when this process of internalization takes place in a society divided among social classes, with unequal and fixed roles in a division of labor, it can only seem rational through some kind of conditioning or ideology.

Why is this inevitably so? In passages that bear at least as much resemblance to the anthropology of Rousseau's *Discourse on the Origin of Inequality* as to Hegel's more figurative discussion in the *Phenomenology*'s chapter on self-consciousness, Marx conceives of consciousness as a fundamentally social phenomenon, consisting in the awareness of one's self as related to, but distinct from, other human beings and nature. He connects its emergence from an undifferentiated herd consciousness to the development of a division of labor, within which "definite" social relations emerge: only when specialized forms of cooperation spur us to reckon with who we are vis-à-vis others do we rise out of the state of animal awareness that characterizes prehistory (GI, 49–50). The particular form that a division of labor takes, and the individual's location within it, deeply imprints itself on consciousness to such an extent that successful fulfillment of the division of labor's established role expectations are liable to furnish the only conception of emancipation that persons have.

So far as Marx is concerned, all pre-capitalist societies have a "socially" organized division of labor, meaning that production and exchange relations are mostly local and personal, based on traditional ascriptions of kinship, caste, gender, etc. Marx certainly recognizes that these "motely ties" are paternalistic: they

---

[11] See Marx, "On the Gotha Program," in *Later Political Writings* (New York: Cambridge University Press, 1996), 213–215.

institutionalize the domination of some groups of human beings by others, sustained by authority and force. For our purposes, however, his point is that their socially determined nature is plain to see. As Marx says of feudalism, it has "immediately a political character" (OJQ, 47); Lukács, emphasizing that in such a society, societal reproduction is ultimately brought about through force, adds that "the state is not a *mediation* of the economic control of society: it is that *unmediated dominance itself*" (CC, 56). Even if the shape of such a socio-economic order is attributed to some non-human source (e.g., divine ordinance), still, it is uncontroversially one within which the productive capacities of some are controlled by others. Motley and oppressive though these ties may be, socially organized divisions of labor give rise to forms of consciousness that allow one to relate to oneself as a social being, with a particular, complementary role in a totality of productive relations. So, there is a qualified way in which feudal societies treat members as individuals: if we imagine that there exists a high degree of value consensus, or collective consciousness (to use Durkheim's phrase), in such a society, they will not experience the kind of aching gap between *who one is* and *what one is forced to become* typical in modernity. At its most seamless, this resembles the individuals' spontaneous identification with their social roles that Hegel attributes to ancient Greek ethical substance, which is both highly determinate (i.e., individuals know what they should do and who they are) and reassuring (i.e., all members of the society recognize what others should do and who they are, and treat them accordingly).[12]

Of course, groups within a given division of labor may at some point cease to identify themselves with their prescribed roles, bringing class struggle to the fore: in the case of the bourgeoisie, Marx thinks that, starting in the late Middle Ages, they acquired a sense of their material interests that went beyond the maintenance of their current (limited, subordinate) status and privileges, and eventually came to see their interests as shackled by the system that prescribed this status. Under these conditions, it is not surprising that the bourgeoisie became architects of "partial," "merely political" revolutions: from their vantage point, the removal of restrictions on the expression of their material interests, which

---

[12] The chink in the armor of Greek ethical life, as both Hegel and Lukács perceive it, is that this mutual reassurance cannot be rational: it aims to confirm the actions and conduct of actual human beings, but since there is no real space for individuality in this society, individuals are for the most part only capable of undertaking actions that garner recognition within the bounds circumscribed by the community's collective consciousness, so real, self-directed human agency cannot be represented or depicted, except in a fictive, aestheticized manner, i.e., in the hero of the epic form. The hero (e.g., Achilles), according to Hegel and Lukács, embodies what it is to be Greek in a fully rounded way that includes the warts and dysfunctions of his form of life, in a way that no actual individual could. See Hegel, A, 476–509; and Lukács, *Theory of the Novel: A Historico-Philosophical Essay on the Forms of Great Epic Literature*, trans. Anna Bostock (Cambridge, MA: MIT Press, 1971), 29–69.

were basically legal-political in nature, seems like emancipation. Unfortunately, Marx contends, this partial, political emancipation in effect depoliticizes the direct power of capital on the lives and prospects of individuals; that is, it by no means abolishes the influence of capital, but allows it free reign to operate in the quasi-natural environment of civil society (OJQ, 38).

b. Law in Class Society

This perspective explains Marx's disdain for Hegel's idea that the law could mediate between the individual, located in a particular place in civil society's division of labor, and the universal: such a thing is simply not in the offing, given the way the state's legal apparatus actually functions in bourgeois society, and the way in which its functionality is so hazily perceived by the public. As discussed in Chapter 1, Hegel does insist on conditions for publicity and responsiveness, in addition to emphasizing (in *The Philosophy of Right's* preface) the importance of authoritative pedigree, which are necessary in order for the law to fulfill this mediational function. Marx does not so much ignore these conditions as argue that the aspirations Hegel has for the law are simply not plausible. For Marx, the legal sphere and the state constitute a fictive world inhabited by shadowy projections of actual persons, husked of their particularity, with a mystified understanding of what the law actually is. He comes very close to formulating the indeterminacy thesis developed much later by legal realists. According to the latter, the ostensible task of judges is to humbly apply existing law, not to make it by substituting their judgment for that of legislators. In practice, however, while legal materials (statutes, precedent, custom, etc.) constrain judges, they experience considerable latitude in defining the scope and content of legal rules, whatever their nominal commitment to a duty of fidelity to law. In other words, to an appreciable degree the content of law is determined in application. Making a virtually identical point, Marx writes that "bureaucracy . . . constitutes itself as an actual power and becomes its own *material* content"; its inhabitants are "the Jesuits and theologians of the state" (CPR, 12). Given his skepticism concerning religion, Marx must mean that legal officials, like the authorized interpreters of religious texts, have a certain public persona: they are trained to be passive vessels for transmitting God's word, or law's meaning, into particular contexts. But, he writes, "'bureaucracy' is a tissue of *practical* illusions," for despite their extensive knowledge of legal materials, legal officials have no real access to their objective meaning, and indeed, the whole notion that there is something like "God's will," or "the Natural Law," lurking behind the text proves hollow. Instead, judges and bureaucrats are that "actual power" determining law's "material content." They may "know" the materials they work with to be purposive human creations whose future application is to some extent indeterminate, but they are compelled by the structural separation between legal creation and application to adopt a dissembling attitude by treating the materials as something fixed and objective whose meaning they are discovering.[13] And insofar as they accept the process of legal application as *de facto* legitimate, legal subjects habitually accede to this picture. All told, the legal order acquires a petrified, thing-like visage. In Marx's terms, "sovereignty, the essence of the state is here conceived to be an independent being; it is objectified" (5). This outlook promotes political passivity by denying the agency of human actors in giving content to law—the connection between "determinate bureau-minds . . . consists of subordination and dumb obedience" (14).

This objectification of the legal order is connected to a perhaps more troubling phenomenon: the reduction of persons to their immediate appearance as bearers of legal rights, and the consequences this has for the ethical quality of social life. Marx gathers that increasingly refined legal systems are made necessary by the decline of the forms of traditional ethical life found in homogenous communities with simpler divisions of labor.[14] But societies that lean heavily on authoritative legal institutions for their integration can fall victim to distorted images of themselves: bourgeois constitutionalism conceives of individuals as independent, rights-bearing property holders with negative liberties against their community to dispose of their property as they will. The self-image fashioned by societies based on these "rights of man" erodes the communal bonds that allow us to thrive as human beings:

> Not only is man not considered in these human rights to be a species-being, but also species-life itself, society, appears to be a context external to individuals, and a restriction of their original independence. The one tie that holds them together, need and private interest, the conservation of their property and their egoistic person. (OJQ, 43)

Depending on one's interpretation of "species-being," one might charge Marx with a kind of prelapsarianism here, wherein our essentially social nature is compromised through participation in a system that alienates it. Marx (the young one, at any rate) may well have something of this sort in mind.[15] But the argument so far only presupposes that the establishment of bourgeois constitutionalism *is* a social act undertaken by an oppressed class that passes off their class interests as the universal interests of society. This social moment of legal

---

[13] See the analysis of "bad faith" and "denial" in legal reasoning in Duncan Kennedy, *A Critique of Adjudication: fin de siècle* (Cambridge, MA: Harvard University Press, 1997), part 3.

[14] See GI, 99: "Civil law develops simultaneously with private property out of the disintegration of the natural community."

[15] See Daniel Brudney, *Marx's Attempt to Leave Philosophy* (Cambridge, MA: Harvard University Press, 1998).

genesis, however, is suppressed in the subsequent day-to-day operation of a legal order, as it stabilizes a system that allows its participants to isolate their own interests and instrumentalize others.[16]

We find no clear account in these writings of why modern legal systems have the power to promulgate such a misleadingly asocial conception of human nature and society. This is probably another instance of Marx implicitly positing that a drive for a freely integrated identity becomes co-opted and adapts itself to existing social conditions. He may also have in mind considerations akin to Hegel's account of ethical decline in forms of life that depend of formal systems of authority exemplified in his distaste for Roman legalism, touched on in Chapter 1. That Marx does not go on to make the criticism of mystifying ideologies of state and legal power more central to his theory could be attributed to several factors. Whatever one takes his commitment to the base-superstructure social theory normally attributed to him by orthodox and analytic Marxists, the dominant position in such circles has been to view legal power as a dressed-up form of economic power. However, role of law in such a theory raises some puzzling issues. For as much as one can insist that law is a superstructural epiphenomenon, it is almost always the case that relations of production are defined in legal categories (e.g., capital owner, wage labor, tenant, landlord, contract, types of property, etc.). Analytic Marxists worried, for a time, about this issue, tending toward the view that these legal categorizations must necessarily occur subsequent to an assertion of raw economic power by one class over another.[17] Whether this leaves the core of historical materialism uncompromised, or not, the points that the economic base of society is shot through with (and can really only be talked about making use of) legal categorizations, and that it is nearly impossible to imagine a minimally sophisticated mode of production functioning for long at all without being stabilized through the repetition of legal concepts, are significant ones that suggest paths for investigating how modern legal orders might crystallize, amplify, and/or independently replicate the commodity form's pattern of mystification and immediacy. Marx's own disinterest in these implications may have been buttressed by the fact that he gives little evidence of being other than a legal formalist, which would be unsurprising, given that that was the overwhelming consensus position in the 19th century. On such a view, property and contract law, as well as the bourgeois rights that undergird civil society, are

---

[16] See Mark Warren, "Liberal Constitutionalism as Ideology: Marx and Habermas," *Political Theory* 17, no. 4 (1989): 511–534.

[17] See H. B. Acton, "On Some Criticisms of Historical Materialism," *Aristotelian Society Supplementary Volume* 44, no. 1 (1970): 143–145; W. Suchting, "On a Criticism of Marx on Law and Relations of Production," *Philosophy and Phenomenological Research* 38, no. 2 (1977): 200–208; and G. A. Cohen, *Karl Marx's Theory of History: A Defense*, expanded edition (Princeton, NJ: Princeton University Press, 2000), chaps. 6 and 8.

more-or-less coherent blocks, the essential shape of which is a necessary consequence of organizing production around capital ownership and free labor, with
ongoing legislative interventions not altering this basic structure (whatever their
consequences for individuals).[18] Under these pre-legal realist premises, the type
of ideological mystification that the legal system is both subject to and inculcates
in its subjects seems a secondary phenomenon that can only be altered through
restructuring putatively more basic economic relations. And such a task can in
turn only be undertaken by a class that has achieved the historically unprecedented standpoint of understanding its emancipation in "real, human," and not
legal-political, terms.

This allows us to make better sense of Marx's pious-sounding insistence
that a proletarian revolution will be genuinely in the interests of all, rather than
just a matter of trading one set of dominant class interests for another (MCP,
11): whereas every other oppressed class may accurately regard their oppression (and, for that matter, their very constitution as a class) as legal or political in nature, it is apparent to proletarians that their existence as workers, and
their oppression by capital, is not directly prescribed by the legal system (these
things are, as Marx slyly puts it, "presupposed" [OJQ, 34]). Nevertheless, they
experience themselves as oppressed, and therefore are in a position to assign
responsibility for this condition to the mode of production as a whole, the total
organization of society, rather than the legal-political apparatus. Lukács adds to
this point when he argues that premodern classes (or really, all classes except the
proletariat) are constituted in part through identifying their interests with their
legal status, which prevents them from perceiving the true nature of their relationship to the social totality (as we will see momentarily, this is the core of genuine class-consciousness for Lukács [CC, 57]). This lends credence to Marx's
view that the formation of a class whose identity maps directly onto its material
interests would be one whose emancipatory aspirations are necessarily radical
in nature.

c. Commodity Fetishism and Capitalism as a Form of Life

But for as much as Marx is remembered for his confidence in the development of
revolutionary class consciousness and the clarity of the modern class situation,
like Weber he is aware that groups in premodern societies are based as much on
cultural status orders as shared material interests, and if it is the latter that in the
long run determines their fates, the former is more often constitutive of their actual self-understanding. In fact, Marx thinks of the development of class, as more

---

[18] See Kennedy, "The Role of Law in Economic Thought: Essays on the Fetishism of
Commodities," *The American University Law Review* 34, no. 4 (1985): 995.

than merely something "in itself" (i.e., rooted in a common relationship to the means of production), but also "for itself" (i.e., consciously based on a group's *recognition* that they participate in such a shared relationship), as a modern phenomenon.[19] Its possibility, he argues, is based on the reduction of productive relations to "naked self-interest," which have "pitilessly severed" status orders (MCP, 3). On the other hand, Marx is equally well known for contending that such developments—the commodification of labor and the transformation of social relations of production into impersonal "relations between things," i.e., "the fetishism of commodities"—put individuals in a position where the social character of their labor, and ties of domination and dependence involved in production, are obscured, which inclines them to view themselves as isolated cogs in a vast, nature-like system of market forces. These considerations imperil the development of class "for itself" and one might plausibly conjecture that the widespread reassertion of status-based forms of common identity would further imperil it—Marx just seems not to think that this is likely.[20]

Unlike an "immediately political" feudal society, capitalism's division of labor is asocially organized, mainly due to its sharp separation of "the sphere of production" from "the sphere of circulation" (or exchange) (C, 167ff). Whereas economic patterns are authoritatively maintained in traditional societies, capitalist production is unorganized, consisting of nominally independent producers who send use values onto the market, in hopes that they will be taken out of circulation by some buyer. Since circulation requires determining commodities' relations to each other (for fixing terms of exchange) irrespective of their origins, participants in the sphere of circulation must understand value in a manner wholly independent from the particular circumstances that led to the commodities showing up in the market—put another way, in circulation, commodities must be understood as objects bearing equivalence relations *to each other* (and all other commodities), absent any relation to their producers or buyers. Hence, Marx's description of exchange value as an "abstraction" that results in "a definite social relation between men" (in the sense that commodities, no matter the form of value they appear under, are still particular, useful objects made by some persons for others) assuming "the fantastical form of a relation between things" (165). When we confront commodities in the sphere of circulation, we grasp them as things that somehow possess value "congealed" or "crystallized" inside of them, as isolated, independent, universally exchangeable objects (128, 131, 135). The fact that, in a capitalist economy, products of social labor appear as things objectively possessing value

[19] See Derek Sayer, *Capitalism and Modernity: An Excursus on Marx and Weber* (New York: Routledge, 1991).
[20] See also CC, 58.

in themselves (and not as expressions of social recognition, dependence, etc. between persons) causes society itself, as a totality of productive relations, to appear, not as a network of socially determined relations reproduced through human action, but as a web of nature-like laws into which individuals find themselves inserted.

These reflections go only so far in Marx, since while he thinks fetishism helps explain how capitalism works, he does not think its prevalence jeopardizes revolutionary class-consciousness. One wonders why not, but unlike Hegel, who puts a great deal of emphasis on how subjects are formed through enculturation and habituation in ethical life in order to explain how they might recognize the rationality embedded in their form of life, Marx puts forth no such general theory of subject formation. Put another way, Marx does not fully theorize capitalism as a form of life. Now, in *The German Ideology*, Marx and Engels do say that a mode of production is more than an instrumental means for societal reproduction: "Rather it is a definite form of activity of these individuals, a definite form expressing their life, a definite *mode of life* on their part" (GI, 37). But however much this may make sense for traditional societies variously geared around agricultural production (which is deeply imbricated with religious ceremony and local custom) and small-scale craftwork (which attaches mostly to households and kinship units), it is less obvious what it would mean in the context of a functionally differentiated, industrial, capitalist society.

There are some fragmentary reflections on what it *might* mean:[21] Marx is sharply aware that there is a form of calculative, reductive rationality embodied in general commodity exchange that has detached from traditional ethical life:

> The bourgeoisie cannot exist without continually revolutionizing the instruments of production, hence the relations of production, and therefore social relations as a whole ... All the settled, age-old relations with their train of time-honored preconceptions and viewpoints are dissolved; all newly formed ones become outmoded before they can ossify. (MCP, 4)

And he is generally aware that this process of rationalization, as it dissolves traditional ethical orientations, can leave in its wake forms of subjectivity that are mangled by meaninglessness and alienation:

> In tearing from man the object of his production, estranged labor tears from him his *species-life*, his actual species-objectivity, and turns his advantage over animals [i.e., the ability to consciously appropriate and

---

[21] See Seyla Benhabib, *Critique, Norm, and Utopia: A Study in the Foundations of Critical Theory* (New York: Columbia University Press, 1986), 123–133.

objectify his essential nature, T.H.] into a disadvantage that his inorganic body, nature, is torn away from him. (PN, 76)

It can also lead to exaggerated egoism:

> The perfected political state is essentially the *species life* of man in opposition to his material life. All presuppositions of this *egoistic* life are retained *outside* of the sphere of the state in civil society . . . Man in his *immediate* reality, in civil society, is a secular being. (OJQ, 36)

Moreover, Marx attributes great significance to commodity fetishism to the extent that it explains the blinkered nature of bourgeois political economy and the everyday ideology of participants in the sphere of circulation; that is, they systematically misunderstand the nature of value, treating it as an objective property of things. Given his conception of consciousness as dependent on cognizing one's place within a set of definite social relations, we can see why he implies that fetishism produces a distorted form of consciousness in which individuals cannot comprehend themselves as participants in a productive totality, nor the real nature of their sociality within it.

Yet, the effect of disembedding production and exchange from what Habermas calls society's "institutional framework" (TRS, 93–100), within which the forces of production have typically been nestled, seems to result, as far as Marx's reflections are concerned, in a kind of cultural confusion about situationally appropriate action norms:

> You must make everything that is yours *saleable*, i.e., useful. If I ask the political economist: do I obey economic laws if I extract money by offering my body for sale, by surrendering it to another's lust? ... Then the political economist replies to me: you do not transgress my laws; but see what Cousin Ethics and Cousin Religion have to say about it . . . Chevalier reproaches Ricardo with having abstracted from ethics. But Ricardo is allowing political economy to speak its own language, and if it does not speak ethically, this is not Ricardo's fault.[22]

This cultural confusion enables (or compels) a kind of hypocrisy, as participants in the sphere of exchange and owners of capital fail to either acknowledge or be aware of the exploitative, basely instrumental nature of their social roles. This is especially on display in the infamous concluding pages of "On the Jewish Question":

> The Jew has emancipated himself in a Jewish fashion not only in that he has acquired financial power, but also in that, with and without

---

[22] Marx, "The Economic and Philosophical Manuscripts of 1844," in *The Marx-Engels Reader*, 2nd edition, ed. Robert Tucker (New York: Norton), 97.

him, *money* has become a world power and the practical Jewish spirit
has become the practical spirit of the Christian peoples. Jews have
emancipated themselves in so far as Christians have become Jews.
(OJQ, 52–53)

Marx's point here seems to be that the contempt that Christians feel toward Jews
contains a good deal of projected self-loathing: what they hate about the Jews are
traits that characterize their own real existence under capitalism.[23] This coheres
with his view that subjects cannot constitute themselves as genuine individuals
by relating themselves to the legal-political structure that furnishes their roles,
since the asocial organization of capitalist society means that individuals, whose
real lives are occupied with the profane struggle for existence in civil society, are
treated as abstractions, whose species-being can only be represented in the abstraction of the state. The effort to understand one's self by relating one's self to
the purported rationality in the state and the sphere of circulation can only lead
to a mystified form of consciousness, with a yawning gulf between what one is
(in civil society and the sphere of production) and how society defines itself and
its members (as free and equal citizens in a self-determining republic).

   If Hegel is contending that the modern socialization process allows people
to recognize (mainly in the law) the rationality *of* that process, Marx moves increasingly toward the view that the real work of social integration takes place
behind the backs of participants, with the more subjective phenomena under
discussion—egoism and atomism, hypocrisy and cultural chaos, the mystification of the law—signifying little beyond the subject's general incapacity to transparently render society as a rational and meaningful totality.[24] In other words, it
is hard to credit Marx with explaining how these phenomena reflect the abstraction of commodity production and exchange, i.e., how capitalism is a form of
life.[25] It may be that Marx gradually became uninterested in this task, thinking it
part and parcel of a philosophical enterprise tacitly resigned to the unchangeable

---

[23] See Wendy Brown, *States of Injury: Power and Freedom in Late Modernity* (Princeton,
NJ: Princeton University Press, 1995), 95–134. Compare Adorno and Horkheimer, DE, 137: "The
Jews are today the group which, in practice and in theory, draws to itself the destructive urge which
the wrong social order spontaneously produces."

[24] Although Marx would almost certainly not agree with his Weberian diagnostic/predictive
points (which argue for the dependency of the capitalist mode of production on a Protestant ethic-
like cultural foundation), there is some resonance between Marx's position here and Daniel Bell's
picture of a culture collapsing into disordered hedonism and narcissism in the wake of the world of
work becoming differentiated from society's more traditional cultural-institutional framework. See
Bell, *The Cultural Contradictions of Capitalism* (New York: Basic Books, 1996).

[25] I believe this substantiates Habermas' early criticism of Marx to the effect that Marx takes
over the German idealist program of conceiving of autonomy as "the self-constitution of the species" but with the twist that labor serves as the medium for this self-constitution. But, Habermas

nature of the world, or he may have thought that, actually, capitalism is *not* a form of life, but the disintegration of previous forms of feudal life, a brief (in the grand scheme of things) historical blip before society self-consciously reconstitutes itself through the free appropriation of labor.[26]

2. Lukács

Since Lukács never explicitly criticizes him, it can be hard to gauge what he takes to be lacking in Marx, but a large portion of *History and Class Consciousness* is devoted to filling the gap just adverted to. I argue in this section that Lukács does succeed in articulating how a capitalist society blocks the actualization of reconciliation between self and society at a systematic level through reification; along the way, he develops some intriguing thoughts concerning how the legal and bureaucratic infrastructure of capitalism reflects and reinforces a reified outlook on society, and how reification could facilitate its own overcoming. Nevertheless, however enticing his conception of reification is, I contend that Lukács simply lacks the account of subject formation or social psychology needed to parry some basic objections to it, for which we need to turn to Horkheimer and Adorno.

a. Reification as the Capitalist Form of Objectivity

At the beginning of *History and Class Consciousness*'s central essay on reification, Lukács is explicit that reification is an "objective" phenomenon that can *subsequently* be connected to a "subjective stance" on the world, i.e., a way of qualitatively experiencing objects, social situations and events, etc. as real. Given that the intuitively resonant dimensions of reification are contained in the phenomenology of its subjective stance, this is what most readers pick up on at the expense of claims about its objectivity—including, as we will see, Honneth. It is, however, important to explore briefly what Lukács means when he refers to reification as a capitalist society's "form of objectivity," since this is essential to his conception of capitalism as a form of life, and hence his ability to link the subject's experience of society to the overall mode of societal reproduction

argues, once the (hitherto subordinate) relation of the system of production to the institutional framework is reversed in capitalism, Marx finds himself with little to say about needs that do not have a straightforward relationship to labor and production. See KHI, 51–56. See also Garbis Kortian, *Metacritique: The Philosophical Argument of Jürgen Habermas* (New York: Cambridge University Press, 1980), 85–92.

[26] For an interpretation of Marx that does have him plausibly conceiving of capitalism as a comprehensive social reality, see Christian Lotz, *The Capitalist Schema: Time, Money, and the Culture of Abstraction* (New York: Lexington, 2015).

more comprehensively than Marx does.[27] Lukács' notion of social objectivity is deeply immersed in now-obscure debates about neo-Kantianism and the status of the social sciences prevalent in Germany after the turn of the century, but the basic idea is something like this: in order for a society to function smoothly, its members must be prepared to render (habitually, spontaneously) all manner of facts, objects, actions, etc. that they undertake or encounter *as meaningful*, i.e., they must deploy some sense of how these varied things figure in the overall way society works (to put it colloquially), or (less colloquially) how they are tokens of types that figure in the way a society coordinates action and reproduces itself. A given society equips its members to do this by socializing them into a cultural milieu that operates, as Andrew Feenberg puts it, as "a kind of naturalized version of the Kantian a priori, a quasi-transcendental precondition of the facts and values it engenders."[28] Only when otherwise isolated social facts are cognized through such a framework do they acquire "objectivity," or the status of social knowledge: "The intelligibility of objects develops in proportion as we grasp their function in the totality to which they belong."[29] Traditional societies do this in what seems like a straightforward (but mystified) way, by relating the various aspects of society together in a way that ultimately is rooted in a cosmology that explains why things are the way they are—the political system is typically central to this narrative and serves as the backstop against breakdowns in social order. Following from some of Marx's reflections discussed previously, it might seem like capitalist societies are precariously deficient at producing this kind of objectivity, in that the way individuals understand their own interactions can be severely disconnected from the way the society actually reproduces itself. Lukács, however, insists that this is not so: reification is the rationality of a capitalist society, i.e., the way in which members of a capitalist society encounter things to render them meaningful (in the sense of "relatable"

---

[27] I am indebted to Andrew Feenberg, *The Philosophy of Praxis: Marx, Lukács, and the Frankfurt School* (New York: Verso, 2014), 61–89, for emphatically underlining the importance of this point.

[28] Ibid., 65. As Feenberg notes, while Lukács had reservations about the reactionary connotations of the term "culture" as it was used in his time, its more contemporary usage as a "unifying pattern of an entire society, including its typical artifacts, rituals, customs, and beliefs" (ibid., 64–65) is basically continuous with the way he talks about reification as a form of objectivity.

[29] Lukács, "What Is Orthodox Marxism?" in *History and Class Consciousness: Studies in Marxist Dialectics*, trans. Rodney Livingston (Cambridge, MA: MIT Press, 1971), 13. Although Lukács cites Marx in this passage, perhaps a better way to understand his point is in relation to Kant's idea of how practical reason provides a framework for making objective judgments about rightness (even though its statements do not refer to entities in the phenomenal world), which Lukács historicizes to epochs. On this notion of objectivity, see Warren Quinn, "Reflections on the Loss of Moral Knowledge and Williams on Objectivity," *Philosophy and Public Affairs* 16, no. 2 (1987): 195–209.

or "comprehensible"—obviously, not meaningful in a more existentially vibrant way).[30] In fact, reification promulgates a quite comprehensive picture of the interrelation of social facts, albeit a highly abstract and distorting one.

In developing his conception of reification, Lukács leverages a bold and expansive interpretation of Marx's commodity fetishism. Just to remind ourselves of the relevant aspects, Marx thinks that in capitalism we encounter products of labor as a type of thing that possesses a certain general, abstract quality—value—as if it were somehow an objective property of it. Commodity exchange compels us to treat the result of a social process (the production of value) as an aspect of the things themselves, without us much being aware that we are doing so (C, 166–167). This furnishes the subject with a general template for relating things to one another: as distinct bearers of abstract value (which, unlike use value, bears no essential relation to the subject) exchangeable for one another on the basis of fixed laws. While Marx is mostly interested in commodity fetishism in order to explain how the system of capitalist exchange seems to most observers and participants akin to a system of (eternal, objective) nature-like laws, Lukács believes that reification represents the subject's global preunderstanding of the subject-object relationship, and comes to characterize the whole bourgeois intellectual outlook. Although reification is in some sense inescapable for members of a modern society, as a phenomenon allegedly more basic than something more affective like "alienation," it is barely noticeable to most affected. Yet, Lukács maintains that reification indoctrinates us into a warped mode of cognizing the world: our relation to self, others, and nature.

Lukács describes the "phantom objectivity" of the commodity with the language of "immediacy": we participate in reification by grasping things in their immediate appearance as being fully what they are ("objective") independently of their relation to anything else (i.e., as "abstract" and "isolated").[31] As a practice, commodity exchange cultivates

> habits of thought and feeling of mere immediacy where the immediately given form of the objects, the fact of their existing here and now and in this particular way appears to be primary, real, and objective, whereas their "relations" seem to be secondary and subjective. (RCP, 154)

In addition to undermining a person's ability to identify with his or her own creative capacities,[32] Lukács explains how reification inculcates a stance toward

---

[30] See Martin Jay, *Marxism and Totality: The Adventures of a Concept from Lukács to Habermas* (Berkeley: University of California Press, 1984), 102–111.

[31] See Andrew Arato, "Lukács' Theory of Reification," *Telos* 11 (1972): 32ff.

[32] It is this aspect of Lukács' writing that so strongly resembles Marx's reflections on alienation from "the act of production" and "species being" in the Paris manuscripts, whose existence Lukács

the world variously described as "isolated," "passive," "contemplative," and "help-less." Reflecting the outlook of a monad encircled by an indifferent and unalter-able reality, bourgeois systems of thought become tied in knots trying to make sense of subjective freedom and collective agency in history: philosophy ends up with Kant's dualisms and antinomies, while history vacillates between fatal-istic determinism and the lionization of world-historical individuals (110–149, 157–158).[33] The reified stance is thus decidedly *individualist* and *apolitical*.[34] Individuals are on their own, as it were, to move through a social world where re-lations are fixed by objective laws that are obstacles to be navigated around: "the personality can do no more than look on helplessly while its own existence is reduced to an isolated particle and fed into an alien system" (90).[35]

The prevalence of reified forms of consciousness thus represents a serious obstacle in the struggle for a more humane and rational world: not only will radical social change appear more or less impossible, but the vehicles through which its plausibility and desirability might be articulated, such as public com-munication exploring shared interests, and class solidarity and conflict, appear unreal to the "isolated," "helpless" subject (CC, 47–48). On this view, closing the gap between theory and practice—the conscious transformation of the so-cial world made possible by grasping its immanent tendencies—should prove impossible unless reification is overcome. On the other hand, reification plays an interesting role in facilitating its own overcoming: Lukács contends that gen-uine, "for-itself" class-consciousness is impossible unless a class can grasp its po-sition within "the totality of existing society." This is something that traditional societies do not at all enable: "Economic and legal categories are objectively and *substantively so interwoven as to be inseparable* . . . There is therefore no possible position within society from which the economic basis of all social relations could be made conscious" (CC, 56). Admittedly, this statement does not cohere well with Lukács' previously discussed point that pre-capitalist societies relied on political force for their integrity, for he here seems to be claiming that *all*

---

was at the time unaware, although, as Shue points out, Lukács was certainly aware of other writings by Marx from the 1843–4 period, as well as the introductory essay to the *Grundrisse*, in which many of these ideas appear. See Henry Shue, "Lukács: Notes on his Originality," *Journal of the History of Ideas* 34, no. 4 (1973): 645–650.

[33] The centrality of overcoming antinomies to Lukács' thought is a point of emphasis throughout Feenberg, *The Philosophy of Praxis*. The theme of overcoming a sense of isolation and passivity through the critique of the dualisms of bourgeois thought is also prominent in Horkheimer's pro-grammatic writings. See Horkheimer, TCT, 198ff.

[34] See Anita Chari, "Toward a Political Critique of Reification: Lukács, Honneth, and the Aims of Critical Theory," *Philosophy and Social Criticism* 36, no. 5 (2010): 587–606.

[35] For an alternative take on this theme of relatedness and isolation, see Rahel Jaeggi, *Alienation*, (New York: Columbia University Press, 2014), 51–67.

social mediations are ultimately economic, whether the societies mediated by them are in any way conscious of this or not. But whether or not Lukács intends to put forth a transhistorically valid theory of social integration, his point here is that reification permits, for the first time, a view of society both immanent (i.e., not rooted in cosmology) and total: it lays bare the essentially economic nature of the ties that bind capitalist society together—it just does so in a way that renders these ties, not as a products and relations of social labor, but as if they were a "second nature" (RCP, 86).

b. Reification in Law and Bureaucracy

This permits Lukács to better conceive of the legal system as a vehicle for transmitting reification throughout society than Marx, and since the legal process plays the crucial role in the "system of mediation" that accomplishes reconciliation for Hegel, it is worth paying attention to what he has to say on the topic. Lukács views the coherence of bourgeois law, which Marx takes at face value, as a surface appearance. Moreover, he links legal formalism to bourgeois thought's tendency to bifurcate, and inability to synthesize, activity (in this case, legislation) and contemplation (the passive deduction of legal decisions from established bodies of law).[36] Following Weber, Lukács notes the tandem modern developments of calculability, planning, and accounting in the capitalist enterprise, on the one hand, and the formalization of legal codes, along with the emphasis on constancy and predictability as cardinal virtues of the rule of law, on the other. These latter features of modern legality demand that law appears "as something permanently established and exactly defined" (97): laws should preserve their meaning across applications by different judges. In order to observe duties of fidelity, judges' decisions must be regarded as passively "contemplative," i.e., a deduction of law's content as it applies to specific cases from basic principles (e.g., the constitution) or coherent blocks of established law (e.g., the common law) (107).

Lukács illustrates these points in a fascinating set of passages contrasting the subjective experience of law in the present with that of the pre-modern world. He notes that the legal code of a traditional society tends to be relatively sparse, and therefore indeterminate ("irrational") in its application ("renewing itself with every new legal decision"), although its official content "has scarcely altered in

---

[36] See RCP, 126: "As long as thought proceeds 'naively', i.e., as long as it fails to reflect upon its activity and as long as it imagines it can derive the content from the forms themselves, thus ascribing active, metaphysical functions to them, or else regards as metaphysical or non-existent any material alien to form, the problem [of the relation of theory to practice—T. H.] does not present itself. Praxis then appears to be consistently subordinated to the theory of contemplation."

hundreds or sometimes thousands of years."[37] In modern societies, on the other hand, continuous innovation in the forces of production prompts frequent legislative change and new dilemmas for established laws, yet despite being "caught up in the continuous turmoil of change," modern law appears "rigid, static and fixed" (97). Lukács has sufficiently distanced himself from the legal formalism of the 19th century to consider this "unbroken continuity"—i.e., the notion that every case has an answer derivable from existing law—to be "purely formal," that is, an illusion (108). Lukács thinks that this fixity and constancy is a necessary appearance for a form of life that regards its mechanisms for action coordination as natural, or machine-like, but that such appearances mask constant developments in law, and the basis of these developments in class conflict.

Lukács moves beyond Marx not only in extending the habits of thought associated with the commodity form to social activities beyond just obviously economic ones, but also by moving toward a more developed conception of how reification is institutionally anchored and transmitted. Lukács believes there to be more than an elective affinity between commodity exchange and modern legal administration: both involve forms of social interaction mediated by legally created, and therefore artificial, concepts (e.g., exchange value, bearer of actionable rights) that reduce particular persons and objects to generic tokens of a type, allowing for standardized processing of situations, but resulting in the reification of social relations mediated through law and exchange. Now, questions of what is supposed to be normatively objectionable about reification raise themselves here, since, in the context of law, abstracting away from the particular social statuses of persons is the central pillar of impartiality in the rule of law, and indeed, might be thought part and parcel of what recognition of autonomous personhood means, in the legal sphere, at any rate.

Although Honneth, as we will see, argues something like this, both Marx and Lukács rebut this point by arguing that modern legal systems indeed tend to be encountered through reified patterns of thought that deny the social activity (and hence need not involve recognition in their operation), and conceal the class bias, involved in legislation and adjudication—abstraction is not the same thing as recognition. What they are less precise about is why this should be the case in the first place, and moreover, why it ought to be considered such an inevitability. Lukács, however, advances matters further than Marx by theorizing that law a) can be an institutional means for consolidating the results of class struggle, which b) subsequently obscures this class domination through

---

[37] Lukács here echoes a point made by Weber: traditional societies frequently lack stable, ongoing practices for adding new law; legal decisions are expected to be based, or at any rate conform to, age-old tradition and custom. See Max Weber, *Economy and Society*, vol. 2, eds. Guenther Roth and Claus Wittich (Berkeley, CA: University of California Press, 1978), 760–761.

the everyday operation of the legal system. Regarding (a), after noting that the legal system's public face of passive consistency is illusory, he writes that the "real basis for the development of law" is not a series of deductions from natural law, as jurisprudential ideologues imagine, but "a change in power relations between the classes" wrought by constantly changing technologies of domination. It is, he writes, "the nature of the legal system . . . to serve purely as a means of calculating the effects of actions and of rationally imposing modes of action relevant to a particular class" (109). But, regarding (b), just as endemic economic crises seem mysterious to bourgeois economics, or are explained away as the result of fetters on the Invisible Hand, jurists ideologically committed to the justness and rationality of bourgeois constitutionalism and property law cannot come to terms with the notion of law's content being determined by the wins and losses of raw power struggles.[38] These profane origins have to be denied or deemed irrelevant (Lukács quotes Hans Kelsen, who writes that legal norms should be considered legitimate regardless of whether "their origin is iniquitous"), such that the origin of bodies of law that are the end results of class struggles "becomes hazy and vanishes into the sciences which study it [i.e., bourgeois jurisprudence—T.H.]."[39] Legal process subsequently represents itself as a neutral and just procedure, with the reified science of jurisprudence able then to attribute the content of law to its relationship to "eternal values," e.g., natural rights embedded in the constitution (109). Legislation and adjudication appear unmediated by history, class dynamics, etc. The unequal distribution of social power resulting from these processes in turn appears to be just the way things are, or the result of morally sound and impartial legal procedures. This, in nugget form, is what Duncan Kennedy calls "the legitimation effect" of adjudication: distributional outcomes appear more natural and/or just than they actually are, due to their being caused and sustained through formal institutions of adjudication and administration, which police a social space whose essential shape has already been determined by class domination, resulting in a formal bias.[40]

---

[38] If Lukács' "paradoxical" picture of modern law—constantly changing on the basis of legislation and class conflict, yet perceived as objective and static—seems odd or implausible, consider that Ronald Dworkin opens *Law's Empire* with an account of what he takes to be the prevailing common sense about law and adjudication, at least in the English-speaking world: the "plain fact" view of law, according to which "there is law in the books decisive of every issue that might come before a judge." Dworkin, *Law's Empire* (Cambridge, MA: Harvard University Press, 1986), 8.

[39] See also Marx, *Grundrisse* (New York: Penguin, 1988), 88: "All the bourgeois economists are aware that production can be carried on better under the modern police than e.g. on the principle of might makes right. They forget only that this principle is also a legal relation, and that the rights of the stronger prevails in their 'constitutional republics' as well, only in another form."

[40] See Kennedy, *A Critique of Adjudication*, chap. 10.

In short, Lukács has a position akin to critical legal realism. His thought on the interplay between law and economic domination builds on Marx's by conceiving of legal creation as the conclusion of class struggles, stabilizing the results in favor of the winners, and casting their victory as the result of impartial and just institutional processes: the law is causally efficacious in bringing about, and rendering impersonal and invisible class domination. But Lukács emphatically does not follow the American legal realists in thinking of an appropriately demystified legal system as a promising tool for social reform, since he views it as "purely" an instrument of class domination. While this, for many, will seem to significantly overstate the extent of formal bias in law, before dismissing Lukács' view as an example of crass Marxist reductionism, we should appreciate the novelty of the position that he arrives at: on the one hand, something like the legal realist critique of law as a dressed-up form of social power applies to the pre-capitalist world, where "legal institutions intervene *substantively* in the interplay of economic forces" (CC, 57), while on the other hand, "immediately political" forms of critique that attempt to expose the class bias of law are beside the point in capitalism, because the pre-capitalist world that is integrated (chaotically and unevenly) by political institutions has been replaced by one of seamless economic integration in which class domination has been stabilized through autonomous mechanisms that render direct political domination secondary.[41] So, modern legal systems develop as a result of class struggle and serve to legitimate its outcomes, while nevertheless being something of an epiphenomenon that merely reflects underlying economic dynamics. Such a position avoids contradiction only if one holds that: a) the integration of societies with a capitalist mode of production is essentially economic, with the commodity form mediating all other social spheres (culture, law, family etc.); and b) the class dynamic of capitalist societies is basically stable, in the sense of having settled into coherent groupings (e.g., workers and owners) with relatively unified class interests. We have seen that Lukács does hold (a) and it convinces him that reification is fundamentally rooted in commodity exchange. And while he recognizes that the bourgeois legal form is necessary to institutionalize commodity exchange and to consolidate the "domination of men" that masks it as "a relation between things," (b) convinces him that the legal system contributes to this in a sort of one-off manner, i.e., that legislation is not continuously re-ordering distributional patters, but only stabilizes class power seized in revolutionary moments.

---

[41] See CC, 55: "The various parts are much less self-sufficient and less closely interrelated than in capitalism. Commerce plays a smaller role in society, the various sectors were more autonomous . . . or else plays no part at all in the economic life of the community and in the process of production . . . In such circumstances the state, i.e., the organized unity, remains insecurely anchored in the real life of society." This thought is prefigured in Marx, *Grundrisse*, 105ff.

As Moishe Postone points out, Lukács' position here may be ultimately untenable, as he wants to have it both ways on the question of whether modern capitalism is a rationally integrated totality, while also an imposition of class power.[42] For present purposes, we can add that elements of his position are themselves questionable. Regarding (b), the notion of a stable, dualistic hierarchy of owners and laborers has not been a convincing description of Western societies, at least not in the postwar era, for well-known reasons, some of which we will touch on at the end of the chapter.[43] The matter is complicated by the fact that, like Marx, Lukács' conception of class—or at any rate, the proletarian class that aspires to be "for itself" instead of merely "in itself"—is by no means a positivistic one. In a way, until it achieves consciousness through revolutionary praxis, the proletariat does not fully exist.[44] He nevertheless seems to feel that the relevant groupings are delineated by legal categories of capital owners and wage laborers; class-consciousness, if it comes about, will develop amongst persons falling within these categories. As for (a), Lukács believes that all forms of bourgeois thought, jurisprudence and ordinary legal consciousness included, are compelled to adapt to the pattern of commodity exchange by representing isolated subjects confronting a recalcitrant, fixed, outer world of homogenous stuff, governed by nature-like laws. As has been noted, the notion that other social spheres are impacted by rationalization in the organization of production is indisputable. But even if it is true that central features of modern law's development were spurred by pressure to facilitate capitalist exchange relations, this by itself does not compel us to conclude that the internal features of the legal order—the value orientation of its participants and their perception of its structural character—need precisely replicate those of commodity exchange, absent an account of the mechanisms by which such a thoroughgoing transformation might take place.[45] Loosening (a) involves softening what seems like a core tenant of Lukács' theory, and rejecting (b) certainly complicates any analysis of economic domination, and the role of class in society's overall power structure. Lukács' conception of

[42] See Moishe Postone, "The Subject and Social Theory: Marx and Lukács on Hegel," in *Karl Marx and Contemporary Philosophy*, eds. Andrew Chitty and Martin McIvor (New York: Palgrave, 2009), 205–220.

[43] See, for example, Anthony Giddens, *The Class Structure of Advanced Societies* (London: Hutchison and Co., 1973); and Luc Boltanski and Eve Chiapello, *The New Spirit of Capitalism* (New York: Verso, 2005), chaps. 4–5.

[44] See Patrick Eiden-Offe, "Typing Class: Classification and Redemption in Lukács' Political and Literary Theory," in *Georg Lukács: The Fundamental Dissonance of Existence*, eds. Timothy Bewes and Timothy Hall (New York: Bloomsbury, 2011), 65–78.

[45] The same point can be made about the relationship of commodity exchange to cultural value spheres. See Habermas, TCA1, 370–372.

reification as a form of objectivity does begin to motivate the plausibility of this picture, i.e., perhaps the contention is that what started as an imposition of class power (the commodity form) has metabolized into the society's overall form of objectivity, which in turn lays bare (albeit in an abstract, one-sided manner) the homogenous (economic) mode of social integration therein. But as I will presently argue, this is not well supported by an account of social-ization or ontogenesis—for as much as reification has struck many readers as psychologically astute conceptualization of the pathologies of modern life, Lukács' explanatory underpinnings are surprisingly thin.

c. Normative and Explanatory Deficits in the Concept of Reification

Despite its powerful portrayal of the modern world as a cold and alien place, where domination and exploitation are foisted on individuals, cloaked in anon-ymous, decentralized systems, Lukács' approach is hampered by problems serious enough to cast doubt on reification's viability, in terms of both its ex-planatory power and normative force. Since he takes a broad (although, as I shall argue in Chapter 4, overly skeptical) survey of the problems with Lukácsian re-ification with an eye toward rehabilitating the concept, I here follow Honneth's lead. The explanatory problems accompany the question of what causes reifica-tion. Lukács' answer seems to simply be "commodity exchange," and certainly the notion, already present in Hegel and Marx, that the insertion of market sys-tems into traditional societies has all manner of disruptive social consequences is amply plausible. Lukács, however, takes a long stride further, arguing that the commodity form imposes itself at such a basic level of consciousness so as to shade the entire self-world relation. And although he does have some sugges-tive thoughts about formal law and administration fostering reification, Lukács' dominant contention seems the more inchoate one that the commodity form, when ascendant, has the power to remake the world in its image. Perhaps this is plausible to him due to his blend of idealism and materialism:[46] on the one hand, Lukács seems to adhere to a materialist social theory, according to which the economy forces functional adaptation to its imperatives in spheres like law and culture. On the other hand, he also maintains that something immaterial like "the universal structuring principle" of the capitalist economy remakes all other social forms—including elemental processes of socialization whereby we acquire the capacity to represent things as interconnected social facts in the first

---

[46] See David Plotke, "Marxism, Sociology, and Crisis: Lukács' Critique of Weber," *Berkeley Journal of Sociology* 20 (1975): 198–199.

place—in its image (RCP, 85). Now, again, I believe that that highlighting the "objective" character of reification makes Lukács' position at least more intuitively plausible, since it shows that he is not pushing the notion that the specific practice of economic exchange wholly colonizes the mature psyche's mode of cognition, which would be hard to defend as an account of ontogenesis. Nevertheless, the idiosyncratic coexistence of materialist and idealist motifs is not well explained in his thought.[47]

The next set of problems that Honneth presses against Lukács revolve around the latter's efforts to specify what, exactly, is normatively problematic about reification. Following the pattern of Marxian theory, Lukács avoids moralizing, appealing instead to what Honneth calls an "undistorted" or "true" form of human praxis (R, 28). That is, Lukács would have us regard reification as a degenerate mode of relating to world—disconnected and nominalistic, blind to the rich dialectical relations between persons, ideas, and things. But this strategy is viable only if we find it credible to believe that the reified stance supplants a more authentically human form of engagement, with the "contemplative" and "detached" features of the former suppressing the "emotional" and "engaged" ones of the latter (24). This invokes a hard-to-defend kind of prelapsarianism: if reification dominates the social world we inhabit, where are we to locate this pre-reified form of praxis? And if we are convinced of its existence, what makes it both more fundamental and normatively superior? Honneth's point is that Lukács' arguments fall short of answering either question. Despite his brilliant conceptual maneuvering, Lukács lacks the philosophical anthropology or ontogenetic account of subject formation that would support the sweeping view of reification he is after.

Moreover, highlighting Lukács' conception of reification as the social rationality of the capitalist epoch pushes us to view it as a totalizing phenomenon, and this has a further pair of consequences that Lukács is willing to embrace, but should give us more pause: first, since he views the commodity form as *the* source of reification, all extensions of formal administration (law, commerce, etc.) that subjects areas of social life to the demands of the economy turn out to be instances of reification and criticizable as such. This is, we might say, a rather jaundiced view of efficient business practices and the impartial rule of law.[48] But Lukács has no criteria for distinguishing justifiable rationalization from

---

[47] For a more general treatment of the issues surrounding idealism and materialism in Lukács, see Timothy Hall, "Reification, Materialism, and Praxis: Adorno's Critique of Lukács," *Telos* 155 (2011): 61–82. Feenberg more sympathetically explores this issue in terms of the way Lukács' thesis about the identity of subject and object is intertwined with his conception of the relationship between society and nature; see *The Philosophy of Praxis*, 121–149.

[48] For a similarly negative take on these practices, see Adorno, *Negative Dialectics*, trans. E. B. Ashton (New York: Continuum, 1973), 309–312.

illegitimate reification.[49] And because it is such an overwhelming phenomenon, reification cannot be disrupted locally, but only overcome through a total social revolution. Lukács himself heartily believed in such possibilities, but there have not been many similarly unabashed defenders of the proletariat's immanent revolutionary potential for a while. Lukács does avoid the indictment—often leveled at Horkheimer and Adorno—that he cannot justify his own critical standpoint, given the allegedly totalizing nature of reification, since he invests so much in the idea of the working class' capacity to penetrate the veil of reification and overcome the social conditions that inculcate it. But, while I can only convey my impression here, Lukács' argument for this point is not impressive, relying mainly on the logic of Hegel's master-slave dialectic: whereas the bourgeoisie inhabit a social world of legal forms and bureaucratic administration that *is already reified*, the proletariat experience themselves *being objectified* and are therefore aware of the social mediations that go into the production of commodities: "Inasmuch as he is capable in practice of raising himself above the role of object his consciousness is the *self-consciousness of the commodity*" (RCP, 168). If they possess a rudimentary class-consciousness, this experience of mediation can flower into the realization that workers occupy a particular class position in the reproduction of what otherwise seems like a uniform and naturally self-reproducing reality. Yet, even if we bracket issues about what this might mean for wage laborers not obviously involved in commodity production, Lukács does not have a clear account—say, a social psychology—that would explain why the awareness of the process of being objectified prompts resistance in the subject. I do not want to suggest here that the real problem with Lukács is that his conclusions are somehow too extreme, but rather that the ambiguities involved—is reification a form of class power, or an immanent development of reason? how are we socialized into it? how does the former question impact the latter?—make it difficult to determine whether they are or not. For as stimulating as Lukács' theory of reification is, in order to understand the conceptual hurdles required for rehabilitating a politically relevant version of Hegelian reconciliation, we require clarification of these issues.

4. Horkheimer and Adorno

Although Lukács was to have a complicated relationship to his best-known work,[50] later 20th-century trends like totalitarianism (described by Hannah

---

[49] See Arato, "Lukács' Theory of Reification," 42; and Honneth, R, 54–55.

[50] See Michael Löwy, *Georg Lukács: From Romanticism to Bolshevism*, trans. Patrick Camiller (London: NLB, 1979); Adorno, "Reconciliation under Duress," in *Aesthetics and Politics*, ed. Ronald Taylor (New York: Verso, 1980), 151–176.

Arendt as "organized loneliness")[51] and the increasingly opaque or "latent" nature of class conflict in late capitalist societies (a frequent meme of mid-century Frankfurt School thought)[52] convince many that Lukács is on to something politically significant. Much of reification's persistent appeal stems from its promise to serve as both a critical and explanatory concept, capable of revealing underlying connections between a swath of pathologies of modern, capitalist societies, e.g., the rootlessness, alienation, and meaninglessness of modern life; the (mis)perception of social structures and inequalities as natural, or inevitable, along with a stunted sense of alternative political possibilities; and trends toward the commodification and objectification of human capacities, linked to a certain anonymity and lack of solidarity in interpersonal and political relations. Horkheimer and Adorno complete the arc I have been tracing in this chapter: they expand Lukács' view of reification as a form of objectivity, deploying it to paint a picture of the legal-political and cultural spheres of modern society as at once volatile, chaotic, and fractured, yet static and repetitive ("Culture today is infecting everything with sameness" [DE, 94])[53]. Moreover, their incorporation of Freudian instinct theory and ontogenesis allows Horkheimer and Adorno to explain the plausibility of something quite like Lukács' thesis that reification is the connective tissue of this form of life. But if Lukács' theoretical maneuvering is intended to rule out the possibility of rationally achieved reconciliation between individuality and sociality absent a definitive resolution to the class struggle, Horkheimer and Adorno inch toward ruling out the very rationality of class struggle or a non-antagonistic relationship between individuality and sociality.

a. False Reconciliation 1: Subject Formation in the Culture Industry

Horkheimer and Adorno's interpretation of the modern state's relationship to the individual as a catastrophe of rationality is rooted in an account of socialization and subject formation missing in Lukács (and Marx), and exemplified in their famous work on "the culture industry." Lukács certainly possesses the idea that reification, as the form of objectivity of modern capitalist life, proffers an

---

[51] Hannah Arendt, *The Origins of Totalitarianism* (New York: Harvest, 1973), 478. See also Adorno, "Freudian Theory and the Pattern of Fascist Propaganda," in *The Essential Frankfurt School Reader*, eds. Andrew Arato and Eike Gebhardt (New York: Continuum, 1982), 118–137.

[52] See Adorno, "Reflections on Class Theory," in *Can One Live After Auschwitz? A Philosophical Reader*, ed. Rolf Tiedemann (Palo Alto, CA: Stanford University Press, 2003), 93–110; and Habermas, LC, 95–117.

[53] For some methodological considerations regarding the delineation and criticism of forms of life, see Jaeggi, "'No Individual Can Resist': *Minima Moralia* as Critique of Forms of Life," *Constellations* 12, no. 1 (2005): 65–82.

appearance of bourgeois institutional patterns as harmoniously related, which conceals an underlying social reality that is violent and antagonistic—in the present context, this is key to his critique of Hegelian reconciliation. Yet we just criticized Lukács for the inadequate underpinnings he provides for this idea. More specifically, Lukács' lack of an account of socialization and subject formation produces two ambiguities:

a) He vacillates on the question of whether reification should be thought of as part of the fateful development of reason itself (which affects different class standpoints in different ways) or the form of social objectivity wrought by a specific form of class domination—one supposes that his preferred answer is "both," yet we cannot really credit him with providing a synthesis sufficient to establish this.

b) Lukács supposes that we (critically attuned persons, in the appropriate class position) can recognize reification as a pinched and narrow conception of rationality, and that being horned into this form of objectivity rankles the subject, which strives toward the fuller, humanized rationality involved in Hegel's "being with one's self in another," and therefore resists reification. Yet this presupposes a prelapsarian philosophical anthropology that would be hard to defend, and in any event, Lukács does not defend it.

Horkheimer and Adorno, with regard to (a), embrace one side of Lukács' vacillation: enlightenment's reversion to myth is the result of a metahistorical process of societal rationalization. They make good on the second Lukácsian gap (b) by incorporating Freud into their theory, which allows them to see (a) as rooted in the natural history of the species: instinctual drives are repressed in the process of ego formation, and while their energy can be appropriated for the rational purposes of dominating inner and outer nature, they possess a rebellious, asocial core that protests against this repression.

As admirers of Freud, Horkheimer and Adorno cannot endorse the kind of Edenic psychology that Marx and Lukács are drawn to. This Freudianism will ultimately prove difficult to square with any Hegelian notion of freedom as reconciliation, however, for according to Freud, the ego—and civilization itself—is constituted through the repression of instinctual nature, and while this repression can be refined and sublimated—indeed, this is what technical and cultural progress amounts to—it never becomes something entirely other than repression.[54] Signaling their allegiance to a Freudian account of subject formation,

---

[54] See Sigmund Freud, *Civilization and its Discontents*, in *The Standard Edition of the Complete Psychological Works of Sigmund Freud*, vol. 21, ed. and trans. James Strachey (London: Hogarth Press, 1961), 64–148.

Horkheimer and Adorno write, "Humanity had to inflict terrible injuries on itself before the self—the identical, purpose-directed, masculine character of human beings—was created, and something of this process is repeated in every childhood" (26). In Freudian terms, the expectation of unrestrained gratification characteristic of infantile sexuality has to give way to the discipline of the reality principle, and all the psychic organization that goes with it (the stressfully maintained identity of the ego, the superego's harsh discipline, the need to control urges emanating from the id).[55] While I do not wish to downplay the importance of the details through which Freud reconstructs this process—namely, the resolution of the Oedipal crisis and the internalization of paternal authority in the superego—it is telling that Horkheimer and Adorno render this process in a much more general and figurative manner, and importantly argue—beyond Freud—that it develops phylogenetically through changing patterns of socialization, not just in the ontogenesis of individuals.

Although Marcuse, in *Eros and Civilization*, is better known for arguing this point, Horkheimer and Adorno also believe the reality principle to be more historically variable than Freud (who regards its form as simply given as an unavoidable consequence of *Ananke* [scarcity]), in terms of the degree of repression it demands and the rigidity of the ego required by this demand.[56] *Dialectic of Enlightenment*'s central thesis, expounded in the first essay and articulated throughout, is that "Myth is already enlightenment, and enlightenment reverts to mythology" (xviii). It is important to understand that this thesis does not mean that myth and enlightenment are somehow the same. Myth is a form of proto-enlightenment in that it involves the imposition of an essentially anthropomorphic pattern of repetition onto what would otherwise be the over-aweing, unconceptualized flux of nature: it renders nature relatable, meaningful, orderly, and (in a very partial and unreliable way) explicable. To this extent, the mythic prehistory of subjectivity involves a formation of the ego that is disciplined for reality by learning to placate mythic powers residing in nature. But because these powers are personal, particular/local, and imbued with sacred meaning that has intrinsic significance for the subject confronting them, the ego's acclimation to mythic reality does not compel it to wholly renounce a mimetic relationship to the environment. For Horkheimer and Adorno, mimesis represents a playfully imitative, open and non-dominative model of subject-object interaction, wherein the subject is active but responsive to the particularity of the object. While Adorno, in particular, wants to argue that the mimetic orientation toward the

[55] See Freud, *Beyond the Pleasure Principle*, in *Complete Psychological Works*, vol. 18, ed. and trans. James Strachey (London: Hogarth Press, 1955), 6–66.

[56] See Marcuse, *Eros and Civilization: A Philosophical Inquiry into Freud* (Boston: Beacon, 1966), chaps. 4 and 6.

object is not just some unenlightened animism lost to the mists of prehistory, it has, for us, come to be associated almost exclusively with the abandoned pleasure principle, due to its orientation toward spontaneous receptivity to the object.[57] Thus, we might say that in mythical prehistory, the reality principle and the form of rational ego required to satisfy it does not involve wholesale renunciation of instinctual gratification, nor a stark, qualitative separation between subject and object; hence it is less repressive, totalizing, and alienated than the modern ego.

Dialectic of Enlightenment's long excursus on Homer's *Odyssey* elucidates the shift in ego formation accompanying the transition to a more modern form of the reality principle. Odysseus represents, for Horkheimer and Adorno, the emergence of the modern, historical ego out of the world of myth. Odysseus is an enlightened, goal-oriented individual operating in a world still populated by nature gods, mythical beasts, and magic, and in order to survive in the pursuit of his goals, he must give the mythical powers their due. But he outfoxes them by recognizing the arbitrary nature of the sacrifices one is expected to perform for them: Odysseus performs sacrifices, but regards them as meaningless (39, 44). Mythic powers become, for him, obstacles to be negotiated around. He adopts what might remind us of a legalistic attitude toward them: he must comply literally with the law, but searches out loopholes, i.e., ways of complying with it that allow him to elude compliance with the "spirit" of the law, which is contrary to his purposes and he does not identify with.

> The formula for Odysseus' cunning is that the detached, instrumental mind, by submissively embracing nature, renders to nature what is hers and thereby cheats her. The mythical monsters under whose power he falls represent, as it were, petrified contracts and legal claims dating from primeval times. (45)

This enlightened, "cunning" attitude is at once tremendously empowering, as Odysseus carves out space for the pursuit of his own interests by learning to manipulate gaps between symbol and object (e.g., tricking the Cyclops with a play-on-words on his own name [50–52]). But enlightenment brings an undertow of less happy consequences:

- It begins the long process of draining the world of innate meaning that could orient actions (Weber's "disenchantment"), forcing the subject to fall back on its own resources in order to direct itself. Yet, at the same time and as a

---

[57] See DE, 4–5. I cannot here do justice to the bevy of issues surrounding Adorno's concept of mimesis. See Albrecht Wellmer, "Truth, Semblance, Reconciliation," in *The Persistence of Modernity* (Cambridge, MA: MIT Press, 1991), 1–35. For a critical discussion of the general issues surrounding mimesis, see Ernesto Verdeja, "Adorno's Mimesis and its Limitations for Critical Social Thought," *European Journal of Political Theory* 8, no. 4 (2009): 493–511.

result of the more intense repression of instinctual drives that the cunning ego requires, self-possessed motives for action are increasingly winnowed down to mere self-preservation (23).[58]

- The ego must accede to the given nature of reality—instead of the mythical powers being potentially responsive interaction partners, they are things, obstacles to navigate through. To traverse them efficiently, the enlightened ego must be prepared to attain an objective, realistic grasp of what they *are*. But notably, this tends to consist in an assessment of the scope of their causal power as it potentially impacts the subject's purposes. This introduces what becomes a key notion for Adorno: the subject must be prepared to think in abstractions, i.e., it must abstract away from the particularity of what the object itself is and cognize it in generic terms that relate it to its causal impact on the subject.

- For Odysseus and his progeny, the repression of the instincts in favor of sublimated and delayed gratification (the main substance of the Freudian reality principle) becomes the primary, constitutive accomplishment of the self, requiring the ability to hold one's self identical and constant in the face of longing to return to a state of untrammeled gratification (dramatized, of course, by the encounter with the Sirens), with all the attendant white-knuckled tension required to accomplish this.

- As a result, while instinctual nature remains present in psychic life, as the unconscious urge to submit to the abandonment of gratification, it becomes alien to the self, representing something fearful, i.e., the dissolution of the self, the loss of one's hard-won identity:

> Mimetic, mythical, and metaphysical forms of behavior were successively regarded as stages of world history which had been left behind, and the idea of reverting to them held the terror that the self would be changed back into mere nature from which it had extricated itself with unspeakable exertions and which for that reason filled it with unspeakable dread. (24)

A general picture emerges from these considerations. Historically prevalent conceptions of rationality are tightly indexed to the existing form of the reality principle, and the ego, as the psychic source of rational self-direction, is formed through the internalization of the reality principle. To be sure, Odysseus' story is not an account of this process of internalization, but a representation of its

---

[58] This is the major theme of *Dialectic of Enlightenment*'s second excursus, "Juliette or Enlightenment and Morality." See also Horkheimer, *Eclipse of Reason* (New York: Continuum, 2004), chaps. 1–2.

result: becoming an enlightened subject is not an unproblematically progressive matter of learning to see the world more objectively, less superstitiously,
but something that the ego must be conditioned for. In particular, the ego has
to shrink and harden by sharply distinguishing itself from outer nature and its
inner drives; while mythic thought renders nature relatable through anthropomorphism, enlightened thought actually involves a more sweeping pattern of
anthropomorphism, in that nature is given in terms of its impact on the subject and is therefore conceived through abstraction.[59] Yet, this is curiously
disempowering: "What appears as the triumph of subjectivity, the subjection
of all existing things to logical formalism, is bought with the obedient subordination of reason to what is immediately at hand" (20). In other words, whereas
the mythical self is geared to engage in interactive communion with its object,
the modern ego asserts its own purposes, but does so by adjusting itself to what
it takes to be the fixed, formal character of external nature—it alienates itself
from its inner nature in order to function within the exigencies of an indifferent
reality. Instead of being defined by the bare fact of scarcity, as Freud has it, the
shape of the reality principle, and the conditioning of the ego to it, depends,
for Horkheimer and Adorno, on how reality is represented (e.g., on its form of
objectivity, as Lukács would put it). In the transition from the mythical to the
enlightened world, mimetic behavior becomes adaptive.

Of course, the ego does not condition itself, nor is it conditioned directly by
sensuous reality. Rather, in Freud's schema, the superego is the agent of the ego's
discipline. Freud famously views the tripartite differentiation of the psyche as
the result of the Oedipal situation, wherein the father figure imposes "reality"
on the child (i.e., that it is not omnipotent, it does not possess or control its
love objects, etc.);[60] with the father figure serving as a stand-in for society, the
superego polices the ego's wishes and desires, restraining it from entertaining
actions at odds with paternal authority with guilt. Although rooted in the personal authority of the father figure, the superego comes to absorb basic demands
of sociality (e.g., conventional sexual morality, conformity to role expectations).
Nevertheless, Horkheimer and Adorno (and Marcuse) deem it vitally important that Freud conceives of the psyche's differentiation as set in motion, and the

---

[59] One can see here why Adorno thinks that the problem of narcissism is prefigured in the form
of modern subjectivity: the ego is geared to understand things in relation to itself, while this "self"
(the ego) becomes emptier and weaker. See, for example, MM, 49–50: "In Hegel self-consciousness
was the truth of the certainty of one's self, in the words of the *Phenomenology*, the 'native realm of
truth'. When they had ceased to understand this, the bourgeois were self-conscious at least in their
pride at owning wealth. Today self-consciousness no longer means anything but reflection on the ego
as embarrassment, as realization of impotence: knowing that one is nothing."

[60] The issue of whether Adorno is guilty of conflating the distinction between the reality principle and the superego is taken up in Chapter 4.

basic dynamic between its elements determined, within the family. As the critical theorists see it, this developmental context allowed Freud's nascent subject to have a personalized relationship to the superego and what it represents, albeit a fraught one. In such a context, behavioral expectations not directly inculcated in the family are less apt to be consciously experienced as prescriptive and disciplinary, since an ego shaped by an "ego ideal" (which usually starts off as a representation of a beloved authority figure) can attain some autonomy vis-à-vis broader social pressures to conform.[61] *But*, the critical theorists, in general (and like Hegel, for whom *Bildung* takes place largely outside of the family, in civil society), conceive of the process of subject formation as a more drawn out one (this is probably already apparent from *Dialectic of Enlightenment*, as Odysseus' subjectivity is formed in the course of his struggle with the mythic powers) as the subject is gradually indoctrinated into the way that their society conceives reality, and in particular, they think that the specific version of the bourgeois family that could have provided the security and insularity needed to make Freud's view plausible existed only for a brief historical moment, for a few people.[62] In their sometimes-odd idealization of high bourgeois culture, Horkheimer and Adorno think that there may have been a time when prosperous heads-of-households in capitalist societies really possessed autarkic authority while supervising their dependents' decisive period of pre-adolescent socialization, during which their ego ideal takes shape, and where the family could operate credibly as the haven-in-a-heartless-world that bourgeois sentimentality (Hegel included) has always taken it to be.[63]

But, the critical theorists hold, this is no longer the case.[64] The transition from liberal/entrepreneurial to administered/monopoly capitalism has markedly diminished the father's autarky, which together with the omnipresence of the culture industry ensures that socialization takes place to a greater extent outside of the confines of the family, by anonymous agencies (peer groups, media, schools, etc.). Essentially, the subject is not socialized in such a way as to reliably develop its ego in relation to an ego ideal. Since for Freud, identification with the

[61] See Freud, "On Narcissism: An Introduction," in *Complete Psychological Works*, vol. 14, ed. and trans. James Strachey (London: Hogarth Press, 1957), 73–104.

[62] See Joel Whitebook, *Perversion and Utopia: A Study in Psychoanalysis and Critical Theory* (Cambridge, MA: MIT Press, 1995), 132–140.

[63] For a critique of the Frankfurt School's view of ego autonomy and the patriarchal family, see Jessica Benjamin, "Authority and the Family Revisited: or, A World without Fathers?" *New German Critique* 5 (1978): 35–57; for a qualified defense, see Christopher Lasch, *Haven in a Heartless World: The Family Besieged* (New York: Norton, 1977), chap. 4.

[64] See Marcuse, *Five Lectures*, trans. Jeremy Shapiro and Shierry Weber (Boston: Beacon, 1970), 44–61; Horkheimer, "Authority and the Family," in *Critical Theory: Selected Essays*, trans. Matthew J. O'Connell et al. (New York: Continuum), 47–131.

father-figure (which becomes possible through the successful resolution of the Oedipal crisis) provides the original basis for one's ego ideal, we can probably say that it ends up being the most transparent portion of the superego, since its source and content is more identifiable, and genesis less murky to the subject than other portions of the psyche. The presence of a robust ego ideal can serve to buffer the ego (although plainly a lot can go wrong when an ego strongly identifies with an ego ideal, too), providing it some critical distance from and resistance to pressures emanating from culture and economy.[65] Its relative absence implies a more alienated, less transparent, less conscious relationship between ego and superego, with the latter becoming a source of opaque, guilt- and anxiety-inducing demands.

Horkheimer and Adorno's perspective on these matters is subtler than the assertion that the late capitalist subject's autonomy is compromised by the vast weight of social pressure to conform[66]—indeed, consciously experienced pressures to conform are probably much less here than in a traditional society with a robust collective consciousness, to use Durkheim's phrase. But, reminiscent of Lukács' reflections on how the patchwork social fabric of a traditional society gives way to the tighter, more homogenous mode of social integration facilitated by reification, "society" becomes something omnipresent in its inhabitants' lives, as they encounter cultural products, cues and stimulations, situation and interaction types, as relatable to each other in terms of equivalence and exchange. The potent expectation upon individuals is that they should fit themselves into this "schema," indeed that being a living, breathing, experiencing member of society *is* a matter identifying things according to it and steering the self through them.

The thing to notice here is that this conditioning—and the attendant instinctual repression—likely does not *feel* overtly disciplinary (like subjection to paternal authority, whether one comes to ultimately identify with it or not, does). There are two reasons for this: first, the unmediated nature of the ego's developmental relationship to society means that ego's experience of society is already schematized—in a minimal way, preinterpreted—by society's form of objectivity, i.e., the exchange/equivalence principle transmitted through the culture industry. There is no equivalent to the transformative reckoning with the father here.

> Even during their leisure time, consumers must orient themselves according to the unity of production. The active contribution which Kantian schematism still expected of subjects—that they should, from

---

[65] See C. Fred Alford, *Narcissism: Socrates, the Frankfurt School, and Psychoanalytic Theory* (New Haven, CT: Yale University Press, 1988), 154–159.

[66] This is, unfortunately, the impression one likely gleans from Adorno's widely read essay, "Late Capitalism or Industrial Society?" in *Can One Live After Auschwitz?*, 111–125.

> the first, relate sensuous multiplicity to fundamental concepts—is denied to the subject by industry . . . To confirm the schema by acting as its constituents is their sole *raison d'être*. (98)

Second, there is an apparent plenitude in the culture industry, in terms of the types of individual particularity, experiences, products, and life paths that are in principle available: thoughts, desires, needs, and impulses that conform to the schema, i.e., are relatable to one another and the broader system of needs as forms of satisfaction/stimulation. "To be entertained means to be in agreement" (115). Because of the imposition of an exchange/equivalence schema at such a basic level of consciousness, however, "disagreement" seems barely possible— what would it even mean?

> On one matter, however, this hollow ideology is utterly serious: everyone is provided for . . . Formal freedom is guaranteed for everyone. No one has to answer officially for what he or she thinks. However, all find themselves enclosed early on within a system of churches, clubs, professional associations, and other relationships which amount to the most sensitive instrument of social control. (120)

The socialization process of modern society thus prepares the subject, from "early on," to conform their experiences, behaviors, expectations, life plans, etc. to the schema of exchange society. Freedom appears here as facility in smoothly navigating this terrain: "But the true masters, as both producers and reproducers, are those who speak the jargon with the same free-and-easy relish as if it were the language it has long since silenced. Such is the industry's ideal of naturalness" (101). Because this schema is so abstract (all things are separate, but comparable/exchangeable/relatable) and the demands of sociality are so rarely concretely prescriptive (one can think and do what one likes, society caters to an amazing plenitude of consumer experiences), the repression and trauma involved in becoming a subject that can fit itself into it is rarely felt as injury. When it is, it seems tendentious to attribute blame to society itself, i.e., its socialization process and basic legal-economic structure.

This proves a significant point, if one recalls the significance for reconciliation that Hegel attaches to individuals' ability to understand their socialization and, generally, how their society works, and that Marx and Lukács attribute to them comprehending the real forces that shape their class position, and their ability to conceive of their real interests beyond the schema of legal categories their society imposes. This is no longer feasible, Adorno writes: "It is the signature of our age that no one, without exception, can determine his own life within even a moderately comprehensible framework, as was possible earlier in the assessment of market relationships" (MM, 37). Given this disconnect between the genesis of individuals and their comprehension of the forces propelling this genesis, the trend in the "re-visionist" Freudian psychoanalysis that Adorno is so contemptuous of is to shunt the trauma of subject formation into the background and focus on the "character" of the mature ego in order to acclimate it to social reality (by making it less selfish, aggressive, more caring/loving, etc.). "The sedimented totality of character, which the revisionists push into the foreground, is in truth the result of a reification of real experiences."[67] While we can sympathize with aims of the revisionists to im-prove clinical practice in an imperfect world, as a theoretical outlook, it naturalizes and normalizes a self conditioned *not* to attend to the antagonism constitutive of its genesis.

We should now be in a position to put together two apparently opposed theses of Adorno's: on the one hand, he writes, "not only the individual but the category of individuality is already a product of society."[68] On the other hand, "inner and outer life are torn apart."[69] In the latter passage, Adorno is interpreting the increasing indifference of academic psychology and sociology from one an-other: fixated on their particular subject matter, psychology (focused on the individual's clinical prospects) finds it unnecessary and impractical to inquire into the general conditions of subject formation characteristic of the epoch, and sociology (in its Parsonian guise focused on social coordination and reproduc-tion) can usually take a base level of compliance with institutional demands as given, postulating an account of motivation that fits this fact. This mutual in-difference is "false" since it "perpetuates conceptually the split between the living subject and the objectivity that governs subjects and yet derives from them."[70] Yet, this academic division of labor accurately reflects a condition where the mediations between individual and society have become reified and opaque: individuals are socialized to schematize reality through abstraction and fit themselves into an apparently universally-accommodating culture industry, and compliance with the demands of exchange society is reliable enough to op-erate at the level of a presupposition.

This "unity" between individual and society, psychology and sociology, "resides in not being unified"[71]—it vitiates the prospects for the rational and transparent mediation between individuality and society that Hegel's con-cept of reconciliation envisages. What we have instead is the following: "The

[67] Adorno, "Revisionist Psychoanalysis," *Philosophy and Social Criticism* 40, no. 3 (2014): 329.

[68] Ibid., 330.

[69] Adorno, "Sociology and Psychology (Part I)," *New Left Review* 46 (1967): 70.

[70] Ibid., 69. See Deborah Cook, *The Culture Industry Revisited: Theodor W. Adorno on Mass Culture* (Lanham, MD: Rowan & Littlefield, 1996).

[71] Adorno, "Sociology and Psychology," 69.

conspicuous unity of macrocosm and microcosm confronts human beings with a model of their culture: the false identity of universal and particular" (DE, 95). Forced identification is obviously a far cry from reconciliation: "The reconciliation of general and particular, of rules and the specific demands of the subject, through which alone style takes on substance, is nullified by the absence of tension between the poles" (102). While both Horkheimer and Adorno give many indications that they continue to view freedom in terms of reconciliation, like Hegel, the picture of modern politics that follows from their assessment of the current state is of a forced, unmediated unity between individual and society that the individual is conditioned not to recognize as forceful: "The relentless unity of the culture industry bears witness to the emergent unity of politics" (96). As we shall presently see, this not only rules out the ongoing reconciliation that Hegel thinks the legal-political system seeks to accomplish, but also seriously undermines the prospects for reconciliation through the sublation of this system through progressive class struggle, á la Marx and Lukács.

b. False Reconciliation 2: State Capitalism as "a Parody of the Classless Society"

Although it would not be credible to claim that the legal-political sphere is of central interest to the mid-century core membership of the Frankfurt School, these authors do outline a more comprehensive view of their political landscape than Lukács, one which conceives of the stalled class struggle and the rise of fascism as the *results* of societal rationalization, rather than breaks with it. In his programmatic essay "Traditional and Critical Theory," Horkheimer declines to follow Lukács in linking the perspective of a critical theory of society to the proletariat, appealing instead more generally (or vaguely) to "reason" and humanity's interest in "the rational organization of society" (TCT 212–213). The motives behind this conceptualization (which denies the current existence of a transformative agent within modern capitalism, making the possibility of an immanent critique of society a perennial problem within the Frankfurt School)[72] may well be historically prompted (based on the fate of working class movements in central Europe during the 1920s and 1930s), but the text attests them to be based on Horkheimer's views concerning structural changes in capitalism that make conceiving of the relationship between owners and workers along the lines of Hegel's master-slave dialectic, as Lukács does, untenable. Horkheimer

[72] See Craig Browne, "The End of Immanent Critique?" *European Journal of Social Theory* 11, no. 1 (2008): 5–24; Maeve Cooke, *Re-Presenting the Good Society* (Cambridge, MA: MIT Press, 2006), 9–71.

observes that lodging research and development ("science") in the heart of the capitalist enterprise renders the "legal owners" of capital rather more marginal:

> Today, however, such ownership has become unimportant, and now there are some powerful mangers who dominate whole sectors of industry while owning a steadily decreasing part of the businesses they direct. This economic process brings with it a change in the way the political and legal apparatus functions, as well as in ideologies. (235)

Horkheimer attributes great significance to the fact that economic domination is increasingly channeled through formal organizations, wherein the visible hierarchical relations are between specialists/managers and workers—or, in the state, between officials and clients—with the former themselves being subject to employee role demands that they neither define nor control. None of this necessarily obviates the basic Marxian point that capitalism is a system where profit is based on the exploitation of labor power, but if Marx's theory of surplus value is supposed to reveal the class-based domination taking place behind the appearances of voluntary market transactions, Horkheimer's point is that it no longer accomplishes this: a stratified class structure is in place, but maintained now through a network of autonomous state and private organizations.[73] Notable also in this regard is Lukács' aside that reification proffered through bureaucratic and legal organization is more resistant to denaturalizing critique because subjects tend to simply find themselves in a social world wherein patterns of interaction have *already* been reified—again, Lukács believes that the experience workers undergo of having their activity objectified is a visceral one that prompts resistance. According to Horkheimer, however, the boundaries between classes of people that experience reification in the latter fashion and those that are simply subject to it in the former have blurred considerably.

In Horkheimer and Adorno's subsequent conception of later stage capitalism, they deem social integration to be heavily dependent on political and cultural power (as opposed to market systems, as in Marx and Lukács), but unlike Hegel, the political process that accomplishes this does not allow individuals to locate themselves within a defined set of relations of production or understand how their interests harmonize with those of differently positioned others; rather it obscures the possibility of this sort of thing. Horkheimer's 1940 essay "The

---

[73] This is a contestable interpretation of Marx's theory of value, as well as how one would verify its contemporary relevance. Since the Frankfurt School's first generation is so cagey in their pronouncements about Marx, one has to suppose that something like this is their view, since they regard the Marxian apparatus of critique to be in need of supplementation through the interdisciplinary research program Horkheimer proposes. Habermas is franker in his views on the limitations of Marx's value theory; see Habermas, TCA2 334–343. See also Georg Lohmann, "Marx's *Capital* and the Question of Normative Standards," *Praxis International* 6, no. 3 (1986): 353–372.

Authoritarian State" reads in many ways like an update of Marx's "18th Brumaire of Louis Bonaparte." If Marx is becoming aware of state capacities to suppress revolutionary trends, in part through the direct administration of populations ("the small-holding peasants") without a direct stake in the class struggle,[74] Horkheimer more unequivocally affirms that the rational organization of society cannot be achieved under the (narrowly rational) social conditions that give rise to the authoritarian state. His and Adorno's position is importantly influenced by Friederich Pollock's writings on "state capitalism."[75] Pollock argues that the concentration of capital and monopolization of industry that Marx anticipated leads to changes in the relationship between state and civil society that he did not: if the "liberal" phase of capitalism is characterized by competition among independent owners of capital, passively overseen by the state's legal apparatus, state capitalism is characterized by a relatively smaller constellation of large, vertically organized, increasingly bureaucratic business concerns whose relationship to each other is less intensely competitive, and more actively managed through the state, which has a recognized interest in preventing economic crises from breaking out. Pollock's essay articulates the Institute's broad agreement at that time about "the primacy of politics," that is, the capacity of administrative, political power to both contain unresolved group antagonisms, and intervene to stabilize the capitalist mode of production to a degree beyond that which Marx contemplated, to whom the Institute ascribed the thesis of "the primacy of economics."[76]

Horkheimer builds on Pollock, defining what he calls an "authoritarian state" by the ability of administrative power to accomplish non-mediational integration by co-opting opposed group interests into the state: "Whatever seeks to exist under a state of domination runs the danger of reproducing it," with organized group interests (including labor groups) falling victim to "the spirit of administration" (AS, 98). If Marx is aware of tendencies toward monopolizing concentrations of power, it is Weber who has a livelier sense of this trend working at all levels of social organization.[77] For Marx, the political organization of class

[74] See Marx, "The 18th Brumaire of Louis Bonaparte," in *Later Political Writings*, 116–125.

[75] See Friedrich Pollock, "State Capitalism: its Possibilities and Limits," in *The Essential Frankfurt School Reader*, 71–94.

[76] The significance of Pollock's writings for the Frankfurt School's development has been widely recognized by its chroniclers; see Helmut Dubiel, *Theory and Politics: Studies in the Development of Critical Theory* (Cambridge, MA: MIT Press, 1985); David Held, *Introduction to Critical Theory: Horkheimer to Habermas* (Berkeley: University of California Press, 1980), 40–76; Rolf Wiggershaus *The Frankfurt School: Its History, Theories, and Political Significance* (Cambridge, MA: MIT Press, 1995), 282–291. It has received less attention in critical analyses of their theories; see, however, Postone, *Time, Labor, and Social Domination: A Reinterpretation of Marx's Critical Theory* (New York: Cambridge University Press, 1993), 84–120.

[77] See Reinhard Bendix, "Inequality and Social Structure: A Comparison of Marx and Weber," *American Sociological Review* 39, no. 2 (1974): 149–161.

interests should counteract their being obscured by commodity fetishism, but Weber and Horkheimer see how this may prove double-edged: the organization of material interests opens the possibility of organizational elites enacting (legally or otherwise) "closure" over their sphere of influence.[78]

Such points about organizations are familiar from Weber,[79] but Horkheimer draws two intriguing implications from them. First, the organized expression of group interests leads almost paradoxically to the atomization of individuals within groups, as the social connections between them are channeled through organizational power, obscuring their social character. Secondly, the prominence of power and formal codes over group interests in the upper echelons of organized social groups creates the potential for a kind of false reconciliation among a society's main classes, as the substantive incompatibility of the different group interests becomes obscured behind the mutually beneficial possibilities for coexistence among elites occupying the upper rungs of organizational hierarchies.[80] This occurs because the institutionalization of group interests leads to a situation where organizations become not so much vehicles for pressing these incompatible interests, and more self-sustaining centers of social power, co-existing in a balance of power under the auspices of the state: "State capitalism sometimes seems almost like a parody of the classless society" (AS, 114). As a result, a numbing of group tensions takes place. Authoritarian states remain characterized by clashes of interests, not only between labor and capital, but also among large industry, small capital owners, and stockholders; and political, military, and cultural elites and the masses. Adorno's quip that class conflict in late capitalism has become "the history of gang wars and rackets"[81] mirrors his colleague Otto Kirchheimer's description of the political sphere in terms of balance-of-power politics conducted by organizational elites, which has come unmoored from any underlying class dynamic.[82] This development—the "refeudalization" of society[83]—represents a serious regression, marking the failure of modernity's public institutions to embody shared ideas and values.

[78] See Weber, *Economy and Society*, vol. 1, 342.

[79] See Weber, "Bureaucracy," in *From Max Weber: Essays in Sociology* (New York: Oxford University Press, 1964), 198–244.

[80] See Weber, *Economy and Society*, vol. 2, 1381–1462. See also Adorno, "Reflections on Class Theory," 99.

[81] Adorno, "Reflections on Class Theory," 100.

[82] See Otto Kirchheimer, "Changes in the Structure of Political Compromise," in *The Essential Frankfurt School Reader*, 49–70; see also Adorno, *Introduction to Sociology* (Stanford, CA: Stanford University Press, 2000), 67–68.

[83] See Volker Heins, "Critical Theory and the Traps of Conspiracy Thinking," *Philosophy and Social Criticism* 33, no. 7 (2007): 787–801.

Pollock's conclusions were hardly uncontested at the time, particularly regarding the degree to which the market had been superseded as an independent source of social integration in state capitalism, and its overall stability. He maintains that the market exists only in a state managed form as a shadow of its former self, resulting in the effective negation of crisis tendencies Marx views as inherent to capitalist accumulation. Conversely, the Institute's "periphery" of legal-political theorists (Neumann, Kirchheimer) holds that, while existing in more politically managed form than before, the market has not been superseded, and that states attempting to directly control the crisis tendencies and conflicts of class society through the co-opting process Horkheimer describes are, in fact, rather volatile.[84] Horkheimer and Adorno basically side with Pollock, although they are dubious of the sanguinity with which he accepts the possibility of state capitalism becoming a stable and efficient social order. The point I would like to highlight, however, is that according to Horkheimer/Adorno/Pollock, Marx's presentation of Hegel's social theory is actually an accurate representation of their present in the following sense: Hegel thinks that while civil society is subject to disintegrating tendencies and incompatibilities of group interests when left to its own devices, in the state, these divisions are mediated through a political process where the different interests that the various estates represent have an ongoing opportunity to mitigate these tendencies and, ideally, reconcile. As Marx argues, contra Hegel, the antagonism of civil society is not sublated in the state and the unity projected onto society by bourgeois constitutionalism is an ideological façade: the rule of law in fact passively regulates an antagonistic accumulation process. However, Marx's characterization *only* holds for the earlier, liberal phase of capitalism, and in fact, Hegel's own vision wherein the state forges a unity among groups, which remain divided by virtue of different relationships to the forces of production, by fusing elements of class and status in the Estates, is actually a rather apt characterization of state and civil society in later stage capitalism—the major difference being that, for Horkheimer and Adorno, this unity is imposed by an amalgamation of power upon subjects conditioned to accommodate themselves to it, rather than being the result of mediation, as in Hegel. They do not dispute the attractiveness of Hegel's vision of political process mediating between individuals in a way that reconciles them to the totality upon which they depend. Indeed, we find Adorno conceiving of "society" as a system of mediation in which individuals, institutions, and situations mutually constitute each other: "Inasmuch as society remains a product of human activity, its living subjects are still able to recognize themselves in it, as from across a great

---

[84] See Franz Neumann, *Behemoth: The Structure and Practice of National Socialism, 1933–1944* (Chicago: Ivan R. Dee, 2009).

distance."[85] But if it is the case that today, as Adorno supposes, the concept of society has ceased to be meaningful (at least to positivistic social science), this is due to the fact that the processes through which individuals relate themselves to one another have lost their social character, becoming opaque or mechanistic, reducing individuals to a bundle of roles and needs. As Horkheimer bluntly puts it: "Mediation has now been abolished."[86]

This flattening of ideological struggle helps explain the apparently reductive nature of Horkheimer's analysis: his view that Western state capitalism, European fascism, and Bolshevism are all variations on the authoritarian state motif.[87] This is not to deny that there are important differences between these various forms—clearly, fascism, for Horkheimer and his circle, is an incredibly dangerous and appalling phenomenon that must be resisted. But all Western societies are, on this view, integrated in a fundamentally similar, non-mediational manner: they are dominated by political power featuring collusion between various powerful interests, and an unmoored, unresponsive, and interventionist state apparatus presiding over an antagonistic society of isolated individuals, containing its tensions without reconciling. The advent of the authoritarian state, for Horkheimer, essentially breaks the wheel of history.[88] So long as Marx and Hegel could conceive (in either idealist or materialist fashion) of a rational relation between state and legal structures, on the one hand, and the underlying social conditions, on the other, the dialectical unfolding of tensions and divisions at one level should produce changes at the other, which, if not predictable, should at least be rationally reconstructable (although, as we saw, Marx is increasingly drawn to the view that this unfolding takes place behind the backs of participants). When the social connections between individuals, groups, and sectors of society break down as a result of becoming a "second nature," resulting in an amorphous and anonymous web of domination, it becomes impossible to have any theoretically grounded sense of future trajectories (AS, 115–116). At least at this dark juncture in their writings, it does not seem plausible to Horkheimer and Adorno to view history as having "reason as its guiding thread" (PoR, 20), as Honneth puts it, except in the negative sense that "socially effective" reason is a pinched, partial, domineering moment of rationality.

[85] Adorno, "Society," in *Critical Theory and Society: A Reader,* eds. Stephen Bronner and Douglas Kellner (New York: Routledge, 1989), 269.

[86] Horkheimer, "The Jews of Europe," in *Critical Theory and Society,* 78.

[87] See AS, 101–103. Horkheimer's position here evolves quickly, as two years earlier he refers to fascism as *the* logical extension of capitalism's monopoly phase. See Horkheimer, "The Jews of Europe," 78.

[88] See James Gordon Finlayson, "Hegel, Adorno, and the Origins of Immanent Criticism," *British Journal for the History of Philosophy* 22, no. 6 (2014): 1142–1166.

Horkheimer and Adorno conclude that while it remains the case that different individuals have vastly different stakes in the preservation of socio-economic status quo, and that their interests can be understood in terms of qualitatively different relations that classes have to the forces of production, the technocratic (or authoritarian) administration of this order reifies the appearance of the social world: the manner in which an individual's identity and place in society is mediated by relations of recognition and domination is obscured, appearing instead as the fate of an isolated individual enmeshed in a vast network of action systems beyond their control and (for the most part) comprehension. Although from a humanitarian perspective, there is a tremendous difference between, say, fascist and non-fascist states, this reification prevents the subject from relating freely and consciously to the social whole, irrespective of the way the state is organized.

5. Reconciliation, Going Forward

Let me close with some reflections about what I have sought to do in this chapter. Chapter 1 argued that Hegel's notion of reconciliation represents a resonant, sophisticated, and plausible rendering of freedom as a universal aspiration, applicable at both the level of personal autonomy and social organization, and which moreover establishes a deep linkage between the two; I pointed out that Hegel places heavy emphasis on the role of the legal and political process in mediating between individual and society. This chapter is initially spurred by wondering what happened to this picture: at least within the critical theory tradition, freedom-as-reconciliation remains a very alluring leitmotif—indeed, almost a haunting one for later figures like Adorno, who are plagued by serious doubts about whether it is realizable in social and psychic life—yet its spokespersons are quite critical of the legal-political mediations Hegel finds important, to the point that this dimension disappears in Horkheimer and Adorno altogether. And it is not just that, from our perspective, Hegel got the political institutions wrong—the deeper critique here is that Hegel has an account of socialization that allows the political process of a compromised, antagonistic society to seem more freedom-actualizing than it is.

In drawing out this trajectory, I have not sought to offer an immanent critique of the positions discussed herein. It may, for example, simply not be part of Marx's agenda to theorize capitalism in a way that connects the mode of socialization to the mode of production—Marx seems to have been looking past such a society, anticipating its demise. I am merely pointing out that this limits Marx's usefulness for the purposes at hand here, namely, for examining reconciliation as a politically relevant aspiration for a society in which an unequal and/or class based division of labor seems unlikely to be decisively sublated in the foreseeable future. Lukács does provide an explanation for why reconciliation is a realizable aspiration only in a society beyond such antagonism: otherwise, we inhabit a reified social reality, and reification effectively short-circuits the nonviolent mediation between self and society that reconciliation involves. I did, however, press something more like an immanent critique against Lukács, since there are real gaps in his theory that he should be answerable for, and which prevent us from moving comfortably from finding reification an intuitively plausible notion to Lukács' very strong conclusion that reification is the fundamental, structuring feature of our social world. I turned to Horkheimer and Adorno in order to provide the account of socialization, or subject formation, that could underwrite something like Lukács' conclusions, although if Lukács takes the idea of socially achieved reconciliation and kicks it down the road, after the revolution, the picture of the political landscape that follows from Horkheimer and Adorno's conception of subject formation all but removes it as a plausible goal. I do not want to suggest either that the Freudian psychology that Horkheimer and Adorno employ is in any comprehensive way correct, or that their consistently grim, sometimes apocalyptic conclusions about politics inextricably follow from any psychology along these lines. For present purposes, however, I do conclude that Horkheimer and Adorno appropriate a plausible account of subject formation in a way that coherently underwrites conclusions about our passive incorporation into a schema of abstraction and exchange, which does indeed make it difficult to see how the law or other social institutions could play the mediational role Hegel envisions. To this extent, then, I think it is reasonable to maintain that anyone attempting to take up Hegel's mantle today owes an account of socialization or subject formation that would underwrite different conclusions about the totalizing nature of reification and the possibility of institutionalized mediation between self and society.

Going forward, I will be examining three major attempts to revive the fortunes of reconciliation as a legally, politically actualize-able aspiration in Rawls, Honneth, and Habermas. Part of the burden of these chapters will be to convince the reader that these three are devoted in one way or another to theorizing reconciliation as a goal, which is not obviously the case with any of them (and turns out not to be really true of Honneth). Following that, I evaluate the success of their endeavors roughly according to the following schema:

Hurdle 1: do they articulate the legal-political system in a way that shows how it could perform the mediational function that Hegel assigns it, but in a more participatory, democratic manner than Hegel?

Hurdle 2: Do they develop a conception of law that is resistant to pathologies of reification?

Hurdle 3: Can they provide an account of subject formation that would support (1) and (2)?

Very roughly, I will argue that Rawls does well with (1), and has an account of (3) that is not nearly as blinkered as those from the critical theory tradition are liable to assume, but that he is very much not alive to (2), which makes his theory very affirmative and seriously weakens its appeal. Honneth, the most frankly neo-Hegelian among the group, has given a great deal of attention to issues surrounding (3), and some to those around (2), but his attempted fusion of post-Freudian psychoanalysis and a Hegelian conception of social freedom does not lead him to the kind of political, process-oriented ideas about the actualization of freedom that were important to Hegel, and eventually undercuts his own account of emancipatory interests. I treat Habermas last because I take him to satisfy (1) and (2) in a way that outstrips competitor theories, and yet considerations of (3) have dropped out of his theory, with serious consequences: it becomes hard to see how to defend Habermas against the charge—which started this chapter, with Kierkegaard, Feuerbach, and Marx leveling it at Hegel—that he locates freedom in something outside the selfhood, agency, or lived experience of individuals.

3

Rawls' Liberal Right Hegelianism

Long a target of agonist political theorists for abstracting bloodless norms of reasonable discourse out of the messiness of political life, John Rawls' work is recently subject to another wave of criticism from political "realists" recoiling from what they deem a pernicious form of "ideal theory."[1] Along similar lines, Amartya Sen views Rawls as the leading proponent of "transcendental institutionalism"—i.e., the position that political philosophy's main task is to outline an ideally just set of institutions—which Sen takes to be an idle exercise, useless for orienting action in the real world.[2] Yet at the same time, a comparably prominent strand of Rawls criticism holds that he is not ideal enough: G. A. Cohen has recently renewed his longstanding critique of Rawls, arguing that Rawls' theory of justice makes undue allowances for non-moral motivations in the construction of its principles.[3] We also witness dissatisfaction with the accommodations Rawls makes to extant social reality in the turn to the more straightforward moralism of "justificatory liberalism," which refuses Rawls' efforts to make his proposals "politically" viable.[4] Some of these critiques have had notable impacts on fields like normative political theory and deliberative democracy where Rawls has been a dominant influence: skepticism about the prospects of reasonable and virtuous citizens deliberating matters of common concern has led deliberative theorists away from the (epistemically challenged) broad public sphere toward proposals for specially designed, small-scale participatory fora, which, whatever their merits, seem to judge as unworkable Rawls'

---

[1] See Geuss, *Philosophy and Real Politics*; Chantal Mouffe, *The Democratic Paradox* (New York: Verso, 2000); and Sheldon Wolin, "The Liberal/Democratic Divide: On Rawls's *Political Liberalism*," *Political Theory* 24, no. 1 (1996): 95–119.

[2] See Amartya Sen, *The Idea of Justice* (Cambridge, MA: Harvard University Press, 2009).

[3] See *Rescuing Justice and Equality* (Cambridge, MA: Harvard University Press, 2008).

[4] See Gerald Gaus, "Reasonable Pluralism and the Domain of the Political: How the Weakness of John Rawls' Political Liberalism Can Be Overcome by Justificatory Liberalism," *Inquiry* 42, no. 2 (1999): 259–284.

aspirations to update the social contract idea of citizens governed by laws that they give to themselves.[5]

These kinds of shifts are to be expected in fields that have labored so long under the shadow of Rawlsianism. However, it would be better if these migrations were guided by an accurate picture about what he is up to in the first place, and given the array of things allegedly wrong with Rawls, one gets the sense that there may be some confusion about this. Anyone basing their impression of Rawls' work solely on critical reactions to it is liable to think it quite distant from the concrete social analyses of Hegelian and left Hegelian thought, and therefore a poor candidate for rearticulating the notion of freedom as reconciliation. Rawls may invite the impression of ideality by stressing the Kantian influence on his work. However, he has always abjured approaches that proceed "from heaven to earth," in Marx and Engel's phrase, e.g., by formulating principles of justice or conceptions of the good society in the abstract and only subsequently turning to see how reality compares to their ideal. Nor does the method of constructing principles out of extant sentiments and intuitions represent a nod to some putatively ineradicable selfishness in human nature. Like authors in the critical theory tradition, Rawls acknowledges that the struggle to articulate a just society takes place within already existing societies, and as philosophers and citizens, we work with the materials at our disposal—laws, traditions, political cultures and practices, institutions—trying to understand their normative potentials and the forces arrayed against their realization.[6] In other words, Rawls is in some deep ways a Hegelian: social reality is not a brute historical given, but a medium through which we collectively acquire a sense of ourselves as free and equal, and strive to actualize these values in social life.

This chapter represents something of an interlude that considers the viability of a program that seeks to reactualize something like Hegel's notion of politically mediated freedom, without reckoning with the criticisms of that vision pressed in left Hegelianism: although Rousseau and Hegel have a substantial influence on Rawls, he is simply not part of the stream of social theory dealt with in the previous chapter. It would be tedious to criticize him simply for failing to respond to, say, the problem of reification, since he never considers it in any direct way. But, the main subject under consideration here is whether the Hegelian idea of freedom through reconciliation represents a viable orienting concept for critical theory today. In this regard, Rawls is hugely important: as I read him,

---

[5] See Simone Chambers, "Rhetoric and the Public Sphere: Has Deliberative Democracy Abandoned Mass Democracy?" *Political Theory* 37, no. 3 (2009): 323–350.

[6] See Kenneth Baynes, "Critical Theory and Habermas," in *A Companion to Rawls*, eds. Jon Mandle and David Reidy (Malden, MA: Blackwell, 2014), 487–503.

he has consistently tied the normativity of his arguments for justice as fairness to a basically Hegelian conception of freedom as being at home with one's self in the social world. He does this by contending that his conception of justice, if consensually agreed to and publicly institutionalized in the basic structure of society, would allow us to recognize that structure as a product of citizens' shared reason. Furthermore, the institutions of such a "well-ordered society" would socialize its members in a way that minimizes psychic conflict between their public duties and private sense of their good—this is overall similar to the sense of wholeness that Hegel believes ethical life provides to those who recognize its rationality. Like Rousseau, Hegel, and some of the left Hegelians canvassed in Chapter 2, Rawls is quite interested in social psychology and believes he can give an account that shows that socialization can mold us to be capable of realizing the kind of autonomy that modern democratic societies seem to promise. For as well-scrutinized as Rawls' thought has been over the last 40-plus years, this portion of it is not all that well understood, probably because Rawls gives the impression of abandoning it in the course of revising his theory during the 1980s. But as I hope to show, what he actually abandons is a small (albeit pivotal) part of *A Theory of Justice*'s social-psychological "stability" argument. He undertakes these modifications for essentially Hegelian reasons and they move his conception of autonomy in a more Hegelian direction, in that he no longer thinks a seamless "congruence" between the moral personality's public and private sides reliably results from normal socialization in a well-ordered society, and so comes to think that the ideal of "political autonomy" requires some politically mediated *reconciliation between* our public sense of justice and privately held comprehensive doctrines.

In short, the case that Rawls is a Hegelian is both sturdy and a neglected angle on his work, as recent scholarship convincingly shows.[7] In a larger sense, however, the fact that Rawls devotes little attention to the issue of overcoming obstacles to freedom's actualization is a significant limiting factor for the purposes of this study. This can be seen in two main ways: a) Rawls' social psychology is very much tailored to support the counterfactual claim that individuals' sense of justice and conception of the good would harmoniously support one another in a well-ordered society, to an extent that makes credible charges of pernicious ideal theorizing; and b) for Hegel, freedom requires reconciliation because society contains a moment of alienation that has to be overcome for people to be at home in their social world, and this figures into Rawls' thinking in, at most, a narrow way. Although I will argue that the modifications Rawls makes to *Theory*

---

[7] See Jörg Schaub, *Gerechtigkeit als Versöhnung: John Rawls' Politischer Liberalismus* (Frankfurt am Main: Campus Verlag, 2009); and Jeffrey Bercuson, *John Rawls and the History of Political Thought: The Rousseauvian and Hegelian Heritage of Justice as Fairness* (New York: Routledge, 2014).

move him toward a conception of freedom as reconciliation, he never considers the need for reconciliation to be driven by the need to surmount alienation or dissolve reification—hence, he tends to have a rather one-sided, affirmative conception of social institutions (in particular, the law) as repositories of value and principle. Rawls is illustrative for our purposes, because by weakening his socialization argument (for what I regard as good reasons), he is compelled to lean heavily on the publicity that law provides in order to make the prospect of mediation between persons' private identity and the public conception of justice credible, and at this point, his affirmative conception of the law becomes a damaging blind spot. This motivates our subsequent consideration of Honneth's efforts to spell out a conception of "social freedom" that deliberately downplays these legal-political mediations.

1. Roles for Political Philosophy

Rawls opens his lectures on the history of liberal political philosophy by enumerating what he sees as the four main "roles" that it has played—tellingly, these concern what it can contribute to "society's public political culture," rather than more purely intellectual efforts to obtain objective truth. They are: a) working out bases for social cooperation amidst "divisive political conflict"; b) "orienting" thought by offering reflections on "social and political institutions as a whole," e.g., their "basic aims and purposes," moral relationships between individual and society, etc.; c) reconciliation, in the specifically Hegelian sense of allowing us to see the rationality of our social world, in order that we might be more content with it; and d) gauging current prospects for social justice and change (LHPP, 10–11; JF, 1–5).

Rawls does not announce clearly which of these role(s) his theory of justice is intended to serve—the tasks are not mutually exclusive and one can make the case that it addresses all four. Nevertheless, the most popular version of Rawls has him focusing on (a): at the beginning of *Theory* (TJ, 4/4),[8] Rawls announces himself as a culmination ("carrying to a higher level of abstraction" [11/10]) of the social contract tradition. While he makes no secret of his preference for later authors (Rousseau and Kant) less apt to consider the social compact a self-interested bargain (á la Hobbes and Locke), he notes that the basic impetus behind contract theory was, in the aftermath of the Reformation, to uncover a shareable basis for political authority amongst confessional traditions (PL, xxvi–xxix, 159; LHPP, 11). Rawls seems to believe that, while

---

[8] References to *A Theory of Justice* are given to the 1971 edition, followed by 1999 revised edition. Where the text differs, quotations are taken from the revised edition.

European liberalism was mostly successful in defusing this kind of conflict by way of the gradual acceptance of principles of toleration and individual rights, it has bequeathed an unresolved conflict between the values of freedom and equality. While this conflict is not, in recent decades, explosive in a way that threatens the state itself, it does make it difficult for citizens divided by ideological disagreement to view the laws they are mutually subject to as reasonably imposed upon them, so long as they cannot recognize them as enacted for reasons consonant with their sense of self, i.e., their values. In this sense, at least as it concerns individuals' relationship to the state, the alienation problematic does make its way into Rawls' thought. As such, the existence of this conflict is not a merely academic point, as Rawls is convinced that a society's ability to furnish a basis for public authority that mediates amongst claims stemming from material inequality and value difference is, in the long term, necessary for sustaining a citizenry's loyalty to constitutional democracy. He draws this lesson from the ill-fated Weimar republic, where, as he recounts, all of the main ideological and class blocks were interested in asserting or defending their parochial interests, not motivated to find common cause, and so none were particularly invested in upholding the constitution itself (PL, lxif; LPP, 7–9). Thus, it is easy to connect Rawls' references to Kant's notion of "philosophy as defense" of Enlightenment political ideals' prospects to his own efforts to spell out a rational basis for hope that a lasting, legitimate constitutional democracy is possible (CP 305).[9]

When Rawls mentions reconciliation, on the other hand, it is with specific reference to Hegel's philosophy (LHPP, 10; LHMP, 331–336; JF, 3–4); since Hegel is, compared to Kant, not one of Rawls' more frequent interlocutors, one gets the impression that he considers an overriding focus on reconciliation to be idiosyncratic to Hegel. I believe that this is misleading: the idea of reconciliation is a profound current through Rawls' philosophy; it is not too much to say that, among the four listed roles for political philosophy, reconciliation is the one he *becomes* overall most oriented toward. As I will indicate, Rawls employs a kind of reconciliatory strategy of justification in *Theory*, though one that departs from Hegel by positing, in a well-ordered society, more of a harmonious "congruence" between the individual's personal desires and interests, and the demands of the social order, than Hegel expected—in this regard, Rawls' early conception of reconciliation is more Marxian, or even Platonic, in the way it sublates tension between the public and private. The revisions that Rawls makes to *Theory*, however, make a more specifically Hegelian idea of reconciliation come to the fore.

---

[9] See Anthony Simon Laden, "The House that Jack Built: 30 Years of Reading Rawls," *Ethics* 113, no. 2 (2003): 367–390.

2. What *A Theory of Justice* Is Really About

To the extent that *Theory* largely still defines Rawls' reputation, he is known primarily for putting forward a certain conception of justice—the two principles of justice, or "justice as fairness"—which he defends by arguing that they (and not competitors like utilitarianism) would be selected in the original position, i.e., a situation where rational deliberators know only generic facts about their society and lack any knowledge of their place or identity within it. Given the vastness of scholarly attention to such matters, I am going to pass lightly over details concerning the two principles' content and how they are specified in the original position. Very briefly, Rawls believes that for people to be free and at home in their social conditions requires them to conceive of society as a "system of fair cooperation." Fairness is not a selfless ideal, but a worldly one in which interlocutors regard the terms of their interaction as giving equal regard to one another's interests. His contention is that the design of the original position, wherein parties choose principles to regulate the major social institutions that impact most everyone's life prospects—"the basic structure of society"—behind a "veil of ignorance" in which they are ignorant of their personal circumstances, is an optimally fair "situation of choice." It is an instance of "pure procedural justice," in which the result is guaranteed to be fair, since parties lack any basis for leveraging the basic structure toward their interests. Such parties would, Rawls argues, insist on a first principle of "equal basic liberties" and a secondary one that secures "fair equality of opportunity" to make use of these liberties—the latter regulates material and status inequalities, allowing them to exist to the extent that they are beneficial to all, in particular to society's least advantaged ("the difference principle"). Altogether, a society consciously and effectively regulated by the two principles would manifest citizens' mutual respect for their separate moral personhood, while ensuring that as one works for oneself, one also works for the benefit of all. Although Rawls is clear that he is not proposing a social revolution in which society would be built from the ground up according to a blueprint specified by justice as fairness, a society that shapes the historical circumstances it inherits according to these publicly acknowledged principles would come as close as possible to actualizing the contractarian vision of society as a voluntary association:

> No society can, of course, be a scheme of cooperation in which men enter voluntarily in a literal sense; each person finds himself placed at birth in some particular position in some particular society, and the nature of this position materially affects his life prospects. Yet a society satisfying the principles of justice as fairness comes as close as a society can to being a voluntary scheme, for it meets the principles which free

and equal persons would assent to under circumstances that are fair. In this sense its members are autonomous and the obligations they recognize self-imposed. (TJ, 13/12)

Past these issues, there is surprisingly little clarity about what the normative force of this argument is supposed to be: in what sense and why does Rawls think we "ought" to shape social institutions according to justice as fairness? What does his avowedly artificial thought experiment contribute to its justification? Rawls' presentation of the original position, and the selection of the two principles of justice therein, occupies the first third of *Theory*, and that portion struck its critical public as the most strikingly innovative part, as well as the most directly engaged with the concerns of moral theory prevalent in Rawls' milieu (i.e., Anglo-American philosophy in the 1970s). Seen in this context, it certainly looks like the original position represents a way of describing something like Kant's universalizability test for generating principles of justice. So, one might surmise that Rawls takes justice as fairness to be normatively binding in more or less the same way that Kant takes the categorical imperative to be, i.e., as an imperative that human beings are unconditionally committed to by virtue of their rational nature.[10] However, it does not take long to realize that this will not do, and that many (to be sure, not all) of Rawls' resemblances to Kant are more surface than methodologically deep-seated: firstly, for Rawls, "Justice is the first virtue of social institutions" (3/3)—he is agnostic about whether his approach could be extended into a defensible ethic for personal conduct ("rightness as fairness" [17/15]). Obviously, this is very different from Kant, whose political philosophy derives from his moral philosophy. Second, Rawls clearly has no interest—even before the "political" turn in the 1980s—in basing his theory on anything like Kant's "two worlds" metaphysics; in fact, he does not put forth any particular metaphysics of the self. Instead, while Kant's noumenal self accounts for receptivity to the demands of pure practical reason, an account of moral psychology plays an equivalent role in Rawls, which Kant would consider heteronomous.

Finally, Rawls early on tells readers that "reflective equilibrium" is his basic concept of justification: reflective equilibrium represents an all-things-considered process of tacking back and forth between our particular judgments and (historically conditioned) moral intuitions, on the one hand, and posited principles that account for the preponderance of those intuitions and judgments, on the

---

[10] For readings of Rawls along these lines, see Dworkin, *Taking Rights Seriously* (Cambridge, MA: Harvard University Press, 1977), 150–183; and Charles Larmore, "The Moral Basis of Political Liberalism," *Journal of Philosophy* 96, no. 12 (1999): 599–625. I have argued against these readings in Hedrick, *Rawls and Habermas: Reason, Pluralism, and the Claims of Political Philosophy* (Stanford, CA: Stanford University Press, 2010), 61–77.

other, until a stable point is arrived at between a coherent set of moral principles and firmly held, "considered judgments" (18–21/16–19). Reflective equilibrium is plainly a context dependent notion: for principles to be normative for
individuals, something corresponding to the process of reflective equilibrium
must actually take place within them, and if the content of reflective equilibrium
is to be broadly shared, certain sentiments and judgments must be common in
"the background political culture."[11] Most important among these "fundamental
ideas" are the ideas that society should be a "fair system of social cooperation,"
and that citizens are "free and equal," in possession of the "two moral powers"
(the sense of justice and conception of the good); the basic notion of constitutional democracy is presupposed. Rawls appears to agree with Hegel that there
is something vainglorious about proceeding as if philosophy were capable of
stepping out of the social world and redrawing it—instead, theory's cogency
is dependent on the accretion of what Hegel calls "right" in the customs and
institutions of that background culture.

Nevertheless, while reflective equilibrium is a contextualist notion, it cannot
be a thoroughly conventional one for the simple reason that one could not very
well defend the normativity of justice as fairness on the grounds of an actual, reflectively stable consensus, since there is nothing approaching this, in the United
States or elsewhere. Moreover, just as Rawls later admits that most people do not
actually have a full "comprehensive doctrine" (PL, 13)—i.e., an articulated, basically coherent moral worldview—reflective equilibrium is itself an aspirational
notion, rather than something that mature adults reliably achieve. It is aspirational in the sense that individuals can be considered "fully" autonomous when
acting from principles that they hold in reflective equilibrium (PL, 77; TJ, 515/
452). In the Hegelian terms I used in Chapter 1, people are free and at home
with themselves in the social world when the political order and its demands are
continuous with their freely articulated and integrated sense of self. For Hegel,
the job of political philosophy is to show that something on this order actually
holds (albeit perhaps in a partial, ongoing manner) in the existing social world.
For Rawls, similarly so: reflective equilibrium is an aspiration that individuals
can approximate, and political philosophy should identify prospective principles that the public could be consensually oriented around, which would in turn
allow individuals to be fully autonomous.

So, while there must be something projective or idealizing about Rawls' argument for justice as fairness, it also must be rooted in a robust sense of how
human beings develop moral convictions and dispositions, how they might
approach a state of reflective equilibrium *qua* individuals, and how groups of

---

[11] See Onora O'Neill, "Changing Constructions," in *Rawls' Political Liberalism*, eds. Thom
Brooks and Martha Nussbaum (New York: Columbia University Press, 2015), 57–72.

individuals might settle on substantially similar principles of justice (although this last question receives much more attention in *Political Liberalism* than in *Theory*).[12] Although Kant was far from unconcerned with such matters, his inquiries into history, moral education, and anthropology are nevertheless auxiliary to his core account of pure practical reason.[13] Despite the fact that Rawls' readers are by now well aware that he never intends his argument to be based on pure practical reason, the fact that parts 2 and 3 of *Theory* are not auxiliaries to a derivation of the two principles of justice has nevertheless been slow to dawn.

Instead of being an articulation of pure practical reason that is subsequently supported by empirical considerations, the account of justice as fairness in *Theory* is a marvelously elaborate coherence argument in which different aspects of the moral personality, in addition to historical experience with institutions, are called on to mutually support the conception of justice. As Samuel Freeman points out, there are actually two standpoints operative in *Theory*, not just the one everyone knows about: in addition to the reasonable, impersonal point of view of the original position, there is the perspective of "deliberative rationality."[14] These standpoints reflect each side of the moral personality: the original position reflects "the sense of justice"; it models the willingness to propose and abide by fair terms of cooperation. Rawls supposes that there is an element of human psychology that supports the development and exercise of the sense of justice, and so he posits a desire "to express our rational nature": "Properly understood, then, the desire to act justly derives in part from the desire to express most fully what we are or can be, namely free and equal rational beings with a liberty to choose" (TJ, 256/225).

The second, less well-known standpoint of deliberative rationality reflects what Rawls later calls the "rational" moral power to formulate a conception of one's good, i.e., what one considers valuable, worthwhile, and satisfying. Deliberative rationality supposes a rational chooser's ability to take a dispassionate, long-term perspective on their adult life, of objectively assessing the likelihood of goals and plans coming to fruition, in order to assess how overall satisfying different "life plans" would be.[15] Unlike the sense of justice, Rawls does not feel compelled to posit a motivational principle in order account for people's willingness to act toward their own good, since it seems obvious that

[12] See Thomas Baldwin, "Rawls and Moral Psychology," in *Oxford Studies in Metaethics*, ed. Russ Schafer-Landau (New York: Oxford University Press, 2008), 247–270.

[13] See Louden, *Kant's Impure Ethics*.

[14] See Samuel Freeman, "Congruence and the Good of Justice," in *The Cambridge Companion to Rawls*, ed. Freeman (New York: Cambridge University Press, 2003), 284.

[15] See Charles Larmore, *The Autonomy of Morality* (New York: Cambridge University Press, 2008), 259–262.

people are generally so motivated. But he does put forward a rule of thumb concerning the level of satisfaction different goods and activities can attain, which guides deliberations in this standpoint: "the Aristotelean Principle." This principle advances the general thesis that people enjoy performing activities that they have some facility with; that is, human beings find the exercise of their distinctive capacities—both their particular talents as individuals and the distinctive capacities characteristic of the human species—satisfying: "other things being equal, human beings enjoy the exercise of their realized capacities (their innate or trained abilities), and this enjoyment increases, the more the capacity is realized, or the greater its complexity" (426/374). Chess is more satisfying than checkers for people skilled at both.

What does this complex of ideas—the rational moral power, the standpoint of deliberative rationality, the Aristotelean Principle—have to do with the articulation and justification of Rawls' conception of justice? Essentially, he supposes that a conception of justice is fully justified if we can see how it would reconcile the reasonable and rational moral powers, i.e., if it proves both optimally fair *and* something that people with a concern for the fruition of a rational life plan would willingly uphold. Rawls' interest in "the question of stability"—that is, his contention that justification involves assurance that a society ordered around the proposed conception of justice could, without coercion, reproduce itself over generations—needs to be understood in light of these requirements. The "stability" element of Rawls' theory has often proved confusing, amounting in many readers' minds to the inappropriate introduction of instrumental considerations near the heart of the theory of justice.[16] But Rawls' language of stability is misconstrued to the extent that it might be taken in either of two ways: a) in a Hobbesian vein, as checking to see whether compliance with justice as fairness, through incentives and state coercion, can be sustained; or b) as an assurance that a constitutional regime centered around justice as fairness is likely to come about, given where we are now.[17] These are not terrible misconstruals, in that Rawls does plan for the partial compliance of some portion of the citizenry with the state's laws (even just ones), and he also (increasingly in *Political Liberalism*) thinks that, for a theory to be normative for us, the well-ordered society cannot strike us as a fancifully distant, radical break with the present. That said, in *Theory*, Rawls' attention to stability revolves around a more holistic, and less bluntly instrumental, set of concerns. There he holds: a) a conception of

---

[16] See Brian Barry, "John Rawls and the Search for Stability," *Ethics* 105, no. 4 (1995): 874–915; and Cohen, *Rescuing Justice and Equality*, 27–87.

[17] See Thomas Hill, Jr., "The Stability Problem in *Political Liberalism*," *Pacific Philosophical Quarterly* 75, nos. 3–4 (1994): 333–352; and Larry Krasnoff, "Consensus, Stability, and Normativity in Rawls' *Political Liberalism*," *The Journal of Philosophy* 95, no. 6 (1998): 269–292.

justice should be rooted in ideals present in public political culture; b) our historical experience with constitutional democracy ought to allow us to envision
how such a conception could be effectively institutionalized in the basic structure of society; and c) a well-ordered society ought to socialize its members to
consciously, willingly comply with the requirements of justice over the course of
their lives. In short, stability represents, not merely holding things together in a
Hobbesian way, but an ideal of lived, social freedom, where people are shaped
by, affirm, and reproduce institutional arrangements that reflect the full breadth
of their moral personality.

These three issues ([a]–[c]) are taken up in *Theory*'s three parts and mirror
the architectonic of Kant's political theory, as they correspond to the latter's
questions about what practical reason prescribes in terms of a political constitution for managing our "unsocial sociability"; what experience tells us about
the historical development of this ideal; and how culture makes us responsive
to the imperatives of practical reason.[18] For Rawls, though, the satisfaction of
(a)–(c) altogether represents an ideal of freedom that resonates strongly with
Rousseau's vision of the general will, where we live in a society known to be
structured by the general will and identify that will with our own, and Hegel's
notion of being at home with ourselves in the social world—both of these ideas
embody a kind of social freedom where we carry out our everyday lives with
the background awareness that our institutions and practices, and the laws that
impact our life prospects, embody fair principles that we endorse along with
our fellow citizens. Rawls' ideal resembles these latter notions more than it does
Kantian moral autonomy, where freedom is a matter of acting on the basis of rational principles, irrespective of how well these actions cohere with the agent's
more prosaic motives, or whether they are effective, reciprocated, etc. (PL, 266;
LHMP, 280–309). In other words, a stable society would be one that actualizes
freedom, in roughly Hegel's sense.

Rawls does not deny that human beings can be moved to act based solely on
the conviction that duty requires X—he thinks that this sort of thing is, if not
commonplace, at least familiar, and so supposes that the sense of justice has an
anchor in "affections" (TJ, 476/416) that separates it from various other desires
to act for the sake of our good. However, he also believes that questions about
the strength of this affection relative to other motives, and whether we have effective second-order desires to prioritize the sense of justice, are questions about
socialization. A stable conception of justice is one that can be seamlessly and

---

[18] See Kant, "Idea of Universal History," in *Political Writings*, ed. Hans Reiss, trans. H. B. Nisbet
(New York: Cambridge University Press, 1991), 41–53; see Freeman, "Congruence and the Good of
Justice," 279.

transparently incorporated into a person's sense of self, during the course of normal maturation, and then sustained through adult life. How well a particular regime scores in these regards will vary based on how visible the conception of justice is in shaping the life prospects of persons in a given context (this is a matter of publicity, and effective lawmaking and administration), and how well the conception meshes with human moral psychology.

3. Moral Psychology and Stability: Non-Hegelian Reconciliation in *A Theory of Justice*

For as much as Rawls announces that he intends to abandon segments of part 3 of *Theory*, the issues raised by (a)–(c), and the ways he proposes to address them, hold mostly steady into his later writings. *Theory*, however, is distinctive in the emphatic way Rawls addresses (c), namely, through the "congruence" argument of chapter 9. This argument incorporates into the ideal of a well-ordered society notions more Platonic, Herderian, or Marxian than Hegelian. Rousseau and Hegel acknowledge that while persons may, *qua* private individuals, evaluate what should be done differently than they would *qua* citizens, freedom requires social organization and a corresponding mode of socialization that eases the tension between these perspectives. As we saw in Chapter 1, a major difference between Rousseau and Hegel is that the former places a lot of weight on conditioning people to put aside their private interests, whereas the latter finds this unrealistic and instead develops a complicated way of revealing to private persons how their interests and identities are folded into a social whole that gives them their due. I want to suggest that Rawls, in *Theory*, splits the difference between these Rousseauian and Hegelian ideas in an interesting way that ultimately goes farther than both in collapsing the potential for the public and private perspectives to be at odds—but that after *Theory*, he sides with Hegel in finding this argument unrealistic.

While not wanting to stake himself to contestable theories of moral development, Rawls thinks that available evidence supports a view of moral consciousness proceeding on a more or less natural path from "the morality of authority" to that of "association" and finally to "principle." He surveys two broad intellectual traditions for conceptualizing the acquisition of moral sensibility: a conditioning model and a rationalist one. On the conditioning model (Hobbes, Nietzsche, Freud), morality is not natural, per se, but something that human beings are indoctrinated into; sanctions and incentives create motives for other-regarding behavior that would otherwise not exist. For rationalists (Rousseau, Kant, Hegel), on the other hand, moral development is not a matter of supplying missing motives, but of activating human beings' potential to take part in rule-governed, reciprocal interactions. Rawls' sketch of moral development gives some weight to both traditions: it supposes that the conditioning model is preponderant early on, as small children are initiated (perhaps painfully) into other-regarding behavior. But, a different dynamic takes hold in the morality of association, wherein children and adolescents start acquiring a substantial sense of self through valuing and being valued by others—associations governed by norms of mutual respect, reciprocity, loyalty, merit, etc. establish a core of self-worth on which a social identity is constructed. Other-regarding actions become a natural extension of this self, rather than a coerced performance. Initially, this only holds true for a circle of intimates and personal connections. But, of course, the personal relationships through which the self initially takes shape are (usually) contained by institutions (e.g., the family, school, eventually work and civic associations), and so, like Hegel, Rawls finds that institutions play an indispensable role in molding natural affections into self-conscious value commitments.

These institutions are, in turn, part of a basic structure of society, and a well-ordered society is one not only in which this basic structure is regulated by a conception of justice, but also one in which there is public awareness of this regulation. In the morality of principle, moral conduct is rationalized as a matter of consistently adhering to certain norms or values, and so is not conditional on the emotional bonds and *quid pro quo* that incubate it in the previous stage. Nevertheless, principles that represent the reciprocity involved in associations engage those emotions—and thereby help to sustain a consistent, long-term commitment to conducting oneself according to principle—in a way that bare imperatives do not. This positions Rawls to claim that a society well-ordered through such principles facilitates the transition from the morality of association to that of principle by transferring the emotional resonance of institutionalized patterns of reciprocity onto the principles that persons come to recognize underlying those institutions. It follows that justice as fairness inculcates a commitment to its principles, and the constitutional regime that institutionalizes them, simply through the socialization process it oversees—this is true of justice as fairness to a degree that outstrips conceptions of justice that do not have the same emphasis on reciprocity or that satisfy transparency conditions less well. This means that justice as fairness is ideally positioned to address stability issues, and to facilitate lived, social freedom.

An interesting angle on this argument is to note how Rawls attempts to show that utilitarianism has serious deficiencies in terms of its stabilization potential, relative to justice as fairness. His contention is not just that utilitarianism would not be selected in the original position (a fact that its defenders may fail to find compelling), or that the original position reveals it to be non-reciprocal or indifferent to individual rights (objections which defenders may regard as dogmatic, or have ways of dealing with). More than this, Rawls argues that the above facts about moral psychology make it difficult to envision utilitarianism functioning as a public conception of justice, due to its lack of transparency and the difficulties it has engaging the affections undergirding the sense of justice. Utilitarianism—which places no particular premium on reciprocity, instead calling for a more rigorously impersonal, self-effacing, at times self-sacrificing, moral outlook—does not engage the emotional core of the sense of justice; it therefore does not cultivate self-respect in the same way that socialization patterns shaped by justice as fairness do (TJ, 499–500/437). By itself, this does not mean that utilitarianism is wrong, that living as a consistent utilitarian is impossible, or that it might not be based on rational insight, but that being one would have to be a matter of discipline and conditioning. All of this is not helped by what Rawls sees as the persistent lack of transparency involved in implementing utilitarian principles: the aggregative, overall manner in which utilitarian principles are satisfied can make it hazy whether some policy, institutional arrangement, etc. satisfies them or not, e.g., whether suffering in one region, or group, is compensated for elsewhere, in the long term, etc. (500/437). All in all, the problems that Rawls sees with utilitarianism surprisingly mirror those that Hegel found in Rousseau: a society ordered by utilitarianism would have to be stabilized through conditioning that subordinates private desire to the public interest, and in large and diverse modern societies, public knowledge about whether laws satisfying the conception of justice is poorly available, which altogether makes its prospects for stabilization dicey and prevents us from thinking of people as autonomous, "at home," under such a regime.

The decisive consideration in favor of justice as fairness from the perspective of stability considerations comes from the depth of reconciliation between the reasonable and the rational that Rawls sees as uniquely possible under it. Prior to this stage of the argument, the two major principles of moral motivation—the desire to express rational nature and the Aristotelian Principle—have more or less independent orbits: it certainly seems that they can compete with each other for priority, but they are not inherently at odds. The Aristotelian Principle calls for the refinement of one's particular talents and abilities, while the desire to express rational nature directs one to perform duty without special regard for one's own interests. Under utilitarianism, Rawls thinks, these two principles of motivation would be at odds in those moments when the greater good would be served by sacrificing individual well-being. But things are otherwise with justice as fairness' well-ordered society: there, our socialization through institutions that promote reciprocity is very deep; it naturally inculcates a thorough commitment to the value of social cooperation among free and equal persons, and inclines us to take special satisfaction in activities in which cooperation is integral.

This goes quite long way toward mitigating frustration that individuals may feel about the partiality of their own existence within a complex division of labor, and not just because they come to see the limited scope through which their particular existence allows them to develop their potentials as well compensated for by participation in institutions and practices that express their rational nature (529/463–464). More than that, in a society where reciprocity is at the core of the individual's identity, the Aristotelian Principle receives a supra-individual twist: Rawls speculates that persons accustomed to finding satisfaction in activities done cooperatively, and which are structured by fair terms of cooperation, have the potential to become radically non-narcissistic, in that their enjoyment is in the cooperative doing, not in having done it, or gotten something out of it, per se.

> In the account of goodness as rationality we came to the familiar conclusion that rational plans of life normally provide for the development of at least some a person's powers. The Aristotelian Principle points in this direction. Yet one basic characteristic of human beings is that no one person can do everything that he might do; nor a fortiori can he do everything that any other person can do. The potentialities of each individual are greater than those he can hope to realize; and they fall far short of the powers among men generally . . . When men are secure in the enjoyment of the exercise of their own powers, they are disposed to appreciate the perfection of others, especially when their several excellences have an agreed place in a form of life all accept . . . [I]t is through social union founded upon the needs and potentialities of its members that each person can participate in the total sum of the realized natural assets of the others. (523/458–459)

Therefore, activities desirable from the standpoint of deliberative rationality—refined and complex ones that fully engage capacities—need not only be ones that individuals perform using their *own* particular talents, but can be undertaken by collectives to which individuals contribute. In a society where individuals see that a fair basic structure enables the flowering of diverse talents and possibilities, which individuals reciprocally enable for each other by supporting just institutions, they can experience the refined complexity that a division of labor makes possible as if (in a sense somewhere between literal and merely metaphorical) they were undertaking this array of activity themselves. Such a society warrants the label of "a social union of social unions."

There is a heady mix here of sublime motifs from the history of philosophy, both classical and romantic. The romantic one, which we might most precisely trace to Herder, is that we can take pleasure in being connected to the flourishing of talents and ways of life that far outstrip what individuals are able to experience

on their own—as a result, they find more value in their own existentially limited rational life plan by seeing it woven into a kaleidoscopic tapestry of human
ways of being. This is not precisely Herder's idea, which is the arguably simpler
one that diversity itself is a value worth appreciating and encouraging, nor Mill's
that being exposed to an unfamiliar array of "experiments in living" contributes
to a widening of one's horizons, although it resonates with both.[19] Rawls' idea
is less cosmopolitan, insofar as it is conditional upon living in a certain kind of
cooperative community: rather than urging that people *should* appreciate the diversity around them, he is predicting that people socialized in a well-ordered
society *would*.

Under these very special circumstances, the Aristotelian Principle supports,
in effect, the sense of justice: in a social union of social unions, individuals experience the flowering of diverse talents as, in a way, part of their self, and so
under these circumstances, a life plan desirable from the perspective of deliberative rationality would be one that experiences this mutual enabling through
just institutions as an integral part of their own good. Thus, Rawls comes very
close to the Platonic conclusion that justice is the human good: supporting and
maintaining just institutions is an integral part of the best human life. Of course,
it is not Platonic in the sense that, for it to be true, just institutions must actually
exist. If Rawls thinks that normally our moral psychology has separate tracks for
the expression of rational nature and the cultivation of excellence, justice becoming the human good requires the counterfactual context of a society ordered
around justice as fairness, in which these tracks converge upon the same object.
The self, in such a society, possesses a degree of unity hitherto unseen: public
morals support private ambitions and *vice versa*—the distinction between doing
one's duty and working for one's self may still exist, and different individuals may
place greater emphasis on one or the other, but they are no longer in any important sense in competition.

As Daniel Brudney has shown, the idea of community that culminates
in chapter 9 of *Theory*'s conclusions that the well-ordered society realizes the
human good is quite similar to Marx's.[20] Recall from Chapter 2 Marx's contention that, in bourgeois society, individuality operates as a legal designation that
sets people formally apart from the social whole, even as the whole dictates, in

---

[19] In a lengthy footnote (TJ, 523–525n4/459–460n4), Rawls recounts that although his idea of
the human good achieved through social union cobbles together some ideas from German romanticism (and those like Mill who were influenced by it), he does not believe that it has a precise historical analog. On Herder, see Taylor, *Philosophical Arguments* (Cambridge, MA: Harvard University
Press, 1995), 79–99.

[20] See Brudney, "Community and Completion," in *Reclaiming the History of Ethics*, 388–415; and
"The Young Marx and the Middle-Aged Rawls," in *A Companion to Rawls*, Jon Mandle and David
Reidy, eds. (Malden, MA: John Wiley and Sons, Inc., 2014), 450–471.

fact, what they can be and do. Only in a communist society do particular persons truly become individuals: they affirm the social whole in their actions, and society licenses the blossoming of their particularity (and everyone else's) as a moment of that whole. Rawls' doctrine of the unity of the self in the well-ordered society is a close rendering of this. Furthermore, according to Brudney, members of Marx's communist society view the existence of that society as an unqualified good that "completes" them as individuals in a way no other could, by giving full expression to their cooperative, productive nature ("species being"). As such, they share a prepotent aim of reproducing the existing social structure (565/ 495).[21] For Rawls, a social union of social unions is fully a community in the precise sense that its members substantially share an end: they see the support of the just institutions that allow them to unify the public expression of rational nature and private cultivation of excellence as an end in itself.

That there is a utopian tenor to this argument should be apparent; it obviously is not just a congelation of conventional moral intuitions. But nor should we understand it as a pure imperative that breaks starkly with the present. The purpose of the argument is to show that such a society, while neither inevitable nor around the corner, is pregnant in the history of liberalism, and despite current ideological disagreements, represents a possible extension of extant political values. And not just possible: the congruence of justice and the good creates a wholeness of self that would be liberatory in a way that most people would find eminently desirable. The twining of justice and individual good is more thorough than anything Hegel contemplated, making the aim of reconciliation (as coming to see "the rose in the cross of the present") hard to ascribe to *Theory* (whose final vision lacks much of a cross), despite other Hegel-like elements—namely, that its normativity derives at least in part from revealing the well-ordered society to be a rational potential of the present, and the two principles of justice's specific normativity derives from being shown to produce the best, most stable, most psychically fulfilling version of the well-ordered society.

The culminating argument of *Theory* is utopian in another sense reminiscent more of Marx than Hegel: the receding of coercive law as a prominent instrument of social organization. I do not want to overstate the case for this point, since it is based more on omission than anything else—there is not a quotable phrase like "the withering of the state" that comes from Rawls' pen. And the vision of community from chapter 9 is always one where citizens' relations are

---

[21] Here, one is also reminded of Aristotle's contention that the best, most virtuous *polis* is one devoted to the "internal" end of reproducing virtue in the citizenry, not "external" ends like war and trade. See Aristotle, *Politics*, trans. C. D. C. Reeve (Indianapolis: Hackett, 1998), 1324a–1326b/ 193–199.

institutionally (and therefore most often, legally) mediated—indeed, the transition from group-oriented morality of association to that of principle depends on this being so. Nevertheless, after satisfying ourselves that history and experience can furnish an institutional skeleton able to bear the actualization of justice as fairness, specific talk of law and policy is largely absent from part 3. By itself, this is not a problem. But I think it indicates this: Rawls holds to the "high" Enlightenment ideal that not only (á la Kant) do citizens have a right to know the laws they are subject to, but (á la Rousseau) they should also have a fairly robust sense of how those laws impact them, as well as similarly and differently situated others, in order to think of themselves as the authors of those laws. But, in the well-ordered society from *Theory*'s chapter 9, Rawls appears not to think that acquiring this knowledge is a major problem. Now, as I showed in Chapter 1, making the operations of the state visible—the ways it mediates between the interests of different groups in civil society, and between civil society and the state generally—is a capital concern for Hegel: because he sees civil society as containing an ineliminable moment of alienation, reconciliation requires an awareness of the state's ongoing efforts to manage, mitigate, and (when possible) sublate this alienation. Rawls, on the other hand, thinks that the well-ordered society solves the stability problem through socialization: individuals, as they graduate from the morality of association to principle, have a powerful collective experience of common dedication to the principles of justice—they experience their good in sharing this dedication with others. In other words, an awareness of a commitment to the principles of justice as a shared end infuses the background political culture (571/500–501). If this is the case, the state advertising, as it were, its ongoing efforts to mitigate alienation through ongoing public legislation is not necessary, since the tensions between public and private that give rise to alienation have *already been mitigated*.

4. Scaling Back the Socialization Argument from
A Theory of Justice: Law Takes Up the Slack
in *Political Liberalism*

As is well known, Rawls eventually finds his solution to the stability problem in part 3 of *Theory* "unrealistic" (PL, xix, xlii). Most commentators have taken this declaration at face value, to mean that Rawls jettisons wholesale the stability argument from part 3, replacing it with the rather different notion of an "overlapping consensus," wherein a conception of justice lies at the center of a Venn diagram representing society's main comprehensive doctrines, which affirm the conception for reasons internal to those doctrines. But actually, this is not so: he retains the notion of the moral personality as comprising a "reasonable" moral power and a "rational" one—the conception of justice still expresses the reasonable power. Although the Aristotelian Principle does not play a vital role in *Political Liberalism*, Rawls continues to suppose that both moral powers are animated by their own motivational sources. And stability is still a matter of individuals being socialized to willingly act on their sense of justice, however they may cognize the justification of its content by the lights of their respective comprehensive doctrines (which include their rational life plans). However different their intellectual rationales for supporting the conception of justice may be, we cannot expect them to be so willing unless reasonableness is supported by, or at the very least not at odds with, their rational interests. But in *Political Liberalism*, Rawls no longer supposes that persons will find the reasonable and the rational to be congruent. To think this, he holds, would be to suppose that individuals will come to a roughly similar "Kantian" comprehensive doctrine.

I would dispute the notion that *Theory* is laying out a specifically Kantian comprehensive doctrine: chapter 9 describes persons who experience doing justice as co-extensive with their own good, and this, if anything, parallels what Kant calls the "*summum bonum*"—a state where moral virtue is perfectly correlated to happiness—and Kant thinks that we should not indulge the belief that this is possible in our earthly existence.[22] In any event, Rawls comes to believe that a diverse, secular society cannot be one in which people's moral personalities converge on a substantially similar life plan, not to mention one in which adherence to a specific conception of justice is integral. This would involve everyone consciously valuing cooperatively achieved, full moral autonomy—in addition to agreeing on the principled content of justice—above other sacred and profane values, and this, Rawls now says, is incompatible with "the fact of pluralism": even if it is plausible to assume that most reasonable people will, when socialized under just institutions, develop some attachment to them, which they somehow relate to their overall conception of the good (an overlapping consensus involves this much, after all), projecting convergence of the above sort is farfetched. We should accept this: a community of shared ends may be desirable from a certain point of view, but features of our social world foreclose it. Moreover, these features are *rational* ones, not bare social facts: the development of individuals' moral powers through "free institutions" does not produce the requisite degree of convergence for *Theory*'s argument to succeed. So, if we pine for a deeper shared experience (just as Hegel acknowledged that the Greek world was more beautiful than ours), we should realize that this can only be accomplished (if it can at all) by making society less rational.

---

[22] See Kant, *Critique of Practical Reason*, in *Practical Philosophy*, 5:129–132/243–246.

A similar conclusion could be drawn by emphasizing the division of labor and its consequences for the psyche, discussed in Chapter 2: from this point of view, Rawls' moral psychology downplays darker, world-rejecting, narcissistic tendencies. From Adorno's Freudian, to Rousseau's and Marx's pre-Freudian social psychology, the sources canvassed in the first two chapters find common cause in arguing that although normal sociality may require the suppression of these tendencies, modern society's functional differentiation prevents them from being substantially overcome, due to the free reign that civil society gives to self-interest. Rawls does argue, along, with Rousseau, that anti-social sentiments like envy would become quiescent in a society where individuals achieve self-possession and self-respect through cooperative activity guided by principles they acknowledge (TJ, 534–538/468–472). But since the institutional structure described in part 2 of *Theory* relies on "background justice" to secure "fair equality of opportunity" in the normal operation of private associations and competitive markets, rather than contracting their scope or transforming the action orientations that functionalize them, it is hard to credit *Theory*'s well-ordered society with ushering in a sea-change in human psychology. In my opinion, Rawls' moral psychology does not, in general, make strong assumptions that all narcissistic or aggressive behaviors are products of dysfunctional socialization, and can be purged through just institutions. But the congruence argument *does* seem to advance this claim, at least to the extent that People would have to regard the thriving of self and other as on par.

Rawls later adheres more rigorously to Rousseau's slogan, "Taking men as they are, and laws as they might be" (SC, 41; LHPP, 206–211). The fact that Rawls no longer thinks citizens experience their good in collectively expressing their sense of justice means, as Brudney observes, that they no longer "complete" one another—they no longer share the "end" of reproducing the just society as among their highest goods. Now, the extent of this last point's departure from *Theory* can be overstated, since *Political Liberalism* repeatedly emphasizes that people still need to treat the maintenance of their political order as "a great good" (albeit not necessarily one at the core of their identity) for an overlapping consensus to be stable. But this means that the "unity of the self," if it is achievable at all in the scaled-back utopia of *Political Liberalism*, is something incumbent on individuals to cobble together for themselves, out of their own biography, as we no longer assume that public life is fully congruent with individuals' private good. This, as Rawls acknowledges, means that *Political Liberalism*'s well-ordered society is not a social union of social unions, and therefore not really a community in Marx's or Aristotle's sense, insofar as they reserve that term for a union held together through an active commitment to creating/preserving a certain kind (for Rawls, egalitarian liberal) of society (PL, 146).

Rawls' argument for this point is not as thorough as one might hope—he usually avers that pluralism makes it implausible to assume any high degree of convergence among comprehensive doctrines (201). But for what it is worth, I think Rawls is right to arrive at this conclusion, for reasons reconstructable from the history of social theory and therefore convivial to the arc of Chapters 1 and 2. Take Durkheim's famous distinction between mechanical and organic solidarity, and his contention that one type of solidarity invariably predominates in a given society. Societies without a far-flung, elaborate division of labor usually have a preponderance of the former: being more culturally uniform and tight-knit, they have a robust "collective consciousness" and generate solidarity through a powerful experience of togetherness. Societies with an intricately specialized division of labor, on the other hand, for the most part do not furnish emotionally nourishing experiences of togetherness on anything like the wide scale that would be needed for social cohesion, and so people must learn to identify with one another by virtue of something more abstract, namely, participating in cooperative productive, legal, and governmental processes, which they (hopefully) can come to recognize as fair and mutually beneficial. Organic solidarity tends not be directly prescriptive (e.g., of lifestyle), nor is it as emotionally visceral as its mechanical counterpart. But it is nevertheless solidarity: it creates a social bond. As Durkheim says, if a traditional society secures legitimacy by delivering its members "a common life as intense as possible, in which the individual is engulfed," a society characterized by the division of labor maintains itself by "inject[ing] an even greater social equity into our social relations, in order to ensure the free development of all those forces that are socially useful . . . Just as ancient peoples had above all need of a common faith to live by, we have need of justice."[23] From this perspective, community in *Theory*, like Marx's conception of postcapitalist community, is based on an intermeshing of organic and mechanical solidarity, or we might say, organically generated solidarity that phenomenologically replicates the mechanical kind—something which Durkheim does not think is possible. And Rawls—who after all, is contemplating nothing on the order of the structural transformations that Marx is—eventually agrees with Durkheim, and finds himself in error for previously thinking this intermeshing is a realistic possibility. The overlapping consensus version of the well-ordered society is stabilized with organic solidarity: its members do not have a vibrant sense of connection; their relations are largely mediated by law; but they do tend to have some regard for one another by virtue of taking part in legally structured processes that are seen to give all parties a fair shake,

<hr>

[23] Emile Durkheim, *The Division of Labor in Society*, trans. W. D. Halls (New York: Free Press, 1984), 321–322.

and work for mutual benefit by making the various types of labor in a division of labor complement one another.

This comparison to Durkheim is instructive for two reasons: first, his notion of organic solidarity captures nicely the kind of social bond that the Hegelian state creates by mediating between the kinds of difference found in civil society. So, if it is true that *Political Liberalism*, in effect, agrees with Durkheim on mechanical and organic solidarity being more or less mutually exclusive, and if *Political Liberalism* abandons a Marxian conception of community and moves toward one rooted in organic solidarity, then it seems likely that the vision in *Political Liberalism* is actually close to Hegel's. Second, Durkheim's way of thinking about the relationship between law and solidarity presages the important compensatory moves that Rawls makes after abandoning the social union of social unions: whereas Durkheim thinks that law *reflects* the collective consciousness in a society of mechanical solidarity, it is responsible for *forging* organic solidarity. Like Hegel, Durkheim sees that the social bonds of a functionally differentiated society do not naturally emerge from socialization—they only come about through individuals becoming aware that their contributions complement those of other segments of society through fair, mutually beneficial interchange. This, in turn, is something that they can be made aware of through public institutions like professional organizations, the welfare state, and the legal process. As a consequence of more fully aligning with this thought in *Political Liberalism*, publicity conditions become a more pressing concern for Rawls, and law comes to the forefront as a means of fulfilling them. In sum, post-*Theory*, Rawls no longer believes that the public/reasonable and personal/rational aspects of individuals' identities align in a well-ordered society, and so the "unity of the self" depends on becoming *reconciled* to this gap. Similar to Hegel and Durkheim, political efforts to fairly mediate between groups with different interests and values become the major vehicle through which this reconciliation takes place—if we come to see the basic structure as shaped by this process, we can reasonably regard the basic laws we are subject to as self-given (albeit, not in the undivided, unreserved way *Theory* envisioned).

5. Rawls on the Complementarity of Law and Democracy

The main feature of Rawls' thought that establishes him as a leading theoretician of deliberative democracy (and keeps him rooted in the political ideals of Enlightenment "high liberalism") is his affirmation of the social contract thesis that freedom in the modern world requires that citizens be able to conceive of themselves as authors of the laws to which they are subject, even as he gives this thesis a more democratic elaboration than the original social contract theorists did, while accounting for increasingly more pluralistic and complex social conditions (PL, xxxviii–xl).[24] There are some discrete ideas that support this contractualist thesis by aiming to articulate a deep level of complementarity between the rule of law and democracy: political autonomy, the "four stage sequence of application," and the publicity conditions for the newly-central idea of "liberal legitimacy."

Political autonomy is an orienting ideal of Rawls' later thought, motivating his attention to articulating a framework within which citizens can recognize the basic structure of society as shaped by their public use of reason (PL, 98, 222, 397).[25] Political autonomy need not amount to self-determination on the basis of practical reason alone (as with Kantian moral autonomy), nor the kind of undivided will that *Theory* posits as ideal (xli). Rather, "it is realized by citizens when they act from principles of justice that specify the fair terms of cooperation they would give to themselves," actualized "by affirming the political principles of justice and enjoying the protections of the basic rights and liberties," and "participating in society's public affairs and sharing in its collective self-determination over time" (77–78). It is therefore a collectively realized value: given the miniscule amount of political influence that individual citizens wield, they can only understand themselves as subject to laws they would reasonably impose on themselves if a series of demanding conditions are met, foremost, that their fellow citizens also largely endorse the same (or very similar) principles of justice, and that this overlapping consensus informs their political constitution and, through democratically enacted law, effectively shapes the major institutions and social policies that impact them.

We are liable to misunderstand something here: in the wake of *Theory*, Rawls allows that it was a mistake to base the justification of a conception of justice on its free acceptance in a comprehensive doctrine that he assumed reasonable citizens would converge toward; since, in that scenario, the conception of justice was tightly woven into both citizens' moral worldview *and* life plan, when complying with it (through the laws, or by being affected by the basic structure more generally) they were exercising autonomy in a full, rounded way—it gave unity to their self. As I put it, in order to highlight what I view as its greater resonance

---

[24] See Michael Frazer, "John Rawls: Between Two Enlightenments," *Political Theory* 35, no. 6 (2007): 756–780. For accounts that are more insistent than most in seeing Rawls as a deliberative democrat, see Joshua Cohen, "For a Democratic Society," in *The Cambridge Companion to Rawls*, 86–138; Freeman, "Deliberative Democracy: A Sympathetic Comment," *Philosophy and Public Affairs* 29, no. 4 (2000): 371–418; and Laden, *Reasonably Radical: Deliberative Liberalism and the Politics of Identity* (Ithaca, NY: Cornell University Press, 2001).

[25] On moral autonomy and the status of political autonomy as a value in political liberalism, see Larmore, *The Autonomy of Morality* (New York: Cambridge University Press, 2008), 139–153.

with the Rousseau-Hegel-Marx axis than with Kant, the well-ordered society in *Theory* chapter 9 achieves an ideal of *lived* freedom. Rawls is careful in *Political Liberalism* to say that autonomy is *political*; to say that someone is politically autonomous is not to presume that he or she has a comprehensive doctrine in which supporting just institutions is a main focus of his or her life plan. As such, political autonomy "must be distinguished from ethical values of autonomy and individuality, which may apply to the whole of life, both social and individual, as expressed by the comprehensive liberalisms of Kant and Mill" (78). When Rawls writes such things, one might conclude that he is surrendering the above ideal of lived freedom, making political autonomy into more of a formal constit-uent of legitimacy. But this is not so. Rather, he is emphasizing that individuals exercise political autonomy when they act publicly, as citizens, to affirm the principles of justice by willingly participating in institutions structured by those principles—this kind of autonomy may well be separate from what they strive for while guided by values local to their private lives and associations. "Justice as fairness . . . affirms political autonomy for all but leaves the weight of eth-ical autonomy to be decided by citizens severally in light of their comprehensive doctrines" (78). But this just means that Rawls is no longer envisioning that the motives behind the sense of justice and the conception of the good, respectively, coalesce in a way that, for all practical purposes, obviates any division between them. In other respects, not much has changed: Rawls still supposes that a stable conception of justice is one that activates the human desire for fair cooperation and is usually internalized such that it, at the very least, does not conflict sharply with the other aspects of the person's life plan (even if it does not sit in an entirely easy, or clear, relationship to it). Otherwise, compliance with the principles of justice would be a matter of habit, coercion, resignation, etc.—i.e., not autono-mous. Political autonomy is a value, and citizens in a well-ordered society have to themselves regard it as such, but depending on their comprehensive doctrine, it may or may not figure centrally in their life plan, or be seamlessly integrated into their motivational set.

This moves *Political Liberalism*'s idea of the well-ordered society into broad agreement with the social freedom actualized in ethical life. Unlike the citizens of Aristotle's *polis* or the members of Marx's free association of workers, Hegel's citizens are not motivated by a particularly tight sense of togetherness: laborers, farmers, land-owners, business and military professionals, and civil servants all have different values and life plans; all find some aspect of their good by indulging their particularity as the rule of law allows; and within these groups, different individuals suffer the burdens of family dysfunction, macroeconomic swings, and interstate conflict unequally and contingently. Their allegiance to the state and its laws is rooted in their own values and perspective, and so they are politically autonomous in Rawls' sense. To nevertheless find their social world to be a home, all of these people have to have a view of the whole in which ethical life strives to comprise a unity of difference. To see things this way, they must be predisposed to "trust" the state, yes, but this trust is not purely a matter of conditioning: they must be able to actually know that the state is striving thusly, through the maintenance of consistent laws, representation of interests in the Estates, and the ongoing interventions of the legislature. So, too, with Rawls.

Since *Political Liberalism* is also less utopian in that Rawls grants that a well-ordered society does not have to be (and likely will not become) one where the political system is clearly oriented toward a uniformly agreed-upon conception of justice, there must be some reliable way for citizens to see the laws they are subject to as either deriving from, or at least consonant with, some approximation of the conception of justice they do adhere to. Given that it would be unreasonable to expect that all will be of one mind concerning what laws are just, even when they agree on principles of justice (TJ, 195–196/171–172), Rawls formalizes a threshold for realizing political autonomy with his principle of liberal legitimacy:

> [O]ur exercise of political power is fully proper only when it is exercised in accordance with a constitution the essentials of which all citizens as free and equal may reasonably be expected to endorse in light of principles and ideals common to their human reason. (PL, 137)

Plainly, this principle (which Rawls explicitly considers part of the conception of justice itself [225]) raises a number of issues concerning how individuals can be in a position to assess the facts relevant to judgments about legitimacy (e.g., the beliefs and goodwill of their fellow citizens, whether their constitution adequately concretizes the more abstract principles of justice, and the goals and efficacy of major social policies) (66).

Some critics hold that in order for individuals to abide by a conception of justice that, while reasonable, is not to their full rational advantage, they should require firm assurances that their fellow citizens will reciprocate.[26] But not only does this seem to set an unrealistic standard; it also neglects the strongly institutional focus of Rawls' thought, which extends from part 2 of *Theory* onward: in order to assess the degree to which a society approximates a genuinely well-ordered one, we should look less to the public professions of representative persons (which can, as Turner and Vallier point out, be hard to distinguish from "cheap talk")[27] and more at institutional history, to see whether it is plausible to think of major laws and policies as if they were enacted in order to satisfy

---

[26] See John Thrasher and Kevin Vallier, "The Fragility of Consensus: Public Reason, Diversity and Stability," *European Journal of Philosophy* 23, no. 4 (2015): 933–954. See also Paul Weithman, *Why Political Liberalism? On John Rawls' Political Turn* (New York: Oxford University Press, 2010), 17–67.

[27] See Thrasher and Vallier, "The Fragility of Consensus," 943–946.

the principles of justice. In other words, we should look to see whether current laws and policies can be traced back through what Rawls calls "the four-stage sequence of application" (TJ, 195–201/171–176). As we have already seen, it has always been Rawls' view that the principles of justice agreed to in the original position should not be regarded as determinations of pure practical reason, categorically binding; their justification depends on flesh-and-blood people freely incorporating the conception into their sense of self and life plan. This is something that is only approximated and varies among persons due to differences in values and background, and other vicissitudes. So too with the application of the conception to an actual society—obviously, no existing political system is capable of gearing all of its laws and policies, from municipal statutes to constitutional law, to satisfy concrete principles, even if the conception of justice in question could be thought to contain a blueprint for its own realization, which it does not.

So, the expectation that laws and policies should directly enact such a blueprint does not lead to a workable conception of legitimacy. In that spirit, the four-stage sequence represents a reasonable way of assessing laws' legitimacy in terms of the basic structure's compliance with the conception of justice. As the sequence models it, once parties behind the veil of ignorance have selected principles of justice, the veil gets lifted, bit by bit, as they deliberate about how to institutionalize them, first in a constitution, then through legislative institutions structured by the constitution, and finally, in an applicative (judicial and administrative) stage. Deliberators are allowed more information about the society they live in because once the principles have been selected in the original position, the issues facing deliberators become more pragmatic ones of institutional design: their goal at the "constitutional convention" is to minimize deviations from the principles of justice (mainly by embedding the basic liberties in a bill of rights [221/194]); at the legislative stage, it is to craft social and economic policies that the ensure the "fair value" of the basic liberties and distribute goods in accordance with the difference principle.[28] Since designing public policy is a matter of specialized (and controversial) knowledge, experimentation, public feedback, etc., perfect compliance is an unreasonable standard and Rawls

---

[28] Rawls treats the first principle of justice as a constitutional issue, while institutional guarantees for the second principle are left to the next, legislative stage, because he thinks that while basic rights are relatively amenable to being constitutionalized, satisfying the difference principle is liable to be a more complex matter of interlocking public policies (TJ, 199–201/175–176). This is primarily a judgment about whether constitutionally mandating levels of equality compatible with the difference principle would be effective. See Frank Michelman, "In Pursuit of Constitutional Welfare Rights: One View of Rawls' Theory of Justice," *University of Pennsylvania Law Review* 121, no. 5 (1973): 962–1019.

assesses liberal legitimacy in terms of whether laws are enacted through a constitutional structure that adequately instantiates an overlapping consensus on
principles of justice.

One of the most important parts of the Rawls-Habermas exchange is Rawls'
clarification about the four-stage sequence's role in his theory.[29] Habermas initially suspects an anti-democratic bias in its order of presentation: actors at later
stages of application (who increasingly resemble actual persons) are bound by
decisions made in previous stages; they are tasked with implementing the conception of justice articulated in the original position—the only stage wholly
constructed by the philosopher.[30] However, just as Rawls intends the original
position to be an expository "device of representation" for concretizing broadly
shared moral intuitions, "the four-stage sequence describes neither an actual
political process, nor a purely theoretical one," but rather "constitutes part of
a framework of thought that citizens in civil society who accept justice as fairness are to use in applying its concepts and principles" (PL, 397). Instead of
maintaining (implausibly) that the principles ordering a society's basic structure
should somehow be determined and fixed prior to a constitutional founding,
Rawls wants to underscore several points: a) our autonomy as citizens cannot
realistically depend on active consent to all of the laws we are subject to; b) there
is an ascending relationship of normative dependency between specific laws/
policies/decisions, the constitutional infrastructure of the state, and the principles of justice ordering the basic structure; c) and our assessment of the legitimacy of laws at "lower" levels on the sequence should be more procedural
in character, depending largely on whether we deem the constitutional system
to adequately embody the conception of justice at the center of an overlapping
consensus.

Elsewhere in his reply to Habermas, Rawls refers to the debate between
majoritarians and constitutionalists in the early American republic, pointing
out that the former did not reject basic rights and principles so much as believe
that popular procedures protect them better than legal ones (PL, 423–424).
Does the four-stage sequence show that Rawls simply holds the opposite view,
or does he have deeper reasons for favoring constitutional procedures over
popular ones? My impression is that the need to satisfy publicity conditions,
which are bearing a heavy burden in actualizing political autonomy in Rawls'
later theory, inclines him toward the latter view, as the optics of constitutionalism and legal certainty become essential for giving citizens a firm grasp of the
laws they are subject to. Constitutional traditions define concretely the context

---

[29] See Jørgen Pedersen, "Justification and Application: The Revival of the Rawls-Habermas
Debate," *Philosophy of the Social Sciences* 42, no. 3 (2012): 399–432.

[30] See Habermas, IO, 69.

within which citizens deliberate about matters of principle and policy, and give them a general sense of how their legal community understands itself and a shared vocabulary to start from. For Rawls, the constitution and its history is a resource for citizens to recognize the existence of a public conception of justice and receive assurances (through the institutional enforcement of constitutional rights and the constitution's public valorization) of everyone's mutual commitment to it.

To this he adds that prominent constitutional courts like the U.S. Supreme Court can offer a model for the forms of discursive justification required by public reason. This argument draws on Dworkin's conception of the Supreme Court as "the forum of principle."[31] Dworkin makes a distinction between "principle" and "policy": policy justifications are couched in terms of collective goals (telic), whereas principled justifications refer to moral rights persons are entitled to (deontic). The former are normally local and aimed at particular groups, industries, locales, etc., whereas the latter aim to treat all citizens fairly, as equals. Dworkin acknowledges that these are styles of justification more than ontological types (advocates often advance both kinds of justification for the same law), and while lawmakers can make principled arguments and policy arguments are used in the courts, duties of fidelity and doctrines of precedent make principled arguments the specialized competence of the judiciary.[32] He argues that the activities of constitutional courts actually enhance the quality of participation in the public sphere, by helping citizens focus on issues of political principle, when they might be otherwise inclined to view them through their own ethical/religious preferences, or as questions of efficiency/expediency. While Rawls does not similarly suggest that the public requires this kind of tutelage, he does affirm that the type of principled, impartial arguments, publicly presented and couched in terms of publicly recognized principles and values, represents the model of justification that he recommends reasonable citizens make use of—the Supreme Court serves as "an exemplar of public reason" (PL, 232)—in order to make visible their shared commitment to principles of justice. Indeed, in the absence of *Theory*'s socialization argument, which holds that citizens acquire their sense of their society's commitment to a conception of justice through a kind of pervasive *esprit de corps*, constitutional law and the kind of civic discourse that swirls around it—including the way that we think constitutional law constrains and shapes more concrete, local policymaking—is the main vehicle for the acquisition of knowledge about whether and how our social world is a home, as Hegel would put it.

---

[31] See Dworkin, *A Matter of Principle* (Cambridge, MA: Harvard University Press, 1985), 33–71.
[32] See Dworkin, *Taking Rights Seriously*, 81–130.

6. Skepticism About the Complementarity of Law and Democracy

Given the burdens that law—constitutional law and high courts, in particular—bear in publicizing and actualizing freedom in his theory, it is important to Rawls that legal institutions be found to make possible and/or bolster the realization of democratic ideals. So, for our purposes, it seems important to get a sense of whether these legal institutions—either as they exist, or in a modestly idealized form—can carry such a load. To that end, I propose to insert here some dissonant notes (which will return in Chapter 5) via the work of Jeremy Waldron and Duncan Kennedy, which introduce some general grounds for skepticism about the complementarity between law and democracy that Rawls seems to suppose: both authors tend to see the law as displacing (often surreptitiously) public deliberations about shared interests and principles into an artificial, elite medium that limits from the outset the scope of disagreements and possible resolutions. Let me note that I do not take Waldron's and Kennedy's points to foreclose the possibility that law could be a vehicle for rendering visible a polity's commitments to principles of justice, as Hegel, Rawls, and to some extent Habermas all imagine. But they show, I believe, that law, presently and historically, carries with it substantial reification effects (what I will be calling a weak ideological distortion), which would have to be reversed, elided, or counterbalanced in order for that possibility to be actual. And given that in Rawls' later theory—which is no longer supported by a full-bodied account of moral education, wherein people acquire their sense of how their self is related to society through experiencing their own good in cooperative actions that reproduce just institutions—commitments to principles of justice are, for all intents and purposes, publicly visible *only* through law. So, the question of under what conditions law serves to enable (rather than undermine through reification) citizens' prospects for being "at home" under the laws they are subject to deserves more attention than he gives it. My eventual conclusion is that, rather than seeking to counterbalance these reification effects, Rawls unwittingly accedes to them.

a. Practical Discourse in a Legal Frame and the Displacement of Disagreement: Waldron

According to Waldron, there are a number of reasons to be suspicious of the idea that modern legal systems operate as vessels for democratic will formation. As we have just seen, Rawls holds that a written constitution with its history and traditions can serve as a shared perspective for democratic deliberations about principles, with the Court's activities serving as a propaedeutic for citizens' exercise of public reason. But for Waldron, treating questions of rights and principle as legal/constitutional issues that courts have something close to a final word on is itself a political choice of the "who decides?" variety, one which undermines rights of participation and the ability of citizens to cognize the moral substance of their polity.[33] He argues that when authors entrench a right or principle in a written constitution that an independent judiciary is subsequently authorized to interpret, they have done several things. They have concretized the right or principle with a unique verbal phrase and entrusted its enforcement to a professionalized body that at least partly understands its job as a technical one of determining the meaning of that text. Constitutional authors furthermore establish a mechanism that is, in the long run, unpredictable: they do not know what the implications of their lawmaking will be and it is to a large extent out of their control. Instead, application will be determined by the vagaries of an elite-driven process. And it is doubly suspicious when the intergenerational nature of constitutional orders is taken into account: even if future courts administer it in a way that is consonant with the will of the ratifiers, it will not be the will of those presently subject to the law. Waldron's intent here is not to deny that there could be advantages in taking the specification and enforcement of basic rights out of the ordinary political process—one need only rehearse warnings about the perils of populism here[34]—but those benefits cannot be cashed out in the language of autonomy, as if we were binding ourselves to our own will.[35] This is especially true of Rawls, who is not a realist about rights *á la* Dworkin, and cannot accept any pre-political definition of them (PL, 379–380).

While it may be true that in a political culture where conflicts concerning rights and principles are frequently settled through constitutional adjudication, the public may adopt the vocabulary that courts and constitutional texts use, it is not clear that this is any great boon for the quality of deliberations. As Waldron observes, the particular phrases that constitutional authors end up selecting often "take on a life of their own,"[36] fixating public discourse around

---

[33] See Jeremy Waldron, "Can There Be a Democratic Jurisprudence?" *Emory Law Journal* 58, no. 3 (2009), 680.

[34] See Alexander Kirshner, "Proceduralism and Popular Threats to Democracy," *Journal of Political Philosophy* 18, no. 4 (2010): 405–424. See also, David Estlund, *Democratic Authority* (Princeton, NJ: Princeton University Press, 2008), 65–97. Waldron (*Law and Disagreement* [New York: Oxford University Press, 1999], 13, 267n31) considers these arguments to be frequently overstated and raises doubts about the effectiveness of judicial mechanisms for, as it were, protecting the people from themselves.

[35] See Waldron, *Law and Disagreement*, 265. See also Richard Stacey, "Democratic Jurisprudence and Judicial Review: Waldron's Contribution to Political Positivism," *Oxford Journal of Legal Studies* 30, no. 4 (2010): 749–773.

[36] Waldron, *Law and Disagreement*, 220.

certain terms: for example, the U.S. Constitution's Eighth Amendment prohibits "cruel and unusual" punishments, so discussions about the merits and morality of penal law frequently become debates about whether something (e.g., capital punishment) qualifies as "cruel" or "unusual." The same goes for debates about what qualifies as "speech," "privacy," "undue burden," and the trimester framework in abortion law, and so on, and all because this is the language that judges and amenders chose, sometimes somewhat arbitrarily.[37] And while portions of the public may have sophisticated views about how rights and principles will be interpreted by constitutional courts, this ability to prognosticate is different from thinking about how they should be resolved as a moral or ethical matter, much less participating in their resolution.[38]

More serious problems emerge when considering ways in which constitutional process can short-circuit democratic deliberations altogether. In the context of constitutional democracies in which freedom of expression, conscience and religion, civil rights, and the welfare state are, with some variation, fairly well entrenched, it may be easy to say that there is at least a thin consensus on these constitutional principles—indeed, such a notion is central to Rawls' belief that an overlapping consensus can develop out of a constitutional one (as well as Habermas' "constitutional patriotism")[39] (PL, 140). At the same time, we are aware of sharp and persistent disagreement about what the concrete meaning of these rights should be when applied and balanced against other rights and common goods. For example, let us say that "we all agree" that freedom of expression is important and individuals have a right to it that should enjoy some legal protection. But with regard to issues like hate speech and pornography, a gamut of seemingly reasonable positions is possible: some think that these kinds of expression have the unacceptable potential to undermine others' freedom; others hold that free speech means tolerating all manner of offensive speech, not just the types of speech we like; still others hold that expression without artistic, scientific or political content does not warrant legal protection, and so on. Waldron stresses the depth of this sort of disagreement: at the time of ratification of constitutional right X, there will be disagreement among the ratifiers about a) whether there is such a right at all, b) whether it warrants legal protection, c) whether it warrants constitutional protection, d) whether the proposed verbal formula intended to capture X is apt, and perhaps most importantly e) what X's implications should be as far as public policy is concerned.[40] Over time, as we grow accustomed to a constitution's way of framing things, some of these

---

[37] Ibid., 289–291.
[38] Ibid., 291.
[39] See Habermas, IO, 225.
[40] See Waldron, Law and Disagreement, 267.

disagreements (i.e., [a]–[d]) may fade, but not in a way that necessarily settles much with regard to (e): such a "constitutional consensus" displaces disagreement into questions of application, promulgating the somewhat misleading impression that a consensus on X itself nevertheless exists, and that settling issues about (e) should boil down to a matter of determining what a text specifying X "really" means.

Most of this picture is familiar to anyone who accepts Rawls' idea that "the burdens of judgment" make moral disagreement a permanent feature of a society "with free institutions" (PL, 54–57). And it might be thought that constitutionalizing a moral issue does have the virtue of making political disputes around it narrower, more deliberative, more focused on finding correct answers.[41] Rawls and Waldron share common ground in urging that the proper response to "the circumstances of justice" is for people to keep talking to one another, attempting to persuade while being open to interlocutors' arguments, with the awareness that any degree of consensus is uncertain and slow to develop. But constitutional law can be a poor medium for fostering this conversation— a possibility Waldron appears more cognizant of than Rawls.[42] Whereas, as Waldron emphasizes, legislative bodies settle disagreements for the time being with resolutions more reflective of citizens' actual disagreements, constitutional adjudication labors under the appearance that, despite disagreement about meaning and application from ratification to the present, "We the People" are committed to this constitution, it has a meaning discoverable through legal reasoning, and the members of the constitutional court are authorized to say what this meaning is.

> The bland rhetoric of the Bill of Rights was designed simply to finesse the very real and reasonable disagreements that are inevitable among people who take rights seriously for long enough to see the Bill enacted. Instead of encouraging us to confront these disagreements directly, an institution of judicial review is likely to lead to their being framed as questions of interpretation of those bland formulations.[43]

Whereas legislative decisions have a certain revisability about them, giving dissenters a stake in the process after a decision has been made,[44] constitutional

---

[41] See Neil MacCormick, "Reconstruction after Deconstruction: A Response to CLS," *Oxford Journal of Legal Studies* 10, no. 4 (1990): 539–558.

[42] See Waldron, *Law and Disagreement*, 11–12, 101–103.

[43] Waldron, "Do Judges Reason Morally?" in *Expounding the Constitution: Essays in Constitutional Theory*, ed. Grant Huscroft (New York: Cambridge University Press, 2008), 64.

[44] See Cristina Lafont, "Is the Ideal of Deliberative Democracy Coherent?" in *Deliberative Democracy and Its Discontents*, eds. S. Besson and J. L. Martí (Aldershot: Ashgate, 2006), 3–25.

adjudication often (less so when rulings are "narrow") carries a pretense of finality, thereby conveying that the issue is settled, the court's conclusions are
demanded by "the law"—even though we know that courts make law by slim
majorities and shift course all the time, and it is certainly possible to doubt
whether high court judges are doing more than voting their policy preferences
much of the time.

b. The "Effects" of Adjudication: Kennedy

Kennedy's book *A Critique of Adjudication* culminates with an account of major
but oft unnoticed "effects" that a political system where relatively large numbers
of disputed political questions pass through adjudication has on perceptions of
social reality: "moderation" (courts tend to grind down the pace and scale of
legislative change), "empowerment" (legal process tends to favor established
interests and groups adept at using adjudication), and "legitimation." For present purposes, "the legitimation effect" is the most pertinent. Kennedy's idea
is in keeping with a broadly Marxist style of critique—drawing on the idea of
commodity fetishism from *Capital* in addition to the ones from "On the Jewish
Question"—which argues that certain systemic ways of reproducing social reality make it seem more natural or inevitable than it really is, and that part of the
reason people accept unjust social conditions is that they misperceive them to
be natural, part of the way things are. Kennedy claims that adjudication coats its
outcomes with a gloss of legitimacy and inevitability. To the extent that mainstream public opinion views the legislative and electoral process as a profane
struggle over power, interest, and ideology, adjudication looks comparatively
more rational, fair, objective, neutral, dignified—in short, more legitimate.[45] In
the context of an open, discursive, legislative process, relatively uncluttered by
thick traditions and precedents, citizens would, under this hypothesis, be more
apt to weigh laws and decisions on their substantive merits. If they believe either
that the process leading to the action was seriously compromised or the result
seriously unjust, they would be disinclined to consider the matter legitimately
settled simply by virtue of its being the upshot of a majoritarian procedure. On
the other hand, if one has some cocktail of the following attitudes toward law,
one would be more inclined to see the decision as rational and legitimate: adjudication is largely rational and relatively "less political" than lawmaking; the
constitutional order bends toward justice, its content fixed in a way that commits
the state to govern in accordance with principles of justice; and the legal process

---

[45] See Jeffrey Mondak and Shannon Smithey, "The Dynamics of Public Support for the Supreme
Court," *Journal of Politics* 59, no. 4 (1997): 1114–1142. Obviously, things would be otherwise in nations where the courts are, for specific historical reasons, held in low esteem.

arrives at decisions by paying fidelity to these principles.[46] Kennedy's hypothesis is that we accept a good deal of distributional inequality because it is the result of a system of rules administered through common and constitutional law, and hence takes on an inevitable, quasi-natural "feel."

Kennedy is quick to add that none of this has to do with the nature of law as such, preferring to draw attention to a series of deep cultural assumptions about politics and legislation, on the one hand, and law and adjudication, on the other:

> At an elementary level, we have a cultural belief in the distinction be-
> tween law application and law making . . . People have associations with
> law, and its development through adjudication that connect to the "nat-
> ural, necessary, just" pole of the duality, with legislation associated with
> the traits at the other end.[47]

Some of this is attributable to surface appearances, e.g., judges dress in robes, surrounded by leather-bound books, occupying columned buildings. Politics, while having its own dignified trappings, is more openly conflictual, its participants more easily regarded as self-seeking.[48] Despite the argumentative character of its process, participants in adjudication appear jointly committed to the discovery of answers ascertainable through interpretation of materials in a way that is "expressive of some underlying spirit of legality," as Waldron puts it.[49]

Kennedy has spilled a great deal of ink urging that this overall appearance of coherence is false and that large bodies of law are really the results of "ideologized group conflict" resulting in mashes of rules reflecting opposed "individualistic" and "altruistic" worldviews.[50] While the degree of incoherence in existing law is a source of dispute between CLS theorists like Kennedy, and camps like Dworkin's and the Law and Economics movement, the important point for our purposes is that political interventions employing positive law not tied to traditional ethical life create high demands for legitimation that can overtax the ordinary political process. And in any event, in the modern administrative state, the job of actually

---

[46] Kennedy, *A Critique of Adjudication*, 237. Habermas also notes that institutions administering justice tend to have lesser burdens of justification than do bureaucracies and legislation, primarily because law is conventionally associated with the restoration of moral order. TCA2, 178.

[47] Kennedy, *A Critique of Adjudication*, 240–241.

[48] See Waldron, *The Dignity of Legislation* (New York: Cambridge University Press, 1999), 31.

[49] Ibid., 25. See also Kennedy's extensive discussion of the "denial" of the presence of ideology in legal work, both in the minds of individual judges as well as the self-understanding and public rhetoric of the legal profession. *A Critique of Adjudication*, 192–212.

[50] See Kennedy, "Form and Substance in Private Law Adjudication," *Harvard Law Review* 89, no. 8 (1976): 1685–1778, and Kennedy, "The Structure of Blackstone's *Commentaries*," *Buffalo Law Review* 28, no. 5 (1979): 209–382. See also Roberto Unger, *What Can Legal Analysis Become?* (New York: Verso, 1996).

fleshing out legislation's implications often falls to the courts.[51] Since the justification of court decisions can at most indirectly draw on discourse in the public sphere, they lean instead on "principled" discourses that seek to draw out the underlying coherence of existing law.[52] But all of this suggests that legitimation deficits in the modern state are being coped with by farming out the real business of lawmaking to the judiciary, thereby transforming unresolved practical issues and group conflicts into more technical ones of legal interpretation, in an institutional setting habitually regarded as legitimate.

7. Rawls, Dworkin's Method of Interpretation, and False Reconciliation Through Law

As I argued a moment ago, Rawls highlights the role of the constitution and the Supreme Court in his theory because of their ability to satisfy a well-ordered society's publicity conditions after crucial elements of *Theory's* socialization argument are abandoned: the constitution represents a public, semi-permanent commitment to a "higher law" of basic rights that is a relatively stable container for the to-and-fro that we have to expect from ordinary legislative and electoral politics. Moreover, the constitutional phase of the four-stage sequence proves crucial for developing an overlapping consensus: it secures important bulwarks against unjust laws at the legislative stage and is the pillar upon which a deepening consensus about the fair value of basic liberties can develop through the public's use of reason, which is informed by the vocabulary and decisions of the constitution and the Court (PL, 356–368). All in all, constitutional law is the solid rock upon which citizens build their joint allegiance to a public conception of justice.

It is, I think, clear that the ideas about law involved here are considerably different from Waldron's and Kennedy's. For one thing, their arguments indicate that the way constitutional law fulfills publicity conditions and structures the lower stages in the sequence of application has consequences that are awkward for Rawls. To be fair to Rawls' side of the argument, no doubt on many occasions

---

[51] Note, however, that the longstanding expectation that this fleshing-out will be done by the courts (or administrative fiat) could conceivably be a cause of a public's low estimation of legislative politics, as well as the incapacity of legislatures to produce effective, binding legislation. See William Scheuerman, "Neumann versus Habermas: The Frankfurt School and the Rule of Law," *Praxis International* 13, no. 1 (1993): 50–67, and Robin West, "Progressive and Conservative Constitutionalism," *Michigan Law Review* 88, no. 4 (1990): 641–721.

[52] Dworkin argues that versions of legal positivism that try to understand law as legislative command lose their relevance "as technological change and commercial innovation outdistance the supply of positive law." *Justice in Robes* (Cambridge, MA: Harvard University Press, 2006), 212.

judicial review has prevented serious legislative injustices;[53] and to take the example of the United States, once-every-few-generations upheavals of a constitutional (Reconstruction) or quasi-constitutional (New Deal, Civil Rights) nature have grappled with the stains of historical injustices.[54] And a lasting constitutional order does provide a certain visible continuity to the law, over time. On the other hand, the combination of Waldron's point about the suppression of disagreement under a veneer of consensus over "bland phrases" and Kennedy's legitimation effect implies that legalistic societies inculcate a weak ideological distortion of social reality—"weak" in the sense that Waldron and Kennedy are describing pervasive habits of mind reinforced by the optics of the legal system rather than the near-total veil that one finds, e.g., with Lukács' conception of reification; but "ideological" in the specifically Marxist sense that they involve cognizing the social world through a lens that filters out discontent and injustice.[55]

The main context in which Rawls discusses ideology is when considering whether justice as fairness runs afoul of Marx's critique of liberalism. He says that it does not: not only because the property-owning democracy he favors secures the fair value of liberty in a way that the "abstract," "merely formal" liberalism Marx targets does not (JF, 176–178), but also because, like Marx's "society of free producers," the well-ordered society would be as free from ideological consciousness as one can be (121–122). This is because the publicity conditions are fully satisfied: a well-ordered society is not sustained by delusions (PL, 66–68). Now, if we understand the well-ordered society to be one where sharp ideological conflict has nearly vanished and the compliance of basic institutions with the conception of justice is a matter of publicly acknowledged fact, then the kind of ideological distortion at issue here would indeed be absent: obfuscating tendencies of the legal system would not be a problem, since there would be nothing to obfuscate. And one obvious rejoinder to the Waldron-Kennedy line of attack on Rawls that I have been proposing is that it describes the legal system of a non-well-ordered society. But it has never been all that clear whether we should understand the well-ordered society as one beyond ideological disagreement—does Rawls really intend that policy disagreements along a left-right spectrum would not exist? This is actually a difficult question to answer. In *Theory*, a well-ordered society is a constitutional democracy: there are competitive elections among political parties, so presumably the parties

---

[53] Though perhaps not as often as we might hope: see Waldron, *Law and Disagreement*, 287–289.

[54] Rawls cites Bruce Ackerman's (2000) work on American constitutional revolutions in this regard: *We the People*, vol. 2, *Transformations* (Cambridge, MA: Harvard University Press, 2000).

[55] For a proposed linkage between ideology critique and deliberative democracy, see Christian Rostbøll, *Deliberative Freedom: Deliberative Democracy as Critical Theory* (Albany: SUNY Press, 2008), 141–153.

disagree about something. The fact that the constitutional convention stage of application only guides and constrains, not determines, legitimacy at the legislative and adjudicative stages indicates the persistence of disagreement here. So, in that sense, the answer must be "no." And yet, Rawls must also think that such disagreements would exist within a framework where all major parties accept:

a) the priority of the liberty;
b) an enumeration of the basic rights and liberties;
c) a balancing approach for ensuring equal basic liberties for all (i.e., ruling out fundamentalism about one or more categories of rights);
d) that the state has some role in ensuring fair equality of opportunity and the equal value of basic rights, and
e) ensuring that inequalities in the basic structure in some way serve less-advantaged groups; and
f) that other political parties also accept (a)–(e).

Since this level of consensus does not undergird current splits between liberal, labor, socialist, and green parties, on the one hand, and Christian democrat, conservative, and nationalist ones, on the other, it is safe to surmise that disagreement in the well-ordered society would be considerably less sharp-edged than they are now. But at this stage in my argument, we are more interested in *Political Liberalism's* well-ordered society, in which there is not a tight, shared socialization process that produces consensus on (a)–(f)—in my estimation, *Political Liberalism's* overlapping consensus really only firmly gathers around (a), probably also includes (b)–(c), loosely overlaps on (d)–(e), and (f), although important, becomes more contestable and fragile. Here—again, given the absence of the socialization argument—the lip service that a society's various groups give to basic laws (especially [a]–[c]) is crucial for establishing the presence of a nascent overlapping consensus that would set a baseline for liberal legitimacy—something akin to the sense of "trust" that underlies Hegelian patriotism. But if *Political Liberalism's* well-ordered society is a "realistic utopia," it is still rather far from where we are now. Rawls' "political" turn after *Theory* only slightly mollified the considerable number of critics who take him to have little of interest to say about less-than-well-ordered societies, or find his theory ideological in the sense of exhorting us to look at our world *as if* it were more well-ordered than it is.[56] I think that Rawls can parry most thrusts of this sort.[57] However, since it is important to him that we be able to see an overlapping consensus as pregnant in what we have now, those keen to defend Rawls here should be troubled that he relies on constitutional law both to inform

---

[56] See Geuss, *Philosophy and Real Politics*, 88–91, and Sen, *The Idea of Justice*.
[57] See James Gledhill, "Rawls and Realism," *Social Theory and Practice* 38 (2012), no. 1: 55–82.

judgments about the legitimacy of existing laws and to facilitate progress toward an overlapping consensus when the points canvassed in the previous section indicate that it militates against both possibilities.[58]

One of the reasons that Rawls favorably receives Dworkin's theory of legal interpretation is that it shares with justice as fairness the ambition of reconciling and synthesizing opposed ideological paradigms like Kennedy's individualism and altruism, thereby serving as an exemplar for how such a thing is possible through public reason (PL, 236–237n23). Indeed, much of what rings false about Rawls and Dworkin to Waldron and Kennedy is that they believe they can anticipate a stage of reasonable agreement beyond ideological conflict. In a paper highlighting a longstanding, but in his view, unresolved, problem with the method of constructive interpretation from *Law's Empire*, Waldron recounts Dworkin's attempts to elide the difficulties that conflicting values embedded in bodies of law represent by urging that the existence of "competing" values in law does not imply that it is "contradictory."[59] Legal correctness depends on the interpreter's ability to synthesize existing legal materials in a way that satisfies criteria of "fit" and "justification." Taken together, these form Dworkin's criterion of "integrity": legal decisions should be as consistent as possible with legal history while presenting the community's standing moral commitments to its members in the most "attractive" light. Waldron observes that when reckoning with cases where significant portions of the legal materials point to opposed decisions, it is almost always *possible* to generate coherent legal arguments in different directions—this is, after all, what advocates do on behalf of their clients. So, Dworkin must show that existing bodies of law furnish us with a consistent possibility for generating interpretations that are uniquely compelling from the standpoint of integrity. If it is too much to ask that he "demonstrate" this, still *something* has to be indicative of legal correctness.[60] But in a divided area of law where interpretations can only aspire to "fit" something like half of the legal materials, what could this be? In such circumstances, Dworkin can only recommend that interpreters settle the case in accordance with their convictions, shunting aside other considerations in order to make the law more morally attractive than it would be had the decision been made to reflect another set of principles—in the judge's opinion.[61] Here, what separates Dworkin's judge of integrity from the sly pragmatist is the former's conviction that the law "really"

[58] See David Ingram, "Dworkin, Habermas, and the CLS Movement on Moral Criticism in Law," *Philosophy and Social Criticism* 16, no. 4 (1990): 237–268.

[59] Dworkin, *Law's Empire*, 225–232.

[60] Waldron, "Did Dworkin Ever Answer the Crits?" in *Exploring* Law's Empire: *The Jurisprudence of Ronald Dworkin*, ed. Scott Hershovitz (New York: Oxford University Press, 2006), 172.

[61] Ibid., 177.

supports his position. Of course, in political life, this sort of situation is hardly uncommon: decisions have to be made all of the time that settle controversies in favor of one side or another, paying heed to certain values and interests to the exclusion of others. But irrespective of the question of whether there are "really" correct answers to such hard cases (a question Waldron and Kennedy consider either irrelevant[62] or a red herring[63]), Dworkin's judge certainly acts like there are. From the perspective of those sympathetic to Waldron's and Kennedy's points, this buttresses the impression that the adjudicative treatment of political controversies in a less-than-well-ordered society serves to enact closure over them on legal grounds that conceal the practical issues and disagreements involved rather than thematizing them.[64]

Now, it is only fair to acknowledge that a friendly footnote in *Political Liberalism* hardly obliges Rawls to defend the theoretical edifice of *Law's Empire* in all its gory details, at least some of which (e.g., grounding integrity in associative obligations) are incompatible with a "political" account of justice. But his hope that the Supreme Court will be able to display justifications for its decisions through public reason does imply that something like the reconciliation of opposed legal paradigms through constructive interpretation in areas of law significantly impacting the basic structure must be consistently possible in a way publicly distinguishable from "cheap talk." Waldron suggests that Dworkin deal with these problems in a way more convivial to the "political" thrust of Rawls by having his judge more modestly attempt to steer the ship between telling rosy "as-if" stories about legal background materials, and the partisan moralism of pragmatism, by admitting that he is just trying his best at a daunting interpretive task in treacherously politicized environment.[65] And yet such a revisionary account of judicial authority and rhetoric is ill-suited to the role that Rawls' publicity conditions and four-stage sequence assigns constitutional law.

8. Conclusion

In Chapter 1, I argued that Hegel faults Rousseau for reconciling us to our sociality without doing much to reconcile us to our actual society, and so his version

---

[62] See Waldron, *Law and Disagreement*, 164–187.

[63] See Kennedy, *A Critique of Adjudication*, 189–190; see also Kennedy, "American Constitutionalism as Civic Religion: Notes of an Atheist," *Nova Law Review* 19, no. 3 (1995): 909–921.

[64] As Waldron points out, a well-ordered society beyond serious ideological conflict would be one where Dworkinian integrity would be inert—there would be no conflicting vales to integrate. *Law and Disagreement*, 188–208.

[65] See James Allan, "The Travails of Justice Waldron," in *Expounding the Constitution: Essays in Constitutional Theory*, ed. Grant Huscroft (New York: Cambridge University Press, 2008), 161–183.

of reconciliation must in the end be based on conditioning, rather than rational insight. Rawls' argument in *Theory* might initially be thought to be vulnerable to the same objection, since there, his well-ordered society seemingly habituates us, through shared experiences of cooperating according to mutually acceptable principles, to deeply value these experiences and the institutions that enable them. But this would be an unfair accusation, since *Theory* attempts to show that a mark of institutions' justness is their capacity to reproduce themselves, transparently and without coercion, and that the well-ordered society of justice as fairness is uniquely positioned to do this. As Rawls eventually did, however, we should find this argument unpersuasive, whether for reasons drawn from social theory (like the Durkheimian ones covered earlier), or psychology (which I did not delve into, though one could), both of which add depth to Rawls' own explanation of why this model of reconciliation is perniciously utopian. *Political Liberalism* does better in this regard: its well-ordered society is neither a rosy description of the present nor a future utopia, but represents an aspiration that is pregnant in what is, while eschewing the more apparently appealing Marxian vision of community from *Theory*—the kind of self-authorship *Political Liberalism*'s well-ordered society facilitates is accordingly more fraught. This position is close to Hegel's view on the state's role in ethical life, and Hegel is happy to think that this kind of setup actualizes freedom. But I criticized Hegel for relying on a fairly profane conception of politics that tended toward interest group pluralism stabilized by elite coexistence, wrapped up in the legitimating optics of the state (of which the law and constitution, along with the crown, are a big part), distancing himself in the process from the conception of lived freedom that makes his view so initially promising. Rawls' theory, while purging itself of the kind of traditionalism and nationalism that runs through Hegel's state, does little to correct these deficiencies, while making publicity depend more on subjects' observation of a distant legal process that the more substantial, intermediary elements of ethical life (absent in Rawls) were meant to correct for.

In this sense, I think of Rawls as offering a kind of liberalized right Hegelianism and an object lesson in trying to update the basically Hegelian idea that modern political institutions can, under the right conditions, actualize freedom, without reckoning with the left Hegelian critique outlined in Chapter 2. While Rawls' initial idea was to elucidate how a higher order consensus on principles of justice could infuse ground level institutions and practices of social life, in *Political Liberalism*, he is bereft of the substantial institutions at the border of civil society and the state that Hegel used to mediate between the individual and the society, which are too prescriptive and anti-pluralistic for the constraints Rawls puts on his theory. As a result, he is forced into overreliance on the legitimating optics of the law to publicize the rationality of the state. One could (as Honneth will) criticize this reliance as myopically fixated on the law as the vehicle for actualizing freedom, at the expense of the broader institutions and practices of socialization that make (or fail to make) an integrated social identity possible. As an internal criticism of Rawls, this neglects his sound reasons for abandoning the argument of chapter 9 of *Theory*, which focused more generally on socialization, not specifically on law. But regardless of whether the abandonment of the non-legalistic version of his argument is well-motivated, Rawls is left with a rather one-sided picture wherein the individuals' autonomy depends on trusting a legal order that projects an appearance of rational coherence over social struggles and ideological disagreements. To that extent, Rawls is led back to the point upon which Hegel criticized Rousseau, and Marx, in turn, Hegel.

4

Actualizing Social Freedom

Normative Reconstruction and Psychoanalysis in Honneth

Among theories I am considering as resources for renewing Hegel's conception of freedom through reconciliation, Axel Honneth's is avowedly truest to Hegel's method: Hegel is the inspiration for Honneth's account of the formation of the self through mutual recognition and its emancipatory interest in a freely developed, integrated set of self-relations. His insistence that "relational social spheres" are inexorably value-laden self-consciously restages Hegel's idea of ethical life. The latter point, combined with his disapproval of Kantian and natural law theories that suffer from "the impotence of the ought" makes Honneth believe that theories of justice are normative—and really, only make sense—when intertwined with a social theory that elaborates how social spheres reproduce themselves (FR, 3–5, 64–65). To that end, he scorns the "juridical" focus of neo-Kantian political theories that screen out issues pertaining to successful socialization that are not obviously related to political organization. He has been equally wary of social theories that erase the layer of value-laden intersubjectivity from their accounts of social integration. Given that these alleged errors have been characteristic of Habermasian and first-generation critical theory, respectively, Honneth has had to move delicately in developing a theory more "critical" than Hegel's, while hewing to it closely enough to evade the deficiencies he finds in more immediate predecessors.

In a lot of ways, I estimate Honneth to be remarkably successful in all this. But he makes for an interesting test case for my purposes, since while he develops a conception of freedom whose basic elements are certainly Hegelian, the concept of reconciliation is not among those elements. To be clear, I am not claiming that there is no place for a notion of reconciliation in Honneth's theory: readers of *Freedom's Right* who find it convincing may well describe this conviction in terms of coming to appreciate the rationality embedded in the modern social order. My claim is rather that Honneth does not see a process of reconciliation as integral to freedom's actualization. At the conclusion of Chapter 1, I argued that the common impression that Hegel's conception of freedom amounts to submission before the status quo is uncharitable; but I also granted it credence to the extent that Hegel is ill-equipped to explain how persons themselves could detect what Honneth calls the presence of a "normative surplus," i.e., ethical life's untapped potential for actualizing freedom.[1] Honneth's neo-Hegelianism is set up to advance through some of these problems. For as much as he thinks of core elements of his critical theory as fairly direct updates of Hegelian doctrines of recognition, "social" or "objective" freedom, and institutional rationality, he is also clear that other key aspects of Hegel should be abandoned. Honneth adheres to a school of Hegel interpretation that identifies the objective teleology ("logic") embedded in both subject and object as the main untenable aspect of Hegel's philosophy.[2] According to this line of thought, we should try to understand as much of Hegel as we can without relying on these elements, among which, for Honneth, is the concept of reconciliation. Of course, he realizes that logic plays a significant role in Hegel's thought and cannot be removed like a vestigial organ, even if one's aims are limited to a methodological reconstruction of *The Philosophy of Right*. In place of this objective teleology, Honneth inserts a naturalized, psychoanalytically informed conception of mutual recognition, which undergirds his accounts of: a) socialization and ontogenesis; b) the impetus for social change and resistance to oppression; and c) societal reproduction.

It is important to Honneth that (a)–(c) be internally related to one another: he takes seriously the notion that a critical theory should be immanent in social reality by attuning itself to real human beings' interest in their own emancipation from unjust, oppressive social conditions. Honneth believes that the Frankfurt School—including Habermas, despite his focus on the problem of "grounding" critique—never successfully developed a conception of emancipatory human

---

[1] I should note that this is not precisely how Honneth sees it: the introduction to *Freedom's Right* defends *The Philosophy of Right* against the charge that it affirms the existing institutional order; FR, 8–10. Honneth notes that Hegel criticizes the guilds and corporations of his time as oppressive and lacking spirit, evidenced by the fact that they do not cultivate pride in labor among their members. It is fair to point out these incidences, but one should also note how few they are, and how they are restricted to what Hegel takes to be pretty clear instances of breakdown in discrete parts of ethical spheres. I think the critical potential of this kind of procedure is less than Honneth would like. In any event, whether Honneth interprets Hegel appropriately here is not of great import, since his own recognition-theoretic accounts of socialization and social change are intended to diagnose the presence of untapped potentials for freedom in the existing framework of ethical life in a way that Hegel's procedure cannot do.

[2] For a critique of Honneth's view of what is and is not viable in Hegel, see Pippin, *Interanimations*, 117–138. For the type of account of Hegel's "metaphysics" that Pippin accuses Honneth of disregarding, see Béatrice Longuenesse, *Hegel's Critique of Metaphysics* (New York: Cambridge University Press, 2007).

interests after the collapse of Marxist philosophy of history, and to that extent did not develop a fully viable alternative to "traditional theory." Accordingly, one of Honneth's main aims has been to spell out an empirically well-grounded emancipatory interest that is normative—in the sense that real human beings identify with and are motivated by it—and capable of diagnosing systematic blockages to freedom's actualization. One of the things that not only makes Honneth relatively unique in the critical theory tradition, but also sharply distinguishes him from Rawls, is his use of what is often called a "philosophical anthropology," or what might more conventionally be dubbed a conception of human nature. Once put in those terms, many critics—sympathetic or otherwise—consider this aspect of Honneth's theory dubious: old fashioned, afflicted by is-ought problems, and otherwise at odds with the general constructivist trend in practical philosophy.[3] I do not view the issue in this light and prefer to think of Honneth's account of emancipatory interests as grounded in theory of socialization, i.e., of how we become thinking, feeling, and acting selves for whom being free or unfree is a meaningful attribution.[4] If one has sympathy for Honneth's reasons for rejecting a freestanding, constructivist grounding for critique, his idea of spelling out those cognitive and affective aspects of psychic life that make oppression and injustice visible has much going for it, even if it hitches itself to a specific (psychoanalytic) account of human nature in a way that Rawls and Habermas have declined to.

My reservations about Honneth's program are overlapping. The first concerns the cogency of his combination of object relations psychoanalysis and a Hegelian conception of the normativity of ethical life. My worry here is not with the idea of combining a philosophical anthropology with the method of "normative reconstruction" utilized in *Freedom's Right*, per se, but with whether the specific psychoanalytic account of ontogenesis and socialization he appeals to supports the notion that the differentiation of social spheres—for Honneth, the hallmark of modernity—can be understood as a result of demands for distinct types of mutual recognition, which work altogether to constitute a freely integrated identity. Here, I think that Honneth moves too easily from psychoanalytic premises to Hegelian conclusions, and is thereby lulled into excessive confidence that deficiencies in the actualization of social freedom in its various spheres produce

---

[3] See Zurn, *Axel Honneth: A Critical Theory of the Social* (Malden, MA: Polity, 2015), 46–54; Renante Pilapil, "From Psychologism to Personhood: Honneth, Recognition, and the Making of Persons," *Res Publica* 18, no. 1 (2012): 39–51.

[4] I use the term "socialization" in a broader way—inclusive of enculturation or *Bildung*—than Honneth, who typically restricts its use to discussions of pre-adolescent development. The reason for this terminological expansion is that I argue for a broader application of concepts of repression and internalization than Honneth's normative reconstruction of ethical life allows.

effective motivations for struggles to realize them. This is, I think, apparent in Honneth's conceptions of ideology and reification, which are innovatively formulated, and yet are not thought to *systematically* undermine the prospects for emancipation. It also—this is my second concern—leads Honneth to essentially reject the conception of freedom as actualized through reconciliation that I am recommending here, toward which he is actually less amenable than either Rawls or Habermas, making his account less centered on the political sphere (something he takes to be a point in favor of his approach). I believe that Honneth has both overestimated the amount of metaphysical baggage that the concept of reconciliation has and underestimated the consequences of orienting critique around a conception of freedom that does not itself involve reflection on society.

1. Anchoring Critique in a Pre-theoretical Interest

Since his earliest writings, Honneth has maintained that the distinctiveness of critical theory lies in grounding its perspective in the feelings and moral convictions of subjects who experience injuries at the hands of society and strive to overcome them. Put another way, critical theory should insist on a tight connection between the normativity of critique and human beings' interest in their own freedom: it is "a particular form of normative critique" drawing on "the pretheoretical resources in which its own critical viewpoint is anchored extratheoretically as an empirical interest or moral experience" (D, 68–69). Honneth calls this interest "pre-theoretical" to indicate that it is not something that human beings are to be informed about by the authorities or philosophical experts, but rather is disclosed through their own feelings of social suffering. In this sense, Honneth stays true to Marx's critique of Hegel: freedom should be something experienced by persons in their everyday lives, rather than a legal or philosophical construct subsumed upon them. It follows, Honneth thinks, that we must have some basis for thinking that an interest in emancipation actually exists, one which real people (to some discernible extent) recognize and are motivated by.

Honneth's major idea here has long been that a theory of recognition allows us to understand socially induced suffering in terms of denials or distortions of types of recognition vital for the human personality's self-realization. He borrows from Hegel a tripartite typology of recognition types:

1) love and care, which individuals typically give and receive in the domain of the family and other intimate personal relationships;

2) respect for one's dignity as a human being, which is typically institutionalized as rights conferred through the legal and political process; and

3) esteem for one's accomplishments, which predominantly occurs in spheres of work and association.

Honneth contends that we can identify these types of recognition as generally necessary preconditions for a successful, freely self-realizing life under modern social conditions, such that their lack severely hinders the prospects for such a life, in the following senses:

1) being recognized as a unique human being in a caring, loving way inculcates a basic trust in one's ability to form volitions of one's own, act appropriately in social space, and intervene effectively in the natural world (self-confidence);

2) being recognized as possessing an innate dignity that entitles one to treatment as a moral equal inculcates moral self-worth that Honneth dubs "self-respect"; and

3) being recognized as a compatriot who makes a socially valuable contribution to the community develops a sense of "self-esteem."

Human beings are intrinsically motivated by felt violations of these preconditions—they are "incapable of reacting in emotionally neutral ways to social injuries" (SR, 138). This ensures that a theory of justice tied to such an account of recognition is bonded to motivating sentiments and judgments.

For as much as this scheme of recognition types has been a perennial feature of Honneth's theory, he has changed how explicitly he thinks of its underlying value in terms of *freedom* (as opposed to something more Aristotelian like "thriving") and whether he thinks of these characterizations as anthropologically grounded (i.e., in human nature), as opposed to hermeneutically (i.e., based on an interpretation of the value orientations that modern people typically have).[5] The general trend of Honneth's writings—especially as *The Philosophy of Right* has come to serve more and more as *the* model for his normative theorizing— has been to insist increasingly on freedom as the exclusive designation for the pre-theoretical interest, and to justify this move hermeneutically. But whether Honneth relies on hermeneutic or anthropological arguments to link his concept of recognition to the human interest in freedom, he believes that this interest is "reconstructible" in a way that can serve as a basis for a theory of social justice, by specifying freedom's fullest meaning as "social freedom," along with

---

[5] Nikolas Kompridis, "From Reason to Self-Realization? On the Ethical Turn in Critical Theory," *Critical Horizons* 5, no. 1 (2004): 323–360.

its structural preconditions. "Social freedom" is a term Honneth borrows from Frederick Neuhouser's work on Hegel—it refers to what both authors take as the straightforward meaning of the kind of freedom that Hegel argues is realized in and through ethical life. Because he thinks that social freedom cannot be understood apart from the formative processes that make it possible, Honneth's critical theory becomes distinctive in the way it links a conception of social justice to a theory of socialization (PIF, 15–18). This linkage allows him to avoid some problems with the normative perspective of early critical theory, on the one hand, and "procedural" or "juridical" theories of justice, which we can associate with Rawls and Habermas, on the other.

2. Objections to Neo-Kantian and Early Frankfurt School Approaches to Normativity

Honneth's critical theory represents a throwback to the Frankfurt School's 1930s interdisciplinary research program in some notable ways, namely, the rootedness of critique in an emancipatory interest, and opposition to "positivistic" social theory. Honneth shares with Horkheimer's original circle the conviction that human beings have a deep, unrenounceable interest in the free development of their self or personality, which carries into an interest in a "rationally" organized society that would enable this. Although Horkheimer, Adorno, Marcuse, and Honneth differ on the details of how this emancipatory interest should be spelled out, there is broad agreement that it should be understood as rational self-determination and/or self-realization pursued without hindrance from repression or domination—"the rational universal of cooperative self-actualization," as Honneth puts it (PoR, 27). Horkheimer, Adorno, and Marcuse believe that the institutional order of society *somehow and to some extent* reflects this interest. That is, society should be understood as the imperfectly and partially realized result of efforts to establish stable patterns of interaction that enable the mutual realization of the emancipatory interest (FR, 3). Indeed, Honneth takes this to be the minimal—and to his mind, plainly true—meaning of Hegelian objective Spirit: "In this weak sense, every society embodies objective Spirit to a certain extent, because its institutions, social practices and routines reflect shared normative beliefs about the aims of cooperative interaction" (4). At the same time, all of them are deeply wary of what they take to be the affirmative, if not outright reactionary, implications of Hegel's *Doppelsatz* ("*What is rational is actual and what is actual is rational*" [PR, 14]) (FR, 8), and so they equip their theories to explain systematic distortions in the actualization of freedom, which include subjects misapprehending the extent to which existing society is actually rational and/or facilitating of the free development of the human personality.

As Honneth stresses, the critical theory tradition comprehends the failure of society to actualize freedom at a level commensurate with its available store of technical and practical knowledge as a pathology, or distortion, of reason: something prevents potentials for freedom from being brought to consciousness, publicly thematized and utilized (PoR, 30ff).

This helps explain a methodological commitment that is probably more apparent in the early Frankfurt School than in Honneth: their shared aversion to "positivistic" social theories.[6] According to Horkheimer, attempts to theorize society as a set of "facts," ascertainable through observation and distilled into nature-like laws, tend to naturalize repressive, domineering patterns of social relations, casting them as just the way things are. This accusation lies behind Horkheimer's famous characterization of "traditional theory" (TCT, 197ff). A similar thought motivates Honneth's dislike of Habermas' and Fraser's systems theoretic accounts of "mediatized" spheres of action: Honneth insists that even social spheres apparently integrated through autonomously self-reproducing systems should really be thought of as, at a deeper level, orders of mutual recognition (RR, 248–256)—and that they therefore (put in the terms of Honneth's more recent theory) aspire to be "relational" or "ethical" spheres (FR, 50). Critics often take this as indicative of a naïve, overly sunny social theory, but Honneth thinks that it has always been important for critical theory to grasp how society has a dialectical/constitutive relationship to individuals—their values, self-understandings, and reasons for action.

As this implies, Honneth is thoroughly committed to an immanent version of critique (FR, 4): he is wary of the pitfalls involved in undertaking a "transcendent" critique of society, that is, one oriented around principles or values justified from a philosophical (or revelatory) standpoint that is indifferent to the extent to which these values are presupposed by individuals themselves, or can be effective in motivating them. Namely, such a critique is guilty of "authoritarianism" and therefore antithetical to a critical Theory tradition that takes seriously the responsibility of speaking on behalf of persons actually subject to the social orders in question.[7] Accordingly, Honneth's argument against utilitarianism and perfectionism—positions he has never much bothered to argue against in terms of their theoretical cogency—is simply that they are disconnected from social reality in a way that critical theory cannot be: perfectionism assumes a paternalistic posture toward its addressees by privileging a particular conception of human excellence. Utilitarianism only avoids similar paternalism if it is the case

---

[6] See Richard Bernstein, *The Restructuring of Social and Political Theory* (Philadelphia: University of Pennsylvania Press, 1978).

[7] On avoiding authoritarianism in critical theory's normative standpoint, see Maeve Cooke, *Re-Presenting the Good Society* (Cambridge, MA: MIT Press, 2006), 16–21.

that human beings are primarily motivated by some perception of their interests. But Honneth considers such notions empirically ill-founded. He does acknowledge that it is often *possible* to describe social struggles undertaken by oppressed or disenfranchised groups as struggles for material advantage, e.g., for a bigger "piece of the pie." And there is a dominant line of social theory, stretching back to Hobbes and Machiavelli, arguably including Marx, which conceives of social struggle as assertions of shared material interests (SR, 160–170). Nevertheless, Honneth points out that for the most part, modern liberation movements—anti-racist and civil rights struggles, workers' struggles for inclusion in social and political life, national liberation and decolonial movements, and feminism, to give an incomplete list—can only be tendentiously characterized in terms of material self-interest, and are much more straightforwardly capture-able in the language of recognition: esteem for a group's unique features and contributions; respect for the dignity that entitles one to participate in social, political, and economic life as an equal.[8]

Honneth has a closer affinity for Kantian theories of justice, if only to the (weak) extent that Kant and his followers consider the autonomy of the individual to be the master standard against which actions and social institutions should be evaluated. However, Kant attempts to build moral recognition of human beings as ends in themselves into the formal structure of practical reason, making it categorically binding on all, regardless of social context or psychological makeup. Against this, Honneth accepts a full range of Hegelian criticisms of Kantian morality, namely, the vacuity of conceptions of ethical behavior that are indifferent to the way those aims are realizable in social life, resulting in the "impotence of the ought":

> [Hegel's] critique of the idea of freedom as rational self-determination is that it conceives of individual freedom as though it was enough for us to have rational intentions, ones supported by good reasons, whereas in fact everything depends on whether we can think of the reality with which we are confronted as already being *itself* an emanation or embodiment of a process of self-determination. (OPL, 163)

This implies that any theory employing individual autonomy (or really, any value) as the standard of evaluation against which existing societies should be judged must be rooted in not only in the consciousness of its members, but in the structure of society itself.

So, Honneth thinks it is plain that a critical theory cannot be content with a wholly transcendent orientation: persons must be able to recognize themselves,

---

[8] See Iris Marion Young's critique of the "distributive paradigm" in *Justice and the Politics of Difference* (Princeton, NJ: Princeton University Press, 1989), 15–38.

with minimal redescription, in the aspirations that the theory propounds in order for it to count as emancipatory. This objection is on display in Honneth's reaction to Habermas' discourse theory. Habermas, Honneth relates, conceives of both legitimacy and moral rightness in terms of discourse procedures: actions and laws are not *inherently* wrong or illegitimate; they are those things to the extent that actors undertaking them (or lawmakers proposing them, etc.) fail (or refuse) to justify them in ways that conform to the invariant, implicit rules of discourse. Such an account is procedural because it does not specify in any substantive way what kinds of considerations count as good reasons, much less what norms are actually justified—it only specifies the procedure that makes norms justified. To put it more bluntly, Habermas thinks that passing through a process of discursive justification *is what rightness is*, i.e., it constitutes it (T&J, 247–248). Honneth has two main arguments against this construal of normativity: first, he thinks that it simply does not resonate with persons' normal (pre-theoretical) sense of what makes something right. Now, this may not always be so: for example, legitimacy often is conventionally treated as a procedural notion, as evidenced by the fact that people will often regard something as legitimate simply because it passed through the proper procedures, even though they personally disagree with it. But this is the exception that proves the rule: Honneth's contention is that localized acceptance of procedural validity is parasitic on persons' larger sense that the procedures themselves support values worthy of recognition (e.g., fairness and equal dignity in the legal system; promotion of social cooperation in the democratic process, etc.). Beyond this, Honneth's dominant contention is that we only acquire a sense of appropriate, obligatory, and praiseworthy forms of conduct by being socialized to give and receive recognition; we develop expectations and habits that ground our sense of misrecognition as something wrong, a painful violation.

Honneth's second objection to the neo-Kantian, constructivist trend in normative theory is that its identification of reasonable agreement as the decisive mark of normative validity leads it to fixate unduly on norms that can be represented as outcomes of a discursive process. In political theory, this usually means laws. Accordingly, domains of social life that are more informal, less voluntary, not easy to legally adjudicate conflicts within or regulate, or are otherwise not legally constituted, tend to recede into the backdrop. Even Hegel, Honneth writes, falls prey to this tendency:

> Hegel seems to have drawn the conclusion that the only interactional relations in modern societies that can be understood as social elements of ethical life are those that fall under the organizational authority of the state and can therefore be institutionalized in terms of positive laws; for without such a possibility of state control the spheres

in question would not possess the foundation of durability, reliability, and implimentability that was necessary to make them a condition of freedom that was available to us and under our control. (PIF, 69; see also RR, 145–146)

By the end of this chapter, I will ask us to consider whether Honneth is right to reject this rationale for Hegel's own juridical focus, in light of Chapter 1's argument that the political process is the main vehicle for reconciliation's activity and publicity. Presently, however (and in light of Chapter 3's conclusions), Honneth has an intuitively powerful case: if, as neo-Kantians agree, the paramount value relevant for normatively assessing society is freedom, then it seems quite artificial to restrict focus to the state and its laws. If, as Honneth thinks, freedom is properly construed as being at home in our social roles in a way that allows us to have a positive, harmonious set of self-relations, then there is a plethora of factors—in particular, ones impacting self-confidence and self-esteem—at least on par with the law. The fact that these types of relationships cannot be directly altered by legal fiat does not mean that they are not matters of public concern.

Even if we were more sympathetic to the contractualist/constructivist view that there must be an element of voluntariness in freedom's actualization, or Habermas' view that normative validity must *ultimately* be cashed out through open and rational discourse, it is still the case that the ability to engage in discourse or make genuinely voluntary choices is undergirded by all those mostly non-voluntary elements of social life that socialize us with the capacity to do so. This line of thought lies behind Hegel's own critique of the social contract, which holds that we misconstrue the individual's relationship to the state by representing it as voluntary—Hegel's point here is not that individuals are inextricably bound to their national unit, but that contractualism ignores the genesis of the perspective from which it is possible to view the relationship to the state as reciprocal in the first place.[9] With this in mind, Honneth's argument is more powerful than just the contention that freedom requires, say, the family in the same way that it requires food, i.e., that it could not exist at all if we were starving, dead, or raised by wolves.[10] It is rather that intentions and desires are only recognizable as rational by being "molded" through historically given institutions (FR, 53). This is not to say that our own interpretations of desires/intentions are unimpeachable, but that we are not in a position to interpret them at all without the aid of concrete socializing institutions. Nor is it to say that we cannot, upon reflection, abstract norms out of their historical genesis to categorize, compare,

    [9] See Robert Pippin, *Hegel's Practical Philosophy: Rational Agency as Ethical Life* (New York: Cambridge University Press, 2008), 239–272.
    [10] Compare, Korsgaard, *The Sources of Normativity*, 100–113.

and otherwise assess them—obviously, such exercises are important for philosophy and critical theory. But given that we deceive ourselves in thinking that this kind of abstraction can arrive at content determined by pure practical reason, this is better thought of as a "reconstruction" than a "construction." Honneth's method of "normative reconstruction" leaves norms bound to their historical context, mainly for the reason that he finds it impossible to make a value-based assessment of social spheres without some sense of how institutions actualize those values, and moreover, how their actualization contributes to a freely self-actualizing life.

3. Social Freedom and Normative Reconstruction: The Transparency and Normal Sociality Theses

So, we have seen that Honneth a) is committed to the idea of a critical theory of society in something like Horkheimer's original sense; b) he rejects as empirically unfounded social theories that deny a significant role to value-laden intersubjectivity in societal reproduction; and c) he rejects as normatively inert neo-Kantian accounts of freedom, which grant pride of place to juridical and discursively justified relations. Against all this, Honneth counterpoises a normative reconstruction of "ethical" or "relational" social spheres as the best candidate for re-actualizing (a). Domains of social life that roughly correspond to the differentiations in Hegelian ethical life can be teleologically understood as embodying freedom and contributing to its full actualization, by examining the underlying "moral principles" in these spheres that move people to voluntarily reproduce them. Earlier, I alluded to an ambiguity in Honneth's theory, namely, the basis of the claim that this array of social spheres (intimate relations, the market, the democratic state and public sphere) should be understood as teleologically oriented to actualize freedom. Since *The Struggle for Recognition*, Honneth has been working with a substantial, empirical, naturalistic picture of a self formed through mutual recognition. In this paradigm, claims about normative deficiencies are grounded in a theory about stable practices of mutual recognition being necessary constituents for a free and affirmative self-relation. This theory is supported by empirical observations about the consequences of systematic misrecognition, in the form of either protest and resistance, or dysfunction in the reproduction of social spheres.

In *Freedom's Right*, however, Honneth gives the distinct impression that this is a basically hermeneutic claim: "Of all the ethical values prevailing and competing for dominance in modern society, only one has been capable of leaving a truly lasting impression on our institutional order: freedom, i.e., the autonomy of the individual" (FR, 15). Of course, the value of this claim could be rather limited, since the concept of freedom permits such a wide manifold of possible meanings. Nevertheless, Honneth is confident that it makes good interpretive sense to gather them under three headings: negative, reflexive, and social. The two most prominent, both intellectually and in terms of popular appeal, are the negative and reflexive varieties, i.e., freedom as absence of obstacles to the realization of one's intentions, and freedom as rational self-legislation, respectively. Both of these conceptions of freedom have, historically, developed along with institutions and cultural practices through which they are "realized," namely, in legally guaranteed freedoms from illegitimate interference and moral conscientiousness or authenticity, respectively. Honneth's way of explaining the deficiencies in these models is as follows: he thinks that both types of freedom plainly have value in terms of securing space for individuals to withdraw from social demands that do not accord with their considered sense of self (their interests and values, respectively). But they become dysfunctional when treated as the final word on what freedom is. Some of the reasons for this have been touched on in Chapter 1: in Rousseau's account of the unfreedom found in "free," but competitive and unequal, societies in which people are driven by *amour propre*, and in Hegel's account of freedom in civil society. In both contexts, individuals are nominally free in that, at least within the boundaries of the rule of law, they may act as they will, and yet because they encounter the social world as an obstacle (or the neutral background) to their wills' realization, they normally do not experience themselves as free *in* social life. Thus, according to Honneth, the nearly inevitable consequence of regarding either negative or reflexive freedom as the apogee of freedom is pathology, in the specific form of an antagonistic relationship to, or disappointed attitude toward, the social world, leading to frustration or anomic withdrawal. This gives him confidence that the kind of freedom realized in and through social life has a definite enough meaning as to give reconstructions of its mode of actualization traction.

The reconstructive method associated with Hegel's *Philosophy of Right* should, Honneth argues, be especially appealing given its ability to evade what Terry Pinkard has called "the Kantian paradox." [11] This is a theoretical impasse confronting approaches to normativity that see it as a matter of freely authoring the norms that bind us: if we assert that only those norms are morally valid that agents freely bind their wills to, and thus presuppose their capacity to freely bind their wills, "we will sooner or later, but inevitably, have to bring moral norms into play so that we may first establish the agential freedom or the communicative accord that we have been presupposing" (NEL, 817). Honneth proposes to bypass this quandary by showing that what serves as the "ground"

---

[11] Pinkard, *German Philosophy, 1760–1860*, 59–61.

for freedom—namely, ethical life—contains "immanent criteria" for confirming (and continually shaping) its constituent practices as "rational," that is, as actualizations of social freedom. Given that Honneth is here explicitly trying to avoid concepts equivalent to Kant's "fact of reason," he may prefer to be agnostic toward anthropological claims about how the structure of modern ethical life satisfies some deep-seated requirements for full human self-actualization. I will, however, be arguing that this bracketing can only hold if, as left Hegelians are unlikely to, one finds Honneth's normative contextualism sound without further ado.

A brief propaedeutic is in order about how this normative reconstruction is supposed to work. Honneth's notion of social freedom is drawn from Hegel's "being at home with one's self in another" formulation. As such, it faces questions similar to the ones that trailed in Hegel's wake: to be free in this sense, is it enough to feel comfortable and affirmed in our social roles, e.g., as parents and lovers, workers, owners, consumers, and citizens? Why should this not just be an indication that we have thoroughly internalized role expectations, which may be neither justified nor all that conscious? Under what conditions can we say that affirming and internalizing the role expectations we are subject to genuinely amounts to freedom? The answer here is that whether role expectations are justified and liberatory depends on their being "ethical" or "objective" in a specifically Hegelian sense. One of Honneth's favorite passages to cite from Hegel is from §7 of *The Philosophy of Right*, where Hegel gestures toward close friendship and romantic love as cardinal instances of freedom. Now, especially if one is intuitively familiar with the paradigm of negative freedom, the very idea here may seem odd, since these are relationships wherein the scope of permissible actions is tightly curtailed; only actions compatible with an overarching norm of mutual care, devotion, affection, etc. are acceptable. And yet Hegel is clearly leveraging an intuition that there is something liberatory about these relationships. Participants in intimate relationships are, when acting toward one another, cognizant of their partners' reciprocity as essential to the realization of their intentions, in a sense deeper than one finds with intentions that just happen to normally require coordination with others. When acting as lovers or friends, persons are not (only) seeking to jostle something—attention, sex, support, etc.—out of the partner: they are expressing a mutual disposition with which both powerfully identify. Thus, the mutuality, the self-consciously shared orientation toward a norm of care/affection, is part of the intention itself. In this way, intentions come to fruition *in* the relationship, not in what one gets out of it. One finds the fruition of intentions associated with one's core purposes in the social world itself, in the requirements and demands that its relationships place upon one. In this way, Honneth seeks to capture what Hegel means when he writes that "in duty the individual finds his liberation" (PR, §149/156–157).

Friendship and love illustrate in an especially vivid way this point about freedom being tied to the essentially relational realization of intentions. But Honneth proposes that we understand ethical social spheres in general as ones that actualize freedom by institutionalizing relationships where intentions come to fruition socially, in the relationship itself. Spheres of action can be considered ethical if they have the following features: a) they are "relational" in that they intertwine partners' intentions—again, in a way that goes beyond coordination—such that they are only realizable in "a complementary fashion" (FR, 48); b) they embody shared values that reflect the sphere's underlying form of mutual recognition (i.e., love and care in the intimate sphere; esteem and fairness in work, exchange, and association; solidarity and dignity in the public sphere and constitutional state); and c) they presuppose norms derived from the underlying value, which interactive partners license one another to employ in evaluating their performance.

I want to draw attention to two other key aspects of ethical spheres that bear on their ability to be freedom actualizing: first, in stretching the formal features of intimate relationships over other types of social relations (i.e., legally mediated forms of association in the market and political sphere), Honneth is denying that social freedom requires the kind of emotional intensity that fuels friendship and romance.[12] Second, practically speaking, the practices of mutual recognition that comprise ethical spheres have to be institutionalized in a publicly recognizable fashion. There are several reasons for this: a) publicity, b) accountability, and c) socialization.

a) Social freedom involves "a common experience," meaning that it requires consciousness of the mutuality and the shared values motivating the actions. The public, stable/permanent, and official or quasi-official nature of institutions provide for this.
b) Interaction partners in ethical spheres are jointly subject to a shared norm according to which they can hold one another accountable for holding up their end of the relationship. Institutions provide (again, formally or informally) specifications of the norms, rules for upholding them, and sanctioning mechanisms for their violation.
c) Honneth agrees with Arnold Gehlen's view that freedom requires institutions to mold urges and desires into a form where they are communicable and regularly realizable—they would otherwise, Gehlen supposes, be too inchoate (FR, 51–54).

Remember that social freedom distinguishes itself from negative and reflexive freedom by virtue of not being indifferent to how intentions are realized in social

---

[12] Honneth thinks that this *is* the idea of some of Hegel's early Jena writings. See SR, 11–63.

reality; rational intentions are ones that can be freely realized through ethical relationships, and thus a rational society is one that socializes its members to give shape to their desires so that they are relationally realizable, and which is institutionally organized to facilitate the common experiences comprising social freedom.

To a lot of readers of *Freedom's Right*, what Honneth does with this framework is the main matter of interest, to wit, his reconstruction of modern ethical life's development over the last two hundred years or so, which informs his assessment of how well personal, economic, and political relations are performing as ethical spheres. This is not my topic here, so suffice it to say that Honneth's assessment is mixed: he mostly lauds the state of personal relationships, seeing real gains in the more tolerant, egalitarian, and exploratory developments that have followed in the wake of postwar sexual revolutions. His appraisal of other spheres is dourer: in the political sphere, greater inclusiveness is counterbalanced by unmoored administrative power, cliques and neo-corporatist arrangements, fracturing and commercialization in the media, and the difficulty that the postwar welfare state has had serving as a credible mediator between conflicting group interests. More alarmingly, the relentless pressure on workers and consumers to treat the economic sphere as a domain of purely instrumental action—one which is, for that matter, weighted against the vast majority's material interests— makes it dubious to reconstruct it as a relational sphere at all.[13]

Let us briefly take stock of what we should make of the theory of social freedom as a methodological proposal for a renewal of critical theory. The reliance on hermeneutic claims might conceivably put Honneth in a similar position as Rawls by involving the acceptance of institutions as straightforwardly reflecting their underlying values. Honneth therefore might be vulnerable to the line of argument I developed in the previous chapter, to the effect that Rawls invests a great deal in progressive, legitimating narratives about our institutions and our relationship to them that are not much assured to reflect an underlying social reality. Given how vociferously Honneth attacks the juridical fixation of normative political theory, however, it would be surprising if he had a similar vulnerability—law plays nothing like the same role in Honneth's theory as it does in Rawls, for whom it fulfills vital publicity conditions. I would argue that this raises not so much the question of what does play the equivalent in Honneth, but whether he thinks he needs an equivalent. My suspicion is that he does not think that he does, and that Honneth is not like the others considered

---

[13] It is, however, not clear that Honneth's theory can account for the possibility of social spheres altogether losing, or failing to actualize in the first place, their relational potential; see Jörg Schaub, "Misdevelopments, Pathologies, and Normative Revolutions: Normative Reconstruction as Method of Critical Theory," *Critical Horizons* 16, no. 2 (2015): 107–130.

in this book who find that the actualization of freedom crucially hinges on consciousness of the relationship between the legal organization of society and individual life prospects. In other words, the publicity conditions so important to Hegel, Rawls, and most others in the left Hegelian tradition (in a negative way) are not so vital in Honneth's theory.

As I see it, Honneth has not, in *Freedom's Right*, jettisoned his long-held, anthropologically-inflected recognition theory in favor of something "political, not metaphysical," to use Rawls' phrase. Rather, that body of theory now serves to a) explain why the contextualist strategy of justification pursued in *Freedom's Right* represents the best understanding of normativity available; and b) assure us that inclusion in functioning ethical spheres is, in fact, sufficient for freedom. In order to accomplish (a) and (b), I propose that we interpret Honneth as defending the following pair of theses:

- *The transparency thesis:* a folk sociological understanding of the modern social order is basically accurate; it is implausible to think of modern persons as deceived or blind, at some fundamental level, about how society reproduces itself. While Honneth does not repudiate concepts from left Hegelian social theory seemingly contrary to this thesis—namely, reification and ideology— he conceptualizes them in such a way that their existence does not threaten this thesis' overall cogency.
- *The normal sociality thesis:* in a modern society, socialization in decently functioning ethical spheres is not normally repressive, not something we need to be emancipated *from* in order to develop an integrated, affirmative self-relation—it is, itself, the actualization of freedom. The thesis denies the psychoanalytic social theory of the early Frankfurt School (as well as Nietzsche, Foucault, Althusser, and Butler), which thinks of normal sociality as repressive and unfree.[14]

Honneth thinks of these theses as encapsulating the Hegelian notions that freedom is being at home with one's self in another and that ethical life is the Idea of freedom actualized. However, as I believe Chapter 1 shows, Hegel does not think that normal sociality in the above sense is, by itself, sufficient for freedom, because he believes there to be a moment of alienation in modern life that needs to be overcome *through reconciliation*. Honneth is aware of this dimension of Hegel's thought, and does not discount problems of alienation, but

---

[14] I take Honneth's point here to be of a piece with what Charles Taylor calls "the affirmation of life"—i.e., the contention that "regular people" participating normally in the gamut of spheres of modern social life are living a full and valuable life—in *Sources of the Self: The Making of the Modern Identity* (Cambridge, MA: Harvard University Press, 1989), 211–305.

he does not find the theoretical apparatus behind Hegel's solution to it credible, and so builds his conception of social freedom with underpinnings that obviate the need for a reconciliation concept. The remainder of this chapter explores those underpinnings and ultimately explains why I do not think they obviate this need like Honneth presumably thinks they do.

4. Reflection vs. Functionality in the Theory of Social Freedom

As he has moved toward greater reliance on hermeneutic claims about freedom being the normative core of modernity, Honneth has at the same time migrated toward seeing our pre-theoretical interest in an integrated social identity more explicitly as an interest in freedom. One might guess that this shift would move Honneth to lay greater emphasis on rational self-authorship. But this hunch is not borne out, at least not insofar as that latter term implies an orientation to the universal, as it does in the German idealist tradition. A well-integrated identity arises out of the types of mutual recognition anchored in ethical spheres; they facilitate the experience of being at home with one's self in another. Ethical spheres' reproduction takes place through individuals finding continuity between what they value in themselves and what ethical relations in the various spheres require of them. Put simply, Honneth closely identifies social freedom with this experience of wholeness, of being at home in the social world. It follows straightforwardly, for him, that if the social spheres of modern societies are, by and large, fulfilling their rational potential, then participants are, to that extent, free—and if not, then not. Unlike in Hegel, reflection does not make a large contribution to freedom in Honneth (qualifications to follow).

In order to underscore this difference with Hegel, consider again the difference that he sees between Greek ethical substance and modern ethical life. As Hegel sees it, ancient Greeks were certainly at home in their social world: their form of life was beautiful and their identification with social roles near total. Despite this, it is unclear whether we should consider them free, for the other side of this is Greek life's incapacity to absorb much personal particularity. This contributed to its unsustainability: when conflicts between social roles *did* arise, individuals had no licensed procedure for adjusting those roles' demands, and so what could have been merely a conflict becomes a tragic contradiction within the form of life. As such, Greek ethical substance is deficient in reason and universality. By contrast, Hegel thinks modern people are *not* unproblematically at home with themselves. To a large extent, this is because of the functional differentiation and elaborate division of labor in a modern society, which make society both tolerate and demand personal particularity—this contributes to society's rationality, but can make individual locations within it seem arbitrary. And the fact that one is compelled to shuffle among the different spheres of ethical life, with their contrasting dispositions and action norms, makes it less than self-evident whether there is any coherence among this disparate array of social roles. To make matters worse, Hegel concedes that certain problems that can severely diminish life prospects are endemic to all spheres of ethical life, and while such slings and arrows were compensated for by an enveloping collective experience in traditional forms of ethical life, this is not true of more anonymous modern societies. So, divorce, war, poverty, etc. can (quite understandably) weaken identification with ethical life among those affected. In sum, Hegel does not think that the question of whether freedom is being actualized can be answered simply by pointing to the stable reproduction of ethical spheres. This is necessary but insufficient: it does not recoup the sense of identity coherence that the contingency and differentiation of modern life fractures.

If one thinks that modern social spheres are doing a good job of fulfilling their rational potential, perhaps a reconciliation concept would not be needed: there might not be enough systematically induced social suffering to undermine free and rational identification with ethical life, hence no pressing need to be *re*-conciled to it. But Hegel does not think this is the case, and Honneth is considerably less bullish than Hegel in his assessment of the present state. If Honneth's diagnoses are supposed to be more than observations in the fashion of traditional theory about the shoddy state of things, we should expect that they are linked to an account of emancipatory interests with an account (one accessible to the persons themselves) of how freedom is thwarted by society and how these obstacles might be overcome. For Hegel, people experience themselves as free by participating in well-ordered ethical spheres, yes, but also through inclusion in the state, which allows them to see how their society works (and doesn't work) to make this freedom possible, adding the self-conscious orientation toward the universal that he considers essential. For all of Hegel's differences with Kant, he never doubts that individuals' action norms must be consciously (albeit as a matter of implicit know-how more than explicit intent) aligned with the universal. Hegel finds that the forms of recognition prevalent in civil society can be very pro forma; they only bloom into a cognitively satisfying form in the ascent toward the more universalistic elements of ethical life—that is, it is only through the activity of the *Polizei*, the Estates, corporations, and, ultimately, the legislature and crown, that we come to recognize the universality present in civil society. It is not recognizable from the nominalistic, individualistic perspective of civil society itself. All of these institutions comprise a complex that mediates between the particular person and the concrete universal of society, by seeking to ensure, in an ongoing, publicly accessible way, that particularity is organized in a way that is mutually beneficial for all. In a more general way, Hegel and Honneth are in accord with the idea that freedom requires being at home with our own will, not alienated from it, as we carry out the various roles involved in family, civil society, and state—we need to grasp these spheres as sites of social freedom: "By emphasizing the intersubjective structure of freedom, we can glimpse the necessity of mediating institutions that inform subjects in advance about the interdependence of their aims" (FR, 65). But Hegel further realizes that the previous point goes not just for relations between persons within social spheres, but among the spheres themselves—and indeed, as far as civil society is concerned, knowledge of this interdependence is needed in order to grasp it as an ethical sphere at all. Being a free individual requires understanding the complementary way social spheres hang together, which enables persons to forge an integrated identity out of apparently disparate social roles. For a functionally differentiated modern society whose unity cannot be represented sensually, only the ongoing, publicly visible activity of the political system can do this. It alone can prevent recognition patterns in individual social spheres from hardening into a second nature—it allows us to see them as moments of an organic totality. A reconciliation concept is needed in order to show how subject and society can be teleologically oriented toward freedom even while the rational potential of social spheres is only partially realized, instead of allowing those deficits to become a second nature that automates patterns of recognition.

Now, it could be that Hegel is wrong to insist on the emancipatory need for an integral, underlying sense of self among the diffuse role performances demanded by ethical life. I do not, however, think that Honneth believes this. He just does not think that this integral wholeness is achieved through reflection on how the universal is mediated through the state (i.e., the concrete universal), as Hegel does. Honneth's conception of the self's coherence is drawn from psychoanalysis, not political theory. The first-generation Frankfurt School also turned to psychoanalysis in order to fill the gap they opened by abandoning a Hegelian-Marxian conception of history, and Hegelian conceptions of reason and reflection. But unlike Horkheimer's circle, Honneth's interest in psychoanalysis elevates ideas supporting the notion that freedom is achievable in ordinary social life, and hence that whatever resources are needed in order for individuals to achieve the degree of ego coherence needed for freedom are available therein.

Although Honneth is usually hesitant to embrace Freud, he does evince sympathy for the following constellation of ideas from the latter:

a)   repression is a regular part of "normal socialization," as urges, desires, and fantasies at odds with "loved objects" are forced into the unconscious (PoR, 137);

b)   mechanisms for repression develop in infancy, but are utilized throughout life to defend the ego against dissonant thoughts and experiences;

c)   the return of repressed mental contents is a primary cause of anxiety;

d)   anxiety undermines freedom, as our will "constantly seems clouded because it is influenced by compulsions or dependencies whose origin we cannot see clearly" (137);

e)   dissolving these "restrictions on the function of the ego" results in a gain of freedom, which all people have an interest in promoting; and

f)   in order to acquire this ability,

> what is needed is . . . a protracted and strenuous process of working through and remembering in which we attempt, against persistent resistance, to appropriate retrospectively the previously separated elements of our will . . . The human self-relation, as Freud's great insight can be summarized, consists in the process of self-appropriation of one's will by affectively admitting to anxiety. (144–145)

As we will presently see, Honneth rejects (a) and has doubts about (b), but otherwise endorses the notion that, for as much as the will's anxious cloudiness can clear by appropriating repressed mental contents, this is mostly a matter of individuals therapeutically working through their own biography (D, 189–191).

For as much as the self's coherence has less to do with attunement to the universal and more to do with dissolving anxiety in this "working through," an interesting strand of Honneth's social analysis asserts that anxiety can arise through social causes, and that socially induced anxiety in turn inflicts real damage to the quality of public life, creating a vicious feedback loop—if these social causes are endemic in modern society, then the normal sociality thesis would be hard to maintain. Honneth is, in this regard, particularly intrigued by the work of Alexander Mitscherlich and Franz Neumann. Neumann and Mitscherlich both operate within a Freudian matrix, but go beyond it in several regards. Although Freud certainly hopes that therapy can train the superego to be less punitive, he also believes that family structure, not cultural values (never mind political organization), sets its basic program; and that the floor amount of repression that civilization requires is fairly constant. Mitscherlich and Neumann, on the other hand, believe that the degree to which repression fosters anxiety depends on the degree of transparency in social life, and the depth of meaningful experience it provides.[15] Here is Mitscherlich: "Social diseases occur if the social matrix becomes too weak to demand a binding socialization of the individual, leaving her thus without guidance in many situations in life, and thereby arousing rather unconscious than conscious anxieties."[16] Neumann, in a complementary vein,

---

[15] See Franz Neumann, "Anxiety and Politics," in *The Democratic and Authoritarian: Essays in Political and Legal Theory*, ed. Herbert Marcuse (New York: Free Press, 1957), 270–300.

[16] Quoted in Honneth, "Diseases of Society: Approaching a Nearly Impossible Concept," *Social Research* 81, no. 3 (2014), 695. Compare to Durkheim's concept of an anomic division of labor; see *The Division of Labor in Society*, 291–309.

argues that both material insecurity, and losses of status or social meaning, lead to the ego compensating for its unconsciously perceived inability to contain an unruly excess of instinctual energy by transferring this excess onto charismatic leadership and mass movements.

Both theorists would do better, according to Honneth, were they not so wedded to Freudian instinct theory, which does not well explain why a loss of social meaning should trigger anxiety of the neurotic, pathological sort, given that Freud does not seem to think that a resource like "social meaning" does much to lower the floor of instinctual repression necessary for social functionality. Here we see Honneth indicating why normative social theory is better served by a psychoanalysis founded on intersubjectivity and recognition than one founded on instinctual drives:

> Neumann could have been much more persuasive in developing this fruitful train of thought if he had introduced the concept of neurotic anxiety in such a way that its correlation with social experiences of loss had been clarified from the outset. Had he drawn on the reflections of object relations theory . . . instead of Freudian orthodoxy, then social anxieties could have been rendered explicable as traumatic anxieties reactivated through experiences of deprivation resulting from the traumatic loss of the constant, security-giving presence of the first, most intimate relation. Within such an explanatory model there exists a kind of psychological continuity between the early forms of childhood anxiety and the social experiences of loss in adulthood, the enduring core of which is constituted by the anxiety-laden endangerment of intersubjectivity. (POR, 152–153)

Honneth is here connecting the psychic development of the individual, on the one hand, to his conception of social freedom, and on the other hand, to a social theoretic explanation of the conditions that can affect the psyche in ways undercutting its prospects for actualizing social freedom.

These suggested modifications to Neumann and Mitscherlich are not entirely innocent translations of their basic points into more up-to-date psychoanalytic concepts. They are writing about anxiety produced by the subject's inability to form a meaningful, coherent identity in the first place due to social conditions that are opaque and meaningless. Honneth, on the other hand, is suggesting that social *losses* cause an anxious, clouded self-relation through perceived threats to identity securing intersubjectivity: anxiety predictably follows when established patterns of intersubjectivity—in particular, solidarity generating patterns of esteem—are disrupted or erode. This implies that identity-securing patterns of recognition are normally in place, and so a reasonable degree of unclouded identity coherence is normally attainable—anxiety only becomes of systematic relevance to social theory in contexts where so-cialization patterns are notably degraded. These contentions are plainly at odds with the Horkheimer circle's.

5. Trading Freud for Winnicott: psychoanalysis in Honneth

Honneth's idea of an emancipatory interest in a freely integrated social identity is not antithetical to Freud. But the version of Freud that Horkheimer, Adorno, and Marcuse favor is the Freud of the late theory of instincts, wherein the life and death drives set in motion an antagonistic intra-psychic dynamic and create a longing for something more than normal social life delivers. As such, the category of repression is a basic element of their social analysis—functionality requires the superego's discipline of the ego, and the ego's repression of unruly instinctual drives, centered around sexuality and destructiveness. As such, emancipation involves liberation of or reconciliation with the instincts, and thus something more than well-ordered, putatively justified social relations.[17] Honneth's appeals to psychoanalysis resist these tendencies: he opposes the notion that society is incapable of gratifying deep-seated human needs, and that it therefore requires the repression of those needs in order to reproduce itself in a quasi-voluntary manner. In order to advance his aim to think of freedom as something achievable in and through society, Honneth swaps Freudianism for the object-relations par-adigm, with special reference to Donald Winnicott's work.

According to Honneth's early work *Critique of Power*, Adorno puts for-ward a hyperbolic, misleadingly reductive vision of a "totally administered so-ciety," which he makes plausible through a conception of subject formation that emphasizes conformity and internalization of authority. For Honneth, the problem elements here are as follows: Adorno and his colleagues mostly ad-here to a Freudian account of ontogenesis as a process punctuated by discipli-nary trauma. Freud's hypothesis of "primary narcissism" allowed a picture to gel in which the ego is an outgrowth of the id.[18] Although the particulars are contested, one of Freud's fundamental premises is that, for some period an infant's mental life is ruled by the pleasure principle, that is, it is impelled by drives for pleasurable mingling and stimulus, free from pain, exertion, and pri-vation. Mental processes governed by "the pleasure principle" are, in this initial

---

[17] See Hedrick, "Ego Autonomy, Reconciliation, and the Duality of Instinctual Nature in Adorno and Marcuse," *Constellations* 23, no. 2 (2016): 180–191.

[18] See Freud, "On Narcissism: An Introduction," in *Complete Psychological Works*, vol. 14, 73–104.

state, unmediated by much if any cognitive organization that distinguishes self and world.[19] There is no real source of intentionality and only the rudiments of what we might call agency. In due course, the ego takes shape as an entity aware of its position in social space and the natural world, which steers the instincts toward some kind of manageable fruition. But this formative process is never placid, since the ego comes into being neither of its own accord nor through the instincts' endogenous development—in most every sense, the instincts themselves *don't* develop, ever. Rather, the ego's organization is imposed on it by pressure to respond, first to privations from external reality that compel it to adopt the reality principle, and then to social authority, initially and most powerfully manifest as parental authority. As Freud makes clear, these impositions both lie at the basis of the psyche's differentiation, which crystallizes during the more or less successful resolution of the Oedipal crisis, and shatters its previously undifferentiated sense of pleasure and omnipotence. This is what Adorno has in mind when he calls the ego a reification of traumatic experiences.[20]

Honneth's initial objection to this Freudian picture of subject formation is that it is essentially monological: the psyche's structure is a byproduct of the way endogenous drive energies necessarily take shape, as it is compelled to come to grips with reality and sociality (IW, 196–197). This fails to reflect evidence that the self's constitution is intersubjective and driven by mutual recognition. There is some justice to the charge, since Freud seems to imply that in pre-Oedipal experience, fantasies of omnipotence hold sway to an extent that there is no recognition of anything distinct from self. It is only when these fantasies are rudely disrupted that the subject is hammered into a shape able to recognize reciprocity and otherness in interaction partners. Neither the pleasure principle nor the fantasy of omnipotence can be wholly renounced and instead drift into the unconscious; since fantasy here has a reality-denying or resisting function, sociality and scarcity necessitate its repression. This colors subsequent forms of intersubjectivity with resentful aggression or defensive, guilty submission.

Honneth simply rejects much of this and instead takes his cues from a tradition that stretches back to Rousseau and Hegel, is sketched by George Herbert Mead, and fleshed out by Winnicott, in which the self is social virtually all the way down: in order to develop into something that could be said to have experience in the first place, one must have a basic self-relation, and this comes about through early interactions with caregivers. In order to develop intentionality and agency, one must recognize one's self as an actor in a social space of reasons, and thus have an ability to take a second person perspective on self. This perspective is, in turn, constituted through relationships where one is recognized as a

---

[19] See ibid., 75–76. See also Freud, *Civilization and Its Discontents*, 68.

[20] Adorno, "Revisionist Psychoanalysis," 328–329.

giver of reasons, entitled to receive them. Winnicott motivates these moves in a subtle, but significant set of modifications to Freudian primary narcissism: he theorizes that the human being's early life is centered around states of symbiosis or fusion with a primary caregiver (usually—though of course not always—the mother). Although the idea here is that, at least on the infant's side of things, the interaction partners are all but wholly absorbed in the interaction and experience themselves as merged with one another.[21] However, the object relations tradition does not think of these fusion states as transcendent or solipsistic like primary narcissism; instead, they incubate a mediated sense of self as an increasingly determinate partner capable of initiating interaction. Winnicott does not represent this formative process as blissful, since there is a fraught tug-of-war between infant and caregiver in which the former has to reluctantly come to terms with the independence of the latter (IW, 199). This resembles the Oedipal process in some respects, but Winnicott thinks that the Freudian story of the father dropping the hammer of social boundaries onto the child is not a necessary element in successful ontogenesis, because the child and caregiver always have enough of a sense of their separateness, and their relationship is saturated in affective dispositions of care and love, such that ego and superego formation are not traumatic events, per se (228–229). As Honneth has it, the fundamental relation to self of self-confidence emerges from being recognized simultaneously as an independent person and an object of care and affection (SR, 98–104). He thinks that Winnicott's reconstruction of ego formation as something rooted in a kind of caring mutuality that oscillates between symbiosis and recognition of otherness not only resonates with, but confirms, Hegel's contention that self-consciousness is the result of a struggle for recognition, and more broadly, his conception of freedom as being with one's self in another.

Honneth also thinks that, in arriving at the conclusion that sociality in late period capitalism has degenerated into unmediated domination, Adorno obfuscates a Freudian distinction that is also significant in object relations theory, namely, between the reality principle and the superego (COP, 86–90).[22] To be precise, the typical Oedipal resolution erects the superego and founds its authority, initially manifest in the father's restrictions on sexuality, eventually expanding into the voice of social mores, writ large. The reality principle, on the other hand, is a more basic piece of ego psychology that precedes the Oedipal complex, directing the ego to delay gratification to cope with scarcity. By running these

[21] See Johana Meehan, "Recognition and the Dynamics of Intersubjectivity," in *Axel Honneth: Critical Essays*, 89–124. Meehan pushes back some against the extent to which some object relations theorists think that caregivers equally participate in this absorption.

[22] See also Jessica Benjamin, "The End of Internalization: Adorno's Social Psychology," *Telos* 32 (1977): 24–64.

two together, Adorno sees subject formation as a matter of the psyche coming to view its relationship to the world—natural and social—in purely instrumental terms, as a relationship of domination.[23] His perspective thereby screens out that part of the psyche constituted through non-instrumentalized recognition relations, and therefore that large part of mental life oriented toward giving and receiving recognition. Since Honneth has gone so far as to say that an "antecedent and very elementary form of recognition" is necessary in order for the subject to be oriented toward reasons at all (RJ, 151), he concludes that interactions where there is a thorough withdrawal or "forgetting" of recognition must be rare, and so Lukács' and Adorno's contention that it is common, and indeed characteristic of our prevailing experience of the social world, strikes Honneth as "improbable" (157).

Adorno's position is not as far-fetched as Honneth suggests. Going along with his view that the superego has become more depersonalized and its formation more drawn out, he supposes that we are not only subject to a repressive social apparatus, but are imperceptibly enveloped by it; as a result, we internalize both a sense of what our social world *is like* and *what it requires of us* without much awareness of doing so.[24] The pressure to adapt to the social world's exigencies has a quasi-moral aura around it, such that nonconformity and failure incites feelings of guilt (DE, 175). Altogether, this has the effect of obfuscating the difference between practical necessity and moral imperative. So, Adorno probably does not simply miss the difference between reality principle and superego. But whether oversight or conscious blurring, Honneth points out that by collapsing the distinction between the ego's capacity for reality coping and the capacity to navigate social space by recognizing interactive role obligations, Adorno erases "the social" from his social theory. His perspective does not allow that any significant portion of social integration is intersubjectively accomplished through more or less voluntarily given mutual recognition. To be fair, of course Adorno is aware that even in late capitalism people interact, and that those interactions involve mutual recognition; but although some degree of care and mutuality is plainly a necessary precondition for subjective development, the subject's constitutive achievement lies in separating itself, and ultimately adopting an instrumental orientation toward, the "mythic" powers of its archaic past. So too with culturally and institutionally mediated social action: Adorno can accept that they contain displays of mutual recognition, which may be necessary for their success, but these displays are not constitutive of the actions or the institutions.

[23] See Honneth, "Postmodern Identity and Object Relations Theory: On the Seeming Obsolescence of Psychoanalysis," *Philosophical Explorations* 2, no. 3 (1999), 229.

[24] See Adorno, *Introduction to Sociology*, 145–154; and MM, §65/102.

What *is* constitutive—what gives them "objectivity" in Lukács' sense—is their being taken as a token of type that fits into the "schema" of mass culture, or "exchange society."

For present purposes, the crux of these disputes about early childhood development is this: Adorno is sympathetic to the Freudian view that there is a pre-social, instinctual core to subjectivity that attunes mind to world, and that sociality is something essentially imposed. This instinctual core is normally co-opted to functionalize the ego for exchange society, but not without repression, and repression has some indefeasible consequences, namely, the pleasure principle's siren call that unsettles the ego from the unconscious. And while the question of whether there is some innate quantum of aggression in the psyche is a vexed one, less controversial is the contention that repression can cause instinctual energy to vent in a hostile or destructive way, either inwardly or outwardly toward others.[25] The Freudian picture also suggests that individuals are ill-positioned, without the benefit of psychoanalytically informed critical theory, to recognize themselves as participant in and victim of an irrational, domineering form of life.

This last point is antithetical to Honneth's critical theory, in particular the transparency thesis; he short-circuits it by denying that either subjectivity or sociality are disciplinary impositions. On the object relations picture he favors, selfhood is the result of something like a proto-social negotiation, as the child is eased and prodded out of its fixation on fusion states. Winnicott's pivotal idea of "transitional objects" captures how the child can move beyond this fixation without repressing the attraction of merging, even though Freud may be correct that the renunciation of experiences of fusion is, if not traumatic, at least discomfiting. This is a complicated idea, but for present purposes its core is that small children tend to invest a great deal of erotic interest in certain beloved objects around the time they grow out of immersion in fusion experiences; they can be observed being absorbed, or "lost" in play, with the object.[26] The transitional object is at once a thing of the world and an object of fantasy that plays a talismanic role in interior life: "one is dealing with ontological links, as it were, that mediate between the primary experience of being merged and the awareness of separateness." Play and imagination serve as a "bridge" between "the painful gap between inner and outer reality" (SR, 103). Once this is appreciated, we can see that transitional objects have lifelong equivalents in the mature psyche (mental habits and rituals, objects/topics of consuming fascination, etc.), which allow it to maintain a playfully immersive relationship to life in a world characterized by

---

[25] See Marcuse, *Negations: Essays in Critical Theory*, trans. Jeremy Shapiro (Boston: Beacon, 1968), 248–268.

[26] Donald Winnicott, *Playing and Reality* (New York: Basic Books, 1971), 18.

scarcity and impersonal forms of human togetherness, which would otherwise be taxing to a potentially crippling degree.[27]

Honneth has a dual purpose in trading Freud for Winnicott: first, he hopes to anchor his theory in an emancipatory interest in a freely integrated identity that does not paternalistically re-describe it, and is therefore compatible with the normal sociality thesis. He also tries to move from a "realistic" (IW, 195) account of the psyche to a social theory that supports the transparency thesis by being receptive to the rationality of modern ethical life, to the extent that its institutions *do* visibly embody patterns of mutual recognition, as opposed to being merely an assemblage of disciplinary power. Such a social theory, in turn, justifies Honneth's immanent, contextualist approach to a normative theory of justice.

All told, this re-engineering of critical theory's account of the psyche is a fascinating gambit, but there are some complicating factors. First, fantasy and the unconscious play a rather different role for Honneth than they do for Adorno. Or, perhaps it would be better to refer to Marcuse here, since he makes a more straightforward appeal to fantasy as the repository of unconscious yearnings for a gratifying existence centered around the pleasure principle: fantasy in *Eros and Civilization* discloses the normative surplus in what might otherwise be a one-dimensional, totally administered social world.[28] For Honneth, following Winnicott, fantasy primarily has a reality-*coping* function (236–237). "Play" in Winnicott may remind some readers of Adornian mimesis, and indeed, Winnicott's research might give lie to Adorno's contention that the post-mythic mode of subject formation shunts the mimetic impulse out of conscious, everyday life altogether. But whether it is fantasy or mimesis, Marcuse and Adorno's contention is that there is an extant, if deeply submerged, impulse in the psyche that longs for a non-dominative relationship between subject and object—this relationship represents a promise of happiness without repression or renunciation, and therefore the attraction to it stands at odds with social reality as it has heretofore existed. It accounts for the possibility of resistance to one-dimensional society. The category of play, on the other hand, is more accommodating to reality—its centrality in Winnicott in effect denies that there is an insuperable opposition between pleasure and reality principle.

This is not necessarily a systematic problem for Honneth, since he clearly rejects the notion that society has become one-dimensional, so he does not need to rely on some impulse to resist oppression and disclose normative surplus. But it does mean that, in order to support the transparency thesis, he is

---

[27] See ibid., 41.

[28] See Marcuse, *Eros and Civilization: A Philosophical Investigation of Freud* (Boston: Beacon, 1955), 140–171.

investing heavily in the idea that deficits in well-ordered patterns of mutual recognition *themselves* generate more or less conscious motivations to overcome
them. It would be overstating things to say that Honneth maintains that because
misrecognition always triggers a negative emotional response in those affected,
that injustice is always identified and resisted. But because persons participate in
the giving and receiving of love, respect, and esteem, and are intuitively aware of
the rational, identity-constituting nature of these practices, recognitional injuries
must evoke social suffering; even if subjects themselves do not identify the
source of their suffering immediately or precisely, it should nevertheless be articulable in a folk-psychological way that they can recognize themselves in. This is a
strange stance for someone steeped in left Hegelian social theory to hold: while
Hegel holds a similar position on societal transparency, even he thinks that this
knowledge of socialization—how our lives come to have the shape that they
do—is not intuitively given through successful initiation into ethical life, but is
instead achieved in the process of reconciliation, through the state.

Before considering the implications of this split from left Hegelianism, we
can ask whether Honneth's neo-Hegelian conception of selfhood and its psychoanalytic underpinnings together support the degree of social transparency
that he requires, in the first place. As Honneth makes clear in *The Struggle for
Recognition*, the self-relation constituted through love is not only a foundational
precondition for a freely integrated social identity; it provides *the* paradigmatic
model of mutual recognition. I think that Honneth is correct in seeing this as
an implication of Winnicott: although Winnicott's notion of symbiotic fusion is
structurally similar to primary narcissism, a crucial difference is that, for Freud,
in order to acquire a functional ego, primary narcissism has to be thoroughly
disrupted, its attraction repressed.[29] Things are otherwise for Winnicott: transitional objects allow us to carry merging experiences with us in the course of
more prosaic everyday existence. Honneth has this in mind when he repeatedly
cites Hegel's allusions to friendship and romantic love as exemplary illustrations
of freedom as being with one's self in another—"love is the structural core of all
ethical life" (SR, 107; see also FR, 44, and OPL, 164). Indeed, Honneth holds
that the full range of self-relations—including respect and esteem—have their
origins in a structural context where love and care are the overarching value
orientation:

> [the] distinction between the main three stages of positive relation-
> to-self—self-confidence, self-respect and self-esteem—should not be
> understood in the strong sense of an ontogenetic sequence; rather we
> can safely assume that all three forms of relation-to-self can develop in

[29] See Honneth, "Postmodern Identity and Object Relations Theory," 231.

unison through the internalization of parental care, and are only experienced later as distinct aspects of one's life by gradually differentiating various partners in interaction. (IW, 205)

In addition to Honneth's belief that such relationships elucidate the formal structure of social freedom in an intuitive way, I gather that the idea here is that people feel most complete, whole, and alive in these emotionally intense relationships, and that this quality serves as a general template for peoples' feelings and judgments about what makes their lives fulfilling. In order for us to experience our social world as meaningful, its demands as continuous with an integrated sense of self, something of the glow that attaches to intimate relations needs to be stretched over the skeleton of contractual, legal, economic, political, and associational relations that make up the rest of society. The consequences of this move are underappreciated, by critics and perhaps by Honneth himself.

Although the cogency of Honneth's point does not depend on its being otherwise, I doubt that the above is all that close to Hegel's rationale for holding that we can be at home with our self in ethical life. The value of recognition in both civil society and the state lies not in their being mediated extensions of love. Hegel has his own reasons for thinking that the types of relationships found in family, civil society, and the state need to be differentiated and institutionalized for freedom to be actual, which have to do with the Idea of freedom's logical structure as a mediation of particularity and universality. This, however, is precisely one of the parts of Hegel's philosophy that Honneth does not want to emulate (NEL, 818), and again, a big part of psychoanalysis' role in Honneth's theory is to provide naturalistic grounding for the theory of recognition that stands in for these "metaphysical" aspects of Hegel. However, if intimate fusion is *the* paradigm instance of mutual recognition, it is unclear why non-intimate relations found in work, association, and law should be something other than repressive derivatives of symbiotic fusion. I do not want to suggest that Honneth is authoring a deeply sentimental social theory that is so literal about love being the structural core of ethical life that it holds that legal and associational relations are essentially just watered down versions of intimacy. But his belief that love and friendship are paradigmatic ethical relationships, together with the idea that transitional objects acclimate us to external reality throughout our lives by infusing more formal and instrumental relations with the aura of merging experiences, makes it fair to say that Honneth thinks of respect and esteem as *sublimations* of love: the impetus to return to a merged state is successfully transformed into forms of intersubjectivity characterized much more by mediated togetherness than fusion.

At any rate, I think this is the best explanation available to Honneth. But there are some matters that require clarification. To begin with what is doubtless a very obvious point, esteem and respect seem rather different than love. Honneth's treatment of Winnicott recognizes that the satisfaction of intimacy is not capture-able just in terms of its mutuality and the twining of intentions (i.e., the formal features of ethical relationships, in general, according to Honneth); more impor-tantly, there is an equilibrium between a moment of acknowledging the other as unique and distinct, and the erotic dissolution of the boundaries between other and self. Intimate relationships that fail to strike a balance between these moments either cease to be intimate or become pathologically consuming (SR, 97–98, 105). These moments are not on par with each other in legally mediated and associational forms of recognition: the togetherness and complementarity of legal, economic/associational, and political relations are premised on the independence of the participants; the twining of intentions is a subsequent af-fair and does not typically approach the eroticism of boundary dissolution. Or rather, when group memberships *do* approach it, as Freud believes can happen in crowd behavior, Honneth is happy to call them regressive (IW, 211)—such forms of togetherness seek unconsciously to return to an unmediated merged state that is at odds with individuation and psychic maturity.[30] So, if we want to think of love as the emotional and structural core of ethical life out of which respect and esteem branch, what is it that makes them sublimations, as opposed to repressive conditioning? And if Honneth is basically right about the actual present state of ethical spheres, is it not the case that most people in fact achieve a decent degree of functionality in social spheres where the forms of together-ness are deficient in terms of their transparency and capacity to ethically twine interaction partners' intentions? So even if it is possible to think of respect and esteem as sublimations of love (and I do not presume that sublimation is easy to distinguish from repression, in the first place)[31], as things currently are, social spheres reproduce themselves through forms of recognition that do not subli-mate intimacy; and since Honneth countenances a tendency toward destructive regression in forms of togetherness that are not rationally mediated, it seems like some kind of repression mechanism is widely operative in the forms of recogni-tion that are stable, yet institutionalized in such a way that the relationships they establish do not realize their rational potential in actualizing social freedom. This would be awkward, since a major part of the case Honneth makes for object re-lations theory is that the struggle for recognition can *replace* repression in its ac-count of ontogenesis. If it does not do this, then it is hard to see the transparency

---

[30] Although Arendt's approach is not psychoanalytically oriented, she similarly emphasizes the attraction toward unmediated togetherness in totalitarian movements. See *The Origins of Totalitarianism*, 464ff.

[31] See Hans Loewald, *Sublimation: Inquiries into Theoretical Psychoanalysis* (New Haven, CT: Yale University Press, 1988).

thesis as well grounded, and the normal sociality thesis would hold only under conditions rather more substantially just than we currently enjoy.

Honneth does nevertheless minimize the role of repression in his social theory, but pays a price for doing so. A further comparison with Marcuse may be instructive here: although Honneth gives no indication of being much influenced by Marcuse, among major figures in the Frankfurt tradition they two are the most committed to psychoanalysis for purposes of both social and positive normative theory. Marcuse, in contrast to Adorno, takes seriously Freud's maxim that Eros is the "uniter of things, builder of ever greater unities," and sees institutions, and social life generally, as manifestations of a basically erotic impulse toward creation and cooperative interaction. Like Freud, he thinks that although Eros provides the impetus for the creation of social orders, its repression is needed for extant ones to reproduce themselves; but unlike Freud, he believes that a liberated society that evolved beyond the need to struggle against scarcity could conceivably allow Eros to flow more freely through everyday life, making it more unreservedly erotic than presently imaginable—this would be an epochal gain in freedom and happiness.[32] The plausibility of a non-repressive civilization sets a yardstick against which the deficiencies of the present can be seen—and not just in the abstract way that, say, utopian socialism condemns capitalism, but concretely, in that we can see how instinctual energies presently co-opted for the reproduction of unequal and repressive social patterns could unfurl more spontaneously. There is much in the details of Marcuse's approach that one would not want to emulate today, not the least of which being his unproblematic view of Eros as inherently rational and liberatory.[33] However, wittingly or not, Honneth emulates many of Marcuse's broader strokes by viewing social life as the product of a basically erotic impulse, to which social institutions give a determinate shape. But the fact that Marcuse is working from a Freudian theory makes a difference here, since according to Freud the very instinctual energy that animates our mental attunement to the world rankles against sociality, either inevitably (Freud) or in any society we are familiar with (Marcuse)—it cannot (presently?) be channeled into orderly forms of togetherness without repression. Winnicott's theory of transitional objects denies this. By incorporating this doctrine into his recognition theory, Honneth denies that recognition is repressive. He maintains that recognition can be unjust by being misrecognition (i.e., denigrating or otherwise violating normative expectations for recognition); that threats to patterns of recognition can produce anxiety; and that anxiety can in turn lead to the repression of desires for the disrupted/unforthcoming

---

[32] See Marcuse, *Eros and Civilization*, 193–221.

[33] See Espen Hammer, "Marcuse's Critical Theory of Modernity," *Philosophy and Social Criticism* 34, no. 9 (2008): 1071–1093.

recognition. But instead of being repressive, the giving and receiving of recognition allows self-relations to take shape; transitional objects allow the merging impulse to sublimate into institutionally mediated respectful and esteeming relations. So, there is a symbiotic impulse driving this process, but unlike in the Freudian tradition, it is not asocial or devouring—in relationships that do not strike an appropriate balance between independence and fusion, there can be an unsublimated excess of this merging impulse, but this only reaches a level where it inhibits ego functioning when patterns of recognition are so dysfunctional or absent as to not produce intact self-relations at all. Under normal, more fortunate circumstances, Honneth—following Mead and Winnicott—represents any unorganized excess of drive energy as a spur prompting the ego to open itself to inner dialogue and intersubjectivity within the existing social world, rather than beyond it.[34]

My sense is that Honneth believes that, in modern societies, spheres of personal relations, work and exchange, and public life exist in a sufficiently intact form that usually allows the self-relations comprising the personality to take shape. Whether those social spheres encourage *affirmative* self-relations and social freedom is a separate, subsequent question addressed by a theory of justice. And whether these self-relations hang together in an integral way that allows an unclouded will to take shape is yet another separate, subsequent question that largely depends on individuals' capacity to work through dissonant and fragmented aspects of their biography and motivational set. By calling these questions separate and subsequent, I do not mean to imply that they are utterly divorced from one another. But the object relations/recognitional account of subject formation that Honneth adopts allows him to dissolve some of the problems that concerned the left Hegelian tradition from Marx through Adorno: they worry that people—in capitalism, or especially in capitalism— are conditioned, mostly without their awareness, to see their social world in an instrumental, dehumanized way; as a result of an impoverished conception of the relationship between self and society, the self tends to become narcissistic and empty, unable to perceive its own lack of freedom. While I do not want to fixate on the category of repression as somehow essential to this perspective, I did argue in Chapter 2 that Horkheimer and Adorno use it to good effect to explain the pervasiveness of reification in a way Marx and Lukács are unable to.

But, on the contrary, Honneth is arguing that it is implausible to hold that persons are pervasively mistaken about the nature of their society and their relationship to it. The fairly commonsensical picture in which society comprises interrelated spheres of action where voluntary (i.e., mutually recognitional) interactions are value-guided is, Honneth thinks, basically correct. Audiences

---

[34] See Honneth, "Postmodern Identity and Object Relations Theory," 232–233.

that are satisfied by this picture may proceed to Honneth's theory of justice without further ado. For audiences skeptical of folk sociology (e.g., most left Hegelians), Honneth has an argument, namely, an object-relations account of subject formation and a neo-Hegelian, recognitional account of society, which combine to elegantly reveal how individuation and social reproduction are complementary, co-dependent processes. In turn, this warrants confidence that society's nature (in particular, the interdependence of individuation and socialization) is transparent enough that threats to freedom—misrecognition and deterioration of recognitional patterns that sustain such self-relations—are normally perceptible, albeit not always with great clarity (e.g., when their major symptom is anxiety).

6. Recognition, Ideology, and Reification

In the previous section, I suggested that Honneth's account of the psyche does not obviate the need for a concept of repression in social theory to the extent that he thinks. He wants to minimize the role of repression in normal socialization and social reproduction because it does not seem compatible with the value-laden, recognitional conception of those things prescribed by the transparency thesis. My preliminary conclusion was that, if a drive for merging intersubjectivity has to be repressed in normal socialization (as would seem to be the case, at least in societies where ethical spheres only partially realize their relational potential), then persons will predictably be plagued by conflicts between unconscious desires and internalized role expectations that cloud the will in a way that prevents them from being at home with themselves. Social freedom would be much more of a utopian possibility than Honneth intends, and he would therefore fail to draw conclusions about its ongoing actualizeability in the modern world. Honneth, therefore, almost stipulates that insofar as recognition serves to constitute self-relations, it *cannot* itself be repressive.[35] He seems to conclude that most any pattern of respectful or esteeming recognition that one is likely to encounter in the modern world *can* serve to sublimate the drive to fuse/merge that is most fully on display in intimate relationships— extant recognition patterns are normally sufficient to develop all three types of self-relations, around which persons internalize expectations and desires for these types of recognition. This is not at all to say that anything close to all persons actually receive an amount of emotionally enriching recognition sufficient to develop well-defined, affirmative self-relations. Nor, again, is it to deny that actual recognition practices too often are denigrating, shallow, and/or

[35] See Lois McNay, *Against Recognition* (Malden, MA: Polity, 2008).

unequal, in ways that frustrate the cultivation of normatively desirable varieties of self-relations—most of *Freedom's Right* is devoted to this topic, after all. It is, however, to say that modern recognition practices do not, at their heart, represent chains that shackle emancipatory impulses for the sake of orderly social integration.

For this reason, Honneth has an arm's-length relationship to Althusser and his followers, for whom recognition is fundamental to subject formation, as with Honneth, but are almost diametrically opposed to him on the previous point. This is apparent in the unorthodox way that left Hegelian concepts like ideology and reification fit into Honneth's theory. Through his theory of recognition, Honneth has a ready way of conceptualizing both: ideology, to start with, is a kind of recognition that binds persons—with their tacit collaboration—to subordinate, oppressive social roles. Honneth does not approve of the sweeping way that the Althusserian tradition has used this concept (IW, 75–81): if one regards a society (e.g., capitalism) as definitively irrational or exploitative, then there seems to be a basis for claiming that the recognition patterns that lead persons to adopt self-understandings that encourage compliance (e.g., the good worker, the good housewife, the good peasant, etc.) are ideological, and criticizable as irrational. It is obviously true that, historically, the vast majority of persons *have* complied, and probably taken identity-securing satisfaction in so complying, with at least some role expectations that we would now regard as lying on a spectrum from senselessly constrictive to monstrously immoral.

Probably, there is nothing incoherent about labeling such forms of recognition ideological, but Honneth finds it distasteful to use what is plainly the benefit of hindsight to criticize compliance with norms that were not obviously surmountable, unethical, etc. at the time (85–89). If ideology criticism is not simply for smug celebrations of the present, it must be useable for criticizing contemporary recognition practices, and this is usually a dubious proposition. For example, there are today cultural expectations for status and benefit in being recognized as a "good worker"; they are not uniform across occupations, neither always clear nor uncontestable, and have changed considerably over recent decades (e.g., from "the good company man" to the flexible entrepreneur).[36] But to recognize a 21st-century American retail worker in the manner of a 19th-century servant or 12th-century serf would be an instance of misrecognition: it would be a felt violation of the implicit norms prevailing in the labor market, and hence immoral on Honneth's terms, not ideological. Nevertheless, one might claim that internalizing recognition of oneself as, say, a good worker (by contemporary standards) creates self-relations that unduly

---

[36] See Boltanksi and Chiapello, *The New Spirit of Capitalism*, 57–101.

constrict, repress, discipline, etc. the self in ways not normally thematized in public. This, on Honneth's terms, would be an example of genuine recognition, not misrecognition, but in a form that causes suffering by unduly diminishing freedom in a way perceptible to the recognized person (at least as shame, frustration, unease, etc.), even while he or she fails to attribute his or her suffering to role obligations/expectations he or she has internalized. This category may justly be called ideological.

But a lot depends on what we mean by "undue": it is probably the case for each and every one of us that some of the social attributions we receive and identify with are unnecessarily limiting, relative to an imaginably more just society, at least in the way they are culturally filled out (for example, being recognized for an honest day's work may be connected to working class subculture that discourages people from pursuing education, talking fancy, etc.). It is entirely fair and worthwhile to point this sort of thing out, but it also seems farfetched to think of this very normal sort of recognition as an infliction of social suffering—after all, people often take great pride in this kind of cultural identification—and the problem seems to be more with the cultural associations surrounding the basic form of recognition (i.e., their implications for things like inclusion and social mobility) than with the recognition itself. Marcuse is in a position to call this kind of attribution ideological and harmful because he thinks that the reality principle itself—and hence the galaxy of social roles institutionalizing it—demands repression, and that fantasy and the unconscious disclose a possibility of a society beyond the present reality principle, hence beyond repression. But as we have seen, this is not Honneth: the fundaments of successful ontogenesis (internalization of recognition in all three dimensions) are not inherently repressive in themselves, and he does not think instinctual drives yearn for existence beyond normal sociality. So, Honneth thinks, to properly call a form of recognition ideological, it would have to be the case that there is a gap between the expectations for status and benefit that the form of recognition inculcates and what it actually delivers. Furthermore, this gap would have to be perceived (at least in an inchoate way), but either denied or excused on account of the satisfaction the self-relation provides. Now, Habermas broached the possibility in 1968's "Technology and Science as Ideology?" that the capitalist "achievement principle"—i.e., the notion that people who work hard and utilize their talents should/will be recognized and rewarded accordingly—might have passed this threshold (TRS, 122).[37] When Honneth concludes that the capitalist market appears

---

[37] Over the decades, Habermas has modified this diagnosis, but not in a way that mollifies the basic point: today, the democratic state to a large extent serves to functionalize the economy

to be breaking down entirely as a possible site of social freedom, he is saying something similar. But by his reckoning, for ideology to be invoked, the gap would have to be yawning and permanent, and this yawning permanency knowable but willfully not known. It is hard, in the present, to conclude with confidence that any particular recognition pattern fits this description.

Honneth's treatment of reification goes similarly. In Chapter 2, we surveyed his contention that Lukács' normative critique of reification depends on an implausible social theory and a prelapsarian psychology. Accordingly, Honneth's efforts to reconceive reification within recognition theory aim to put it on sounder empirical and normative footing. In his view, recognition involves a subjective stance wherein we encounter others as minded, feeling beings in a way that reciprocally engages faculties of judgment and emotion.[38] Not only is this stance central to successful ontogenesis; the ability to cognize the world in an objective, neutral manner already presupposes, at a deeper level, engaged care with it: "recognition precedes cognition" (R, 40–52).[39] This positions Honneth to reinterpret reification as a suspension, or "forgetting," of the recognition extended to others, as a normal matter of course, during everyday social interaction, which becomes pathological when habitual. Reification is morally criticizable when the suspension of emotional engagement with others amounts to a neglectful failure to recognize them as persons. By largely psychologizing reification, Honneth removes its concrete, historical dimension; for previous left Hegelians, reification is specific to (or at least reaches its apogee in) capitalist modernity, whereas Honneth does little to connect reification to historical forms of social organization.[40]

While Honneth's idea of reification as a forgetting of recognition is immensely suggestive, much of the intent behind the concept's original formulation in Marx and Lukács is lost when it is interpreted as a morally objectionable form of intersubjectivity. Clearly, Honneth thinks that reification is a widespread enough phenomenon to warrant comment, but we have seen enough of his social theory to guess that he will not countenance it as the predominant mechanism through

---

in accordance with the imperatives of globalized finance, giving them a gloss of legitimacy, even though they pay remarkably little heed to expectations for status and benefit correlated to "achievement." See Habermas, *The Crisis of the European Union: A Response* (Malden, MA: Polity, 2014), 12–52.

[38] In this regard, see Honneth's appeal to Heidegger's notion of "care": R, 32–36.

[39] On the connection between reification and "the priority of recognition," see Alessandro Ferrara, "The Nugget and the Tailings: Reification Reinterpreted in the Light of Recognition," in *Axel Honneth: Critical Essays*, ed. Danielle Petherbridge (Boston: Brill, 2011), 371–390.

[40] See Anita Chari, "Toward a Political Critique of Reification: Lukács, Honneth, and the Aims of Critical Theory," *Philosophy and Social Criticism* 3, no. 5 (2010): 587–606; and Andrew Feenberg, "Rethinking Reification," in *Georg Lukács*, 101–119.

which individual actions and social spheres interlock, as it is for Lukács. His interest in reification lies elsewhere, namely, in trying to understand the calculating coldness that enabled some of Europe's 20th-century moral catastrophes, and what he takes to be a trend toward the manipulation of one's own emotional states ("self-reification") (R, 82–84; RJ, 158). For Lukács and Adorno, on the other hand, reification is not primarily an intersubjective phenomenon: it is not so much persons as "social relations" that are rendered thing-like,[41] and while persons may come to seem thing-like, this is a *consequence* of being encountered *within* social structures that appear as a second nature, and hence do not appear to be sustained through ongoing practices of mutual recognition. So, understanding the institutional aspects of reification seems essential to its role in a critical theory of society.

Such a project, however, runs counter to Honneth's in key respects, as he views the legal infrastructure of capitalist societies as providing recognition of autonomous personhood, which buffers individuals against dehumanization. As noted earlier, he regards capitalism not as an autonomous, norm-free functional system, but as an order of recognition that reflects the normative expectations of its participants. Although such thoughts are initially of a piece with the contention that Marxist social theory tends to overestimate the degree to which market forces have superseded traditional hierarchies,[42] Honneth takes them in a more affirmative direction: in addition to seeing the recognition of value-added labor in the economy as embodying (very partially) a normative "principle of achievement,"[43] he argues that economic interactions take place within a legal framework, where employment and exchange contracts embody mutual recognition of the contractors as rational and responsible agents, entitled to guarantees of fairness and security.

> The very fact that . . . we only reify other persons if we lose sight of our antecedent recognition of their existence as persons should suffice to demonstrate just how unconvincing Lukács' equation of commodity exchange and reification is, given that the persons with whom we interact in the process of economic exchange are normally present to us, *at least legally*, as recognized persons. (R, 75, italics mine)

I think that, at this juncture, something has gone wrong in Honneth's theory. It turns out that the conditions for a legally mediated or associational interaction to

---

[41] Although Lukács does discuss "self-objectification" (RCP, 92) as an aspect of reification, it plays a minor role in his work.

[42] See Heidi Hartmann, "The Unhappy Marriage of Marxism and Feminism," *Capital and Class* 3, no. 2 (1979): 1–33.

[43] See David Borman, "Labor, Exchange, and Recognition: Marx contra Honneth," *Philosophy and Social Criticism* 35, no. 8 (2009): 935–959.

count as genuine recognition are pretty minimal: they do not have to be particularly conscious, sincere, emotionally potent, etc.; it is enough that they involve a performance that is generally understood as recognition. This is in keeping with Honneth's contention that a kind of incipient, proto-recognition—amounting to an attunement to others' personhood—sustains engagement with world while underlying virtually all interactions, even while he denies that there is anything particularly warm, altruistic, etc. about it (RJ, 151–153). It is also in keeping with his view that patterns of recognition are entirely capable of allowing the psyche's core structural self-relations to take shape, even though they may not fare all that well in terms of successfully actualizing social freedom.

Honneth's use of the transitional objects concept indicated that our ability to feel at home with our self in the wide social world depends on carrying with us a memory of intimacy that infuses more mediated, formal, anonymous interactions. And yet surely there are limits to this, that is, points past which the use of this reality-coping mechanism becomes either solipsistic and unhealthy, on the one hand, or simply unsustainable, on the other—otherwise, Honneth would be materially indistinguishable from the "revisionist" Freudians that Adorno and Marcuse savaged for equating psychic health with adaptability to existing reality. I do not want to deny that it is possible for law to function as Honneth conceives it in the above quote, as a delivery vehicle for recognition, even under conditions (like the present, according to Honneth) where the social sphere of labor, consumption, and contract is at best partially functioning as a relational one—*but only to the extent that the law is itself encountered by its subjects as a social relation, and not a reified thing*.[44]

Because Honneth thinks of reification as something that takes place in person-to-person interactions, he does not sufficiently consider the notion that patterns of recognition themselves could become reified. But there is nothing stopping him from doing so, and indeed, in *Freedom's Right*, Honneth basically endorses Hans Kelsen's idea that citizens' identification *with the law* instead of charismatic leadership defuses potentials for regressive irrationality in the political sphere, suggesting that how we perceive a pattern of recognition (i.e.,

---

[44] In her debate with Honneth, Fraser draws a useful distinction between the affirmation of existing rights, statuses, and identities in social struggles, as opposed to their deconstructive transformation; see RR, 76–77. Fraser's point is that, while strategies of affirmation may be sometimes useful, they risk reifying rights and identities by applying fixed schema to persons, potentially cementing existing forms of subordination. Transformative strategies, on the other hand, while generally riskier, are "by their nature dereifying." Fraser's accusation that Honneth makes no room for such a distinction is, I believe, of a piece with the line of criticism I am advancing here. In more recent work, Honneth comes closer to acknowledging this problem in a discussion of the ethically troubling consequences of pervasive instrumentalization of the legal system by its participants. See FR, 172.

as either reified second nature or consciously shared value commitment) can profoundly affect the quality of social life (FR, 315–317). And if we look back to Hegel, the ossification of institutional patterns is precisely the kind of reification that he is concerned with. When, at various points in his work, Hegel hazards that Roman life, modern Christianity and secular conscience, or the *Phenomenology*'s "unhappy consciousness," may somehow be failing as shapes of Spirit, he is not saying that they no longer establish relationship patterns wherein human beings recognize one another as responsible for certain role performances—clearly, they do that much. He is saying that the conferrals of recognition have become automated, that is, something that subjects have internalized as simply what is to be done as an unreflective matter of course, a bare fact about social life. Subjects are unable to conceive of these recognition patterns as concretely embodying a shared way of life, consciously reproduced for good reasons—the social world cannot be a home under such a description. To put it in Honneth's terms, in situations like these, patterns of recognition are intact enough for self-relations to coalesce around, but do little to facilitate the affirmative self-relations that need mutual respect and esteem in order to grow;[45] and too often they leave individuals on their own as far as articulating an integrated, coherent set of self-relations is concerned, which is the key requirement for an unclouded will to emerge.

Honneth does not have a solid reason for not theorizing this type of reification—his innovations to the tradition of left Hegelianism do not rule its existence out. His combination of recognition and object-relations theory directly opposes the notion—present in Lukács and Althusser, given a Freudian inflection by Adorno—that subjectivity is constituted by submitting to a certain schema through which the social world is encountered. It therefore moderates the Lukácsian conception of reification wherein social phenomena are only knowable through the "form" of reification. But it has less of an impact on Adorno's version, at least on one of his key points, namely, that anonymous, diffuse social pressure is increasingly responsible for superego formation, making its discipline both more enveloping and opaque. This, Adorno insists, reduces capacities for reflection and spontaneity in the ego, automating interactions and thereby diminishing freedom. It is true that Adorno makes these points in a Freudian framework, but it is hard to see how Honneth's object relations paradigm refutes them: for Honneth, patterns of recognition that are ultimately unconducive to social freedom nevertheless are normally intact enough to allow self-relations to form; however, if we grant Adorno's point, the socialization

---

[45] See IW, 205: "The experience that one's own needs, judgement and, above all, skills are regarded as valuable is one that subjects must constantly renew and re-concretize so that they do not lose their strength and vitality in the anonymity of a generalized other."

process through which they form would tend not to inculcate much definition or reflexivity in the self-relations. Meanwhile, as object relations theory has it, the psyche has imaginative capacities that preserve the memory of emotionally nourishing intimate recognition for purposes of reality coping. All told, this adds up to a picture that is not too different from Horkheimer and Adorno's culture industry: it suggests a capacity for approximating social functionality (in Honneth's normative sense) amidst a condition where the self's relation to its social roles is conditioned and unreflective, therefore more disciplinary than a matter of being freely "at home." When self-relations are unreflective and conditioned, we may say that the subject experiences a deficit of social meaning, which stems from ethical life not supplying resources for understanding the interrelation between social roles as complementary; this causes ethical life's action-orienting power to weaken. When this happens, we would expect a concomitant deficit in the subject's capacity to sublimate drives for merging experiences into satisfyingly mutual relationships, which would have to mean that repression would be necessary for functionality in everyday social life, in a way Honneth does not envision.

I do not have any precise sense of how much closer the typical experience of modern society is to this type of scenario than to Honneth's more idealized counterfactual of social spheres reliably realizing their rational potential. But unless we are much closer to the latter than the former (and this certainly does not seem to be Honneth's position), I do not think that the transparency or the normal sociality thesis will be true enough to support a conception of social freedom that can do without a reconciliation concept. Honneth's normative perspective—a contextualist theory of justice whose orientation toward the value of freedom is justified by a hermeneutic claim about what the institutions of modern life are all about—depends on the cogency of seeing modern social orders as, altogether and overall, working to actualize freedom. But if the incorporation of individuals into multiple, mutually inscrutable social spheres in a way that is not affirmed by an underlying, coherent` identity becomes a bare, reified fact about social life, then Honneth's normative reconstruction threatens to become an idle, counterfactual exercise.

Some of Honneth's writings recognize this possibility—his essay "Organized Self-Realization," for example.[46] There, in a formulation strikingly close to Horkheimer and Adorno's culture industry, Honneth argues that three apparently liberatory postwar trends in Western societies have conspired to actually disempower the subject: a) the rise of consumer culture as an important medium for self-realization; b) loosening restrictions on sexuality; and c) the breakdown of

---

[46] See also RR, 118–120.

stable working- and middle-class career arcs. Ever since romanticism penetrated mainstream bourgeois culture during the 19th century, together with the relative lack of direct lifestyle prescriptions that were typical of more traditional forms of ethical life, individuals are subject to a diffuse cultural expectation that they should be the authentic source of their own biography. In this context, we can agree with Honneth's contention that Freudian self-appropriation represents an ideal for what the formation of a coherent will would look like, but given the above diagnosis, we have to suppose that it is normally only achievable as a shallow simulacrum: "The demands that subjects voiced once they began to interpret their lives as an experimental process of identity-seeking have now returned to them as diffuse external demands, compelling them—implicitly or explicitly—to keep their biographical aims and options open" (IW, 165). This process of "transforming ideals into constraints" takes place behind the backs of individuals, implying both that patterns of recognition are leading to self-relations that are anxiously ill-defined and alarmingly bereft of social meaning, even while the cultural demand for authentic self-realization as occupational flexibility comes to functionally serve "as a basis for legitimizing the system" rather than a basis for criticizing the oppressive burdens society foists on the individual (157). Honneth has his reasons for not invoking ideology to characterize this, but describing the situation in terms of a reified pattern of esteeming recognition seems irresistible.

So, I think that Honneth can accommodate within his theory a more robust conception of reification, but not its antidote, either in the form of revolutionary *praxis* (Marx and Lukács) or reconciliation (Hegel and—so I will argue—Habermas). Honneth has never considered the former, and he rejects the parts of Hegel's philosophy that support the latter. Now, it follows from Chapter 1 that Honneth misjudges the kind of "baggage" attaching to reconciliation, i.e., that it is less abstruse and contemplative, more political and process-oriented than he, like most, thinks. Given, however, that Honneth has arranged his theory to conceive of freedom's actualization without mediation through the universal (i.e., the state), we are not in a position to simply amend it by fastening to it the politicized conception of reconciliation I have been pressing for, since this would re-center the idea of social freedom in the political sphere, contrary to Honneth's non-state-centric picture of normative theorizing. This is not to say that there is something objectionable about Honneth's reconstruction of the political sphere, which is substantially similar to Habermas'. The main role of the state in this is to provide a foundation of legal freedom, an avenue for the specific form of membership involved in being recognized as a citizen entitled to deliberate on public affairs, and to respond to normative demands in the other spheres of ethical life. In order to function as a genuinely relational sphere, democratic will formation, which should largely be a product of the less formally institutionalized ranges of the public sphere, would have to be embedded more deeply in the legislature than it is in its presently unequal, commercialized, and insider-dominated form. And, constitutional and parliamentary authority would have to be embedded more deeply in administration, which presently exists in overly bureaucratized form. That said, although the state has a unique role in establishing a baseline of order in other social spheres, Honneth treats it as a co-equal site for the actualization of social freedom, and thinks it a great distortion of the human emancipatory interest to think that it somehow culminates in the state (RR, 144–145; FR, 329–332). Honneth does not accept that the coherence of an identity's constitutive self-relations depends significantly on mediation through the political process—his theory cannot accommodate this point without a foundational overhaul.

7. Conclusion

Honneth is therefore mired in the following quandary: like Marx in "On the Jewish Question," he is committed to the idea that freedom should be conceived as something lived and experienced in everyday life, not a legal or philosophical construct—hence his hostility to "juridical" theories of justice. Despite the fact that Marx saw Hegel as a failure in this regard, Honneth wants to think of normativity in basically Hegelian terms: ethical life is normative in that it inculcates reasonable expectations for being treated as a free being with interests that warrant account; since ethical life is rational, by consciously acting in accordance with the norms embedded in its spheres, we mutually confirm ourselves as free beings. There is obviously some reflective dimension in all this: the fact that ethical life should and (hopefully) does actualize freedom needs to be a matter of publicly accessible knowledge. But Honneth foreswears the philosophy of Spirit that supported Hegel's account of how we come to see the rationality of modern ethical life, and the concept of reconciliation is contained in this account. Absent this reflective element, Honneth's account of normativity has to stake itself to one of the following to be successful:

a) A sunny, optimistic construal of ethical life. There are surely problems that Honneth's theory of justice picks out, but on the whole, modern ethical life's bones are structurally sound and represent indelible progress. Moreover, its deficits are discernible as injuries to these affected, i.e., as violations of generally accepted expectations for recognition. All of this is intuitively accessible.

b) A less optimistic construal of the contemporary state of ethical life, in which (some of) its spheres are only tenuously identifiable as relational, but with the caveat that the intersubjective constitution of the subject ensures that ideology and reification remain peripheral problems. They cannot systematically obscure the extent to which ethical life actualizes freedom.

In (a), the transparency and normal sociality theses are unproblematically true (or at any rate, true enough to support Honneth's conclusions). In (b), their veracity is less obvious, but Honneth's recognition and object relations account of the psyche seeks to ensure that neither ideology nor reification can poison social relations to such an extent that the freedom on offer in ethical life is an entirely false construct.

While I tend to think that Honneth would favor (b), this interpretive choice is immaterial, since neither (a) nor (b) is viable. In a world where patterns of recognition reproduced themselves transparently, and allowed self-relations to form non-repressively, without systematic deprivation, we could imagine—as Marx did—that the political may come to serve more as backdrop for social freedom's actualization in intimate, vocational, and associational life, rather than itself being an important site for it. Alternatively, we can imagine a social theory (e.g., Marcuse's) that countenanced reification and/or ideology as significant contributors to normal social reproduction, but was linked to a social psychology in which drives and instincts themselves rankle (independently of their political mobilization) against the constraints of sociality. In both scenarios, politically mediated reconciliation need not be an important vehicle for actualizing freedom. But neither can hold for Honneth. In a world like ours, where neither the transparency nor the normal sociality theses seem that firmly entrenched, reification effects and repressive sociality foster social identities more haphazardly than coherently integrated, under conditions where subjects are incorporated into social spheres in involuntary ways that do not necessarily allow them to experience their will as their own in their actions. It is not that Honneth's perspective is too blinkered see this—I think he is right to be annoyed with the posture of critics who deem his approach insufficiently radical and a status quo apologetic.[47] My argument, rather, has been that his effort to simultaneously maintain that social freedom is actualize-able in modern ethical life, even while its individual social spheres only partially manifest their underlying rationality, ultimately does depend on a reconciliation concept that he has arranged his theory to avoid. Although I want to preserve large elements of both Honneth's method in normative social theory of reconstructing social spheres in light of their underlying values, and his revisions to critical theory's relationship to psychoanalysis, my conclusion is that a Hegelian conception of freedom as being at home

---

[47] See Honneth, "Rejoinder," *Critical Horizons* 16, no. 2 (2015), 204–205, and *The Idea of Socialism: Towards a Renewal*, trans. Joseph Ganahal (Malden, MA: Polity, 2017), viii.

in the social world requires an element of reflection on society, which Honneth denies, and furthermore, as I will argue in the next chapter, that the kind of required reflection needs to be institutionally anchored (to avoid degenerating into something purely contemplative) in a way that he is also not prepared to accept.

5

Reification and Reconciliation in Habermas' Theory of Law and Democracy

Some of the early critical reactions to Habermas' *Theory of Communicative Action* made explicit a tension in the conception of communicative rationality developed there, one that reverberates through his writings since, as he tries to explain why a philosophy that has become centered around a "quasi-transcendental" reconstruction of formal structures of communication should still be regarded as a critical theory.[1] On the one hand, Habermas claims to occupy the perspective of a hermeneutic interpreter of a communicatively integrated "lifeworld," where, in the course of lived life, considerations of truth, rightness, and authenticity are indistinct, deeply intertwined in deliberations on what to do and how to live. On the other hand, from the point of view of reconstructive theory, in modernity this lifeworld has become "functionally differentiated," with different forms of practical reason developing into freestanding specialized discourses, some of which are institutionalized in sprawling systems of action coordination within which different, incompatible action orientations predominate. Habermas wants to be neither a mournful romantic decrying this differentiation as fracture and alienation,[2] nor a blasé modernist settling for the view that the rise of markets, sciences, and bureaucracies represents an unvarnished gain for reason and progress. A persistent critic, however, may press the question: which is it? Is

---

[1] See Charles Taylor, "Language and Society," and Martin Seel, "Two Meanings of 'Communicative' Rationality: Remarks on Habermas' Plural Concept of Reason," in *Communicative Action: Essays on Jürgen Habermas' Theory of Communicative Action*, eds. Axel Honneth and Hans Joas (Cambridge, MA: MIT Press, 1991), 23–35 and 36–48.

[2] This is, at any rate, how Habermas tends to regard attempts at problematizing differentiation itself. See Jay Bernstein, "Art Against Enlightenment: Adorno's Critique of Habermas," in *The Problems of Modernity: Adorno and Benjamin*, ed. Andrew Benjamin (New York: Routledge, 1991), 49–66.

the differentiation of the lifeworld reifying and alienating? Or is that view basically Luddite, with the real problem one of distinguishing these different types of validity claims, assigning them proper object domains, and institutionalizing them appropriately?[3] The "colonization of the lifeworld" thesis from *Theory of Communicative Action* suggests that the answer is "a bit of both." Although sometimes seeming to end up with an appeal to an image of balance between everyday communication and societal rationalization, Habermas' deeper method of adjudicating issues about freedom and autonomy, on the one hand, and the rationalization of society, on the other, is to maintain that individuals should be able to a) recognize the development of the differentiated systems in which they (with gradations of voluntariness) participate as an advance in societal rationality, and b) understand—rationally, without self-deception—actions dictated by the prescribed codes of subsystems as good reasons *for them* to act. The task of a critical theory becomes one of identifying systemic obstacles that prevent individuals from being able to do these things. In other words, Habermas is restaging Rousseau's problem (how can I be free while obeying society?), while trying to muster a more satisfactory answer than he did (i.e., by making the general will my own). I claim that Habermas is the best candidate among the theories under consideration here for successfully updating Hegel's answer to Rousseau's problem, while addressing the problem of reification more satisfactorily than Rawls and Honneth. I regard Habermas in this way for the following reasons: he has come to see a democratically and constitutionally organized legal system as the crucial vehicle for mediating between communicative action and systems rationality, and making reconciliation between these perspectives an ongoing possibility, while allowing that law can be reifying, but conceiving of a form of legal practice resistant to this.

That Habermas represents some kind of departure from Horkheimer and Adorno's gloomy mid-century reflections on modern society is a commonplace, but less clear is the matter of how, and how much, of a break it amounts to. The relationship between Habermas and his predecessors is often misunderstood, to some extent due to a selection of topics that did not much occupy Horkheimer's circle (e.g., moral and legal theory), to some extent because of his choice of allies (Kant, Rawls) and enemies (poststructuralism). But rather than viewing him as countering Horkheimer and Adorno by offering a more upbeat account of reason's universality and emancipatory potential, we can treat Habermas— especially when *Theory of Communicative Action* and *Between Facts and Norms* are

---

[3] Amy Allen characterizes this tension as one between a Kantian/transcendent and Hegelian/contextualist/historicist strategy for grounding normativity, which she sees him—despite occasional professions to the contrary—resolving in the latter direction. See *The End of Progress?*, 50–67. I am in agreement with this reading.

taken together[4]—as an attempt at a dialectical synthesis of Hegel and Adorno/Horkheimer that conceives the political process as aiming to mediate amongst and reconcile differentiated group interests *amidst* a condition of "latent class conflict" (LC, 31ff).

The broad interpretive thesis of this chapter is that this is an illuminating, cohesive way of approaching Habermas' *corpus* that brings out the distinctiveness of positions he arrives at in legal and political theory (which can be difficult to discern if one reads *Between Facts and Norms* as a stand-alone work about deliberative democracy). Specifically, the fullness of such a synthesis only comes into view when "the proceduralist paradigm of law" is introduced (more suggestively than in detail) at the end of *Between Facts and Norms*: the proceduralist legal paradigm's importance—as well as what is puzzling about it—only comes into focus, I contend, when understood as of a piece, generally, with the line of "social philosophy" passing through Rousseau and the young Marx, which is convinced that the individual's autonomy is dependent on conditions of what Honneth generically calls "cooperative self-actualization" (PoR, 27), and, specifically, with Hegel's notion of the state providing the site for a complex process of mediation between differently positioned individuals and social groups that contains the fraught possibility of reconciliation.

I acknowledge that this represents a revisionary appropriation of Habermas, at least to the extent that the focal concepts of this study (reconciliation, reification) are not a huge part of his vocabulary. Although I will urge that the centrality of the problem of reification to *Theory of Communicative Action* is underappreciated, systematic uses of the term are infrequent in his work before and since. With regard to reconciliation, Habermas has mostly foresworn appeal to it: he usually links it either with a kind of regressive utopianism that he suspects lies in crevices of Marcuse's and Adorno's work, or with Hegel's finality and triumphalism.[5] Since, as I argued in Chapter 1, Hegel's disrepute in this regard is to some degree a result of conflating ideological discomfort with *The Philosophy of Right*'s account of the state with incredulity at the heady rhetoric of culmination in the *Phenomenology*'s conclusion—disambiguating reconciliation's relationship to these legacies shows it to be neither a closed nor a utopian notion. That said, Habermas is consistently (and strangely) wary of Hegel, and I am in accord with the claim that Habermas has adopted an understanding of Hegel (i.e., that he made a wrong turn during the Jena period, moving away from an

---

[4] On through-lines between these texts, see Daniel Gaus, "Rational Reconstruction as a Method of Political Theory between Social Critique and Empirical Political Science," *Constellations* 20, no. 4 (2013): 553–570.

[5] See Fred Dallmayr, "Critical Theory and Reconciliation," in *Habermas, Modernity, and Public Theology*, eds. Don Browning and Francis Fiorenza (New York: Crossroads, 1992), 119–151.

intersubjective theory and toward a macrosubjective "philosophy of consciousness")[6] that prevents his thought from finding affinities with Hegelianism that
would be clarifying to it.[7]

According to the evaluative schema formulated at the end of Chapter 2,
Habermas' theory is geared to explain how the democratic legal-political system
could be a system of mediation in Hegel's sense (hurdle 1), is intensely interested
in the depoliticizing effects of reification in law, and concomitantly in developing a dereifying conception of politics and legal practice (hurdle 2). However,
Habermas does not like to describe his aspirations in these terms, and while to
some extent a matter of rhetorical choice, I also contend that this creates some
knotty problems for his theory. More serious is the relative absence of a plausible, supporting account of subject formation (hurdle 3)—or rather, as I will
argue, the account that Habermas does develop is tailored to address hurdles 1
and 2, but makes it hard to see, in light of considerations raised by Horkheimer
and Adorno, what distinguishes genuine from "false" reconciliation.

1. Reassessing the Adorno-Habermas Relationship: Latent Class Conflict and Differentiation as a Threat to Individual Autonomy

Although some aspects of Horkheimer's and Adorno's analyses of modernity's
culture and politics, and the fate of the individual within it, can easily strike
readers as reductive or apocalyptic, the concerns they raise about the unre-
sponsiveness of governing institutions to rational will formation, the opacity
of the conditions under which individuals are socialized, isolation and lack
of genuine communication between persons, and the ominous threat of collective irrationality—plus the implausibility of real democracy—under such
conditions are hardly alien. For as much as Habermas seems to have split with
his predecessors in offering a more buoyant take on modernity, it is striking to
observe the degree to which he accords with their more ground-level assessment
of advanced capitalism's social structure.

Like Marx, Habermas stands in the tradition of classical social theory
whose great preoccupation has been the epochal transition from traditional
to modern societies: the differentiation of exchange markets, professionalized

[6] For early and late statements of this interpretation, see KHI, 7–42 and T&J, 175–211.
[7] For critical evaluations of what the authors take to be Habermas' unsympathetic misreading
of Hegel, see Pippin, *Idealism as Modernism: Hegelian Variations* (New York: Cambridge University
Press, 1997), 157–184; and Espen Hammer, "Habermas and the Kant-Hegel Contrast," *German
Idealism: Contemporary Perspectives,* ed. Hammer (New York: Routledge, 2007), 113–133.

bureaucracies, and specialized discursive institutions out of traditional ethical life; and the decline of the public authority and explanatory power of "metaphysical" (usually religious) worldviews. For Habermas, the nodal phenomenon here is "the functional differentiation of the lifeworld," i.e., the increasingly refined parsing of reason into discourses with distinct object domains and modes of validity (truth, rightness, and truthfulness/authenticity) (TCA1, 164–178). As Hegel already intimated, this enables a crisper segmentation of life into public and private spheres, and the development of specialized forms of institutional discourse (e.g., natural science; the administration of justice; therapy and cultural criticism). This segmentation and the institutionalization of discursive logics facilitates the differentiation of society into a lifeworld where action coordination depends on achievements of mutual understanding, and social systems where "mediatized" exchanges (money or formally codified power) allows action coordination without such achievements (TCA2, 179–185).[8] Obviously, there is a great deal to unpack here, but for present purposes it serves to note, first, that this reaffirms *Dialectic of Enlightenment*'s basic conclusion, namely, that "with every step enlightenment entangles itself more deeply in mythology" (DE, 8): the development of reflexivity in socio-cultural institutions has all of the tradition-dissolving power oft-observed by theorists of modernity ("all that is solid melts into air"), but instead of replacing the power of authority with that of reason, Enlightenment ends up conjuring far-flung systems of action coordination that are by no means self-limiting, operate behind the backs of those affected, and compel participation within them in a way that inclines individuals toward ideological self-understandings to cope with opaque, coercive social conditions.[9]

Second, as the dilapidation of tradition's "sacred canopy" exposes individuals to disenchanted life, the task of "becoming a person" is increasingly thrown back upon individuals, in their private lives. For Habermas, following one of German idealism's great insights, it is far from accidental that the distinctive values of modernity turn out to be self-determination and self-realization: modernization is experienced as deeply ambiguous by those caught up in it, as it both liberates persons from ascribed social roles and deprives them of traditional sources of meaning. It creates an environment in which they are expected

---

[8] Although I am going to be treating the system-lifeworld distinction's soundness as "good enough" to advance present purposes, it is not without problems. See Hugh Baxter, "System and Lifeworld in Habermas' *Theory of Communicative Action*," *Theory and Society* 16, no. 1 (1987): 39–86; and Joseph Heath, "System and Lifeworld," in *Jürgen Habermas: Key Concepts*, ed. Barbara Fultner (New York: Routledge, 2014), 74–90.

[9] Adorno's interest in varieties of modern fatalistic outlooks, and their ideological content, is instructive in this last regard. See Adorno, *The Stars Down to Earth and Other Essays on the Irrational in Culture*, ed. Stephen Crook (New York: Routledge, 2002), 152–166; and MM, 238–247.

to "find themselves" amidst a potentially bewildering swirl of roles and contingency (BFN, 94ff). The social conditions under which they can reliably
accomplish this turn out, on most accounts (aside from ones like possessive
individualism), to be fairly demanding. Habermas is quite close to Adorno
when he seriously weighs the following hypothesis: "Progressive inclusion in
increasing numbers of functional systems does not imply any increase in autonomy, but at most a transformation in the mode of social control" (PT, 195).
"Conventional" ego identities that cling unreflectively to given social roles will
find their autonomy diminished when thrown into a world of differentiated
systems. As in Rousseau and Hegel, "post-conventional" individuation requires
not just greater "flexibility," but an ability to affirm one's dependence on others
without losing one's self in the process. It is worth reminding ourselves here that
this is the type of individuation that Marx judges to be possible in a modern
society only as a semblance, a point that Horkheimer and Adorno flesh out
one hundred years later when they argue that the modern, enlightened ego has
been conditioned by the post-mythical reality principle to accept the discipline
of the social roles it finds itself subject to, and to conceive of its autonomy—
which Horkheimer and Adorno, like Marx, think is an unmediated, false reconciliation between particular and universal—as a matter of smoothly navigating
through the apparent plenitude of (mostly consumerist) social roles that the
culture industry makes available. Given that Habermas accepts at least the surface definition of this problem, he must have some reason for thinking that it
is nevertheless possible for individuals to have a two-sided, appropriative relationship to their social roles. Individuals must, he writes, "themselves generate
their socially integrated forms of life by recognizing each other as autonomous
subjects capable of action and, beyond this, as individuated beings who vouch
for the continuity of the life histories for which they have taken responsibility"
(199). Such thoughts are not exactly new with Habermas—it is, rather, the
"social philosophy" tradition that gives the slogan "no one is free unless everyone is" a plausible, secular meaning: autonomous personhood is in some way
something for individuals to accomplish or not, but one whose prospect for
success depends on the availability of socio-cultural practices stable and reciprocal enough to garner mutual recognition. What he, along with Hegel, wrestles
with more deeply than most is the question of what this all could mean for
the real world not just of socialization practices, but also, political institutions.
Habermas has in mind that persons individuated through mutual recognition
must occupy some culturally or institutionally anchored vantage point from
which their plethora of roles and action types, their place in some larger totality
that makes these roles and activities available to them, can be comprehended
as a reasonable way for a community to organize social cooperation among free
and equal persons.

The suggestion that I would like to put forward here is that this process of politically configuring social roles, together with Habermas' suggestion that autonomy depends on the individual forging some kind of rational identification with this process, plays a role equivalent to that of the ego ideal in Horkheimer and Adorno's appropriation of Freud. As described in Chapter 2, Horkheimer and Adorno draw from Freud the idea that the autonomy of the ego to some large degree depends on its relationship to the disciplinary force that the superego brings to bear on behalf of society: is that relationship transparent, rationally reconstructable, interactive and revisable, or is it essentially opaque and one-sided? While they think that, in general, the modern, enlightened ego tends to be alienated from its instinctual drives, Horkheimer and Adorno extrapolate from Freud the more specific point that the ego ideal (which usually begins as an idealized representation of a father-like figure) is the portion of the superego most likely to manifest the former set of "good" qualities—but they further argue that the process of subject formation in the culture industry of post-liberal capitalism tends to lack the mediation of an ego ideal and be more a matter of the direct imposition of opaque demands to think in abstraction and adapt to role expectations. As we will see, Habermas thinks that this is not inevitable, and that it is possible for modern individuals to reflectively shape their own conceptions of who they are in relation to a discursive, democratic process of configuring social roles through which they are incorporated into systems of action; this, I will argue, is the essential core of Habermas' conception of reconciliation between individuality and sociality. Plainly, it depends not only on a certain construal of the democratic political process, but also on a conception of subject formation that would support the idea, contrary to Horkheimer and Adorno's, that the modern subject is formed in such a way as to be able to engage with its social roles in a reflective, dialogical, non-coercive way and thereby cultivate its freedom. Displayed here is an argumentative trope that one sees often with Habermas, especially when considering his relationship to the first generation of the Frankfurt School: he takes what is, for someone like Adorno, an issue about elemental processes of subject formation, for which political solutions are all but foreclosed, and treats it as an issue of social organization amenable to political interventions. Since I have already indicated in Chapter 2 that there is a good deal of plausibility to the way Horkheimer and Adorno employ Freudian ego psychology to underwrite sweeping Lukácsian claims about the pervasiveness of reification, we will have to ask whether Habermas' conceptualization of the political configuration of social roles as functionally equivalent to the role of the ego ideal in the development of autonomous ego identity is credible.

If they are to operate as functional equivalents to an ego ideal, the degree to which genuine cultures of self-determination and self-realization are developing in modern societies is unclear. But given the way in which Habermas thinks of the socialization processes that develop autonomous personhood as dependent upon the rational and responsive configuration of social roles through the political process, many of his reflections on the political structure of modern states are not encouraging. Like his predecessors, he affirms that modern societies are characterized by a divisive class structure that has been "repoliticized" in the sense that it owes its existence to extensive state intervention and administrative maintenance. At the same time, it is "depoliticized" by the anonymity of bureaucratic systems that maintain it, as well as an apparent lack of viable alternatives to the current system. If an acceptable, traditional justification for social stratification is lacking, the absence of open class conflict does not quell the demand for legitimation and/or transformation to address inequality and exclusion. The idea of democracy as responsive and participatory implicitly promises to address this demand, but such a thing is perpetually deferred in technocratic mass democracies, leading to a non-mediational form of social integration based, in the last analysis, on distorted or foreshortened communication (LC, 23, 36).[10] Meanwhile, the political system seems to have the steering capacity to contain the worst crisis tendencies of the capitalist mode of production.[11] The end result is an appraisal reminiscent of Adorno's "gang warfare" characterization of social conflict: unequal and antagonistic structures are sustained by political "pseudo-compromises" between classes, which are not rationally satisfying in that they take the partial interests of opposed groups (i.e., their interests *within the context of the system*) as given and fail to explore possibilities for uncovering generalizable interests (112–113).[12]

None of this is to downplay the significant renovation of critical theory that Habermas has undertaken since the late 1960s, as it has great significance for his later legal theory.[13] Notable in this regard, Habermas is leery of a point

[10] Habermas updates and reaffirms this conclusion in "Further Reflections on the Public Sphere," in *Habermas and the Public Sphere*, ed. Craig Calhoun (Cambridge, MA: MIT Press, 1992), 429–441.

[11] Habermas acknowledges that the 2008 financial crisis, and subsequent global recession, throws the solidity of this assumption into question. See *Europe: The Faltering Project*, trans. Ciaran Cronin (Malden, MA: Polity, 2009), 184–197.

[12] See also TRS, 102. In discourse theory's more evolved iterations, bargaining and compromise *can* be legitimate, but only if modes of consensual decision-making on the basis of shared interests are genuinely unavailable and the need for a collectively binding resolution is pressing; see BFN, 168–186.

[13] I do not attend here to the role of Habermas' "linguistic turn" in understanding his distance from the critical theory's first generation, although it clearly has importance in this regard. See Seyla Benhabib, *Critique, Norm, and Utopia: A Study in the Foundations of Critical Theory* (New York: Columbia University Press, 1986), 224–278; Axel Honneth, *The Fragmented World of the Social*, ed. Charles Wright (Albany: SUNY Press, 1990), 92–120; and Peter Uwe Hohendal "From the Eclipse of Reason to Communicative Reason and Beyond," in *Critical Theory: Current State and Future Prospects*, eds. Peter Uwe Hohendal and James Fisher (New York: Berghahn Press, 2001), 3–28.

that Adorno often seems convinced of: if Adorno suspects that individuals in late capitalism are so overwhelmed by "abstract," reified institutional domination that they are nearly ceasing to be centers of spontaneous action altogether (MM, 123–124), Habermas insists that the reproduction of large swathes of social life continues to hinge on achievements of uncoerced mutual understanding through ordinary language, which has an interpersonal, recognitional structure that renders it resistant to reification. Those aspects of societal modernization, then, that increasingly demand that actions be coordinated on the basis of discursively redeemed validity claims represent a distinct form of social evolution, corresponding to the development of universalistic moral outlooks and democratic decision-making, and which is related to, but separate from, the development of sophisticated forms of instrumental rationality (CES, 95–129). The unfortunate hitch in Enlightenment forecasts is that social evolution along the former track by no means necessarily accompanies the latter, which has, in fact, outpaced and supplanted the former.

Given the rather extreme-sounding nature of *Dialectic of Enlightenment*'s conclusions, one can understand how Habermas' moves could garner a sympathetic readership. He accuses Horkheimer and Adorno of completely missing "the rational content of cultural modernity," which demands a continuous process of self-reflection in the arts and sciences, social organization, and the administration of law, and belies the picture of impotent subjects suspended in frozen relations of domination (PDM, 113). Although we can credit Habermas with enriching the critical theory tradition by articulating a framework that elucidates the liberating power of reflection without denying that societal rationalization can lead to Weber's "iron cage," there is another level at which he simply does not engage with Horkheimer and Adorno: presumably Horkheimer and Adorno are not unaware that there is communication and reflection going on in "cultural modernity," but they are arguing that this reflection does not penetrate into the structural interrelations of the psyche itself as "real, human emancipation" would require, since the basic mode of subject formation characteristic of the modern reality principle very early on alienates ego from instinctual nature and subjects it to the discipline of a superego centered around, not an ego ideal, but the depersonalized schematism of the culture industry.

When Habermas discusses these issues, his preferred reference point is George Herbert Mead's social psychology, in particular, the relationship between the "I" (as the center of spontaneous urges and drives) and the "me" (the sense of one's self as it relates to others) (PT, 177–182). This, more than his appeals to the potentials of the bourgeois public sphere, is his real counterpoint to the culture industry. Unfortunately, it relies on some simplifying abstractions. While from a Freudian perspective we need not deny Mead's point that individuals may largely acquire their sense of who they are from the "me" (roughly equivalent here to the superego), nevertheless the psychic architecture of Mead's "I" and "me" seems reductive, since it basically identifies superego with ego ideal—that is, the "me" represents the expectations and demands of sociality, generally, like the superego, but functions within the psyche like the ego ideal. For as much as Freud thinks that the relationship between the ego and ego ideal is fraught, bound as it is to the Oedipus complex, it can nevertheless enable the flowering of the ego's rational autonomy. However, we also saw that, crucially for Horkheimer and Adorno, the enlightened ego of post-liberal capitalism is not primarily oriented toward an ego ideal that the subject can develop an ongoing, reflective relationship to, but the opaquer and anonymous conditioning of the culture industry, to which the ego is simply exposed.

Since Habermas tends to identify superego with ego ideal and does not take very seriously the more one-sided, alienated construal of the ego-superego relationship that Horkheimer and Adorno think is the norm, he can hold that the structural interrelations of the psyche are open to reflective transformations that can extend into mature psychic life. In his most substantial discussion of Freud, this is all manifest: Habermas thinks Freud has a "scientistic" misunderstanding of his own work insofar as he tends to ontologize id, ego, and superego, treating them as different entities (KHI, 247–250).[14] Habermas, on the other hand, argues that the fact that a "talking cure" *can* be effective shows that these agencies are linguistically constituted—metapsychology does not need, and should not have, its own metalanguage, disconnected from the originary language through which the self (as ego) communicates with itself (as id) (265). Freud, Habermas adds, also tends to ontologize and reify the instinctual drives along similar lines, thinking of them as asocial and prelinguistic.[15] But, Habermas claims, in order for instinctual nature to enter the psychic economy of the linguistically socialized subject, it must be interpretable, i.e., in order to be affective, drives have to be at least potentially encountered as meaningful by the ego:

> Impulse potential, whether incorporated in social systems or suppressed instead of absorbed, clearly reveals libidinal and aggressive tendencies. This is why an instinct theory is necessary. But the latter must preserve itself from false objectivism. Even the concept of instinct that is applied to animal behavior is derived privately from the preunderstanding of a linguistically interpreted, albeit reduced human world: in short, situations of hunger, love, and hate. The concept of

---

[14] See also Ernst Tugendhat, *Self-Consciousness and Self-Determination*, trans. Paul Stern (Cambridge, MA: MIT Press, 1986).

[15] See Peter Dews, "The Paradigm Shift to Communication and the Question of Subjectivity: Reflections on Habermas, Lacan, and Mead," *Revue Internationale de Philosophie* 49, no. 4 (1995): 483–519.

instinct, when transferred back from animals to men, is still rooted in the meaning structures of the lifeworld, no matter how elementary they may be. They are twisted and diverted intentions that have turned from conscious motives into causes and subjected communicative action to the causality of "natural" conditions. This is the causality of fate, not of nature, because it prevails through the symbolic means of the mind. Only for this reason can it be compelled by the power of reflection. (256)[16]

The goal of analysis, as a specialized, depth-hermeneutic form of self-constituting reflection, is to *restore* communicative relations between psychic agencies, which have developed (through the repression of trauma) systems of private meaning indecipherable to the ego (255ff). Although the ego's capacities for intentionality and signification can apparently be influenced by archaic memories (id) and conditioning (superego) without its awareness, these things only enter into the psychic economy by being interpret-*able* in ordinary language. The successful restoration of channels of ordinary, public language between psychic agencies renders their structure and content (including, in principle, the difficult-to-access paleocontent of the id and superego) "communicatively fluid" (CES, 93).[17] Habermas' self is one that is primed for reconciliation—this makes his social psychology closer to Rawls' than Adorno's. Here, reconciliation is an essentially political task of institutionalizing reflection in the basic structure of society in a form that the subject could perceive, identify with, and appropriate in its drive for an integrated ego identity. This is admittedly a hugely difficult enterprise (and one that I argued Rawls neglects critical aspects of by not being attuned to the reification problematic), since Habermas does think that capitalist societies resist institutionalizing reflection across the basic structure of society, by spinning out nature-like systems of action.

There is, of course, much to be said about these signature pieces of Habermas' critical theory, but in this context, we can observe that maintaining them allows him to think of rationalization ("enlightenment") as potentially emancipating or dominating, *depending on how it is politically institutionalized.* He thus absorbs much of what Weber, Horkheimer, and Adorno say about the creeping nature of instrumental rationality (while implicitly denying that it affects the basic

---

[16] This is a point which Joel Whitebook has been especially critical of; see "The Marriage of Marx and Freud: Critical Theory and Psychoanalysis," in *The Cambridge Companion to Critical Theory*, ed. Fred Rush (New York: Cambridge University Press, 2004), 91–97, and *Perversion and Utopia*, 179–196.

[17] For criticism of Habermas' association of the communicative permeability of the psyche with autonomy, see Alford, *Narcissism*, 173ff; see also David McIvor, "Pressing the Subject: Critical Theory and the Death Drive," *Constellations* 22 (2015): 405–419.

structural interrelations of the psyche), and accepts that the modern state has the capacity to indefinitely contain economic crises without resolving class-based antagonism, while nevertheless maintaining that this form of social integration, which relies on stunted, deferred communication and pseudo-compromises, cannot be accomplished without cost.[18] Modern societies find themselves in a curious situation where demands for the discursive justification of the social structure are heightened—if Habermas is right that it has been repoliticized in late capitalism—yet the political system stubbornly "suppresses" open, potentially transformative communication concerning generalizable interests. Habermas reasons that societies so organized can expect to suffer chronically from "rationality crises," in which state policies fail to accommodate incompatible group interests, and "legitimation crises," in which citizens' spontaneous identification with the state's authority as consonant with their wills drops below a threshold to become, in Hegelian terms, an "external," "merely positive" system of command and authority (LC, 74ff).

2. Reification as Colonization: Habermas Between Lukács and Weber

Like his predecessors, Habermas views the latency of class conflict as a "reification effect": pseudo-compromises seem to be the best form of legitimation available in modern societies, to the extent that the class structure is naturalized and class-based injustices relatively invisible. He, however, has a rather different conception of reification than his predecessors, viewing it as a "colonization" of the communicatively integrated lifeworld by market and administrative systems that disrupt the "symbolic reproduction" of the lifeworld.[19] While I lack space here to give a full account of the way that Habermas uses these terms, the basic idea is that when some action coordination or socialization process previously dependent upon the achievement of mutual understanding through ordinary language is replaced by steering media (i.e., money or administrative codes), this *can* have pathological side effects, most notably in the forms of

---

[18] In this regard, Habermas takes his lead more from Marcuse than Weber-Horkheimer-Adorno, although Marcuse's reasons for thinking that society will not become *seamlessly* "one-dimensional" are more speculative, based on his revisionary appropriation of Freud's drive theory. See part 2 of Marcuse, *Eros and Civilization*, and *An Essay on Liberation* (Boston: Beacon, 1969).

[19] Despite the fact that Habermas concludes *Theory of Communicative Action* by making a conception of reification the centerpiece of his critical theory of society, few commentators emphasize this, focusing much more on aspects of the book like his universalistic theory of rationality, contributions to sociological action theory, and criticisms of Western Marxism. See, for example, the selection of topics in Honneth and Joas, eds., *Communicative Action*.

discontent and disconnection (alienation, anomie, etc.) (TCA2, 140–148).[20]
Since *rationalization* only crosses into *reification* if it disrupts symbolic reproduction, and because whether or not it does is, he reckons, an empirical
question, there are no a priori criteria for distinguishing the two. Nor can reification be identified with a distinct phenomenology, as it manifests in a variety of fatalistic worldviews; instrumentalized self-concepts; anomic distress;
and so on.[21] I am not inclined to view these features as shortcomings in and
of themselves: rejecting the all-or-nothing nature of the Lukácsian approach
implies that the intrusion of formal codes and logics of exchange into everyday
life should not be criticizable as such, but only to the degree that it shifts the
balance between communication and abstract domination in the reproduction
of an area of social life in such a way that tends to atomize and depoliticize the
perception of social suffering. Although Habermas does not much address either the phenomenology of reification or the process through which anomic
suffering becomes an "effect" of it, Honneth's models of misrecognition and
social pathology (more so than his own more phenomenologically attuned
theory of reification) can be put to good use here:[22] reification tends to render
persons ill-equipped to grasp the extent to which individual outcomes and
circumstances are impacted by group conflict (or in extreme cases, the existence of such impacts in the first place), producing the likelihood that feelings of
injury and frustration will be misdirected or internalized.[23] All that said, these
departures from Lukács come at a price: although we had cause to be critical of
his position, Lukács does not merely assert that reification is a totalizing phenomenon: he thinks that it possesses a self-reinforcing dynamic. Although he
believes reification to be rooted in commodity exchange, institutional patterns
(law, bureaucracy, administration) and intellectual life (jurisprudence, social science) are manifestations of it, in addition to the subjective stance most
readers associate with reification. Altogether, this causes reification to saturate
the social world while creating a nexus of conditioning that is nigh-impossible
to penetrate except for persons (i.e., workers) that experience the objectification of their labor. Horkheimer and Adorno, I argued, better substantiate this
perspective by elaborating how the dialectic of enlightenment culminates in
the formation of a social subject geared to adapt itself to a social reality that it

[20] The "can" is notable here, since it represents a departure from the Lukácsian conception of
reification, wherein patterns of modern rationalization (in law, administration, culture, etc.) are fundamentally rooted in the commodity structure, and therefore by nature reifying.

[21] Rahel Jaeggi's *Alienation*, trans. Frederick Neuhouser (New York: Columbia University Press,
2014) goes a long way toward capturing this phenomenology in an ecumenical spirit.

[22] See Zurn, "Social Pathologies as Second Order Disorders," in *Axel Honneth: Critical Essays*,
345–370.

[23] Neumann's "Anxiety and Politics" contains an interesting precursor to this idea.

receives as merely given—in other words, reification takes root in the process of socialization. I recall this analysis here in order to point out that, if there is anything to it, Habermas' perspective on reification is likely to give it short shrift, since he picks up at the point where the nominalization and de-signification of social phenomena has discernible consequences for societal reproduction. This probably does not seem like much of a problem to Habermas, since as we have just seen, his construal of the self allows him to think that reification does not operate in the structural interrelations of the psyche itself—again, the issues raised by Adornian reflections on subject formation are taken up by Habermas as ones about social organization. Independent of whether these are defensible moves within social psychology, however, they will come back to haunt Habermas, as they tend to empty out any notion of an emancipatory interest being at stake in the process of overcoming reification through reconciliation.

Despite significant departures from the Marx-Lukács all-or-nothing take on the conditions for social freedom, it should be stressed that the basic architecture of Habermas' theory is very Lukácsian: for both, a fundamental level of normatively regulated, rational, human sociality (social labor for Lukács, communication for Habermas) is overlaid with (and potentially supplanted or "colonized" by) autonomous systems of instrumental action. Habermas is more catholic than most of his predecessors in holding that markets and administrative systems may equally produce reification effects. Although more inclined than Lukács to see legal-administrative rationalization as the dominant form that this overlay takes (TCA2, 338–343), what more starkly separates him from the tradition of Western Marxism is—given the ambiguity of his conception of societal rationalization—the relative sanguinity with which he regards this legally enabled spread of systems rationality, which apparently shares more with Weber than with Lukács, et al.

On the whole, Habermas' account of modern legal development is indebted to Weber, for whom the spread of markets and bureaucratic systems is an inexorable tendency of an increasingly complex world, and while Weber allows that we may regret its side effects (i.e., diminishing the prospects for public freedom and ethical orientation as a result of "the disenchantment of the world" and "the iron cage")[24], he regards it as normatively unimpeachable in the sense of being both rational and inevitable. A critic of "ultimate values," Weber resists the idea that modern legal administration should be justified by reference to "external" moral criteria. Instead, law's legitimacy stems from its formal rationality, i.e., its coherence in treating like cases alike. A striking aspect of Weber's account of legal validity is his de-emphasis of the importance

---

[24] See Weber, *The Protestant Ethic and the Spirit of Capitalism*, trans. Talcott Parsons (New York: Routledge, 1992), 155–183.

of justifications for laws' enactment, e.g., through public deliberations, parliamentary procedures, etc. Legitimacy instead stems directly from conformity to standards of "legality."[25]

Weber contends that this perspective is inescapable: for social orders to function over time, participants need to regard the norms to which they are subject as de facto legitimate. Educated news consumers can have some sense of the body of law particularly relevant to their situation, major past and pending legislation, highlights of constitutional history, etc. But overall, individuals are impacted by a bewildering amount of law, with new legislation added all the time by an array of legislative and administrative agencies. Practically speaking, they usually know very little about the "economic and social conditions" shaping social outcomes—as Weber comments, the "primitive" knows "infinitely more" about such things. And if we think about it (which Weber assumes we usually do not), the origins, purposes, and justification of most law is quite obscure:

> Once a rule is familiar practice, the meaning more or less uniformly intended by the founders can be so completely forgotten or concealed through change in meaning that only a minute fraction of judges and attorneys grasp the "purpose" for which complicated legal norms have been agreed upon or imposed.[26]

We can only cope with this obscurity by accepting it:

> Inevitably, the notion must expand that the law is a rational technical apparatus, which is continually transformable in light of expediential considerations and devoid of all sacredness of content. This fate may be obscured by the tendency of acquiescence in the existing law, which is growing in many ways for several reasons, but it cannot really be stayed.[27]

What could motivate this acquiescence? The best case that Weber makes for its rationality is an appeal to a thin version of Hegelian ethical life, i.e.,

> the generally established *belief* that the conditions of civilized everyday life, be they the streetcar or lift or money or court of law or military or medicine, are in *principle* rational, that is, are human artifacts accessible to rational knowledge, creation, and control.[28]

[25] See the critique of Weber on this point in TCA1, 264–267, which I largely follow here.
[26] Weber, "On Some Categories of Interpretive Sociology," *Sociological Quarterly* 22, no. 2 (1981), 178.
[27] Weber, *Economy and Society*, vol. 2, 895.
[28] Weber, "On Some Categories of Interpretive Sociology," 179.

In other words, law's legitimacy rests on little more than our sense that it is based, somewhere down the line, on efficient technologies and reliable knowledge. Weber is convinced that this is a fate for elites to face bravely and the masses to half-consciously accept.[29]

While Habermas accepts a good deal of this as a description of legal development, his stoicism regarding the tendency toward obscurity does not extend nearly so far. Habermas, on the contrary, has long defended the thesis that any society featuring group-based stratification in status, wealth, and power is subject to functional demands for legitimation, on the hypothesis that participants in social systems that produce unequal outcomes require justification for this inequality as a condition for their compliance, in the long run (CES, 178–188). Traditionally, such requirements have been met by overarching (usually religious) worldviews—Marx's "ideology in general." However, Habermas contends that the differentiation of society into lifeworld and market and administrative subsystems, along with the functional differentiation of the lifeworld itself into specialized discourses, prevents modern societies from being graspable (and hence, legitimated) through "basic religious and metaphysical concepts" (TCA2, 189; BFN, 66–75). This point will become very significant momentarily: the idea is that traditional societies remain traditional in their mode of production and culturally stable over often long periods of time due to a) a shared sense of the sacred, which restricts the scope of actions that either can or must be justified reflexively, as opposed to being ascribed by authority; and b) the fact that boundaries between the realm of the sacred and everyday practice are relatively indistinct. This is not to say that a metaphysical/religious/cosmological worldview in a traditional society cannot be enormously complicated, subject to local variation; but it *is* to assert that such worldviews do manage to explain the interrelation of various institutions, social classes, practices, etc., through a sacred narrative upon which there is significant consensus. If something like Hegel's ethical life could perform an equivalent function in modern society (with its sharp separation between social spheres with different and incompatible action types), it could only recoup a sense of unity in a much more procedural, formal way, and at a more abstract level, than traditional sacred narratives do.[30] Again, Durkheim's distinction between mechanical and organic solidarity captures this point well.

[29] See Weber, "Politics as Vocation," in *From Max Weber*, 77–128.

[30] Lukács also has this idea in his early work, where he contrasts classical epic to the modern novel: the former is capable of expressing a social totality (e.g., a sense of what the Greeks were all about as a civilization), whereas, at its highest, the latter discloses fracture and alienation. See Lukács, *Theory of the Novel*. For accounts that links this theme from Lukács' earlier career as a cultural critic to his later Marxist social theory, see Martin Jay, *Marxism and Totality*, 81–127; and Jay Bernstein, *The Philosophy of the Novel: Lukács, Marxism, and the Dialectics of Form* (Minneapolis: The University of Minnesota Press, 1984), 44–76.

If tradition, religion, and ideology cannot furnish a comprehensive, publicly shared sense of the modern legal-political order's legitimacy, this raises the question of how and whether these functional demands are being met. Following from the above conclusions, and in accord with Weber, Habermas accepts that the only ultimately stable, publicly shareable source of the modern social order's legitimacy is the rational acceptability of legal decision-making procedures, rather than some conviction that it reflects a substantial moral order (as with religious ideas of social order, secular natural law, etc.) (TCA2, 178).[31] And yet, against Weber, Habermas insists that this acceptance needs to be a continuously renewed achievement based on intersubjective justification, not a mere background assumption "normatively ascribed" on the basis of the legal order's putative rationality and necessity—or rather, to the extent that such a demand *can* be met by the latter sort of technocratic ideology, this cannot *per hypothesis* be accomplished without dysfunctional consequences (LC, 113; BFN, 436).

It is within this context that Habermas offers his own take on the venerable Frankfurt School theme of the fate of transformative class dynamics in advanced capitalist societies: they are still, as Marx held, structured by an unequal and antagonistic class structure. However, more than in Marx's time, these divisions are less the visible result of class conflict, than of a diffuse and anonymous system of administration, resulting in faded class-consciousness. Class-based exploitation continues to exist, but the discontent it engenders tends to be displaced—again, mainly into alienation and anomic social pathologies—rather than channeled directly into political discourse about what Habermas calls the crucial "interchange roles" between system and lifeworld of "employee and consumer" (economy), "client and citizen" (state): "conflicts that do not appear primarily in class-specific forms and yet go back to a class structure that is displaced to systematically integrated domains of action" (TCA2, 350). To the extent that the spread of the legal regulation that supplants more direct applications of social power is understood by those affected as an autonomous, quasi-natural process, the normative expectations of persons—in their roles as workers and consumers, citizens and state clients[32]—are (in Habermas' somewhat ambiguous phrase)

[31] The issue of whether it makes sense to regard procedures and "substance" as sufficiently distinguishable, such that procedures of discursive decision-making can be regarded as, in themselves, normatively valid, is a complicated issue in Habermas. See James Gledhill, "Procedure in Substance and Substance in Procedure: Reframing the Rawls-Habermas Debate," in *Habermas and Rawls: Disputing the Political*, eds. J. Gordon Finalyson and Fabian Freyenhagen (New York: Routledge, 2011), 181–199. See also Hedrick, *Rawls and Habermas*, 125–148.

[32] See Timo Jütten, "The Colonization Thesis: Habermas on Reification," *International Journal of Philosophical Studies* 19, no. 5 (2011): 701–727. I am indebted to this piece overall, but in particular for underscoring the importance of the interchange roles in Habermas' theory.

"normalized," i.e., "rendered innocuous" as sites of contestation and democratic self-determination (TCA2, 349).[33]

If this is correct, it follows that administratively driven reification tends to neutralize recognition of social power operating through legislation and adjudication: the immediate appearance of inequality is the product of largely opaque forces operating through institutions that present themselves (as with Kennedy's "legitimation effect") as fair, just, and/or apolitical in the sense of being above the partisan fray. It is in this regard that Habermas' statements about class conflict becoming "normalized" are so potentially misleading: it may be the case that along with the amelioration of pauperization in advanced capitalist societies accomplished by the welfare state, the legal mediation of class conflict has neutralized it as the sort of transformative social conflict that so much Marxist theory held it to be. But at the same time, it has diminished the scope for democratic self-determination by ossifying and naturalizing the interchange roles through which persons participate in systemically organized domains of action, which in turn undermines, as Honneth puts it, "the communicative infrastructure which is the basis of a cooperative mobilization and elaboration of feelings of injustice" (D, 89).[34] This is certainly a discouraging conclusion, but it seems unnecessary to draw the further one—which Habermas admittedly suggests in *Theory of Communicative Action*, as well as subsequent writings that seem to treat low-simmering class conflict as a fixed reality—that this "normalization" is such a firmly established feature of modern societies that social movements could not persuasively ascribe greater political agency to the existence of unequal outcomes that are presently seen as the quasi-natural result of legal administration.

Readings of Habermas' application of the system-lifeworld conception of society to critical theory often understand it as circumscribing the possibilities for effective political contestation to only include publicly recognized lifeworld disruptions (e.g., this is what "New Social Movements" are supposed to be about [TCA2, 391–396]). This is misleading for two reasons: a) while the

---

[33] In what appears to be a break from the Marxian tradition, Habermas contends that the normative expectations for remuneration and recognition centering around the roles of employee and state client are more fungible than the ones around consumer and citizen roles, largely because the former pair are more fully defined by "legal fiat," whereas the latter, while "organizationally dependent," ineluctably involve the exercise of subjective preferences that cannot be wholly programmed; see TCA2, 322. See, however, RCP, 171–172, where Lukács makes the point that the reification resulting from bureaucratic systems of administration may be more stubbornly entrenched in consciousness than that engendered by markets, for much the same reason. I am uncertain how this squares with Habermas' thesis that current (late 1970s, early 1980s) protest potentials are clustered around the client interchange.

[34] On "disturbed normative expectations" as initiating spurs for moral discourse, see MCCA, 48.

distinction between system and lifeworld itself is piece of generally applicable social theory, most of what Habermas says in *Theory of Communicative Action* about social movements amounts to an assessment, circa 1980, of where potentially transformative social conflict is taking place, and given that he judges them to be located at system-lifeworld interchanges, to his mind this current state of play lends credence to his theory of society. But, b) this assessment, if accurate, is not a natural fact about where transformative social conflict is possible—the fact that some forms of inequality, deprivation, exclusion, and denigration are either not experienced as political injustices or, if they are, are not articulable in a widely resonant way, is to some degree (it is hard to say in advance, or in general, how much) due to reification effects: interchange roles have become naturalized. As I shall emphasize later, *this* is a huge problem that a critical theory of society should be very concerned with. If Habermas minimizes or elides this point, he should be criticized for it, although I do not think reversing this elision requires denying anything essential about the system-lifeworld theory of society, or the colonization thesis. Moreover, it can be hard to understand the impetus, or appreciate the distinctive appeal, of the positions Habermas stakes out in the discourse theory of law and democracy without bringing this problem to the fore.

In order to set the stage for this argument, let us briefly bring together several ideas that propel discourse theory's diagnosis and aspirations. First, Habermas is elaborating a social theoretic position triangulated among Rousseau and Hegel, on the one hand, and Horkheimer and Adorno, on the other. He clearly sides with the latter pair at some level of empirical description: modern societies are integrated to a significant extent by way of a mass of "abstract" institutional power that obscures group conflict; they are highly fractured and differentiated in a way that threatens the autonomy of the individual. However, reason itself has not broken apart into mutually inscrutable subsystems; anchored in natural language and oriented toward mutual understanding, it draws on idealizations of transparent communication that overshoot particular contexts (PT, 115–148). Hence, there is a moment in Habermas that is very un-Marxian: for Marx and Lukács, the fact that civil society is a world of class conflicts means that the universalistic discourse of citizenship found in Hegel and Rousseau is bound to be a sham—a genuinely universalistic mode of being related to others could only come about in a classless society. For Habermas, however, the fact that existing social reality is conflict-riven does not foreclose the possibility of universalistic discourses that justify norms through the articulation of generalizable interests—socialization processes that still take place through ordinary language bear enough of a trace of existing reason to make this possible.

On the other hand, Habermas seeks to avoid the sort of naiveté that arguably prevails in Rousseau (and in a subtler way, as I argued in Chapter 3, Rawls), where such a universalistic discourse (e.g., the general will) is capable of shaping the polity's basic organizational norms while hovering behind the institutions of government like a spectral presence. In order to actualize any of its meditational potential on a society-wide scale, Habermas, like Hegel, holds that universalistic discourse must be concretized in positive institutions. But this proves to be tremendously problematic for him to acknowledge, given the degree to which he follows Weber, Horkheimer, and Adorno in viewing modernity's public institutions as dominated by functional rationality. So, the struggle to find a credible institutional anchor for rational discourse concerning generalizable interests has been a difficult one. After downgrading initial hopes that a revitalized bourgeois public sphere might play this role, Habermas spent the bulk of two decades developing his theory of communicative action, which seems to hold that rationality continues to have a universalistic, emancipatory moment that sadly lacks an immanent basis in the social structure of modernity.

3. From Estates to Interchange Roles: The Nexus of Social, Critical, and Normative Theory

But even as a conclusion about Habermas' work from *The Structural Transformation of the Public Sphere* through the end of the 1980s, this is a simplifying one. To illustrate, consider how Habermas' interchange roles could (if not subject to reification effects) function in a manner that in important ways resembles Hegel's Estates. The Estates, recall, mediate between particular individuals (their needs, abilities, statuses, and values), and the larger economic and political systems into which their actions are incorporated. They do this by providing an institutionally anchored vantage point from which individuals become cognizant of how their particularity contributes to the universal. The Estates are normative in the double sense of being prescriptive (i.e., giving one a sense of the particular values and conduct appropriate to one's estate) and recognitive (i.e., giving a sense of what one is owed, in terms of esteem and material security for one's particular contribution), and Hegel holds that the harmonious interplay of state and market systems depends on participants internalizing these responsibilities and expectations. Although Habermas' frequent use of system-theoretic language of "autonomous" systems of "norm-free sociality" can cloak this point, the presence of normatively laden interchange roles shows that his view cannot just be that individuals are plugged into mediatized systems of action, which then operate solely according to their own logic and momentum (TCA2, 15):[35] systems

---

[35] This phraseology is unfortunate in that critics have honed in on it, taking it to imply that Habermas is resigned to markets and thinks that there lacks a basis for criticizing fairly extensive use of them. See Thomas McCarthy, *Ideals and Illusions: On Reconstruction and Deconstruction in*

need to coax semi-voluntary performances to function, and the internalization of interchange roles facilitates this, just as the disappointment of normative expectations associated with them can create dysfunctions, either in the systems themselves, or in the form of anomic social pathologies.[36]

By conceiving of the Estates as positive, political institutions, Hegel makes the state directly responsible for addressing such disruptions in the satisfaction of internalized role expectations. Clearly, there are some significant differences here with Habermas' interchange roles, since the latter are more general (most everyone inhabits them, in one way or another), not institutionalized in this directly positive manner, and thus do not confer the same sense of belonging: the social identity conferred by estate membership contributes to the concreteness central to Hegel's notion of freedom, something with no direct analog in Habermas. But one of the reasons that makes overcoming the sense that the Estates are authoritarian institutions difficult is that membership in them involves the ascription of a concrete identity, which, while not fully determinative, is nevertheless prescriptive in terms of occupation, lifestyle, and ethical values. For Habermas, on the other hand, the modernization processes associated with the ambiguous, liberating-yet-dislocating phenomena of the decline in the public authority of traditional worldviews creates a context in which being self-determining and -realizing is both an individual responsibility and diffuse cultural expectation.[37] If Hegel hopes that persons will become reconciled to contingency and role differentiation through inclusion in traditional organizations like estates, for Habermas any similar such reconciliation must be an ongoing achievement among participants themselves—interchange roles can abet this, but the division of labor between institutions and individuals has clearly shifted toward the latter.

Given that Habermas has settled on the view that class stratification and cultural pluralism are indefeasible consequences of the differentiation of society into system and lifeworld, this is a process that can never be completed. Modern persons are subject to a complex division of labor, sometimes-Kafkaesque bureaucratic and market systems, and a class structure that, if not wholly determinative of life prospects, nevertheless massively impacts them. It is through the interchange roles that individuals conceive of themselves as (to some minimal

Contemporary Critical Theory (Cambridge, MA: MIT Press, 1991), 152–180. Honneth, for example, repeatedly quotes this phrase when contrasting Habermas' understanding of markets to his own conception of them as "orders of recognition." See RR, 251; IW, 58–63; FR, 190ff.

[36] As Heath points out, Habermas does tend to assume that these sorts of breakdowns of symbolic reproduction inevitably result in a more Kafkaesque/alienated world, rather than a Hobbesian/chaotic one; see "System and Lifeworld," 89.

[37] See Joel Anderson, "Autonomy, Agency, and the Self," in *Jürgen Habermas: Key Concepts*, 90–111.

degree) voluntarily participating in these (to some degree divisive and unequal) structures: they norm behavior and shape expectations (for preference satisfaction, material security, public esteem, civic participation, etc.) that can be satisfied or frustrated. Reconciliation with one's integration into these systems crucially hinges on the ability to conceive of one's self as a participant in a political process that aims at the rational, consensual organization of the domains of work and consumption, citizenship and the regulation of the public and private spheres for the common good, in a way that reasonably balances competing interests, and more ambitiously, seeks to articulate generalizable interests among differently positioned and abled others—or at least discloses the possibility of such a thing. It is mainly through the political configuration and contestation of these interchange roles that the class and status inequality we are subject to can appear as something other than just a "second nature," a cruel or fortunate contingency, and therefore something that reconciliation with can appear as a (no doubt fraught) possibility.

This is, to be sure, not a new idea for Habermas. In 1971, he writes:

> [I]n an industrially advanced society private autonomy can be maintained and assured only as a derivative of a total political organization. The rights to freedom, property, and security . . . are based on an integration of the interests, of all the organizations acting in relation to the state, and in turn controlled by an internal as well as external public sphere. This integration has to be continually constituted in a democratic manner. (TP, 117)

A decade later, in *Theory of Communicative Action*, Habermas specifies the system-lifeworld interchanges as the mediators between particular individuals and organizations, and general interests embodied in the constitution and state, with the normative expectations attaching to the interchange roles being the site at which this "continual constitution" through democratic discourse ought to take place. The consciousness of oneself as active and included in this process would be as close to "reconciliation" with "totality" that Habermas (who is leery that functionally differentiated societies can be conceived along the lines of a "totality" at all)[38] allows. But even this seemingly weak version of reconciliation is blocked by reification effects: interchange roles are, as Habermas puts

---

[38] Although not without reservations; see Jürgen Habermas, "Questions and Counterquestions," in *Habermas and Modernity*, ed. Richard Bernstein (Cambridge, MA: MIT Press, 1985), 216: "I do not want to pass over in silence the fact that McCarthy and Whitebook both touch on a basic philosophical problem, which, if I am correct, still awaits an adequate resolution this side of Hegelian logic: How is it possible to weaken the claims of statements about totalities so that they might be joined together with stronger statements about general structures?" See also, Jay, *Marxism and Totality*, 462–509.

it, "rooted" in the lifeworld, meaning that their articulation, interpretation, internalization, etc.—and ultimately, the normative validity of the duties and entitlements they entail—are dependent upon shared understandings of situation types consensually developed through the use of natural language. But, the hypothesis of the colonization thesis is that the interchange roles start to appear as a "second nature," wholly determined by the functional requirements of the systems themselves, compelling individuals to understand themselves merely as subject to demands foisted upon them by systems of disparate action types with their own internal logics.

We find Habermas echoing Adornian thoughts on the opacity of the processes through which individual and society mutually constitute one another when reflecting on the naturalization of the interchange roles wrought by colonization:[39] one might predict that the injury and disrespect felt by individuals as a result of alienating labor and income inequality, commodified consumerism, bureaucratic paternalism, and the lack of meaningful opportunities for civic participation (among the dysfunctions possible at the site of the interchange roles) would force "competition between forms of social and systems integration" to "openly come to the fore." However, colonization has the effect of "preventing holistic interpretations [of society] from coming into existence" (TCA2, 355). Thus, to the extent that colonization shrouds possibilities for the interchange roles becoming sites of democratic discourse, inequalities and injuries resulting from the operation of market and administrative systems tend to become depoliticized rather than perceived as class-based injustices.[40]

Habermas' turn toward normative legal and political theory in the 1990s is often thought to represent more abandonment than continuation of the critique of reification. Although he has done some things to buttress this impression, it is neither necessary nor accurate. As we have just seen, Habermas accords with the long line of left Hegelian thought that views the freedom and autonomy of the individual as dependent upon reconciliation between the particularity of the individual and the demands of sociality.[41] Moreover, like Hegel, he views the possibility for such a thing as dependent upon the existence of some institutionally anchored perspective from which persons can perceive the group differences to which they are subject as being consensually configured. He eventually arrives at the thought that a society's legal constitution could offer

[39] See Adorno, "Reflections on Class Theory," 97.

[40] Relatedly, this is a large part of the reason that Lukács believes that persons with reified conceptions of self and society cannot achieve genuine class-consciousness; see CC, 47–48, 52. See also Robert Castel, *From Manual Workers to Wage Laborers: Transformation of the Social Question*, ed. and trans. Richard Boyd (New Brunswick, CT: Transaction Publishers, 2003).

[41] See Kenneth Baynes, "Freedom and Recognition in Hegel and Habermas," *Philosophy and Social Criticism* 28, no. 1 (2002): 1–17.

this perspective, provided that it be understood, interpreted, and applied in a manner that counteracts the reifying effects that often result from the day-to-day operation of market and administrative systems—this would be as close to a re-covery of a "holistic interpretation" of society that could be conceived of under "postmetaphysical conditions." The impression exists that this intensified focus on normative legal theory and constitutional rights amounts to a reversion to a Rousseauian-Kantian model of politics, behind Hegel's suspicion of abstract universalism and Marx's critique of "the rights of man," and thereby retreating from the Hegelian aspiration toward a politically mediated reconciliation of the division of labor, and the Marxian one of contesting class domination. But this impression should begin to dissolve when we observe that Habermas, like Hegel before him, has a broad conception of constitutionalism that connotes the spine of institutions through which a society recognizes itself as an integrated whole:

> [The] problem of "law and freedom" cannot be solved without im-plicitly defining the roles the that the economy, as the basic functional system, and civil society, as the arena in which public opinion and po-litical will are formed, are supposed to play in relation to the adminis-trative powers of the state. (BNR, 328)

Thus, in order to actualize this mediational function, constitutional discourse should be seen as a vehicle for the ongoing construction of generalizable interests in the face of persistent cultural difference and class/status inequality.[42]

Before moving on to the topic of what, in light of the preceding, a proceduralist paradigm might mean for institutional structure and legal practice, I want to em-phasize that, on this reading, the Habermasian framework is most cohesive and aspirational if we treat the system-lifeworld interchanges as the connective hub between the system-lifeworld theory of society, a critical theory of reification as lifeworld colonization, and a normative discourse theory of democracy. The rec-onciliatory potential of a proceduralist paradigm of law requires conceiving of the interchange roles from the *Theory of Communicative Action* as contested sites of justificatory discourse, in a way that Habermas does not make plain, possibly because of the flanks of his position that he has been most concerned to defend. For example, a frequent criticism of his work is that the theory of communica-tive action, with its idealizing presuppositions and emphasis on consensus, is overly idealized.[43] This is an objection that Habermas has been at pains to serve rejoinders to, and as a result his legal and democratic theory has trended toward the thought that, however severe the normative presuppositions for genuinely

[42] See Dieter Grimm, "Integration by Constitution," *International Journal of Constitutional Law* 3, nos. 2–3 (2005): 193–208.

[43] See McCarthy, *Ideals and Illusions*, 181–199.

legitimate democratic deliberations may be, we ought not be overly idealistic in spelling out the conditions for the possibility of a proceduralist model of law—which always, after all, exists "between facts and norms"—being relevant to actually existing democracies. He hopes that it makes sense to think of existing constitutional orders as "self-correcting learning process[es]" where, at some level, there is a productive (if attenuated) interaction between the periphery of informal civil society and the legally constituted core. This interaction and development is supposed to ease the formulation of, and make the state responsive to, justice claims, amidst class stratification and cultural pluralism, rather than conceiving of overcoming those divisions as a precondition for any legitimate discourse, as the Marx-Lukács all-or-nothing model would have it.

There are two problems with this drift: a) it becomes easy to read more recent work as resigned to social stratification; and b) it becomes rather unclear what the "subjectless" circulation of political discourse in the ether between the informal communication at the periphery and the state has to do individual efforts to live self-determining, self-actualizing lives. Ambitious social justice advocates are likely to find (a) discouraging, whereas (early) Rawls and Honneth both do a better job of conveying the relevance of their theories to prospects for lived, individual freedom. Although I think (a) can be overstated as a criticism of Habermas and regard (b) as a persistent concern that I am not sure can be fully mollified within the framework of his theory, the way I am proposing to arrange its pieces intends to address both. We should be more clear that the stabilization of large-scale group conflicts over the appropriate expectations attached to employee/consumer and citizen roles (Habermas thinks that—again, circa 1980—dissatisfaction with welfare state paternalism *is* being articulated and contested)[44] is as much a cause for concern as celebration, so long as we think that this stabilization is based, at most, on pseudo-compromises, or at worst, on the interchange roles vanishing as topics on the political agenda due to reification effects. Probable consequences of these reification effects include social justice concerns becoming more intractable and socialization processes serving to internalize passive relationships between self and social roles that are deleterious to freedom.

While it would be implausible to hold that all current struggles for social justice can be conceived within its orbit, I hope to have credibly indicated why the conception of reification attaching to Habermas' system/lifeworld social

---

[44] See William Scheuerman, "Capitalism, Law, and Social Criticism," *Constellations* 20, no. 4 (2013): 571–586. I believe the line I am advancing here either mollifies Scheuerman's valid concerns about discontent with juridification syphoning away attention from economic injustice, or suggests the need for dereifying critique of consumer and employee interchange roles that have become naturalized through law, thereby exacerbating this lack of attention.

theory (which members of the post-Habermasian "third generation" of critical theory often give the impression of wanting to discard) has unexplored potentials and ought to play a vital role in critical social theory today: following Horkheimer, and more recently Nancy Fraser, we can agree that status-based hierarchies, rather than becoming relatively epiphenomenal as Marx predicted, are re-entwined with class-based exploitation in contemporary capitalist societies (RR, 54–59). Habermas may acknowledge the analytic dualism between distributional and recognitional justice claims that Fraser urges (BNR, 294)—after all, as we will see momentarily, the reflexivity in his proceduralist paradigm of law demands that participants themselves should be free to thematize their discontent with the laws that affect them in terms of denials of formal and/or material equality, depending on their experience.[45] But the integrated perspective on Habermas' theory developed here permits a kind of diagnostic/explanatory depth not present in his successors, for we can also employ his conception of reification to critically analyze possible reasons why such discontent may be hazily perceived by individuals and/or not effectively thematized at the group level. In this way, Habermas avoids the charge that Honneth levels at Fraser (which, in a way, mirrors the Horkheimer circle's trepidation toward Lukács), namely, that in abjuring an explanatory account of why social conflicts and experiences of injustice take the shape that they do (or fail to take shape at all), she hitches her theory to the actual mobilization of social movements, thereby "merely affirming the existing level of conflict" (RR, 134). Habermas' framework, however, can preserve the aspiration of Marxian critique to gather individual pathologies (e.g., alienation) and distributional injustice within the same theoretical framework, as does Honneth, but Habermas' stress on the legal system's role both in producing reification effects at the site of the interchange roles, as well as in orienting normative aspirations for reconciliation through these role expectations adds a level of historical/institutional specificity to the diagnostic end of the theory that Honneth tends to neglect. Finally, regarding the normative dimension, Habermas' assumption that class stratification is inevitable in functionally differentiated societies may or not be the case,[46] but drawing from Hegel's Estates model, I have also sought to show that modern states' aspirations for legitimacy substantially depend on ongoing efforts to configure differential statuses and material outcomes (if they cannot be presently overcome, altogether) in a reasonable and visible manner that strives for the construction of common goods and shared interests. As Hegel acknowledges, at least in moments, this may involve as much contestation as reconciliation. Seen

[45] See Fraser, *Scales of Justice*, 48–75.

[46] See Joseph Heath, "Habermas and Analytic Marxism," *Philosophy and Social Criticism* 35, no. 8 (2009): 891–919.

in this light, it would be desirable for class stratification to be politicized rather than normalized, and if, as Habermas' conceptual apparatus suggests, this normalization is a result of "juridification," then we need theoretical methods and practical strategies for highlighting the role of the legal system in the production of social inequality.

But we should also be aware, at this point, of the toll that Habermas's evasion of Horkheimer and Adorno's problem of the ego-superego relationship—by appealing to Mead and reducing the superego to the ego ideal—takes on any effort to articulate an emancipatory interest: it leaves him without much to say about (b). He sees no structural obstacle to individuals incorporating the "subjectless" circulation of communication into their construal of the ego ideal, but nor is there much to suggest that this will happen. Hegel and Rawls here appeal to ideas about affect: they think that being socialized in a community of mutual recognition produces sentiments of trust, patriotism, and solidarity that facilitate this incorporation, hence an identification of self with the substantial practices of mutual recognition in ethical life, hence reconciliation. Habermas has little inclination for this path—for him, it smacks of nationalism, is un-cosmopolitan, and appeals to notions of the good life or moral realism he seeks to avoid. His preference—and to this extent, interpretations of his theory as liberal and neo-Kantian ("Kantian republicanism") are not wrong—is to assess the basic structure of society in terms of whether it is worthy of identification through the democratic principle. But as I will indicate as this chapter progresses, Habermas shows that this assessment never achieves any repose. I will support this conclusion, but it makes the task of saying something about (b) more urgent, and the fact that Habermas has arranged things to excuse himself from addressing it becomes a real deficit in his approach.

4. Hegelian Constitutionalism-as-Mediation Revisited: Promising Ideas and Follow-through Problems in Habermas

Understanding that Habermas' discourse theory of law and democracy is motivated by a desire to unravel the normalization of class stratification and naturalization of system-lifeworld interchange roles belies the common impression that the move from the critical theory developed in *Theory of Communicative Action* to the rational reconstruction of *Between Facts and Norms* involves basically abandoning immanent critique. I want to argue that the constitutionally ordered legal system on display in the latter text comes to represent the vantage point from which persons' reconciliation with a social totality is disclosed as an ongoing possibility. While in some sense one system among others, the legal system has a special capacity to shape the environments of other systems, regulating their interaction. Of course, it is not the only system capable of affecting other systems' environments, but law is uniquely open to inputs from ordinary language, and thus potentially more pliant and responsive to democratic will formation: "Normatively substantive messages can circulate *throughout society* only in the language of law ... Law thus functions as the 'transformer' that guarantees that the socially integrating network of communication stretched across society as a whole holds together" (BFN, 56).[47] This allows for the possibility of the consensual, social regulation of domains ranging from the economy to the family where actors are presumed to be motivated by their private interests instead of respect for the law, while allowing persons directed toward such interests to nevertheless be cognizant that their privately oriented behavior is compatible with respect for generally valid norms. While we should be cautious about automatically viewing the constitution as the fulcrum of the legal order, its status as basic law is significant in this respect, for reasons explored in Chapter 1, with Hegel's distinction between a broad conception of constitutionalism and the narrow, "political" one. For, recalling Hegel's broad conception, constitutions not only define the structure of government and "the relationship between citizens and the state" (as with Hegel's "political" constitution): they also "implicitly prefigure a comprehensive legal order," that is, "the totality comprised of an administrative state, capitalist economy, and civil society" (BNR, 327–328). So, while these social spheres can be treated as distinct functional subsystems, their boundaries are legally defined in ways that affect their interaction: "The political constitution is geared to shaping each of these systems by means of the medium of law and to harmonizing them so that they can fulfill their functions as measured by a presumed 'common good'" (329–330). Thus, constitutional discourses should be less exclusively a matter of interpreting a positive legal text, and more an attempt to articulate legal norms that could shift the balance between these systems in a manner more reflective of generalizable interests.

A constitution's status as positive law is nevertheless important, also for fundamentally Hegelian reasons relating to his narrower sense of constitutionalism: its norms must be public and concrete, such that differently positioned citizens have at least an initial sense of what the shared hermeneutic starting points for discourse might be. But these concrete formulations should be understood to embody principles in the interests of all, so that constitutional discourse can be the site of effective democratic will formation concerning the basic norms that mediate between particular persons and the general interests of free and

---

[47] See Klaus Günther, "Legal Adjudication and Democracy: Some Remarks on Dworkin and Habermas," *European Journal of Philosophy* 3, no. 1 (1995): 36–54.

equal citizens. And this, in turn, recalls Hegel's point that while constitutions fulfill their mediational function by being sufficiently positive so as to be publicly recognizable, their substance cannot not be exhausted by this positivity—the content of the constitution is filled in through ongoing legislation. In order to avoid Hegel's foreshortened conception of public participation in this process, Habermas highlights the importance of being able to conceive of basic constitutional norms as themselves the products of public contestation and discourse. In order to elaborate this idea, he draws on legal theorists like Robert Cover and Frank Michelman who characterize this process of legal rearticulation as "jurisgenesis":[48] the production of legal meaning by way of a community's continuous rearticulation, through reflection and contestation, of its constitutional project's meaning.

Habermas explicitly conceives of the democratic legal order in such a way when, in the context of questioning how a constitution that confers legitimacy on ordinary legislation could itself be thought to be democratically legitimate, he writes:

> I propose that we understand the regress itself as the understandable expression of the future-oriented character, or openness, of the democratic constitution: in my view, a constitution that is democratic—not just in its content but also according to its source of legitimation—is a tradition-building project with a clearly marked beginning in time. All the later generations have the task of actualizing the still-untapped normative substance of the system of rights. (CD, 774)

A constitutional order and its interpretive history should represent a community's attempt to render the terms under which they can give themselves the laws that shape society's basic structure. Although rational reconstruction can provide a grasp of the presuppositions of a practice of legitimate lawmaking, this framework of presuppositions ("the system of rights") is "unsaturated" (BFN, 126). In Hegelian fashion, to be meaningful it must be concretized through actual discourse, and not in a one-off founding moment that fixes the terms of political association once and for all, but continuously, as new persons become included in the community, and new circumstances, problems, and perspectives emerge.

This point is obscured by the fact that, although he notes its circular, dialectical character, Habermas' shorthand represents the system of rights as if it were

---

[48] See Robert Cover, "*Nomos* and Narrative," in *Narrative, Violence, and the Law: The Essays of Robert Cover*, eds. Martha Minnow, Michael Ryan, and Austin Sarat (Ann Arbor, MI: University of Michigan Press, 1992), 95–172, and Frank Michelman, "Law's Republic," *The Yale Law Journal* 97, no. 8 (1988): 1493–1537. See also, Drucilla Cornell, "Institutionalization of Meaning, Recollective Imagination, and the Potential for Transformative Legal Interpretation," *University of Pennsylvania Law Review* 136, no. 4 (1988): 1135–1229.

the result of a presuppositional analysis of the conditions for legitimate popular sovereignty. To put a rather elaborate argument schematically, the rule of law figures in Habermas' account of democracy in the following way:[49] he distinguishes various forms of practical discourse (moral, ethical, pragmatic) that correspond to different validity claims (rightness, goodness/authenticity, efficiency/expediency). Although these discourse types have rules of argumentation specific to them, they share a generic concept of normative validity, which Habermas captures with his "discourse principle": "Just those actions are valid to which all possibly affected persons could agree as participants in rational discourse" (BFN, 107). He maintains that the possibility of persons coming to an understanding in a way that satisfies the discourse principle requires that they observe certain norms and be relatively confident that interlocutors will do likewise—otherwise it would not be worthwhile to engage in discourse in the first place. These include logical rules pertaining to the evaluation of arguments, but also norms with moral import: for example, participants must regard one another as rational and responsible persons, be open to topical inputs from their interlocutors, refrain from coercion or manipulation, and the like (MCCA, 56–68). If citizens are to view the political process as one that makes mutual understanding concerning the laws that govern them possible, they must be reasonably confident that such conditions are adequately satisfied in that process. At the most abstract level, citizens attain freedom and autonomy by institutionalizing the discourse principle in "the legal medium." This application generates a procedural standard of legislative legitimacy dubbed "the democratic principle": "only those statutes may claim legitimacy in a discursive process of legislation that has in turn been legally constituted" (BFN, 110). Simultaneously, institutionalizing the discourse principle necessitates an ongoing commitment to secure the conditions for a communicative lawmaking process. A constitution's function in this is to set out these conditions—this is the sense in which Habermas thinks of democracy and basic rights as "co-original." Actions by majorities that abrogate these conditions are unconstitutional (e.g., majorities cannot be regarded as legitimate if they limit franchise, manipulate elections, quash free speech, etc.): the integrity of majoritarian decisions requires that citizens respect one another as private persons responsible for their conduct and entitled to their individuality, that their right to access the process of collective will formation be secure, and that they have equal opportunities to make effective use of these freedoms.

At this point, though, an account of democracy that began by focusing on its procedural aspects is liable to start sounding something like Dworkin's, which insists that democracy cannot define the conditions for its own legitimacy.[50]

---

[49] See Hedrick, *Rawls and Habermas*, 103–124.
[50] Rawls makes a very similar point; see PL, 238–239.

For Dworkin, the moral authority of majoritarian procedures depends on the character of the political community in question. If it is constituted in such a way as to respect the freedom, equality, and independence of its members, it can claim legitimacy; if it is not, it cannot.[51] To return to terminology from Zurn, Dworkin (and Rawls, on my reading) has a "threshold" conception of legitimacy: certain substantive conditions must be satisfied in order for procedures to have legitimacy in the first place. But several features of his theory keep such a position at bay for Habermas: first, he argues that modern reason provides nothing like a "direct blueprint" for how to instantiate democratic community through concrete constitutional provisions, and there are no rationally intuitable or a priori constructible answers to questions about what rights democracy requires (BFN, 5)—their specification, at the very least, will vary in different times and places, and the question of whether citizens have the rights that they should have in order to license confidence in the rational acceptability of the legislative process' outcomes is subject to ongoing reasonable disagreement. Second, concrete moral and legal principles can only be justified through an actual process of discourse leading to rational acceptance among those affected by their observance.[52] And thirdly, discourse has a transformative effect on the need interpretations of affected parties, which should not be regarded as pre-political (T&J, 247–248). Philosophers and citizens are always *in medias res*: the democratic process depends on the prior embeddedness of individual rights securing public and private autonomy, yet we are constantly having to work out, using fallible reason within a presently compromised democratic process, what those rights are and how we should actualize them.[53] It would seem that there is no stance from which anyone can claim to know in any firm way whether the conditions of democratic legitimacy are adequately instantiated at a given place or time.

Now, this would be a rather large problem for Habermas if he maintained all of this in conjunction with a threshold conception of legitimacy: legitimacy would become a completely empty, indeterminate concept. But as Zurn has argued, legitimacy on the Habermasian account (and Hegel's as well) is a "developmentalist" conception operating as a "regulative ideal" toward which the legal system as a whole aspires. To the extent that it makes sense to think of legitimacy as something individual laws possess, it is a byproduct of being a procedurally valid result of a legitimate legal-political system. So far, this is

---

[51] See Ronald Dworkin, *Freedom's Law: The Moral Reading of the American Constitution* (Cambridge, MA: Harvard University Press, 1996), 15–20.

[52] See David Borman, "Actual Agreement Contractualism," *Dialogue* 54, no. 3 (2015): 519–539.

[53] See Simone Chambers, "Can Procedural Democracy Be Radical?" in *The Political*, ed. David Ingram (New York: Blackwell, 2002), 168–190; and Waldron, *Law and Disagreement*, 232–254.

similar to Rawls' principle of liberal legitimacy, but unlike Rawls, assessments of the legitimacy of the whole cannot depend on it firmly embodying substantive principles of justice at basic levels of social organization, but rather on our sense of how the legally and informally constituted dimensions of the political process develop, altogether and over time, to produce laws on the basis of communicatively achieved mutual understanding: "the procedures and communicative presuppositions of democratic opinion- and will-formation function as the most important sluices for the discursive *rationalization* of the decisions of an administration bound by law and statute" (BFN, 330, emphasis added; see also IO, 249–250). Elsewhere, he writes, "the permission for legal coercion must be *traced back* to the *expectation of legitimacy* . . . The positivity of law is bound up with the promise that democratic processes of lawmaking justify the presumption that enacted norms are rationally acceptable" (BFN, 33). I have emphasized the holistic, future- and process-oriented language in these formulations: the justifiable expectation that legislative outcomes will be rationally acceptable hinges upon a belief that the political system is constituted in a responsive way that channels legislation through discursive "sluices"—assessments of legitimacy are based on this constellation of expectations and beliefs. While not relative, such assessments are clearly debatable and holistic, dependent on interpretations of historical trajectories, i.e., whether a given constitutional order actually is unfolding as "a process of self-correcting attempts to tap the system of rights more fully" (CD, 776).[54]

The stakes involved in sustaining this sort of broad and inclusive constitutional discourse turn out to be significant, in ways that go beyond functional considerations of stability or formal ones of normative validity, since it should be clear by now that such discourse is the nodal center for generating the conditions for social freedom. Habermas has more recently invoked the concept of dignity in this regard, linking it to the process through which society politically constitutes itself as a reciprocal order of free and equal citizens. Internalized through status ascriptions rather than being an inherent/inherited property, the "dignity that accrues to all persons equally preserves the connotation of a *self-respect* that depends on *social recognition*" (CHD, 472). Rather than being understood as a quality some persons possess by virtue of their proximity to the divine, the modern universalistic conception of dignity is social status dependent upon ongoing practices of mutual recognition. Such practices, Habermas posits, are most fully instantiated in the role of citizens as legislators of the order to which they are subject.

> [Dignity] can be established only within the framework of a constitutional state, something that never emerges of its own accord. Rather,

---

[54] See Zurn, "The Logic of Legitimacy," 217–218.

this framework must be *created* by the citizens themselves *using the means of positive law* and must be protected and developed under historically changing conditions. As a modern *legal* concept, human dignity is associated with the status that citizens assume in the *self-created* political order. (473)

It should be noted that the implications of invoking dignity (as opposed to, say, autonomy) as the normative core of democratic constitutionalism are unclear: it appears to suggest a more moral-foundational account of the system of rights, which is not obviously compatible with the conception of procedural rationality that undergirds it.[55] But, plainly Habermas remains committed to strongly intersubjective conceptions of such things, an intersubjectivity that continues to be legally and politically mediated—a dimension largely absent in Honneth's successor theory of intersubjectivity, where identity-forming modes of recognition are politically regulated, but not on his reckoning politically constituted.

All of this suggests a role for constitutional politics that citizens are empowered to take part in, and which meaningfully impacts the terms of their cultural, economic, and political relations to each other. Such a politics would need to be considerably less legalistic and precedent bound, less focused on the democracy constraining aspects of constitutionalism than in most liberal rule of law models. The sense of incompleteness and revisability that marks this approach to constitutionalism represents a point at which it may claim to be more radical and revisionary than forms of liberal and deliberative democracy. It implies a sharp critique of more familiar models of bourgeois constitutionalism: whether they conceive of a constitutional order as having a foundation in moral rights or natural law, or in an originary founding moment, such models a) tend to be excessively backward-looking in their justifications, seeing the legal order as founded on an exogenously determined moral order; b) tend to represent the law as an already determined container, within which ordinary politics takes place; and c) represent the content of the law as ascertainable through the specialized reasoning of legal professionals. In Habermas' conception of constitutionalism, this presumption of completeness and technicity amounts to the reification of a constitutional project, where a dynamic social relation is misperceived as something fixed and objective.[56] And we can see why this should be immensely problematic for him: constitutional norms are supposed to concern the generalizable interests of free and equal citizens, and if it is overall the case that generalizable interests are at least partially constituted *through* discourse, and therefore not given in any pre-political sense (T&J, 266–271), this is especially so in a

---

[55] Habermas seems to recognize and defer this potential difficulty. See CHD, 470n10.
[56] See Warren, "Liberal Constitutionalism as Ideology."

society like ours with an unreconciled class structure sustained by pseudo-compromises. Therefore, discursive rearticulation of basic norms is necessary for the very emergence of generalizable interests.

Despite offering an admirably systematic synthesis of radical democracy and the constitutional rule of law, Habermas' theory is hobbled by the cautious way that he embraces these ideas. Given a commitment to proceduralism and the view that, in order for constitutionalism to perform its mediational function, actual discourses among those affected must take place during the production of legitimate law, as well as his opposition to foundational or backward-looking models of political justification, we might expect that Habermas would advocate constitutional discourses critically interrogating laws that structure the distribution of rights and social benefits to be circulating continuously and broadly in civil society, with some appreciable effect on the way constitutional projects develop through ongoing legislation. In that way, citizens should be able to see the links between their political constitution (narrowly construed), the effects that democratic discourse has on the shape that it takes, and the role of the political constitution in regulating and transforming the broader institutional skeleton of society in accordance with the common good. At least in the abstract, this is what the "two track" conception of democracy in *Between Facts and Norms*, with its model of discourses circulating between the informal public sphere and more formal legislative institutions, seeks to capture.[57] So, Habermas' version of constitutionalism seems a natural ally of theories of "popular constitutionalism"[58] from the American legal academy, or those skeptical of the merits of legalistic constitutionalism like Waldron's or Robin West's,[59] which press for democratic participation in the ongoing rearticulation of constitutional norms. Indeed, I would submit that the preceding pages demonstrate that the left Hegelian, social theoretic backdrop of Habermas' theory supplies a deeper normative justification for more democratic conceptions of constitutionalism than have heretofore been given by their proponents (who are, to be fair, primarily legal theorists seeking to uncover the basic commitments of American constitutionalism, a project more interpretive than normative)[60]. Given that such

---

[57] See BFN, chaps. 4, 7, and 8.

[58] See Larry Kramer, *The People Themselves: Popular Constitutionalism and Judicial Review* (New York: Oxford University Press, 2004).

[59] See Jeremy Waldron, "Constitutionalism—A Skeptical View," in *Contemporary Debates in Political Philosophy*, eds. Thomas Cristiano and John Christman (New York: Blackwell, 2009), 267–282. See also Robin West's arguments to the effect that progressive social justice agendas are, despite some landmark successes in the United States, hamstrung by the nature of adjudicative process: "Progressive and Conservative Constitutionalism," 713–721; and "Constitutional Skepticism," *Boston University Law Review* 72, no. 4 (1992): 765–799.

[60] See, for example, Michelman, "Law's Republic," 1500.

theories have revisionary views on the appropriate method and scope of judicial review, and the role of constitutions in public life, it is surprising that Habermas evinces a mild critique of the constitutional practices and institutions in actually existing democracies, and skirts around the likelihood that institutions of constitutional review administered by legal elites are paternalistic and undermine the impetus among the public for the actual discourses that he prizes.[61] In fact, institutional questions of where we would like to see constitutional discourse taking place and how the power to make authoritative determinations of constitutional meaning should be shared among civil society, legislative, and judiciary, are mostly abstracted away in Habermas' post-*Between Facts and Norms* writings, while that work is mostly content with the professional administration of constitutional issues as it exists in the United States and Germany.

Habermas does not present an independent theory of judicial decision-making, but, like Rawls, Dworkin's "law as integrity" is warmly received in his writings. To some extent, this affinity makes sense, given Dworkin's sensitivity to the hermeneutic dimension of interpretation and because his concept of integrity mirrors discourse theory in holding that legal decisions should be justifiable to those affected in terms of publicly recognizable principles. Habermas does follow Michelman in criticizing the "monological" reasoning that Dworkin's exemplary Judge Hercules employs (BFN, 222–225), replacing it with the interpretive activities of a specialized legal public sphere, which is presumably supposed to be more responsive to the public than Hercules. But this substitution does little to alleviate other aspects of Dworkin that make a match between him and Habermas awkward: the standard of integrity directs judges to interpret law as if it were a complete, coherent whole, resting on a foundation of moral rights.[62] Because Dworkin regards deontic rights in a strongly realistic manner, and as an unwritten part of the law, there is a finished, retrospective, "already there" quality to his picture of law. Thinking of moral rights as existing independently of their social articulation is what moves Dworkin to conceive of them as, at least in principle, accessible to the right reason of individual judges.[63] Legal correctness can be achieved when lawyers and judges combine specialized knowledge of precedent with potentially objective insights into deontic rights—fashioning the law in accordance with the demands of integrity becomes the province of legal elites, with the public, discursive construction of generalizable interests in

[61] I owe this point to its treatment in Christopher Zurn, *Deliberative Democracy and the Institutions of Judicial Review* (New York: Cambridge University Press, 2007), 239–252.

[62] See Dworkin, *Law's Empire*, chaps. 6, 7, and 11.

[63] See Dworkin, "Objectivity and Truth: You'd Better Believe It," *Philosophy and Public Affairs* 25, no. 2 (1996): 87–139. For a useful critical discussion, see Jon Mahoney, "Objectivity, Interpretation, and Rights: A Critique of Dworkin," *Law and Philosophy* 23, no. 2 (2004): 187–222.

principle unnecessary. This helps explain Dworkin's un-participatory conception of democracy and his comfort with entrusting vast amounts of decision-making power with the judiciary.[64]

There is more than a little here that should make Habermas uncomfortable. Firstly, on his account, legitimate law is the product of actual discourses that weave together the full spate of pragmatic, ethical-political, and moral discourse types. If the task of judicial decision-making is to reconstruct the types of discourse that went into the production of law, Dworkin's vision of filling in the gaps between legal rules exclusively with moral rights and principles (other considerations are filed under the heading of "policy")[65] makes little sense.[66] And while Habermas distances himself from Dworkin's moral realism, which he calls "hard to defend" (CD, 774), he appears not to appreciate the extent to which Dworkin links his account of legal correctness to this very possibility of individual insight into objective moral order. If Habermas wishes to maintain his long-held position that constitutional projects involve the ongoing construction of generalizable interests through the democratic process, which is really the heart of his program, he needs an account of legal correctness that puts some distance between it and Dworkin's picture of legal elites discovering the content of law through technical interpretation and rational intuition into a fixed moral order.

5. The Proceduralist Paradigm as an Anti-paradigm of Law

As I argued in Chapter 3, Rawls ends up favoring a model of adjudication like Dworkin's for deep-seated reasons: although he does not share Dworkin's moral realism, he does share a threshold conception of legitimacy, and as a result, public reason and constitutional discourse suppose a standpoint from which this threshold is satisfied—this notably involves anticipating the principled resolution of ideological conflict. If we recall Marx's contention that *The Philosophy of Right* projects a false unity onto the state, thereby functioning as an ideological façade, we can see why this sort of exercise might have bad results when used as a model for understanding our world.

What separates Habermas from Rawls and Dworkin in this context is that his legal theory harbors no such synthetic ambition. The proceduralist paradigm is

---

[64] See Dworkin, *Freedom's Law*, 32–36.

[65] See Dworkin, *Taking Rights Seriously*, 90–100.

[66] It is possible that Habermas is more cognizant of this point than I here credit him with being. See BFN, 229ff.

essentially a public understanding of law that directs citizens to think of their legal order as a pliant, unfinished medium through which to continue their conversation with one another about how to deepen the freedom and equality of their political union in light of new experiences, changing circumstances, and greater inclusivity—it is supposed to be a conception of law that builds in resistance to the reifying tendencies that Weber is resigned to.[67] Sociologically, the proceduralist paradigm is motivated by the recognition that the more that complex, modern societies use law for political steering and social planning, the greater the burden of legitimation on its democratic genesis, i.e., for persons to grasp law as a social relation, continuously reconstituted through intersubjective justification and rearticulation. This contention is behind Habermas' curious-sounding claim that existing paradigms of law (liberalism and the welfare state) fail in this, by virtue of being wedded to a "productivist image of society" (BFN, 407): they conceive of rights as a kind of pre-political good, to be distributed in accordance with formal (liberal) or material (welfarist) conceptions of equality. But the history of constitutional democracies strongly suggests that affected groups (e.g., workers, cultural and racial minorities, women) justifiably experience the application of pre-determined conceptions of legal equality as injustice, or as an external, random imposition (400–409)—when the latter occurs, "the dialectic of legal and factual equality coalesces into a second nature" (430). This impels the need for democratic society to be oriented around a reflexive legal paradigm that makes the criterion of legal equality appropriate for adjudicating in a certain context itself an object of deliberation among those affected:

> It must therefore be decided from case to case whether and in which respects factual (or material) equality is required for the legal equality of citizens who are both privately and publicly autonomous . . . [The proceduralist paradigm] privileges all the arenas where disputes over the essentially contestable criteria of equal treatment must be discursively carried out if the circulation of power in the political system is to stay the course set by constitutional regulation. (415)

The last two hundred years or so of legal history has witnessed a fractious dialectic between formal and substantive/material equality that Habermas casts as a clash of legal paradigms. The program of dissolving legally maintained status orders, creating frameworks for transactions based on free contract, and curbing

---

[67] This concept has not, in my view, received the attention it deserves. See David Ingram, "The Sirens of Pragmatism versus the Priest of Proceduralism: Habermas and American Legal Realism," in *Habermas and Pragmatism*, eds. Mitchell Aboulafia, Myra Bookman, and Cathy Kemp (New York: Routledge, 2002), 83–112; and *Habermas: Introduction and Analysis* (Ithaca, NY: Cornell University Press, 2010), chaps. 7 and 8. See also Hedrick, *Rawls and Habermas*, 146–183.

arbitrary state powers coalesces in a liberal legal paradigm (roughly equivalent to Kennedy's "individualism"): law centers around a formal set of individual liberties enabling free choice and insulating against state interference (396–401). Political discontent with systemic crises and inequalities engendered by market systems spurs a reformist response in the form of a "welfare state" paradigm (e.g., Kennedy's "altruism") wherein law's *telos* is reformulated in terms of distributing goods (employment, income, access to basic goods, etc.) in ways that level material inequalities and meet minimum standards (401–404).[68] Habermas makes the familiar point that injurious consequences follow when norms of either formal or material equality are allowed to solidify into fixed standards to be mechanically applied: formal equality is blind to actual differences, and advantages already advantaged groups; material equality is fixated on collective outcomes, indifferent to personal liberty, and enables discretionary and paternalistic administrative powers. As we have seen, Rawls would like to reconcile these two paradigms within justice as fairness and institutionalize this reconciliation through the four-stage sequence of application. But Habermas' proceduralist paradigm is instead something like an anti-paradigm of law, driven by the conviction that neither form of equality should be allowed to harden in the way just described, by leaving the determination of the appropriate type of equality up to those affected.

So far, so good. If we understood the legal order in this manner, many of the ideological distortions involved in pervasive adjudication and legalism described in Chapter 3 (legal technocracy, the legitimation effect, the filtering out of disagreement and felt injustice in the resolution of conflicts) would ebb: we would be disinclined to see the legal process as a fixed moral order, professionally administered on our behalf, or to accept decisions merely because they were the upshot of some adjudicative process, and more open to challenges from subordinated perspectives to received interpretations of constitutional doctrine. However, it is not immediately obvious what it would mean to "believe" in a proceduralist paradigm as Habermas describes it: whereas the other paradigms correspond to worldviews with an "implicit image of society" (BFN, 389), the same cannot be said of it.[69] It is, if anything, supported by the (discouraging?) conviction that there is no comprehensive worldview within which these

---

[68] See also, Habermas, "Law and Morality," in *The Tanner Lectures on Human Values*, vol. 8, ed. S. M. McMurrin (Salt Lake City: University of Utah Press, 1986), 224.

[69] Here, Habermas accords with Kennedy ("Form and Substance in Private Law Adjudication," 1774ff), who also thinks of individualism and altruism not just as collections of opposed propositions, but as relatively comprehensive visions of the individual-society relation. See also Waldron, "Did Dworkin Ever Answer the Crits?" 33–34; and West, "Progressive and Conservative Constitutionalism."

conflicting value orientations can be synthesized. Among those craving unified value theories (Dworkin being an arch-example)[70], Habermas likely conveys the impression of simply punting on the decisive question. It is, however, well in line with his characterization of the Enlightenment as a perpetually "unfinished project" (PDM, 336–367), opposition to "macrosubjective" (or, in Dworkin's term, "personified") conceptions of society (T&J, 187–193), and contention that traditional, overarching worldviews are unable to supply comprehensive justifications for functionally differentiated modern societies (TCA2, 179ff).

Given these longstanding commitments, and Habermas' rejection of threshold conceptions of legitimacy, we cannot plausibly understand the proceduralist paradigm to aim for integrity (Dworkin), nor does the conception of political autonomy associated with it require viewing laws as issuing from a conception of justice that reconciles legal ideologies like Kennedy's individualism and altruism (Rawls) (BFN, 220–222). This returns us to Zurn's characterization of Habermas' "developmentalist" conception of legitimacy as a feature of the lawmaking system as a whole: the rational acceptability of laws among all affected is a regulative ideal toward which it aspires. Seen from this perspective, as individuals, we will have our own reasons for thinking that laws are wise, just, good, or not, but legitimacy depends more on a holistic assessment of whether the system's overall trajectory warrants the present and future expectation that outcomes be rational acceptable. Since all legal orders have contingent and morally compromised origins, more than anything, acceptability depends on the presence of "reflexivity" in law, i.e., its facility in responding to arguments and testimonies in the public sphere, allowing those to inform decisions about the mode of legal equality (formal or material) appropriate to the situation. Given the preceding, the "expectation of rational acceptability" that the democratic principle requires cannot mean the expectation that legal process reliably applies a unified moral-ethical worldview (this would be the triumph of one legal paradigm over its competitors) or a coherent synthesis of them (á la Rawls and Dworkin), but more like the refusal to cede primacy to any concrete legal paradigm in the application of law.

Habermas' programmatic continuity notwithstanding, something begs explanation here, namely, how people convinced by his arguments for the proceduralist paradigm could actually be participants in legal discourse—if traditionalists and ideologues are informed and motivated by some image of the just society, why should the Habermasian proceduralist get to be any different? The line of defense most likely to recommend itself is Habermas' contention that postmetaphysical practical reason remains committed to the idealizing presupposition of shared

---

[70] See Ronald Dworkin, *Justice for Hedgehogs* (Cambridge, MA: Harvard University Press, 2011).

object domains (i.e., "objective," "social," and "subjective" worlds [TCA1, 99–102]), which ensure that mutual understanding through discourse is a standing possibility, even across deep ideological cleavages. Whatever the success of this argument as a riposte to generalized skepticism regarding practical reason, however, it does not cut to the real concern:[71] however much we water down these conditions, the conception of freedom as reconciliation at issue here must be participatory, self-conscious and non-self-deceptive—reconciliation cannot be something that takes place behind the backs of participants—and it is not clear how such conditions can be satisfied by participation in a discursive practice that one has an ironic attitude toward the truth claims of, or indeed how such a social practice could be sustained at all without self-deception, given the paucity of moral substance undergirding it.[72]

To see why Habermas seems to be barreling into this sort of dilemma, note that he has no real alternative to Dworkin's method to recommend to the judiciary. If we share Habermas' concern for reflexivity in law, we might hope that the judiciary on the whole resembles Michelman's model of the democratic judge (toward which Habermas nods with approval [CD, 769–771]) exposed "to the full blast of sundry opinions and interest articulations in society"[73] more than Dworkin's Hercules or Kennedy's ideologue-in-denial. But it is not much in the spirit of Habermasian legitimacy as a justifiable expectation of rational acceptability, nor for that matter Hegelian patriotism as "trust" in law, to pin hopes on the virtue of leaders. Looking at the lawmaking system more expansively, it seems that rationally justifiable confidence in law's reflexivity depends minimally on being able to assure ourselves that political decisions with significant practical important are not being settled with any finality by a system of adjudication that resembles a closed field of combat between legal intelligentsias,[74] whose public perception is filtered through the legitimation effect. Habermas' proposal for elevating reflexivity in law by leaving appropriate standards of equality to situational determinations will be disappointing, if it just amounts to a license for greater administrative or judicial discretion—as Waldron points out, for as much as democrats should resist any "content-based jurisprudence," they should be equally wary of turning adjudication into more of a publicly inscrutable practice than it already is.[75] Moreover, I do not think

---

[71] There is some overlap here with Dworkin's arguments about the irrelevance of "external skepticism" to interpretation. See *Law's Empire*, 76–86.

[72] See Gledhill, "Constructivism and Reflexive Constitution-Making Practices," *Raisons Politiques* 51, no. 3 (2013): 63–80.

[73] Michelman, *Brennan and Democracy* (Princeton, NJ: Princeton University Press, 1999), 60.

[74] See, for example, the types of scenarios described in Mark Tushnet, "Constitutional Hardball," *John Marshall Law Review* 37, no. 2 (2004): 523–553.

[75] See Waldron, "Can There Be a Democratic Jurisprudence?," 695–699.

that we can avoid the conclusion that Habermas' conceptions of legitimacy and proceduralist law imply either significant changes to the legal system that would make it substantially more receptive to inputs from the public sphere (in ways that would diminish the legitimation effect),[76] and/or would deprive the judiciary of authority to enact closure over issues of significant moral-political import.[77] And although Habermas does not highlight this point, it would seem to follow from all of this that the proceduralist paradigm demotes many of the stabilizing virtues associated with the rule of law: if fidelity and consistency have been subordinated to reflexivity, it may be hard to avoid the conclusion that the rule of law has been subordinated to democracy, rather than co-original with it, as on his preferred formulation. Although he insists that, as in any practical discourse, participants in legal discourse should be oriented toward "single right answers," he distinguishes his theory from legal positivism by substituting re-flexivity for fidelity to existing legal materials as the rule of law's cardinal virtue.[78] And it would also seem to follow that law, as conceived by the proceduralist paradigm, does not contain *any* settled criteria for legal correctness (a further difference with Dworkin), making it difficult to see what "single right answers" would amount to. Given Habermas' commitment to law being responsive to the actual discourses and interest articulations of those involved in its production and affected by it, it seems to me that he should avoid granting specialized legal discourse authority to settle questions of laws' meaning in a way that would trump destabilizing discourses of application from outside of the legal sphere. This should block him from fully embracing another ally's—Robert Alexy's—position that legal discourse is a "special case" of "general practical discourse" with an internal "claim to correctness."[79]

[76] Although the proposal is vague, this seems to be the idea behind conceiving of the judiciary as specialists in "discourses of application" that would employ formal or material conceptions of equality variably depending on the need interpretations of affected groups. See Habermas, *Justification and Application: Remarks on Discourse Ethics*, trans. Ciaran Cronin (Cambridge, MA: MIT Press, 1994), 38–39; and BFN, 217–221. A similar idea is at work in Catherine MacKinnon's concluding reflections on what a feminist jurisprudence would amount to; see *Toward a Feminist Theory of the State*, 237–249.

[77] See Christopher Zurn "Judicial Review, Constitutional Juries and Civic Constitutional Fora," *Theoria* 58, no. 2 (2011): 63–94.

[78] I am substantially in agreement with John McCormick ("Three Ways of Thinking 'Critically' about the Law," *The American Political Science Review* 93, no. 2 [1999]: 413–428) when he criticizes CLS for having a critical program that is one-sidedly directed against liberal legalism, and a nearly non-existent positive program, while regarding Habermas as superior in both regards, though only marginally so in the latter. I have sought to show here that amplifying the role of the proceduralist paradigm of law in indicates how that deficit could be improved upon.

[79] See Robert Alexy, *A Theory of Legal Argumentation: The Theory of Rational Discourse as the Theory of Legal Justification* (New York: Oxford University Press, 2010). Habermas gives a quick indication that he does not endorse Alexy's proposal in "A Short Reply," *Ratio Juris* 12, no. 4 (1999), 447.

6. Incongruity Problems: Narrow and Broad Constitutionalism, Legal Practice, and Everyday Life

In order to bring this chapter to a provisional summation, I would like to highlight two large and interrelated problems that confront Habermas' theory: a) the problem of reciprocally entwining what I have been calling, following Hegel, the narrow, political constitution, on the one hand, and the broad constitution of society's subsystems and their lifeworld interchanges, on the other, through a rational, transparent, and participatory process; and b) possible incongruities between the everyday life/participant perspective on this process, on the one hand, and the perspective of a normative reconstruction of the legal system as whole, on the other—incongruities of these sorts here become problematic, since the prospect for reconciliation hinges on self-conscious harmonization between these perspectives. I will continue to argue that the Habermasian framework holds promise for dealing with these problems (which afflict Hegel and Rawls, as well), but that (a) is a perennially thorny one, and that there are unresolved puzzles surrounding a Habermasian approach to (b) that threaten to breach a hole in its prospects for articulating a conception of reconciliation that is both politicized and emancipatory.

a. The Problem of Totality: Linking the Narrow and Broad Constitutions

It is not my intention to overstate the positive contributions that constitutions make to actually existing democracies, where they can serve to entrench political systems experiencing paralysis in the face of long-term fiscal, environmental, and inclusion problems, and where engagement with them more often than not invokes visions of society that are more nostalgic, ethno-nationalist, authoritarian, or reactionary than what Habermas presumably has in mind.[80] But I take the Hegelian leitmotif from Chapter 1 relevant here to be this: modern persons ought to be able to comprehend their social order as the work of reason; the spine of institutions through which their relations to differently abled and

---

For an instructive treatment of the issues between Alexy and Habermas (which defends the opposite conclusion), see Maeve Cooke, "Law's Claim to Correctness," in *Law, Rights, and Discourse: The Legal Philosophy of Robert Alexy*, ed. George Pavlakos (Portland, OR: Hart Publishing, 2007), 225–248.

[80] For a more transformative model of constitutionalism along Habermasian lines, see Benhabib, "Democratic Iterations: The Local, the National, and the Global," in *Another Cosmopolitanism*, ed. Robert Post (New York: Oxford University Press, 2008), 45–80. I have commented on the benefits and limitations of Benhabib's approach in "Democratic Constitutionalism as Mediation: The Decline and Recovery of an Idea in Critical Social Theory," *Constellations* 19, no. 2 (2012), 395–396.

positioned others are mediated ought to be responsive to their interests as fully-rounded persons; and comprehending this system of mediation can contribute to becoming reconciled to the partiality of one's roles in modern life. Though modern life is differentiated, seen through the lens of a constitutional ordering of the interchange roles, it can be understood as a result of the citizens' collective rationality, when certain conditions are met—conditions more stringent than Hegel realized (but less so than Marx and Lukács insist). In this light, a strikingly deficient aspect of modern politics is the number of issues deeply impacting citizens' social and economic relations to one another that range from marginal to invisible in terms of airing that they receive in the public sphere, and the degree to which they are treated as mostly settled or non-questions in the legal system: the intrusion of market logic and technology into everyday life; the commodification of public goods; the legal standing of consumers, residents, and citizens; the role of shareholders, workers, and public interests in corporate governance; vast income inequality; the status of collective bargaining arrangements; and so on. The other side of these legal-political issues' neglect, I have been maintaining along with Honneth and Habermas, is grinding alienation and anomic sociality. I have argued that we can extract from Habermas a potent conceptual apparatus for a) diagnosing this collection of phenomena (as a naturalization of interchange roles, a reification effect of colonization); b) understanding their consequences (anomic social pathology, legitimation problems); c) why those consequences are normatively problematic (they make social justice concerns more intractable than they otherwise would be, and stymie prospects for reconciliation); and d) at least an indication of how they might be addressed (the proceduralist paradigm of law).

As this phraseology suggests, I find that most of the serious problems emerge with (d). Both of the overarching areas of concern highlighted at the beginning of this section may be construed as issues about how mediation between particularity and universality can be accomplished on an ongoing basis—a conceptualization I have lauded Hegel for thematizing. A brief recap of the problem, as it has developed through previous chapters: pejorative views of Hegel often have it that he thinks of the individual as being derivatively free through an anti-individualistic political theory (e.g., an organic theory of state)[81] and an anti-individualistic metaphysics (e.g., individuals are really just vehicles of Spirit). These versions of Hegel unduly marginalize the category of mediation: they have him conceiving of the individual as less real than the whole of which they are a part, and then regarding the whole as that which strives to be

---

[81] On the role that organic motifs *do* play in Hegel's political thought, see Sally Sedgwick, "The State as Organism: The Metaphysical Basis of Hegel's *Philosophy of Right*," *The Southern Journal of Philosophy* 39 (2001): 171–188.

free. On Hegel's mediational understanding of such matters, however, it is not a metaphysical issue of the whole being "more real" than the parts; rather, individual and whole become what they are through exchanges—which can be more or less reciprocal, more or less transparent—of role performances and recognition: Spirit is "the 'we' in the 'I' and the 'I' in the 'we'" (PhG, §177/110). In Chapter 1, I argued that in *The Philosophy of Right*, Hegel develops a quite nuanced account of how mediation between particular persons and larger systems occurs (i.e., through the activity of the Estates and the ongoing articulation of the constitution), *and* how this mediation can be brought to consciousness, since after all, reconciliation only gets off the ground if this process of mediation becomes transparent to those experiencing it. In the context of Hegel's political philosophy, I described this as an interchange loop between the narrow and broad constitutions that is grounded in a representative and publicized political process. Hegel's elitism in this area prevents him from regarding the passive sense of mass participation that he countenances as a problem, but despite this objectionable element, his conceptualization is a coherent one for the society he was familiar with. Ideological distortions wrought by the segmentation of society and the increasing autonomy and scale of systems, however, have more and more intruded over the last two hundred years, making it harder to see how interchanges between the political system and social subsystems might be regulated on the basis of consensus-oriented participation. As we have seen, Marx and Lukács recognize this problem and think it tractable, but only through a dramatic societal reordering. In the absence of this revolutionary option, Rawls represents, we might say, a one-sidedly top down attempt to sort this issue out: the center of reconciliatory activity occurs in an institutional core, with citizens identifying themselves with that core. Simplifying somewhat, Honneth may be thought to represent a version where the dependency is weighted in the other direction: institutions may variously amplify, preserve, reinforce, or distort intersubjective patterns of recognition, but overall, they are reflections of those patterns. Along these lines, we might look at Habermas' apparent acquiescence to liberal legalism as suffering from "top-down" problems.

Now, I do not find this to be an unmanageable obstacle for Habermas: his commitments to a liberal version of the separation of powers, which largely confines the articulation of constitutional meaning to an institutional core, are either overstated or inessential, revisable in light of the preceding considerations. At which point, we would be left with the problem of how to link in a plausible and transparent way the more professionalized discourse in the constitutional state to everyday attempts to articulate social subsystems' boundaries in response to experiences of social suffering. This is quite simply a problem that no one unwilling to invoke revolution can claim a clean solution for. Yet it is a serious one that demands attention: since the early 20th century, we have seen the rise of large-scale state programs with massive distributional effects; industrial and monetary policy; the development of a worldwide "risk society" requiring long-term planning, and interstate bargaining and cooperation arrangements—all of this and more renders the federalism of the early American republic quaint. And all of it makes a certain kind of legal indeterminacy inevitable:[82] major legislative initiatives require extensive "fleshing-out" that usually occurs in courts and administrative agencies, and often without much input or awareness from the legislature (even bracketing concerns about the responsiveness of the legislature itself). Although such trends may have accelerated in recent decades, none of this is new, and at one level, classical legal paradigms have served to cope with it: they seek to impose a coherent teleology on law, guiding application and making public accountability more feasible than it otherwise would be. At another level, however, they are of little help at all:[83] classical liberalism more and more resembles an insurgent perspective on the modernity's evolving legal order, committed to various invisible hand/civic privatist motifs, and to viewing large amounts of state activity as barely legitimate. Welfarism's strained relationship to classical rule of law ideals has acquired a quality of stoic acquiescence: resigned to administrative discretion, while banking on the cultivation of competence and an orientation to the common good among legal-political elites. Neither paradigm encourages the idea that more expansive participation in legislation or application is likely to help much of anything. A significant takeaway from this study, however, should be that these classical paradigms have become resigned to a pervasive condition of legal reification that cannot be maintained without high costs: such a condition is, relatedly, normatively deficient; corrodes law's powers of social integration; and undermines the sort of holistic view of society that would help a democratic public grapple with 21st-century problems. Although not very eye-catching compared to a revolutionary program, we do have with a proceduralist paradigm a revisable collection of more or less revisionary small-ball proposals that this nascent paradigm gathers into focus: constitutional fora, forms of legislative supremacy, arbitration forums; collective bargaining; more creative and responsive forms of administration; less imperious and managerial courts.[84]

---

[82] See Klaus Günther, "The Pragmatic and Functional Indeterminacy of Law," *German Law Journal* 12, no. 1 (2011): 407–429.

[83] It is in this context that Habermas reintroduces the language of crisis ("crisis tendencies in the constitutional state")—mostly absent since the 1970s—back into his theory. BFN, 432ff.

[84] To this we would have to add the development of postnational forms of governance that retain strong elements of democratic accountability. This topic has been a major preoccupation of Habermas' for the last fifteen or so years and not one, I admit, that I have been able to devote attention to in this study. For a brief primer on how Habermas sees the discourse theoretical framework from *Between Facts and Norms* extending to this sphere, see *The Lure of Technocracy* (Malden, MA: Polity, 2015), 51–60.

b. Minding the Gaps: Contemplating Totality, Elite Practice, and Everyday Life

Once views of Hegel either as a theorist of the organic nation-state or a macrosubjective metaphysician are put aside, we can see that he is full-throatedly behind the notion that individuals' freedom requires more than just *feeling* at home in their social roles, namely, a rationally grounded sense that those roles are the work of reason in history. A bothersome element in his thought, however, is the apparent answer to queries about how self-conscious and articulate this sense can and should be. Even on a pragmatic rendering of what Science entails, it almost certainly involves apprehending that the framework for rational inquiry that modern life furnishes is both fully adequate for theoretical and practical deliberation; further, we can only understand this by having some notion of how this framework is the culmination ("result") of a society-wide learning process. Together, this is the core of what it means to grasp "the True not only as *Substance* but equally as *Subject*" (PhG, §17/15)—where the formal framework for rational inquiry and deliberation, plus their concrete institutional practices, is the substance, and the societal leaning process is the subject. And although art and religion can give one an intimation of what modern life is all about, understanding the adequacy of the substance of modern life through an account of its dialectical development requires, for Hegel, philosophy's exposition of this substance. To be sure, he never says that only the readers of the *Phenomenology* are fully, actually free. Indeed, at least by the time of *The Philosophy of Right*, his answer to the question of how erudite, articulate, and self-conscious this grasp needs to be seems to be "not very," with the main components being some sense of how the Estates work together through the constitutional state more or less harmoniously to reproduce the whole; to find one's self completed by participation in the three spheres of ethical life; and a habituated trust (i.e., patriotism) toward the laws. Now, on the one hand, this goes to show that Hegel's conception of the masses is appreciably different than, say, Plato's view of the iron and bronze people in *Republic*—Hegel thinks that we *are* free in the modern world, and that being free requires knowing (in the same way everyone else knows) that we are. On the other hand, it seems clear that philosophy represents the most refined expression of such a knowing, and that reconciliation with totality, fully grasping it as the work of reason, depends on elaborating the structure of modern life not merely as substance, but also as subject. And *this* is *not* the sort of knowing that falls out of reflective participation in the practices of modern life—it requires philosophy.[85]

---

[85] As Hegel puts it, "The Spirit that, so developed [i.e., 'in and for itself'—T. H.], knows itself as Spirit is *Science*; Science is its actuality and the realm it builds for itself in its own element" (PhG, §25/21).

To this we should add: for as much as Hegel does not hold that affective identification with the substance of objective Spirit is at all sufficient for freedom, it is necessary. If Hegel is to be defended against the charges that Kierkegaard, Marx, and Feuerbach leveled at him in the 1840s—that he abstracts away from individuals' lived, sensuous experience—we have to point out that he does not think that previously myopic individuals drifting in the atomism of civil society become free simply by having it pointed out to them that the society that made them this way is, in the grand scheme of things, rational. Hegel does think that comprehension of the ethical life's rationality needs to be rounded-out by citizen dispositions of galvanizing solidarity in order to achieve the sense of personal wholeness that reconciliation represents. Fortunately, Hegel believes that these two dimensions (comprehension and affect) are not unrelated: socialization within institutions one recognizes as rational (or just, to reframe it in Rawls' terms—and as evidenced in Chapter 3, it is really Rawls who grounds and spells out this argument) tends to activate these dispositions.

Now, it is safe to say that there is little in the previous two paragraphs that Habermas would enthusiastically second. However, consider two issues that have percolated to the surface during this Hegelian-hued elaboration of Habermas' proceduralist paradigm of law: first, it is hazy what conception of truth, objectivity, or "single right answers" it is compatible with—natural law clearly is not, nor, I argued, are more apparently convivial versions of objectivity/correctness like Dworkin's or Alexy's. If this is right, we have to concede that specifically *legal* discourse has no fixed internal criteria for correctness, and that the notion of single right answers can only represent a receding horizon. Second, the proceduralist paradigm does not correlate—as do preceding paradigms— with an image of the just society, i.e., a worldview with a concrete vision of the individual-society relation. This proved to be a more substantial claim than it might at first seem, having to do with the role of ideology in functionally differentiated societies. Here I want to underscore this further: for legal practice within previous paradigms, these worldviews are not epiphenomena: they guide practice and motivate belief. So, the question of what does motivate and guide participation in legal practice (professional or otherwise) as conceived by the proceduralist paradigm is so far unresolved. For it seems that the kind of comprehension that discloses the possibility of social-freedom-as-reconciliation is not something internal to the practices themselves, but depends on some articulated view of the whole. And from this perspective, which still seems appropriate to call distinctly philosophical,[86] a certain degree of ironic distance toward the

---

[86] See Baynes, "Modernity as Autonomy," *Inquiry* 38, no. 3 (1995): 289–303. Although Baynes may be right that conceptions of self-grounding reason remain bedeviled by Hegelian bootstrapping problems, the thrust of my argument suggests a less modest task for philosophy than some of

validity claims of legal discourse (as opposed to other forms of practical reason) looks inevitable.

This means that, even if he were more amenable to the affirmative, affective social psychology that Hegel and Rawls develop, Habermas could not use it like they do to claim that the subject's rational identification with the substance of ethical life (Hegel) or the basic structure (Rawls) completes the process of rec-onciliation. He thinks that a rationally organized legal-political order does not have a substantial moral/ethical core of this sort—the insistence that it does results in reification effects. If Habermas is left with the idea of identification of self with a fluid, subjectless flow of communication operating to reconfigure so-cial roles that incorporate individuals into systems of action, in accordance with inputs from the public sphere, it is hard to see how that could provide the sub-stance for an ego ideal around which to constitute an autonomous ego identity. The fact that Habermas does not shy away from facing Adorno's thesis that the fluid incorporation of the ego into its social roles can represent a repressive sem-blance of autonomy, plus the fact that his social psychology characterizes eman-cipation as the exposure of the psyche's structures to the transparency of public communication, means that while Habermas' self is primed for reconciliation, it is also primed for the false reconciliation Adorno feels is prevalent, while he has largely divested himself of substantive criteria that Honneth and (early) Rawls might use to distinguish one condition from the other.

A possible conclusion at this point would be the negative one of conceding that reconciliation is only a concept that can be developed as a compromised, ideologically foreshortened semblance (Hegel, Rawls), or as a post-political/utopian notion (Marx, Lukács, Adorno). Indeed, this may be Honneth's conclu-sion: for as much as he is more directly inspired by Hegel's practical philosophy than anyone else discussed herein, as I argued in Chapter 4, the political di-mension of reconciliation is not something he seriously attempts to reactualize. I criticized Honneth for this at the time, but now his perspective looks more rea-sonable. And it seems, too, at this point that Habermas' reservations about the rhetoric of reconciliation, adverted to at the beginning of this chapter, may have also been justified. Such a negative conclusion would be a substantial one, but while I do not take myself to be in a position to adjudicate what does and does not count as a "critical" theory, it also seems like Habermas and Honneth do wish to combine a more measured take on modernity than one finds in the first generation of the Frankfurt School with a robust conception of an emancipatory interest. But we see here how this combination is fraying apart, with Honneth

Habermas' deflationary statements (see, e.g., MCCA, 1–20) would suggest. Whether such a task is compatible with philosophy as detranscendentalized rational reconstruction at all is a question I will touch on in the conclusion, but cannot resolve here.

opting for a more individuated, psychologized conception of the emancipatory interest and Habermas with a more depersonalized one that is resigned to a disconnect between the life of individuals and the subjectless communication circulating above them. Since I opened this book arguing in favor of reconciliation as a political concept for critically reckoning with the existing world—and that this was the untapped core of *The Philosophy of Right*—the concluding section to this book will explore whether this conclusion is inexorable. As I see it, Habermas is left with a series of uncomfortable alternatives: if Hegel believes that knowing the truth about society results in reconciliation with it, Habermas may be in the position of admitting that such knowing is tinged with irony that borders on resignation; if this is unpalatable, Habermas' theory may have to find a way to open itself to more revisionary ideas of the emancipated ego.

Concluding Remarks

Almost from the moment that Horkheimer claimed critical theory's advantage over traditional theory on the basis of its integral relationship to human beings' interest in their own emancipation, authors in this tradition have struggled to spell out such an interest in a way that—per Horkheimer's intention—makes it immanent in society, while pointing beyond it. The reasons for this are various, and idiosyncratic to individual authors, but I would hazard, generally, that theorizing an emancipatory interest entails both an account of what it *is* (e.g., how it is rooted in the nature of the subject, developed and repressed during socialization) and how it is *actualized* in social institutions. In the Frankfurt School, psychoanalysis has often been called on to address the former issue and normative social theory (a philosophy of history, a theory of social freedom, discourse, democracy, etc.) the latter. These two sides have hitherto failed to mesh: either authors emphasize society's suppression of the emancipatory interest (in which case its actualization appears utopian, blocked by the pervasiveness of reification), or the actualization of freedom through society (in which case the interest itself appears too malleable and accommodating to really be emancipatory). If Adorno is exemplary of the former tendency, Hegel, Rawls, Honneth (despite his more intense interest in psychoanalysis), and Habermas all fault toward the latter. A guiding intuition behind this project has been that rehabilitating Hegel's concept of reconciliation, while underscoring and updating the legal-political mediations that are a part of it, could bridge this gap.

The answer as to whether it has, in fact, helped is more ambiguous than an author might like. Certain negative points, to be sure, have been established: Rawls represents an object lesson on what happens when updating a conception of Hegelian reconciliation that bypasses the left Hegelian critique of reification; Honneth represents a lesson about restaging a Hegelian conception of freedom that does not include a reconciliation component. In light of these examples, Habermas embodies the closest thing to a theory that combines reconciliation (concretized through the democratic legal system) with attention to the problem of reification (as it is proffered by legally ordered systems whose organization is democratically deficient). This book's order of presentation was, after all, meant to suggest this arching narrative. Yet Habermas' theory was just seen to have significant shortcomings of its own: it tends to evacuate the emancipatory interest by identifying it with inclusion in "subjectless" flows of discourse percolating through the political sphere, thereby distancing itself from individuals' lived freedom, and washing out in potentially alienating conclusions about irresolvable ideological conflict within the legal system.

Since there are a number of outstanding problems and holistic considerations pertaining to any final evaluation of reconciliation as an appropriate characterization of freedom's actualization, and a critical concept for assessing the legitimacy of social orders, in lieu of declaring a winner or carrying out a full synthesis of the "good" parts of Rawls, Honneth, and Habermas, I will canvass the most significant issues pertaining to such an evaluation.

1. Is Reconciliation Enough?

Chapters 3–5 may have given the impression that Honneth's conception of freedom (and early Rawls') should elicit praise for being solidly grounded in peoples' pre-theoretical sense of what makes their lives worthwhile and authentically their own (what I have been calling "lived freedom" for shorthand), but that the same cannot be said of Habermas and (later) Rawls, whose conceptions have an unfortunately attenuated relationship to lived freedom, due to their focus on the commanding heights of the political system. This impression needs to be corrected in two ways. First, I have been arguing that reconciliation integrally involves (beyond what is on offer in Honneth) reflection on society, namely, on how society shapes individuals into what they are. Hegel, Rawls, and Habermas all focus on the political sphere here, since it provides the lens through which society's organization can appear as something other than a nature-like set of givens. And it is just inevitably the case that making freedom's actualization depend upon political mediations puts it at some remove from peoples' usual first order notions of meaning and value. But this, by itself, is not grounds for criticism, since I faulted Honneth precisely for the lack of reflection on society in his conception of social freedom. Of course, in some abstract sense, it would be nice if these mediations were dispensable, and freedom actualize-able either through individuals' rational, conscientious conduct of life, or via the possibility that they could—normally and without deception—identify in an unproblematic way with the social conditions shaping their life prospects. The former is a Kantian option that has not been under serious consideration here, and the latter either echoes Rousseau's and Hegel's nostalgia for ancient Greece, or is utopian in a way that reaches beyond reasonably envisage-able prospects for what even a post-revolution society would be like. The need for reconciliation arises from perceiving one's contingent relationship to a division of labor that produces unequal outcomes and requires taking up roles that only narrowly realize a form of life's (and one's own) possibilities. Such conditions would exist even in a society substantially more just than our own—although we can say that, in a more just society, the objective possibilities for individuals to become reconciled would be closer to universal, the process less vexed, and the results more easily distinguishable from resignation.

So, a theory of social freedom that makes its actualization dependent upon reconciliation does, in some sense, abstract away from a more visceral sense of lived freedom that does not involve mediating reflection on society, but the latter has never been seriously on the table in this inquiry. Which brings us to the second potential misimpression to be corrected: if Rawls' and Habermas' conceptions of freedom through reconciliation are liable (like Hegel's) to seem arid and bloodless by virtue of their mediations, these appearances are not accurate to the same degree or in the same way. For Rawls, people attain political autonomy primarily by coming to see the basic structure of society as embodying a reasonable conception of justice, and self-consciously affirming this conception. While there is room for interpretive disagreement about whether describing a situation in which people could be cognitively and affectively at home with themselves is a conscious goal of Rawls' (the later Rawls, at any rate—there is a strong textual basis for thinking that *A Theory of Justice* does intend this), from the perspective of this book's concerns, it does seem that identification with the basic structure and its laws has a directly freedom-actualizing power, for him. Here, Honneth's observation that people rarely think of themselves as "following the law" in most of the social spheres in which human interests can be freely actualized (especially intimate, personal relations and vocational/associational pursuits) is sound, and so too are his protests against theories that fixate on law as the major vehicle for actualizing freedom.[1]

But this objection does not cut Habermas so deeply, since he does not attribute the same kind of directly freedom-actualizing power to the democratic legal system. To illustrate this, let us recur to the example of the modern professional person's "self-directing dignity" from the introduction: a person aspiring to such a thing will usually acquire, in the course of his or her life, all manner of personal loyalties, familial responsibilities, ethical codes of personal conduct, civic and professional norms, ideological commitments, and so on. Actualizing freedom here hangs on not only living up to these norms and commitments, but a reflective sense that there are good reasons for having

---

[1] See Honneth, "Beyond the Law: A Response to William Scheuerman," *Constellations* 24, no. 1 (2017): 126–132.

had internalized them in the first place. The fact that law, in a modern society, does not directly prescribe very many of these norms and commitments does not gainsay its massive background role in shaping and, over time, modifying the institutional expectations attaching to them. Equally important for our purposes, law delivers public reference points that specify putatively justified baselines for role obligations and entitlements: for example, individual parents may not *need* legal obligations to conclude that they should get their kids to school, not discipline them corporeally, etc.; vendors *can* be convinced without the prodding of legal sanctions that they should accurately inform customers about the nature of their services, not vary price and quality on a discriminatory basis, etc. But expectations like these being normalized obviously has something to do with legal institutionalization; furthermore, a person's sense that a norm ought to be reformed (or rejected) usually involves reference to the manner of its institutionalization, together with the belief that it is changeable through law (though not necessarily by legal fiat). In turn, law's responsiveness to changing public sentiments is a powerful, de-reifying signal to those undertaking this internalization that normative role expectations should be based on reasons, and internalized through conscious acceptance of those reasons, as opposed to unconscious conformity.

In short, although in the background of most interactions, law is the central node for the process of inculcating and changing normative role expectations, on the one hand, and serving as a public reference point for the kind of critical reflection that is vital for differentiating autonomous self-cultivation from the blind acceptance of oppressive codes. Although figures like Rousseau and Rawls may present a simplified vision of actualizing freedom directly through identification with the law, Hegel's and Habermas' perspectives better capture these reasons for thinking that law is central to both reification and the kind of reflection that facilitates reconciliation. Whether it does more of the former than the latter depends on the degree of transparency and democratization that the legal system enjoys.

2. What Kind of Psychoanalysis Complements the Idea of Reconciliation?

So, the claim that freedom is actualized through reconciliation, and that a significant volume of reconciliation's work is mediated through law, can be defended against the objection that it conceives of freedom too aridly. But this raises another issue: the trend among theorists who have made these moves (Hegel, Rawls, Habermas) is to endorse, in a manner that one suspects is rather stipulative, accounts of ego formation in which the internalization of role expectations takes place consciously and non-repressively. It is hard to say how objectionable this is, since all of us tend to gravitate toward theories that support our general outlook, and I do not want to grant intra-psychoanalytic disputes veto power over the theories of freedom being considered here. So, for example, I do not want to say that if Freud's account of ego formation were true, it would wholesale falsify ideas about freedom being actualized through reconciliation. However, since the theorists under consideration (including more Kantian ones like Rawls and Habermas) all reject the notion that freedom is actualized through the formulation of rational intentions, they hold that society and affect must meet these intentions halfway in order to generate the sense of at-home-ness they consider important. And since reconciliation, as I am characterizing it, is not a stable state with formal, externally observable features to distinguish it from repressive conformity, we should not be indifferent to what psychoanalytic theories say about the social conditions for unhindered ego function that could inform such a distinction. As such, were the basics of Freudian ontogenesis true, it *would* put theories involving reconciliation under pressure to explain how a process of reconciliation can sublimate impulses that would otherwise be re-pressed or vented in pathological, socially disruptive ways.

That said, we should not find the Freudianism of Horkheimer, Adorno, and Marcuse to be all that viable. In particular, there is broad consensus that Freud's solipsistic account of primary narcissism is not well-supported by empirical evidence, and so explanations of impaired ego function that concentrate on re-pressed archaic memories (and such ideas do play an important role in *Dialectic of Enlightenment*'s Odysseus excursus) should be discounted. But abandoning this tenant of Freud does not come close to discrediting the notion that instinc-tual drives are resistant to the molding of impulses needed for self-directing ego functions. This can be seen in my contention that Honneth's appropria-tion of Winnicott (who abandons Freud's monological, trauma-laden picture of ontogenesis) by no means obviates the need to grant a systematic role to re-pression in the normal reproduction of social life. If my conclusions are sound that the major problem with the psychic underpinnings in Hegel's, Rawls', and Habermas' theories is that they see the psyche slotting too smoothly into puta-tively well-ordered social relations, then we need to retain something of Adorno's contention that normal functionality too often involves a false reconciliation between individual and society, which reproduces unjust and oppressive social relations—whether we think of blindness and narcissistic indifference, or sub-conscious attachment to hierarchy, as the main mechanism for this reproduction. Holding to this central insight from "the culture industry" means endorsing the idea that instinctual drives have an asocial core. This need not involve invoking a death drive, per se, but minimally that instinctual drives are not merely coex-tensive with what I was calling "normal sociality" in Chapter 4, and that they can become reconcilable to normal sociality only through sublimation that reckons with one's place in the social world and how one receives its imperatives.[2] In order to support my contention that reflection on society is integral to reconciliation, any such account of sublimation should deny that therapeutically working through one's own biography is sufficient for these purposes.

Resolving some of the tensions in Honneth's appropriation of psychoanalysis can contribute to this effort. Honneth is well on-board with trends in post-Freudian psychoanalysis (which are not just confined to the object relations school he is most interested in)[3] toward a more interactive conception of ontogenesis, in which the self is less of a disciplinary, conventional imposition than it is for Freud. Yet, Honneth also resists Daniel Stern's research conclusions concerning the presence of a distinct proto-self in very early mental life, with all of their implications about the existence of a natural intuition of self.[4] Although Honneth does not stress the recalcitrance of the instincts, desires for merging and fusion represent for him drives that have a tense, lifelong relationship to normal ego functioning. While in Chapter 4, I was critical of the use to which Honneth puts Winnicott's notion of "play" for easing this tension, my complaint there was not so much with this very intriguing and productive idea, but that Honneth does not do enough to disambiguate the ways in which play can serve as an obfuscating, reality-coping mechanism from its potentially emancipatory uses. By remaining equivocal here, Honneth comes uncomfortably close to the revisionary Freudianism that Adorno and Marcuse condemn, wherein psychic health is equated with social functionality. This failure is related to the stretched-thin relationship between theory and practice in Honneth: the theory of justice in *Freedom's Right* is a form of macrosocial reflection that does not mirror the subject's efforts to work through its own genesis with emancipatory intent; rather, emancipation is a matter of inclusion in well-functioning ethical spheres, while Honneth's macrosocial reflections are a theoretically informed survey about how those spheres are functioning—the former in no way requires the latter.[5] One of my specific hopes for this project going forward is that the

---

[2] Although in many circles, the notion of a death drive is treated incredulously, I believe it should be taken seriously. See Benjamin Fong, *Death and Mastery: Psychoanalytic Drive Theory and the Subject of Late Capitalism* (New York: Columbia University Press, 2016); see also Hedrick, "Ego Autonomy, Reconciliation, and the Duality of Instinctual Nature in Adorno and Marcuse," *Constellations* 23, no. 2 (2016): 180–191.

[3] For a helpful overview, see Richard Ganis, "Insecure Attachment and Narcissistic Vulnerability: Implications for Honneth's Recognition-Theoretic Reconstruction of Psychoanalysis," *Critical Horizons* 16, no. 4 (2015): 329–351.

[4] See Honneth and Joel Whitebook, "Omnipotence or Fusion? A Conversation between Axel Honneth and Joel Whitebook," *Constellations* 23, no. 2 (2016), 175.

[5] On the importance of connecting critical-theoretical reflection to the subject's activity of emancipating itself, see Frieder Vogelmann, "Measuring, Disrupting, Emancipating: Three Pictures of Critique," *Constellations* 24, no. 1 (2017): 101–112.

most developed form of macrosocial reflection considered here—Habermas' proceduralist paradigm of law and affiliated conception of dereifying critique—can be joined to the conception of play that Honneth appeals to, in order to bring out its emancipatory potential.

3. Reconciliation, Irony, and Reflection on Society

I propose—at this juncture, I can only pose it as a suggestion—that we consider a certain kind of cultivated irony as an attitudinal stance that could link a subjective orientation toward play with macrosocial reflection on objective conditions in a way that could open possibilities for reconciliation. Recently, some interesting scholarship has reconsidered Hegel's relationship to German romanticism, in particular, the stance of irony considered normatively appropriate by that group of authors.[6] Hegel's posture toward these close contemporaries tends to be more unremittingly hostile than the consideration that he gives to philosophical worldviews deeper in the past. He has little time for the subjectivism and skepticism toward intersubjective validity associated with Novalis and Schlegel, nor the end of personal authenticity (as opposed to public engagement) flowing from these views. This dismissive stance may obscure important ways in which, as he does with most positions he encounters, Hegel incorporates something of romanticism into his thought. Like the romantics, Hegel thinks that the most sophisticated modern effort to redeem the concepts and norms that make sense of cognitive and moral life—Kant's transcendental philosophy—collapses into skepticism. So, the subjectivism in romanticism's stance toward the world does not lack a rationale. But Hegel clearly thinks that the concepts, and institutional values and norms, that modern society prescribes *are* redeemable, albeit only through his reconstruction. This is to say that Hegel thinks that modernity's framework for belief formation, action guidance, and self-understanding—natural science, law and ethical life, romantic art and reformed Christianity—are amenable to an overarching metanormative justification. But, as with Habermas' insistence on the distinction between discourses of justification and application, Hegel does not think that metanormative justification directly validates first order claims about *this* hypothesis, *these* laws, etc., with which the bulk of practical justification is concerned. Now, Hegel's views about the interplay between first order and metanormative justification is complicated—and as Robert Pippin makes clear, it is appreciably different

---

[6] See Fred Rush, *Irony and Idealism: Rereading Schlegel, Hegel, and Kierkegaard* (New York: Oxford University Press, 2016); and Jeffrey Reid, *The Anti-Romantic: Hegel Against Ironic Romanticism* (New York: Bloomsbury, 2014).

from Habermas'[7]—but their present upshot is that first order claims can only be supported by the balance of available reasons, making them provisional in light of contravening evidence, new interpretations, etc.; the metanormative framework informs *what counts* as evidence, good reasons, etc. While this reinforces Hegel's conviction that the question of whether we consider our-selves self-determining cannot turn solely on having rational grounds for belief and action, the kind of open-mindedness about the ultimate justifiability of our commitments that follows does not by itself recommend a retreat into irony. He considers the metanormative context of first order claims—ethical life—to be firm and substantial enough, publicly knowable as the work of reason, such that the claims, despite their provisional nature, can be considered actualizations of freedom. Indeed, I argued that the political system's revisability is part of what allows us to consider modern social roles to be actualizations of freedom, even in a world riven by deprivation, injustice, and uncertainty. So, the fact that poli-tics for Hegel is somewhat open-ended does not entail indeterminacy about its basic substance that might nudge one to adopt an ironic stance toward it. Nor does Honneth recommend this move: despite his suspicion about whether the market (and to a lesser extent, the constitutional state) has ever really served as a vehicle for actualizing freedom through exchange relations, he thinks of socialism as a viable (albeit in need of revitalization) program for correcting this deficit.[8] And anyway, not being a theorist of reconciliation, Honneth does not consider macrosocial reflection integral to making institutionally mediated interactions realizations of freedom.

The procedural character of Habermas' theory, however, does make irony the alternative to resignation, as the orientation toward social existence that opens one to reconciliation. Insofar as reconciliation is a matter of coming to see norms, values, and commitments as internalized for good reasons, for Habermas, in the final analysis, the ongoing operation of the democratic legal system provides a public backstop for justifying this confidence. But the basis for this confidence in Habermas is slimmer and more hesitant than in Hegel. It is not just that Habermas' interchange roles are less substantial than Hegel's Estates: he maintains that the legal system—the chief vehicle for society's

---

[7] See Robert Pippin, *Hegel on Self-Consciousness: Desire and Death in the* Phenomenology (Princeton, NJ: Princeton University Press, 2011), 18n1. For his larger account of the interac-tion between metanormative frameworks and first order judgments, see Pippin, *Hegel's Practical Philosophy: Rational Agency and Ethical Life* (New York: Cambridge University Press, 2008), chaps. 5–9.

[8] See Honneth, *The Idea of Socialism: Towards a Renewal,* trans. Joseph Ganahal (Malden, MA: Polity, 2017). It should be noted that Honneth's contention that socialism will have to be con-tent with Deweyan social experimentation through ongoing democratic legislation (51–75) puts his proposal less at odds with Habermas' proceduralist paradigm of law than it might seem.

reflection on itself—is not teleologically oriented toward a form of life in which freedom subsists in coherent, widely actualized form (á la socialism in Honneth).[9] A proceduralist paradigm of law is not undergirded by the vision of an emancipated form of life, but rather a sense that the law is responsive to concrete experiences of injury and deprivation that, through the work of social movements and dereifying critique, continually come to light. Joined with this is the awareness that this kind of reflexivity—the airing of moral injuries in the public sphere, responses to them through the introduction/modification of legal rules—spirals into its own set of pathologies, in the form of estrangement from cultural certainties and repressive normalization resulting from administrative controls, with no end in sight. And this is in a good-case scenario in which the political order credibly instantiates a proceduralist paradigm of law, in the first place—something that can hardly be taken for granted, presently. If this is basi-cally correct, reconciliation would need to incorporate, first, an awareness of this state of affairs, and second, a kind of acceptance of it that does not amount to cynical or world-weary resignation.

On the awareness question, we should pause to consider whether the already counterfactual view of society associated with a proceduralist paradigm is an ac-cessible or a counterintuitive one. This is important, since one of the aspects of reconciliation in Hegel's original conception that I am recommending reten-tion of is its insistence that society's manner of reproducing itself and socializing members should be publicly knowable. I am sure that the proposition that Habermas' theory of society (or Hegel's) is intuitively accessible strikes many readers as laughable, given the volumes of dense prose that have gone into it. But the issue is not whether one needs to have read Habermas' books, but whether the conception of society laid out in them is resonant, or at odds, with the know-how one usually acquires in the course of learning to participate in the various spheres of social life. I will confess that I am unsure how to answer this ques-tion plainly. On the one hand, it seems clear that Habermas is not defending anything akin to the "transparency thesis" that I attributed to Honneth in Chapter 4. Nor is he adopting Rawls' face-value understanding of how the legal order constitutes society. Neither seems possible because the introduction of steering media (money and administrative power) into the lifeworld allows sys-tems to "functionally integrate" (i.e., materially reproduce themselves and main-tain their boundaries vis-à-vis their environment) in ways that bypass the usual

---

[9] Maeve Cooke's perspective on critical theory has consistently emphasized the need for theory to engage the motivations of empirical subjects through compelling presentations of utopian visions. See her *Re-Presenting the Good Society*. My argument here and in the last chapter suggests that this perspective is more continuous with Honneth's critical theory (at least once *The Idea of Socialism* is taken into account) than Habermas'.

need for social actors to develop shared ways of understanding their situation. He urges that both the rational progress and problems attending societal modernization result from the functionalist rationality of systems becoming distinct from the rationality of social action undertaken by individuals. This is the point of departure for Marx's contention that the integration of modern societies takes place increasingly "behind the backs" of social actors. Now, this does not mean that persons cannot (with the help of social science) learn how social actions (e.g., fair exchange, familial care and loyalty, civic behavior guided by ideological convictions) contribute to functional integration, nor that actions apparently oriented toward norms and values are not "really" that, but rather responses programmed for the purposes of systems maintenance. To the latter hypothesis, Habermas has long opposed Western Marxism's critique of instrumental and "subject-centered" reason, which holds that the logic of systematic imperatives can overwrite communicative action (e.g., exchange logic in Adorno). But without revisiting the guts of this issue, we can note that Habermas has to concede that a preponderance of systemic and functional integration crowds out (or renders delusional) "holistic" interpretations of society. If we understand a holistic interpretation of society to be one in which parts contribute to a whole, and the whole is oriented toward the promotion or preservation of norms and values, then holistic interpretations represent a straightforward way of making norm- and value-guided actions within specific subsystems meaningful; this kind of meaning is, in turn, integral to the modern professional's aspiration of "self-directing dignity." All of this underscores a point from Chapter 5 (and echoed in some of Honneth's darker reflections on individuation): the rejection of Lukács' and Adorno's conceptions of instrumentally-oriented "subject-centered reason" does not mean that the culture industry's basic picture of the individual's relationship to society is not substantially on target. So, the question of whether an individual's incorporation into diffuse systems of action validates the culture industry, or not, depends to a large extent on whether society's democratic bona fides (in terms of the gamut of issues mentioned in the last chapter, from developing reflexive, procedural understandings of the constitution, to administrative responsiveness to injuries resulting from overly formalized, materialized, or discriminatory applications of rules) are strong enough to counterbalance the reified picture of individuals indoctrinated into frozen hierarchies.

If these bona fides are robust enough, the subjective side of the equation remains: how could awareness of this state of affairs positively, tangibly impact the realization of individuals' freedom? To repeat, Habermas does not have much to say on this question—he inclines toward the view that incorporation into non-reified institutions that are democratically organized, and toward which one can have a critical, appropriative relationship, actualizes freedom. I have indicated, at some length now, both that I think this actualization is best conceived in terms of reconciliation, and that Habermas' rationale for thinking that this relationship between the individual and society is sufficient for freedom is itself not sufficient. As we have seen, his view of the individual-society relationship as, under relatively ideal conditions, institutionalizing an open-ended learning process provides somewhat tenuous assurances about the correctness of norms and duties attaching to contemporary social roles. Moreover, reflection on the way the democratic legal process shores up these assurances is further unreassuring: it reveals that claims of correctness advanced in legal argumentation, however unreservedly they are intended by speakers, cannot be taken at face value. Kennedy's characterization of legal practitioners probably has more than a grain of truth to it: they are constrained by institutional conventions to couch their rulings and advocacy full-throatedly, as definitive, neutral interpretations of the legal materials, while being aware at some level that their arguments can usually be flipped by advocates from other ideological persuasions. Although, at the end of the previous chapter, I raised the possibility of a rift between this irony- and/or denial-laden perspective and that of lay-participants in democratic will formation, enough of the public seems comfortable thinking of the constitution as an evolving, "living" order, such that the self-understanding of legal insiders is not, on its own, a major source of concern. Knowledgeable citizens are not trapped in a naïve view of law, even if the general obscurity of legal system's inner workings remains a problem for the view I am advocating. But it does indicate that macrosocial reflection serves more to confirm, at a higher level, the contingency and attendant uncertainty about the way social roles are presently configured, unease with which spurred the need for reconciliation in the first place. On the one hand, this conclusion can serve as a negative answer to the question of whether Habermas' macrosocial reflection on the role of the democratic legal system in society's reproduction is at odds with the hermeneutic one of lay-participants. On the other hand, it falls short of providing the kind of reassurance that Hegel's metanormative account of modernity intends—e.g., that all of our personal efforts and commitments could be seen as progressively contributing to the universal—beyond indicating that this deeper level of assurance is not forthcoming.

This should temper our sense that our commitments and norms are as they should be, only that they seem well-supported here and now, and thus, at best, may justly be regarded as a worthy effort to live a life that is integrated into society, but on one's own terms, despite the fact that it may seem misguided (though hopefully not monstrously so) in retrospect. There actually can be something reassuring about this kind of negative realization, namely, that the thing you have been pining over in vain is not real, attainable, cogent, etc., and so you can stop bothering and be more satisfied with what you have. But on the other hand, Habermasian macrosocial reflections could equally easily have the effect of estranging those who absorb them from the norms and commitments themselves: there is a kind of "bad" irony that flows from coming to believe the pretensions of modern social practices, and the legal order undergirding them, to be realizations of freedom are a sham, not to be taken seriously, even if it is expedient to publicly pay them lip-service. Whether or not they have this effect on those who absorb them is, at some level, a matter of temperament. But the kind of "good" irony inspired by Socrates and Kierkegaard—taken up more recently by authors like Richard Rorty, Jonathan Lear, and Richard Bernstein[10]—suggests not that truth, justice, and freedom are false pretenses to be discarded, but that our efforts to realize them may not amount to what we imagine and that we cannot sensibly think of those efforts as steps toward a full realization of those values. Irony here involves internalizing an acceptance of this ambiguity, without thereby diminishing one's commitment to realizing the values embodied in one's social roles as best as one can, through critical appropriation and creative interpretation.[11]

From a certain angle, this call for acceptance of ambiguity is somewhat banal, at least among those assenting to the basics of postmetaphysical reason—for that matter, it is not all that different from Rawls' characterization of the reasonable person's acceptance of the fact of pluralism. And this apparent banality might suggest that, at the end of the day, the concept of reconciliation cannot be extricated from the initial left Hegelian charge against it, namely, that it perversely maintains that peoples' best path for liberating themselves from the strictures of their circumstances is to contemplate those circumstances from the right perspective. But I have throughout been arguing against a conception of reconciliation that amounts to enlightened cognition, and "acceptance," as I intend it here, is not something achievable through those means. As any therapist, any analysand struggling to move through trauma or deep-seated discontent, or any addict

---

[10] Richard Rorty, *Contingency, Irony, and Solidarity* (New York: Cambridge University Press, 1989); Jonathan Lear, *A Case for Irony* (Cambridge, MA: Harvard University Press, 2011); Richard Bernstein, *Ironic Life* (Malden, MA: Polity, 2016).

[11] One issue that I have not given as full of an airing as the issue warrants is whether reconciliation is premised on a general narrative of social progress. Allen has persuasively argued that the strategy for grounding the normativity of critique in left Hegelian theory has problematically hitched itself to a notion of progress that unwittingly reproduces the domineering side of European Enlightenment. See *The End of Progress?*. The notion of reconciliation that I have been advocating for does indeed suppose that the internalization of social roles can be based on good reasons that represent moral progress, at least in a local way (i.e., the adoption of these roles is better justified than relevant historical alternatives), and more globally, that the de-differentiation of modernity's metanormative framework (e.g., collapsing the distinction between state and civil society, and/or between institutionalized forms of practical reason) would be regressive. However, the posture of irony and acceptance toward the unfinished and uncertain nature of social roles' justification that I am recommending here goes at least some way toward accommodating Allen's concerns.

will attest, enlightenment by itself can more easily serve as a defense mechanism than a source of freedom: a way of coping with something that has come to be irrefutably at odds with one's well-being, while going on as before ("I realize that fixating on this memory/ingesting this substance won't do me any good; I should stop, I know ... ").[12] However, as successful anaysands and recovering addicts can also attest, acceptance is absolutely crucial to getting better, *can* be liberating, and indeed is quite at odds with complacency. What makes acceptance liberating is a difficult question to answer, and as far as clinical cases are concerned, a deeply personal one. But we need not leave it at that, by saying that the ironical accept- ance is therefore just a matter of personal character, or worse, a refuge for those in possession of secure class and status privilege. Honneth, after all, has laid some groundwork for treating play as an emancipatory form of self-relation that ego can have vis-à-vis its social roles, even if he does not do enough to distinguish it from defensive coping. Hopefully there is more to say about how play and Habermasian macrosocial reflection could combine in an ironic, but not world- weary stance toward one's empirical roles and the society that furnishes them. For one thing, dereifying critique as Habermas undertakes it would be crucial for steering acceptance toward liberation and reconciliation, since a subject's iron- ical acceptance of its social roles' incomplete justification is unlikely to issue in anything more than withdrawn, inner-worldly coping, so long as those roles, and the society that foists them, appear as the demands of an unchangeable reality. More work needs to be done to spell out the general conditions of socialization that would allow subjects to approach their role commitments with a clear-eyed sense of their contingency and incompleteness, but without emotional with- drawal. Play, as Honneth, following Winnicott, describes it, allows the self to find the impersonal and straining aspects of the social world tolerable and mean- ingful by creatively restaging them in ways that draw on emotionally nourishing experiences from its biography. It is important that we be able to describe this orientation such that play picks up on objective features of the social world—i.e., genuine patterns of mutual recognition—albeit ones that exist often in a formal, institutionalized form, rather than projecting a hallucinatory, artificially com- forting visage onto the world.

I would also like, here at the end, to caution against another kind of banality toward which not just critical theory, but philosophy and the humanities, more generally, may be prone: pieties about openness to difference and contingency, experimentation in ways of being, being critical and modest about our own commitments, etc., trip easily off of the tongues of contemporary humanities academics, most of whom, like myself, have been afforded the space and security

---

[12] See Allen, "Psychoanalysis and the Methodology of Critique," *Constellations* 23, no. 2 (2016): 252.

to cultivate this kind of attitude toward our own social existence. In order to avoid moralistic exhortation, we should not discount the extent to which this is a pretense that masks deeply felt needs for identity assurance that academics are subject to as much as anyone else, and not think of play as an attitude that one can simply decide to adopt (e.g., after a university education has expanded one's horizons, etc.), but realize that it rather has a lengthy incubation period, during which the ego learns to sideline the defensive (and often narcissistic) orientation toward the world that Horkheimer and Adorno see as an elemental feature of post-mythic, enlightened subjectivity. Although Adorno hangs onto a notion of mimesis that is intriguingly similar to play in object relations theory, he only thinks that it is really applicable in the modern period to interaction with works of art, a circumspection that would have to be dismantled if the possibility of reconciliation is to be extended into normal sociality.[13] Horkheimer and Adorno's reflections on the paucity of real ego strength in late capitalism, due to the way socialization takes place in the culture industry, continue to have real bite, even if we decline to accept the totalizing view of society accompanying them, and the specific theory of ego formation undergirding them. In order to conceptualize reconciliation as a plausible way the rational, democratic organization of society actualizes freedom, the universal availability of which serves as a regulative ideal the legitimacy of modern social orders should be assessed against, we have to revise that picture of socialization in a more thoroughgoing way than Habermas and Honneth do (and more plausibly than Rawls and Hegel). But there are limits to this, since it seems to me that Horkheimer and Adorno are rather on point with their observation that the psyche in our time is, from very early on, awash in largely unfelt pressures to adjust itself to a plethora of social imperatives that do not issue from clear, authoritative sources (i.e., are abstract), poising the more mature self to "find itself" through adaption to these demands—it is primed for a reified social reality. If we are not counting on a sweeping social revolution that decisively puts an active, human face on reality to disrupt this picture, then a theory that still wants to see its way clear toward a more genuine kind of reconciliatory freedom needs to explain not just how more just social conditions might mitigate the pervasiveness of reification (in pre- and post-adolescent life), but also how participation in processes of democratic will formation that felicitously transform social roles is capable of affecting mid-life (i.e., post-adolescent) transformations of the self's relation to society in an ironic, playful, but still committed direction, that *re*-conciles the former to the latter.

---

[13] For a helpful account of Adorno's circumspection of mimesis, which sees it as a consequence of the way social orders tend to organize the drive for self-preservation, and which emphasizes mimesis' non-oppositional relationship to reason, see Owen Hullat, "Reason, Mimesis, and Self-Preservation in Adorno," *Journal of the History of Philosophy* 54, no. 1 (2016): 135–151.

BIBLIOGRAPHY

Achen, Christopher and Larry Bartels (2016), *Democracy for Realists: Why Elections Do Not Produce Responsive Government* (Princeton, NJ: Princeton University Press).

Ackerman, Bruce (2000), *We the People*, volume 2: *Transformations* (Cambridge, MA: Harvard University Press).

Acton, H. B. (1970), "On Some Criticisms of Historical Materialism," *Aristotelian Society Supplementary Volume* 44, no. 1: 143–145.

Adorno, Theodor (1967), "Sociology and Psychology (Part I)," *New Left Review* 46: 67–80.

—— (1973), *Negative Dialectics*, trans. E. B. Ashton (New York: Continuum).

—— (1980), "Reconciliation under Duress," in *Aesthetics and Politics*, ed. Ronald Taylor (New York: Verso), 151–176.

—— (1982), "Freudian Theory and the Pattern of Fascist Propaganda," in *The Essential Frankfurt School Reader*, eds. Andrew Arato and Eike Gebhardt (New York: Continuum), 118–137.

—— (1989), "Society," in *Critical Theory and Society: A Reader*, eds. Stephen Bronner and Douglas Kellner (New York: Routledge).

—— (1993), *Hegel: Three Studies* (Cambridge, MA: MIT Press).

—— (2000), *Introduction to Sociology* (Stanford, CA: Stanford University Press).

—— (2002), *The Stars Down to Earth and Other Essays on the Irrational in Culture*, ed. Stephen Crook (New York: Routledge).

—— (2003), "Late Capitalism or Industrial Society?" in *Can One Live After Auschwitz? A Philosophical Reader*, ed. Rolf Tiedemann (Stanford, CA: Stanford University Press, 2003), 111–125.

—— (2003), "Reflections on Class Theory," in *Can One Live After Auschwitz?*, 93–110.

—— (2005), *Minima Moralia: Reflections on a Damaged Life*, trans. Edmund Jephcott (New York: Verso).

—— (2014), "Revisionist Psychoanalysis," *Philosophy and Social Criticism* 40, no. 3: 326–338.

Adorno, Theodor and Max Horkheimer (2002), *The Dialectic of Enlightenment: Philosophical Fragments*, ed. Gunzelin Noerr, trans. Edmund Jephcott (Stanford, CA: Stanford University Press).

Alexy, Robert (2010), *A Theory of Legal Argumentation: The Theory of Rational Discourse as the Theory of Legal Justification* (New York: Oxford University Press).

Alford, C. Fred (1988), *Narcissism: Socrates, the Frankfurt School, and Psychoanalytic Theory* (New Haven, CT: Yale University Press).

Allan, James (2008), "The Travails of Justice Waldron," in *Expounding the Constitution: Essays in Constitutional Theory*, ed. Grant Huscroft (New York: Cambridge University Press), 161–183.

Allen, Amy (2016), *The End of Progress? Decolonizing the Normative Foundations of Critical Theory* (New York: Columbia University Press).

—— (2016), "Psychoanalysis and the Methodology of Critique," *Constellations* 23, no. 2: 244–254.

Anderson, Joel (2014), "Autonomy, Agency, and the Self," in *Jürgen Habermas: Key Concepts*, ed. Barbara Fultner (New York: Routledge), 90–111.

Arato, Andrew (1972), "Lukács' Theory of Reification," *Telos* 11: 25–66.

Arendt, Hannah (1973), *The Origins of Totalitarianism* (New York: Harvest).

Aristotle (1998), *Politics*, trans. C. D. C. Reeve (Indianapolis: Hackett).

Baldwin, Thomas (2008), "Rawls and Moral Psychology," in *Oxford Studies in Metaethics*, ed. Russ Schafer-Landau (New York: Oxford University Press), 247–270.

Barry, Brian (1995), "John Rawls and the Search for Stability," *Ethics* 105, no. 4: 874–915.

Baxter, Hugh (1987), "System and Lifeworld in Habermas' Theory of Communicative Action," *Theory and Society* 16, no. 1: 39–86.

Baynes, Kenneth (1995), "Modernity as Autonomy," *Inquiry* 38, no. 3: 289–303.

—— (2002), "Freedom and Recognition in Hegel and Habermas," *Philosophy and Social Criticism* 28, no. 1: 1–17.

—— (2014), "Critical Theory and Habermas," in *A Companion to Rawls*, eds. Jon Mandle and David Reidy (Malden, MA: Wiley Blackwell), 487–503.

Beiser, Frederick (2005), *Hegel* (New York: Routledge).

Bell, Daniel (1996), *The Cultural Contradictions of Capitalism* (New York: Basic Books).

Bendix, Reinhard (1974), "Inequality and Social Structure: A Comparison of Marx and Weber," *American Sociological Review* 39, no. 2: 149–161.

Benhabib, Seyla (1986), *Critique, Norm, and Utopia: A Study in the Foundations of Critical Theory* (New York: Columbia University Press).

—— (2008), "Democratic Iterations: The Local, the National, and the Global," in *Another Cosmopolitanism*, ed. Robert Post (New York: Oxford University Press), 45–80.

Benjamin, Jessica (1977), "The End of Internalization: Adorno's Social Psychology," *Telos* 32: 24–64.

—— (1978), "Authority and the Family Revisited: or, A World without Fathers?" *New German Critique* 5: 35–57.

Bercuson, Jeffrey (2014), *John Rawls and the History of Political Thought: The Rousseauvian and Hegelian Heritage of Justice as Fairness* (New York: Routledge).

Berlin, Isaiah (1990), *Four Essays on Liberty* (New York: Oxford University Press).

Bernstein, Jay (1984), *The Philosophy of the Novel: Lukács, Marxism, and the Dialectics of Form* (Minneapolis: The University of Minnesota Press).

—— (1991), "Art Against Enlightenment: Adorno's Critique of Habermas," in *The Problems of Modernity: Adorno and Benjamin*, ed. Andrew Benjamin (New York: Routledge), 49–66.

Bernstein, Richard (1978), *The Restructuring of Social and Political Theory* (Philadelphia: University of Pennsylvania Press).

—— (2016), *Ironic Life* (Malden, MA: Polity).

Boltanski, Luc and Eve Chiapello (2005), *The New Spirit of Capitalism*, trans. Gregory Elliot (New York: Verso).

Borman, David (2009), "Labor, Exchange, and Recognition: Marx contra Honneth," *Philosophy and Social Criticism* 35, no. 8: 935–959.

—— (2015), "Actual Agreement Contractualism," *Dialogue* 54, no. 3: 519–539.

Brandom, Robert (2002), *Tales of the Mighty Dead: Historical Essays in the Metaphysics of Intentionality* (Cambridge, MA: Harvard University Press).

Brint, Steven (1996), *In an Age of Experts: The Changing Role of Professionals in Politics and Public Life*, 2nd ed. (Princeton, NJ: Princeton University Press).

Brooks, Thom (2012), "Natural Law Internalism," in *Hegel's Philosophy of Right*, ed. Thom Brooks (Malden, MA: Blackwell), 167–179.

Brown, Wendy (1995), *States of Injury: Power and Freedom in Late Modernity* (Princeton, NJ: Princeton University Press).

Browne, Craig (2008), "The End of Immanent Critique?" *European Journal of Social Theory* 11, no. 1: 5–24.

Brudney, Daniel (1997), "Community and Completion," in *Reclaiming the History of Ethics: Essays for John Rawls*, eds. Andrews Reath, Barbara Herman, and Christine Korsgaard (New York: Cambridge University Press), 388–415.

——— (1998), *Marx's Attempt to Leave Philosophy* (Cambridge, MA: Harvard University Press).

——— (2014), "The Young Marx and the Middle-Aged Rawls," in *A Companion to Rawls*, 450–471.

Brunkhorst, Hauke (2005), *Solidarity: From Civic Friendship to Global Legal Community*, trans. Jeffrey Flynn (Cambridge, MA: MIT Press).

Bubner, Rudiger (2003), *The Innovations of Idealism*, trans. Nicholas Walker (New York: Cambridge University Press).

Buchwalter, Andrew (2001), "Law, Culture, and Constitutionalism: Remarks on Hegel and Habermas," in *Beyond Liberalism and Communitarianism: Studies in Hegel's Philosophy of Right*, ed. Robert R. Williams (Albany: SUNY Press), 207–228.

Castel, Robert (2003), *From Manual Workers to Wage Laborers: Transformation of the Social Question*, ed. and trans. Richard Boyd (New Brunswick, CT: Transaction Publishers).

Chambers, Simone (2002), "Can Procedural Democracy Be Radical?" in *The Political*, ed. David Ingram (New York: Blackwell, 2002), 168–190.

——— (2009), "Rhetoric and the Public Sphere: Has Deliberative Democracy Abandoned Mass Democracy?" *Political Theory* 37, no. 3: 323–350.

Chari, Anita (2010), "Toward a Political Critique of Reification: Lukács, Honneth, and the Aims of Critical Theory," *Philosophy and Social Criticism* 36, no. 5: 587–606.

Cohen, G. A. (2000), *Karl Marx's Theory of History: A Defense*, expanded ed. (Princeton, NJ: Princeton University Press).

——— (2008), *Rescuing Justice and Equality* (Cambridge, MA: Harvard University Press).

Cohen, Joshua (1997), "The Natural Goodness of Humanity," in *Reclaiming the History of Ethics*, 102–139.

——— (2003), "For a Democratic Society," in *The Cambridge Companion to Rawls*, ed. Samuel Freeman (New York: Cambridge University Press), 86–138.

Cook, Deborah (1996), *The Culture Industry Revisited: Theodor W. Adorno on Mass Culture* (Lanham, MD: Rowan and Littlefield).

Cooke, Maeve (2006), *Re-Presenting the Good Society* (Cambridge, MA: MIT Press).

——— (2007), "Law's Claim to Correctness," in *Law, Rights, and Discourse: The Legal Philosophy of Robert Alexy*, ed. George Pavlakos (Portland, OR: Hart Publishing), 225–248.

Cornell, Drucilla (1988), "Institutionalization of Meaning, Recollective Imagination, and the Potential for Transformative Legal Interpretation," *University of Pennsylvania Law Review* 136, no. 4: 1135–1229.

Cover, Robert (1992), "*Nomos* and Narrative," in *Narrative, Violence, and the Law: The Essays of Robert Cover*, eds. Martha Minnow, Michael Ryan, and Austin Sarat (Ann Arbor: University of Michigan Press), 95–172.

Cullen, Bernard (1988), "The Mediating Role of Estates and Corporations in Hegel's Theory of Political Representation," in *Hegel Today*, ed. Bernard Cullen (Brookfield: Gower), 22–41.

Dallmayr, Fred (1992), "Critical Theory and Reconciliation," in *Habermas, Modernity, and Public Theology*, eds. Don Browning and Francis Fiorenza (New York: Crossroads), 119–151.

Dews, Peter (1995), "The Paradigm Shift to Communication and the Question of Subjectivity: Reflections on Habermas, Lacan, and Mead," *Revue Internationale de Philosophie* 49, no. 4: 483–519.

Dubiel, Helmut (1985), *Theory and Politics: Studies in the Development of Critical Theory* (Cambridge, MA: MIT Press).

Durkheim, Emile (1958), *Professional Ethics and Civic Morals*, trans. Cornelia Brookfield (Glencoe, IL: The Free Press).

——— (1984), *The Division of Labor in Society*, trans. W. D. Halls (New York: Free Press).

Dworkin, Ronald (1977), *Taking Rights Seriously* (Cambridge, MA: Harvard University Press).

——— (1985), *A Matter of Principle* (Cambridge, MA: Harvard University Press).

——— (1986), *Law's Empire* (Cambridge, MA: Harvard University Press).

——— (1996), *Freedom's Law: The Moral Reading of the American Constitution* (Cambridge, MA: Harvard University Press).

——— (1996), "Objectivity and Truth: You'd Better Believe It," *Philosophy and Public Affairs* 25, no. 2: 87–139.

——— (2006), *Justice in Robes* (Cambridge, MA: Harvard University Press).

——— (2011), *Justice for Hedgehogs* (Cambridge, MA: Harvard University Press).

Dzur, Albert (2008), *Democratic Professionalism: Citizen Participation and the Reconstruction of Professional Ethics, Identity, and Practice* (University Park: The Pennsylvania State University Press).

Eiden-Offe, Patrick (2011), "Typing Class: Classification and Redemption in Lukács' Political and Literary Theory," in *Georg Lukács: The Fundamental Dissonance of Existence*, eds. Timothy Bewes and Timothy Hall (New York: Bloomsbury), 65–78.

Engels, Friederich and Karl Marx (1996), "Manifesto of the Communist Party," in *Later Political Writings*, ed. Terrell Carver (New York: Cambridge University Press), 1–30.

——— (1998), *The German Ideology* (Amherst, NY: Prometheus).

Estlund, David (2008), *Democratic Authority* (Princeton, NJ: Princeton University Press, 2008).

Feenberg, Andrew (2011), "Rethinking Reification," in *Georg Lukács*, 101–119.

——— (2014), *The Philosophy of Praxis: Marx, Lukács, and the Frankfurt School* (New York: Verso).

Ferrara, Alessandro (2011), "The Nugget and the Tailings: Reification Reinterpreted in the Light of Recognition," in *Axel Honneth: Critical Essays*, ed. Danielle Petherbridge (Boston: Brill), 371–390.

Finlayson, James Gordon (2014), "Hegel, Adorno, and the Origins of Immanent Criticism," *British Journal for the History of Philosophy* 22, no. 6: 1142–1166.

Fraser, Nancy (2010), *Scales of Justice: Reimagining Political Space in a Globalizing World* (New York: Columbia University Press).

Fraser, Nancy and Axel Honneth (2003), *Recognition or Redistribution? A Philosophical Exchange* (New York: Verso).

Frazer, Michael (2007), "John Rawls: Between Two Enlightenments," *Political Theory* 35, no. 6: 756–780.

Freeman, Samuel (2000), "Deliberative Democracy: A Sympathetic Comment," *Philosophy and Public Affairs* 29, no. 4: 371–418.

——— (2003), "Congruence and the Good of Justice," in *The Cambridge Companion to Rawls*, 277–315.

Freud, Sigmund (1955), *Beyond the Pleasure Principle*, in *The Standard Edition of the Complete Psychological Works of Sigmund Freud*, vol. 18, ed. and trans. James Strachey (London: Hogarth Press), 6–66.

——— (1957), "On Narcissism: An Introduction," in *The Standard Edition of the Complete Psychological Works of Sigmund Freud*, vol. 14, ed. and trans. James Strachey (London: Hogarth Press), 73–104.

——— (1961), *Civilization and its Discontents*, in *The Standard Edition of the Complete Psychological Works of Sigmund Freud*, vol. 21, ed. and trans. James Strachey (London: Hogarth Press), 64–148.

Galanter, Marc (1974), "Why the 'Haves' Come Out Ahead: Speculations on the Limits of Legal Change," *Law and Society Review* 9 (1974): 95–160.

Ganis, Richard (2015), "Insecure Attachment and Narcissistic Vulnerability: Implications for Honneth's Recognition-Theoretic Reconstruction of Psychoanalysis," *Critical Horizons* 16, no. 4: 329–351.

Gaus, Daniel (2013), "Rational Reconstruction as a Method of Political Theory between Social Critique and Empirical Political Science," *Constellations* 20, no. 4: 553–570.

Gaus, Gerald (1999), "Reasonable Pluralism and the Domain of the Political: How the Weakness of John Rawls' Political Liberalism Can Be Overcome by Justificatory Liberalism," *Inquiry* 42, no. 2: 259–284.

Geuss, Raymond (2008), *Philosophy and Real Politics* (Princeton, NJ: Princeton University Press).

Giddens, Anthony (1973), *The Class Structure of Advanced Societies* (London: Hutchison and Co.).

Gledhill, James (2011), "Procedure in Substance and Substance in Procedure: Reframing the Rawls-Habermas Debate," in *Habermas and Rawls: Disputing the Political*, eds. J. Gordon Finlayson and Fabian Freyenhagen (New York: Routledge), 181–199.

——— (2012), "Rawls and Realism," *Social Theory and Practice* 38, no. 1: 55–82.

——— (2013), "Constructivism and Reflexive Constitution-Making Practices," *Raisons Politiques* 51, no. 3: 63–80.

Goodfield, Eric Lee (2014), *Hegel and the Metaphysical Frontiers of Political Theory* (New York: Routledge).

Grimm, Dieter (2005): "Integration by Constitution," *International Journal of Constitutional Law* 3, nos. 2–3: 193–208.

Günther, Klaus (1995), "Legal Adjudication and Democracy: Some Remarks on Dworkin and Habermas," *European Journal of Philosophy* 3, no. 1: 36–54.

—— (2011), "The Pragmatic and Functional Indeterminacy of Law," *German Law Journal* 12, no. 1: 407–429.

Habermas, Jürgen (1970), "Technology and Science as Ideology?" in *Toward a Rational Society: Student Protest, Science, and Politics* (Boston: Beacon Press).

—— (1971), *Knowledge and Human Interest*, trans. Gary Shapiro (Boston: Beacon Press).

—— (1973), *Legitimation Crisis*, trans. Thomas McCarthy (Boston: Beacon).

—— (1973), *Theory and Practice*, trans. John Viertel (Boston: Beacon).

—— (1979), *Communication and the Evolution of Society*, trans. Thomas McCarthy (Boston: Beacon).

—— (1984), *Theory of Communicative Action*, vol. 1: *Reason and the Rationalization of Society*, trans. Thomas McCarthy (Boston: Beacon).

—— (1985), "Questions and Counterquestions," in *Habermas and Modernity*, ed. Richard Bernstein (Cambridge, MA: MIT Press), 192–216.

—— (1986), "Law and Morality," in *The Tanner Lectures on Human Values*, vol. 8, ed. S. M. McMurrin (Salt Lake City: University of Utah Press), 219–279.

—— (1987), *Theory of Communicative Action*, vol. 2: *System and Lifeworld: Toward a Critique of Functionalist Reason*, trans. Thomas McCarthy (Boston: Beacon).

—— (1987), *The Philosophical Discourse of Modernity: Twelve Lectures*, trans. Frederick Lawrence (Cambridge, MA: MIT Press).

—— (1990), *Moral Consciousness and Communicative Action*, trans. Christian Lenhardt and Shierry Weber Nicholsen (Cambridge, MA: MIT Press).

—— (1992), "Further Reflections on the Public Sphere," in *Habermas and the Public Sphere*, ed. Craig Calhoun (Cambridge, MA: MIT Press), 429–441.

—— (1992), *Postmetaphysical Thinking: Philosophical Essays*, trans. William Mark Hohengarten (Cambridge, MA: MIT Press).

—— (1994), *Justification and Application: Remarks on Discourse Ethics*, trans. Ciaran Cronin (Cambridge, MA: MIT Press).

—— (1996), *Between Facts and Norms: Toward a Discourse Theory of Law and Democracy*, trans. William Rehg (Cambridge, MA: MIT Press).

—— *Inclusion of the Other: Studies in Political Theory*, trans. Ciaran Cronin and Pablo De Greiff (Cambridge, MA: MIT Press).

—— (1999), "A Short Reply," *Ratio Juris* 12, no. 4: 445–453.

—— (2001), "Constitutional Democracy: A Paradoxical Union of Contradictory Principles?" *Political Theory* 29, no. 6: 766–781.

—— (2003), *Truth and Justification*, trans. Barbara Fultner (Cambridge, MA: MIT Press).

—— (2008), *Between Naturalism and Religion*, trans. Ciaran Cronin (Malden, MA: Polity).

—— (2009), *Europe: The Faltering Project*, trans Ciaran Cronin (Malden, MA: Polity).

—— (2010), "The Concept of Human Dignity and the Realistic Utopia of Human Rights," *Metaphilosophy* 41, no. 4: 464–480.

—— (2014), *The Crisis of the European Union: A Response* (Malden, MA: Polity).

—— (2015), *The Lure of Technocracy* (Malden, MA: Polity).

Hall, Timothy (2011), "Reification, Materialism, and Praxis: Adorno's Critique of Lukács," *Telos* 155: 61–82.

Hammer, Espen (2007), "Habermas and the Kant-Hegel Contrast," *German Idealism: Contemporary Perspectives*, ed. Hammer (New York: Routledge), 113–133.

—— (2008), "Marcuse's Critical Theory of Modernity," *Philosophy and Social Criticism* 34, no. 9: 1071–1093.

Hardimon, Michael (1994), *Hegel's Social Philosophy: The Project of Reconciliation* (New York: Cambridge University Press).

Hartmann, Heidi (1979), "The Unhappy Marriage of Marxism and Feminism," *Capital and Class* 3, no. 2: 1–33.

Hartmann, Martin and Axel Honneth, "Paradoxes of Capitalism," *Constellations* 13, no. 1 (2006): 41–58.

Heath, Joseph (2009), "Habermas and Analytic Marxism," *Philosophy and Social Criticism* 35, no. 8: 891–919.

—— (2014), "System and Lifeworld," in *Jürgen Habermas*, 74–90.

Hedrick, Todd (2010), *Rawls and Habermas: Reason, Pluralism, and the Claims of Political Philosophy* (Stanford, CA: Stanford University Press).

—— (2012), "Democratic Constitutionalism as Mediation: The Decline and Recovery of an Idea in Critical Social Theory," *Constellations* 19, no. 2: 382–400.

—— (2016), "Ego Autonomy, Reconciliation, and the Duality of Instinctual Nature in Adorno and Marcuse," *Constellations* 23, no. 2: 180–191.

Hegel, G. W. F. (1970), *Encyclopedia of the Philosophical Sciences*, part 2: *The Philosophy of Nature*, trans. A. V. Miller (New York: Oxford University Press).

—— (1975), *Early Theological Writings*, trans. T. M. Knox (Philadelphia: University of Pennsylvania Press).

—— (1975), *Aesthetics: Lectures on Fine Art*, vol. 1, trans. T. M. Knox (New York: Oxford University Press).

—— (1977), *Faith and Knowledge*, trans. Walter Cerf and H. S. Harris (Albany: SUNY Press).

—— (1977), *The Phenomenology of Spirit*, trans. A. V. Miller (New York: Oxford University Press).

—— (1995), *Lectures on Natural Right and Political Science*, trans. J. Michael Stewart and Peter Hodgson (Berkeley: University of California Press).

—— (1995), *Lectures on the History of Philosophy*, vol. 3: *Medieval and Modern Philosophy*, trans. E. S. Haldane and Frances Simson (Lincoln: University of Nebraska Press).

—— (1999), *Political Writings*, eds. Laurence Dickey and H. B. Nisbet, trans. H. B. Nisbet (New York: Cambridge University Press).

—— (2008), *Outlines of the Philosophy of Right*, ed. Stephen Houlgate, trans. T. M. Knox (New York: Oxford University Press).

—— (2010), *Encyclopedia of the Philosophical Sciences in Basic Outline*, part 1: *Science of Logic*, ed. and trans. Klaus Brinkmann and Daniel Dahlstrom (New York: Cambridge University Press).

Heidemann, Dietmar (2008), "Substance, Subject, System: The Justification of Science in Hegel's *Phenomenology of Spirit*," in *Hegel's* Phenomenology of Spirit: *A Critical Guide*, eds. Dean Moyar and Michael Quante (New York: Cambridge University Press), 1–20.

Heins, Volker (2007), "Critical Theory and the Traps of Conspiracy Thinking," *Philosophy and Social Criticism* 33, no. 7: 787–801.

Held, David (1980), *Introduction to Critical Theory: Horkheimer to Habermas* (Berkeley: University of California Press).

Hill, Thomas, Jr., (1994), "The Stability Problem in *Political Liberalism*," *Pacific Philosophical Quarterly* 75, no. 3-4: 333–352.

Hohendal Peter Uwe (2001), "From the Eclipse of Reason to Communicative Reason and Beyond," in *Critical Theory: Current State and Future Prospects*, eds. Hohendal and James Fisher (New York: Berghahn Press), 3–28.

Honneth, Axel (1990), *The Fragmented World of the Social*, ed. Charles Wright (Albany: SUNY Press).

—— (1991), *The Critique of Power: Reflective Stages in a Critical Social Theory*, trans. Kenneth Baynes (Cambridge, MA: MIT Press).

—— (1996), *The Struggle for Recognition: The Moral Grammar of Social Conflicts*, trans. Joel Anderson (Cambridge, MA: MIT Press).

—— (1999), "Postmodern Identity and Object Relations Theory: On the Seeming Obsolescence of Psychoanalysis," *Philosophical Explorations* 2, no. 3: 225–242.

—— (2001), *Pathologies of Individual Freedom: Hegel's Social Theory*, trans. Ladislaus Löb (Princeton, NJ: Princeton University Press).

—— (2007), *Disrespect: The Normative Foundations of Critical Theory* (Malden, MA: Polity).

—— (2008), "Reification and Recognition," in *Reification: A New Look at an Old Idea*, ed. Martin Jay (New York: Oxford University Press), 17–94.

—— (2008), "Rejoinder," in *Reification*, 147–159.

—— (2009), *Pathologies of Reason: On the Legacy of Critical Theory*, trans. James Ingram (New York: Columbia University Press).

—— (2012), *The I in the We: Studies in the Theory of Recognition*, trans. Joseph Ganahal (Malden, MA: Polity).

—— (2014), "Diseases of Society: Approaching a Nearly Impossible Concept," *Social Research* 81, no. 3: 683–703.

—— (2014), "The Normativity of Ethical Life," *Philosophy and Social Criticism* 40, no. 8: 817–826.

—— (2015), *Freedom's Right: The Social Foundations of Democratic Life*, trans. Joseph Ganahal (New York: Columbia University Press).

—— (2015), "Rejoinder," *Critical Horizons* 16, no. 2: 204–226.

—— (2016), "Of the Poverty of Our Liberty: The Greatness and Limits of Hegel's Doctrine of Ethical Life," in *Recognition or Disagreement? A Critical Encounter on the Politics of Freedom, Equality, and Identity*, eds. Katia Genel and Jean-Phillipe Geranty (New York: Columbia University Press), 156–176.

—— (2017), *The Idea of Socialism: Towards a Renewal*, trans. Joseph Ganahal (Malden, MA: Polity).

—— (2017), "Beyond the Law: A Response to William Scheuerman," *Constellations* 24, no. 1: 126–132.

Honneth, Axel and Joel Whitebook (2016), "Omnipotence or Fusion? A Conversation between Axel Honneth and Joel Whitebook," *Constellations* 23, no. 2: 170–179.

Horkheimer, Max (1972), "Authority and the Family," in *Critical Theory: Selected Essays*, trans. Matthew J. O'Connell et al. (New York: Continuum), 47–131.

—— (1972), "Traditional and Critical Theory," in *Critical Theory*, 188–244.

—— (1982), "The Authoritarian State," in *The Essential Frankfurt School Reader*, 95–117.

—— (1989), "The Jews of Europe," in *Critical Theory and Society*, 77–94.

—— (2004), *Eclipse of Reason* (New York: Continuum).

Houlgate, Stephen (1986), *Hegel, Nietzsche, and the Critique of Metaphysics* (New York: Cambridge University Press).

—— (1997), "Hegel's Critique of the Triumph of *Verstand* in Modernity," *Hegel Bulletin* 18, no. 1: 54–70.

Hullat, Owen (2016), "Reason, Mimesis, and Self-Preservation in Adorno," *Journal of the History of Philosophy* 54, no. 1: 135–151.

Ingram, David (1990), "Dworkin, Habermas, and the CLS Movement on Moral Criticism in Law," *Philosophy and Social Criticism* 16, no. 4: 237–268.

—— (2002), "The Sirens of Pragmatism versus the Priest of Proceduralism: Habermas and American Legal Realism," in *Habermas and Pragmatism*, eds. Mitchell Aboulafia, Myra Bookman, and Cathy Kemp (New York: Routledge), 83–112.

—— (2010), *Habermas: Introduction and Analysis* (Ithaca, NY: Cornell University Press).

Jacobs, Lawrence and Robert Shapiro (2000), *Politicians Don't Pander: Political Manipulation and the Loss of Democratic Responsiveness* (Chicago: University of Chicago Press).

Jaeggi, Rahel (2005), "'No Individual Can Resist': *Minima Moralia* as Critique of Forms of Life," *Constellations* 12, no. 1: 65–82.

—— (2014), *Alienation*, trans. Frederick Neuhouser (New York: Columbia University Press).

Jay, Martin (1984), *Marxism and Totality: The Adventures of a Concept from Lukács to Habermas* (Berkeley: University of California Press).

Jütten, Timo (2011), "The Colonization Thesis: Habermas on Reification," *International Journal of Philosophical Studies* 19, no. 5: 701–727.

Kant, Immanuel (1991), "Idea of a Universal History with a Cosmopolitan Purpose," in *Political Writings*, ed. Hans Reiss, trans. H. B. Nisbet (New York: Cambridge University Press), 41–53.

—— (1996), *Critique of Practical Reason*, in *Practical Philosophy*, ed. and trans. Mary Gregor (New York: Cambridge University Press), 135–276.

—— (1996), *Groundwork of the Metaphysics of Morals*, in *Practical Philosophy*, 39–108.

—— (1996), *The Metaphysics of Morals*, in *Practical Philosophy*, 360–540.

Kelly, Christopher (1987), "'To Persuade without Convincing': The Language of Rousseau's Legislator," *American Journal of Political Science* 31, no. 2: 321–335.

Kennedy, Duncan (1976), "Form and Substance in Private Law Adjudication," *Harvard Law Review* 89, no. 8: 1685–1778.

——— (1979), "The Structure of Blackstone's *Commentaries*," *Buffalo Law Review* 28, no. 5: 209–382.

——— (1985), "The Role of Law in Economic Thought: Essays on the Fetishism of Commodities," *The American University Law Review* 34, no. 4: 939–1001.

——— (1995), "American Constitutionalism as Civic Religion: Notes of an Atheist," *Nova Law Review* 19, no. 3: 909–921.

——— (1997), *A Critique of Adjudication: fin de siècle* (Cambridge, MA: Harvard University Press).

——— (2008), *Legal Reasoning: Collected Essays* (Aurora, CO: The Davies Group, 2008).

Kierkegaard, Søren (2000), *Concluding Unscientific Postscript*, in *The Essential Kierkegaard*, eds. Howard Hong and Edna Hong (Princeton, NJ: Princeton University Press).

Kirchheimer, Otto (1982), "Changes in the Structure of Political Compromise," in *The Essential Frankfurt School Reader*, 49–70.

Kirshner, Alexander (2010), "Proceduralism and Popular Threats to Democracy," *Journal of Political Philosophy* 18, no. 4: 405–424.

Kompridis, Nikolas (2004), "From Reason to Self-Realization? On the Ethical Turn in Critical Theory," *Critical Horizons* 5, no. 1: 323–360.

Korsgaard, Christine (1996), *The Sources of Normativity*, ed. Onora O'Neill (New York: Cambridge University Press).

Kortian, Garbis (1980), *Metacritique: The Philosophical Argument of Jürgen Habermas* (New York: Cambridge University Press).

Kramer, Larry (2004), *The People Themselves: Popular Constitutionalism and Judicial Review* (New York: Oxford University Press).

Krasnoff, Larry (1998), "Consensus, Stability, and Normativity in Rawls' *Political Liberalism*," *The Journal of Philosophy* 95, no. 6: 269–292.

Laden, Anthony Simon (2001), *Reasonably Radical: Deliberative Liberalism and the Politics of Identity* (Ithaca, NY: Cornell University Press).

——— (2003), "The House that Jack Built: 30 Years of Reading Rawls," *Ethics* 113, no. 2: 367–390.

Lafont, Cristina (2006), "Is the Ideal of Deliberative Democracy Coherent?" in *Deliberative Democracy and Its Discontents*, eds. S. Besson and J. L. Martí (Aldershot: Ashgate), 3–26.

Larmore, Charles (1999), "The Moral Basis of Political Liberalism," *Journal of Philosophy* 96, no. 12: 599–625.

——— (2008), *The Autonomy of Morality* (New York: Cambridge University Press).

Lasch, Christopher (1977), *Haven in a Heartless World: The Family Besieged* (New York: Norton).

Lear, Jonathan (2011), *A Case for Irony* (Cambridge, MA: Harvard University Press).

Leopold, David (2007), *The Young Karl Marx: German Philosophy, Modern Politics, and Human Flourishing* (New York: Cambridge University Press).

Loewald, Hans (1988), *Sublimation: Inquiries into Theoretical Psychoanalysis* (New Haven, CT: Yale University Press).

Lohmann, Georg (1986), "Marx's *Capital* and the Question of Normative Standards," *Praxis International* 6, no. 3: 353–372.

Longuenesse, Béatrice (2007), *Hegel's Critique of Metaphysics*, trans. Nicole Simek (New York: Cambridge University Press).

Lotz, Christian (2015), *The Capitalist Schema: Time, Money, and the Culture of Abstraction* (New York: Lexington).

Louden, Patrick (2000), *Kant's Impure Ethics: From Rational Beings to Human Beings* (New York: Oxford University Press).

Löwith, Karl (1991), *From Hegel to Nietzsche: The Revolution in 19th Century Thought* (New York: Columbia University Press).

Löwy, Michael (1979), *Georg Lukács: From Romanticism to Bolshevism*, trans. Patrick Camiller (London: NLB).

Lukács, Georg (1971), *History and Class Consciousness: Studies in Marxist Dialectics*, trans. Rodney Livingstone (Cambridge, MA: MIT Press).

—— (1971), *Theory of the Novel: A Historico-Philosophical Essay on the Forms of Great Epic Literature*, trans. Anna Bostock (Cambridge, MA: MIT Press).

MacCormick, Neil (1990), "Reconstruction after Deconstruction: A Response to CLS," *Oxford Journal of Legal Studies* 10, no. 4: 539–558.

MacKinnon, Catherine (1989), *Toward a Feminist Theory of the State* (Cambridge, MA: Harvard University Press).

Mahoney, Jon (2004), "Objectivity, Interpretation, and Rights: A Critique of Dworkin," *Law and Philosophy* 23, no. 2: 187–222.

Marcuse, Herbert (1966), *Eros and Civilization: A Philosophical Inquiry into Freud* (Boston: Beacon).

—— (1968), *Negations: Essays in Critical Theory*, trans. Jeremy Shapiro (Boston: Beacon).

—— (1969), *An Essay on Liberation* (Boston: Beacon, 1969).

—— (1970), *Five Lectures*, trans. Jeremy Shapiro and Shierry Weber (Boston: Beacon).

—— (1999), *Reason and Revolution: Hegel and the Rise of Social Theory* (New York: Humanity Books).

Marx, Karl (1967), *Capital: A Critique of Political Economy*, vol. 3 (New York: International Publishers).

—— (1978), "The Economic and Philosophical Manuscripts of 1844," in *The Marx-Engels Reader*, 2nd ed., ed. Robert Tucker (New York: Norton), 66–125.

—— (1988), *Grundrisse*, trans. Martin Nicholaus (New York: Penguin).

—— (1990), *Capital*, vol. 1, trans. Ben Fowkes (New York: Penguin).

—— (1994), "Critique of Hegel's *Philosophy of Right*," in *Early Political Writings*, ed. and trans. Joseph O'Malley (New York: Cambridge University Press), 1–27.

—— (1994), "From the Paris Notebooks," in *Early Political Writings*, 71–96.

—— (1994), "On the Jewish Question," in *Early Political Writings*, 28–56.

—— (1994), "Theses on Feuerbach," in *Early Political Writings*, 116–118.

—— (1996), "On the Gotha Program," in *Later Political Writings*, ed. and trans. Terrell Carver (New York: Cambridge University Press), 208–226.

—— (1996), "The 18th Brumaire of Louis Bonaparte," in *Later Political Writings*, 31–127.

McCarney, Joseph (2000), *Hegel on History* (New York: Routledge).

McCarthy, Thomas (1991), *Ideals and Illusions: On Reconstruction and Deconstruction in Contemporary Critical Theory* (Cambridge, MA: MIT Press).

McCormick, John (1999), "Three Ways of Thinking 'Critically' about the Law," *The American Political Science Review* 93, no. 2: 413–428.

McGregor, David (1992), *Hegel, Marx, and the English State* (Boulder, CO: Westview).

McIvor, David (2015), "Pressing the Subject: Critical Theory and the Death Drive," *Constellations* 22, no. 3: 405–419.

McNay, Lois (2008), *Against Recognition* (Malden, MA: Polity).

Meehan, Johana (2011), "Recognition and the Dynamics of Intersubjectivity," in *Axel Honneth: Critical Essays*, 89–124.

Michelman, Frank (1973), "In Pursuit of Constitutional Welfare Rights: One View of Rawls' Theory of Justice," *University of Pennsylvania Law Review* 121, no. 5: 962–1019.

—— (1988), "Law's Republic," *The Yale Law Journal* 97, no. 8: 1493–1537.

—— (1998), "Family Quarrel," in *Habermas on Law and Democracy: Critical Exchanges*, eds. Michel Rosenfeld and Andrew Arato (Berkeley: University of California Press), 309–322.

—— (1999), *Brennan and Democracy* (Princeton, NJ: Princeton University Press).

Miller, Jason (2016), "The Role of Aesthetics in Hegelian Theories of Recognition," *Constellations* 23, no. 1: 96–109.

Moland, Lydia (2007), "History and Patriotism in Hegel's *Rechtsphilosophie*," *History of Political Thought* 28, no. 3: 496–519.

—— (2011), *Hegel on Political Identity: Patriotism, Nationality, Cosmopolitanism* (Evanston, IL: Northwestern University Press).

Mondak, Jeffrey and Shannon Smithey (1997), "The Dynamics of Public Support for the Supreme Court," *Journal of Politics* 59, no. 4: 1114–1142.

Mouffe, Chantal (2000), *The Democratic Paradox* (New York: Verso).

Neuhouser, Frederick (2000), *The Foundations of Hegel's Social Theory: Actualizing Freedom* (New York: Cambridge University Press).

—— (2008), *Rousseau's Theodicy of Self-Love: Evil, Rationality, and the Drive for Recognition* (New York: Oxford University Press).

Neumann, Franz (1957), "Anxiety and Politics," in *The Democratic and Authoritarian: Essays in Political and Legal Theory*, ed. Herbert Marcuse (New York: Free Press), 270–300.

—— (2009), *Behemoth: The Structure and Practice of National Socialism, 1933–1944* (Chicago: Ivan R. Dee).

O'Connor, Brian (1999), "The Concept of Mediation in Hegel and Adorno," *Bulletin of the Hegel Society of Great Britain*, 39/40, nos. 1–2: 84–96.

O'Neill, Onora (2015), "Changing Constructions," in *Rawls'* Political Liberalism, eds. Thom Brooks and Martha Nussbaum (New York: Columbia University Press), 57–72.

Pedersen, Jørgen (2012), "Justification and Application: The Revival of the Rawls-Habermas Debate," *Philosophy of the Social Sciences* 42, no. 3: 399–432.

Pilapil, Renante (2012), "From Psychologism to Personhood: Honneth, Recognition, and the Making of Persons," *Res Publica* 18, no. 1: 39–51.

Pinkard, Terry (1994), *Hegel's Phenomenology: The Sociality of Reason* (New York: Cambridge University Press).

—— (2002), *German Philosophy, 1760–1860: The Legacy of Idealism* (New York: Cambridge University Press).

—— (2008), "What is a 'Shape of Spirit'?" in *Hegel's* Phenomenology of Spirit: A Critical Guide, 112–129.

—— (2012), *Hegel's Naturalism: Mind, Nature, and the Final Ends of Life* (New York: Oxford University Press).

Pippin, Robert (1997), *Idealism as Modernism: Hegelian Variations* (New York: Cambridge University Press).

—— (2008), *Hegel's Practical Philosophy: Rational Agency and Ethical Life* (New York: Cambridge University Press).

—— (2011), *Hegel on Self-Consciousness: Desire and Death in* The Phenomenology of Spirit (Princeton, NJ: Princeton University Press).

—— (2015), *Interanimations: Receiving Modern German Philosophy* (Chicago: University of Chicago Press).

Plotke, David (1975), "Marxism, Sociology, and Crisis: Lukács' Critique of Weber," *Berkeley Journal of Sociology* 20: 181–232.

Pollock, Friedrich (1982), "State Capitalism: its Possibilities and Limits," in *The Essential Frankfurt School Reader*, 71–94.

Postone, Moishe (1993), *Time, Labor, and Social Domination: A Reinterpretation of Marx's Critical Theory* (New York: Cambridge University Press).

—— (2009), "The Subject and Social Theory: Marx and Lukács on Hegel," in *Karl Marx and Contemporary Philosophy*, eds. Andrew Chitty and Martin McIvor (New York: Palgrave), 205–220.

Quinn, Warren (1987), "Reflections on the Loss of Moral Knowledge and Williams on Objectivity," *Philosophy and Public Affairs* 16, no. 2: 195–209.

Rawls, John (1971), *A Theory of Justice* (Cambridge, MA: Harvard University Press).

—— (1996), *Political Liberalism*, 2nd ed. (New York: Columbia University Press).

—— (1999), *Collected Papers*, ed. Samuel Freeman (Cambridge, MA: Harvard University Press).

—— (1999), *A Theory of Justice*, rev. ed. (Cambridge, MA: Harvard University Press).

—— (2000), *Lectures on the History of Moral Philosophy*, ed. Barbara Herman (Cambridge, MA: Harvard University Press).

—— (2001), *Justice as Fairness: A Restatement* (Cambridge, MA: Harvard University Press).

—— (2007), *Lectures on the History of Political Philosophy*, ed. Samuel Freeman (Cambridge, MA: Harvard University Press).

Reid, Jeffrey (2014), *The Anti-Romantic: Hegel Against Ironic Romanticism* (New York: Bloomsbury).

Riley, Patrick (2001), "Rousseau's General Will," in *The Cambridge Companion to Rousseau*, ed. Riley (New York: Cambridge University Press), 124–153.

Rorty, Richard (1989), *Contingency, Irony, and Solidarity* (New York: Cambridge University Press).

Rostbøll, Christian (2008), *Deliberative Freedom: Deliberative Democracy as Critical Theory* (Albany: SUNY Press).

Rousseau, Jean-Jacques (1997), "Discourse on the Origin and Foundation of Inequality among Men," in *The Discourses and other Early Political Writings*, ed. and trans. Victor Gourevitch (New York: Cambridge University Press), 111–231.

—— (1997), *The Social Contract and other Later Political Writings*, ed. and trans. Victor Gourevitch (New York: Cambridge University Press).

Ruda, Frank (2011), *Hegel's Rabble: An Investigation into The Philosophy of Right* (New York: Continuum).

Rush, Fred (2016), *Irony and Idealism: Rereading Schlegel, Hegel, and Kierkegaard* (New York: Oxford University Press).

Sayer, Derek (1991), *Capitalism and Modernity: An Excursus on Marx and Weber* (New York: Routledge).

Sayers, Sean (2011), *Marx and Alienation: Essays on Hegelian Themes* (New York: Palgrave Macmillan).

Schaub, Jörg (2009), *Gerechtigkeit als Versöhnung: John Rawls' Politischer Liberalismus* (Frankfurt am Main: Campus Verlag).

—— (2015), "Misdevelopments, Pathologies, and Normative Revolutions: Normative Reconstruction as Method of Critical Theory," *Critical Horizons* 16, no. 2: 107–130.

Scheuerman, William (1993), "Neumann versus Habermas: The Frankfurt School and the Rule of Law," *Praxis International* 13, no. 1: 50–67.

—— (2013), "Capitalism, Law, and Social Criticism," *Constellations* 20, no. 4: 571–586.

Schneewind, J. B. (1998), *The Invention of Autonomy: A History of Modern Moral Philosophy* (New York: Cambridge University Press).

Sedgwick, Sally (2001), "The State as Organism: The Metaphysical Basis of Hegel's *Philosophy of Right*," *The Southern Journal of Philosophy* 39: 171–188.

—— (2012), *Hegel's Critique of Kant: From Dichotomy to Identity* (New York: Oxford University Press).

Seel, Martin (1991), "Two Meanings of 'Communicative' Rationality: Remarks on Habermas' Plural Concept of Reason," in *Communicative Action: Essays on Jürgen Habermas' Theory of Communicative Action*, eds. Axel Honneth and Hans Joas (Cambridge, MA: MIT Press), 36–48.

Sen, Amartya (2009), *The Idea of Justice* (Cambridge, MA: Harvard University Press).

Shue, Henry (1973), "Lukács: Notes on his Originality," *Journal of the History of Ideas* 34, no. 4: 645–650.

Siep, Ludwig (2004), "Constitution, Fundamental Rights, and Social Welfare in Hegel's *Philosophy of Right*," in *Hegel on Ethics and Politics*, eds. Otfried Höffe and Robert Pippin (New York: Cambridge University Press), 268–290.

Stacey, Richard (2010), "Democratic Jurisprudence and Judicial Review: Waldron's Contribution to Political Positivism," *Oxford Journal of Legal Studies* 30, no. 4: 749–773.

Stern, Robert (2015), *Kantian Ethics: Value, Agency, and Obligation* (New York: Oxford University Press).

Suchting, W. (1977), "On a Criticism of Marx on Law and Relations of Production," *Philosophy and Phenomenological Research* 38, no. 2: 200–208.

Taylor, Charles (1985), *Philosophical Papers*, vol. 2: *Philosophy and the Human Sciences* (Cambridge, MA: Harvard University Press).

—— (1989), *Sources of the Self: Making of the Modern Identity* (Cambridge, MA: Harvard University Press).

—— (1991), "Language and Society," in *Communicative Action: Essays on Jürgen Habermas' Theory of Communicative Action*, eds. Axel Honneth and Hans Joas (Cambridge, MA: MIT Press), 23–35.

—— (1995), *Philosophical Arguments* (Cambridge, MA: Harvard University Press).

Thalos, Mariam (2016), *A Social Theory of Freedom* (New York: Routledge).

Thrasher, John and Kevin Vallier (2015), "The Fragility of Consensus: Public Reason, Diversity and Stability," *European Journal of Philosophy* 23, no. 4: 933–954.

Tomasello, Michael (2001), *The Cultural Origins of Human Cognition* (Cambridge, MA: Harvard University Press).

Tugendhat, Ernst (1986), *Self-Consciousness and Self-Determination*, trans. Paul Stern (Cambridge, MA: MIT Press).

Tushnet, Mark (2004), "Constitutional Hardball," *John Marshall Law Review* 37, no. 2: 523–553.

Unger, Roberto (1996), *What Can Legal Analysis Become?* (New York: Verso, 1996).

Verdeja, Ernesto (2009), "Adorno's Mimesis and its Limitations for Critical Social Thought," *European Journal of Political Theory* 8, no. 4: 493–511.

Vogelmann, Frieder (2017), "Measuring, Disrupting, Emancipating: Three Pictures of Critique," *Constellations* 24, no. 1: 101–112.

Waldron, Jeremy (1999), *Law and Disagreement* (New York: Oxford University Press).

——— (1999), *The Dignity of Legislation* (New York: Cambridge University Press).

——— (2006), "Did Dworkin Ever Answer the Crits?" in *Exploring Law's Empire: The Jurisprudence of Ronald Dworkin*, ed. Scott Hershovitz (New York: Oxford University Press).

——— (2008), "Do Judges Reason Morally?" in *Expounding the Constitution: Essays in Constitutional Theory*, ed. Grant Huscroft (New York: Cambridge University Press), 38–64.

——— (2009), "Can there be a Democratic Jurisprudence?" *Emory Law Journal* 58, no. 3: 675–712.

——— (2009), "Constitutionalism—A Skeptical View," in *Contemporary Debates in Political Philosophy*, eds. Thomas Cristiano and John Christman (New York: Blackwell), 267–282.

Walker, Margaret (2003), *Moral Contexts* (Lantham, MD: Rowman and Littlefield).

Walsh, Katie Padgett (2010), "Reasons Internalism, Hegelian Resources," *Journal of Value Inquiry* 44, no. 2: 225–240.

Warren, Mark (1989), "Liberal Constitutionalism as Ideology: Marx and Habermas," *Political Theory* 17, no. 4: 511–534.

Waszek, Norbert (2011), "Hegelianism and the Theory of Political Opposition," in *Politics, Religion, and Art: Hegelian Debates*, ed. Douglas Moggach (Evanston, IL: Northwestern University Press), 147–163.

Weber, Max (1964), "Bureaucracy," in *From Max Weber: Essays in Sociology*, eds. and trans. Hans Gerth and C. Wright Mills (New York: Oxford University Press), 198–244.

——— (1964), "Politics as Vocation," in *From Max Weber*, 77–128.

——— (1978), *Economy and Society*, vol. 1, eds. Guenther Roth and Claus Wittich (Berkeley: University of California Press).

——— (1978), *Economy and Society*, vol. 2, eds. Roth and Wittich (Berkeley: University of California Press).

——— (1981), "On Some Categories of Interpretive Sociology," *Sociological Quarterly* 22, no. 2: 151–180.

——— (1992), *The Protestant Ethic and the Spirit of Capitalism*, trans. Talcott Parsons (New York: Routledge).

Weithman, Paul (2010), *Why Political Liberalism? On John Rawls' Political Turn* (New York: Oxford University Press).

Wellmer, Albrecht (1991), "Truth, Semblance, Reconciliation," in *The Persistence of Modernity* (Cambridge, MA: MIT Press), 1–35.

West, Robin (1990), "Progressive and Conservative Constitutionalism," *Michigan Law Review* 88, no. 4: 641–721.

——— (1992), "Constitutional Skepticism," *Boston University Law Review* 72, no. 4: 765–799.

Westphal, Merold (1998), "Kierkegaard and Hegel," in *The Cambridge Companion to Kierkegaard*, eds. Alasdair Hannay and Gordon Daniel Marino (New York: Cambridge University Press), 101–124.

Whitebook, Joel (1995), *Perversion and Utopia: A Study in Psychoanalysis and Critical Theory* (Cambridge, MA: MIT Press).

——— (2004), "The Marriage of Marx and Freud: Critical Theory and Psychoanalysis," in *The Cambridge Companion to Critical Theory*, ed. Fred Rush (New York: Cambridge University Press), 74–102.

Wiggershaus, Rolf (1995), *The Frankfurt School: Its History, Theories, and Political Significance* (Cambridge, MA: MIT Press).

Williams, Robert (1997), *Hegel's Ethics of Recognition* (Berkeley: University of California Press).

——— (2013), "Freedom as Correlation: Recognition and Self-Actualization in Hegel's *Philosophy of Spirit*," in *Essays on Hegel's* Philosophy of Subjective Spirit, ed. David Stern (Albany: SUNY Press), 155–180.

Winnicott, Donald (1971), *Playing and Reality* (New York: Basic Books).

Wolin, Sheldon (1996), The Liberal/Democratic Divide: On Rawls's *Political* Liberalism," *Political Theory* 24, no. 1: 95–119.

Wood, Allen (1990), *Hegel's Ethical Thought* (New York: Cambridge University Press).

Young, Iris Marion (1989), *Justice and the Politics of Difference* (Princeton, NJ: Princeton University Press).

Zurn, Christopher (2007), *Deliberative Democracy and the Institutions of Judicial Review* (New York: Cambridge University Press).

——— (2010), "The Logic of Legitimacy: Bootstrapping Paradoxes of Constitutional Democracy," *Legal Theory* 16, no. 3: 191–227.

——— (2011), "Judicial Review, Constitutional Juries and Civic Constitutional Fora," *Theoria* 58, no. 2: 63–94.

——— (2011), "Social Pathologies as Second Order Disorders," in *Axel Honneth: Critical Essays*, 345–370.

——— (2015), *Axel Honneth: A Critical Theory of the Social* (New York: Polity).

INDEX